Confronting the
Mystery of God

Confronting the Mystery of God

Political, Liberation, and Public Theologies

Gaspar Martinez

CONTINUUM
New York • London

2001

The Continuum International Publishing Group Inc
370 Lexington Avenue, New York, NY 10017

The Continuum International Publishing Group Ltd
The Tower Building, 11 York Road, London SE1 7NX

Printed in the United States of America

Library of Congress Cataloging-in-Publication Data

Martinez, Gaspar, 1949–
    Confronting the mystery of God : political, liberation, and public theologies / Gaspar Martinez.
        p. cm.
    Includes bibliographical references and index.
    ISBN 0-8264-1239-4
    1. Catholic Church – Doctrines – History – 20th century. 2. Rahner, Karl, 1904- 3. Metz, Johannes Baptist, 1928- 4. Gutiérrez, Gustavo, 1928- 5. Tracy, David. 6. Political theology – History of doctrines – 20th century. 7. Liberation theology – History of doctrines – 20th century. I. Title.

BX1751.2. M338 2001
230'.2'0922 – dc21

00-064408

Contents

Foreword

There are two notable facts about this unique book by Basque theologian Gaspar Martinez. First, the author's educational background not only in Christian theology but also in economics, politics, and culture has freed him to write the kind of book long needed: a culturally specific study of the significant similarities and differences among European political theology, Latin American liberation theology, and North American public theology. All three forms of these distinct but related theologies render explicit what most theologies leave implicit: the relationship to a particular "world" (in theological terms) of any "logos" or "theos," that is, any *theo-logia*. Professor Martinez has accomplished this, first, by studying with representative theologians of these three traditions: Johann Baptist Metz (political theology), Gustavo Gutiérrez (liberation theology), and the present writer, David Tracy (North American public theology). It is extraordinary how a scholar from a fourth culture, Basque culture, could immerse himself intellectually, linguistically, and existentially in three such different cultures as that of Germany, Peru, and the United States. The opening sections of the three principal chapters of this book show how well the author succeeds in each case: a study of the economic, political, and cultural differences that deeply influence (he never claims they determine) three distinct politically committed theologies (generally of the Left). He examines Latin American liberation theology in Peru to show the central insights of this theological model—a model developed widely in Latin America and in the important African American, Native American, and Hispanic theologies of North America, as well as in the distinct liberation theologies of Africa, Asia, Palestine, Oceania, and (we hope) eventually in the theologies of the Roma (Gypsy) people and other marginalized peoples (e.g., *Gastarbeiter*) in Europe itself. The author goes on to demonstrate how, within the elites of the rich nations of western Europe, the same kind of political commitment gives rise to political theologies and again, within the United States and Canada, to public theologies (the latter deeply influenced by the African American, Hispanic, and Native American indigenous theologies in North American culture).

The second fact about this singular book is equally important. Although Professor Martinez could also have written on the parallel Protestant theologies in Latin American liberation theology (e.g., José Míguez Bonino), European political theology (e.g., Jürgen Moltmann), or North American public theology (e.g., Schubert Ogden, Martin Marty, Ronald Thiemann, or Cornell West), he has wisely chosen to delimit the discussion by demonstrating the remarkable resurgence of Roman Catholic theology since the Second Vatican Council (1961–64) and especially the influence of the incomparable Karl Rahner—a major theologian of Vatican II—as an opening to the modern world of a Catholic theology once disastrously closed to modernity. Rahner, along with his contemporary Bernard Lonergan and the noteworthy French theologians of *la nouvelle theologie* such as Henri de Lubac, Yves Congar, and M.-D. Chenu, not only influenced the three theologians Martinez analyzes in this book but also set in motion a new theological paradigm in Catholic theology further developed by members of the next Vatican II generation such as Edward Schillebeeckx, and even the third such as Hans Küng, Gregory Baum, Claude Geffré, Charles Cunear, Rosemary Radford Ruether, Elisabeth Schüssler Fiorenza, Francis Schüssler Fiorenza, and Brian Hehir. This brief list should include many others, especially because—as the feminist, womanist, and *mujerista* theologians say with the exactitude needed—the second, third, and now fourth generations of Vatican II inspired liberation, feminist, womanist, *mujerista*, political, and public theologies. The Catholic contribution to liberation, political, and public theologies, as Martinez shows, is indeed amazing: Vatican II achieved, for all times, the crucial step needed: the rapprochement, from both sides, of the best of Western modernity and the classic Catholic tradition. It is scarcely an exaggeration to state that, with some notable and sometimes tragic exceptions (e.g., Teresa of Avila, Ignatius of Loyola, Archbishop Fénélon, Madame Guyon, Sor Juana Inés de la Cruz, and others), Catholicism, in its official (and therefore most powerful) form, successfully resisted modernity for four centuries (sixteenth to twentieth) and then finally embraced it (at Vatican II) at the very moment when modernity began to distrust itself in the 1960s— the era of Vietnam and the May events in Paris, Mexico City, Prague, and Washington. Vatican II affirmed Catholicism's relationship with modernity, and the great generation of theologians (namely, the French, German, Dutch, Belgian, and Austrian) helped to bring about that remarkable sea change. No one was more influential in those heady days or the days following than Karl Rahner, with his turn to the "modern subject" and his increasingly profound turn to a radicalized sense of mystery. All the theologians who gathered around the reforming journal *Concilium* followed Rahner's lead but took the reform movements in directions (political, liberationist, feminist, hermeneutical, postmodern) to which Rahner himself opened the door, made excursions into, but left to future theological generations to work out. And so they did. Three examples of such post–Vatican II and post-Rahner Catholic theologies can be found in the three theologians Gaspar Martinez chooses to study from the last thirty years in the progressive branch of post–Vatican II Catholic theology in the modern world.

For my own part, the most remarkable fact about Martinez's study of these three post–Vatican II and post-Rahner contextual theologies is not merely to show the amazing similarities and equally amazing differences among Peruvian, German, and U.S. theologies but to demonstrate a startling fact. Each of these three theologians quite independently (even though they were friendly and sometimes critical readers of one another's work during their many years together as editorial colleagues on the journal *Concilium*) returned, in the last fifteen years, to Rahner's central question, the question of God. Theology, after all, no matter how political, liberationist, or public it may prove to be, should always find its center of gravity in the reality of God. And so, as Professor Martinez shows with brilliance in his final chapter, the mystical-political character of theology became more and more (not less and less, as some conservative critics of the *Concilium* theologians alleged it had) concerned with the ultimate mystery of God as the ultimate mystery of the world.

I was personally amazed and instructed by this final point of Martinez's brilliant study: the radical turn to God and to mystery in three representatively "worldly" theologies without loss of the political, liberationist, or public character of modern theology. In sum, this book was deeply instructive to me, even about my own work, as well as about the work of other progressive Catholic theologians since Vatican II. I am deeply grateful to have learned so much from Professor Martinez's exceptional insights. I heartily recommend this study to all theologically interested readers that they might learn as well from the sharp intelligence, exceptionally broad knowledge, and theological acumen of yet another distinguished Basque theologian, Gaspar Martinez.

DAVID TRACY

It is important to emphasize that this work is not simply a presentation of theological perspectives coming from different places and a critical analysis of their similarities and differences. The project is far more ambitious and original. It tries to establish a fruitful dialogue among three different theological models. This dialogue, always against the background of Vatican II, focuses on the continuities and discontinuities in the major avenues that were opened up by Karl Rahner's thought.

Bearing in mind this central concern, each author is analyzed with a profound respect for his ideas. The result is a personal and insightful work that issues in highly valuable viewpoints about some of the central questions facing theology today: theological method, salvation in Jesus Christ, the relationship between history and eschatology, the people of God as the bearer of hope in the historical journey of humanity. The author never gives up reasoning his central point: all these questions are related, in the last analysis, to the only question of theology, that is, the mystery of God. Those who wrote the works analyzed in this book will be the ones who will benefit most from it.

GUSTAVO GUTIÉRREZ

Preface

The origin of this work can be traced to the sweeping changes that have taken place in the Catholic Church since the Second Vatican Council, at the beginning of the 1960s. These changes have been of two main, interrelated orders: pastoral and theological. This work focuses on the second, the theological order, although it refers to pastoral issues in several places.

This study argues that Karl Rahner was a turning point in Catholic theology. His theology, together with that of other crucial authors on the eve of Vatican II, shaped the theology of the council and paved the way for a fruitful dialogue between modernity and Catholic theology.

Taking Rahner's theology as the starting point, this work has a three-fold aim. First, it seeks to show that a very fruitful Rahnerian heritage can be found in the work of three theologians who have developed their own theological projects in three different cultural and social contexts: Johann Baptist Metz in Germany, Gustavo Gutiérrez in Peru, and David Tracy in the United States. Metz is widely considered the founder of political theology. Gutiérrez fathered liberation theology in the late 1960s and has been, since then, one of its main proponents. Tracy, in turn, represents the best effort at shaping a public theology in the United States from a Catholic perspective.

Second, the study aims at showing that there is an important commonality among these three post-Rahnerian theological enterprises. Each project can be clearly traced to Rahner and maintains a fruitful relationship with Rahner's theology throughout its development. However, unlike Rahner's theology, each of them is directly related to the concrete culture and society in which it was born and with which it seeks to establish a fruitful and critical dialogue on strictly Christian theological grounds. In this respect, all three of them replace Rahner's transcendental approach with a more historical and concrete one.

The final aim of the study is to reveal the depth of the theo-logical substance of all three enterprises. Like Aquinas in his time, Rahner was criticized for being "too anthropological" and, consequently, for risking the dissolution of the religious substance of Christian theology. This critique has been also addressed to the three authors who form the core of this work. However, as the study tries to establish, far from getting theologically lost, these authors intensify their theo-logical core, and, like Rahner, each one of them finds his own route to the mystery of God on the basis of his own theological approach.

The work is divided into five chapters. The first one is a sort of referential chapter, devoted to outlining the central tenets and method of Rahner's theology. The next three chapters focus on the analysis of the theology of Metz, Gutiérrez, and Tracy, paying special attention to the social, cultural, and ecclesial context of each. The fifth and last chapter compares the theology of the three authors, both in method and in content, keeping always the reference to Rahner.

First and foremost, I am deeply grateful to Professor David Tracy for his constant support and advice throughout all the stages of the present work, for having read the manuscript and its revisions, and for his invaluable suggestions. I am also deeply grateful to Professors Anne Carr and William Schweiker for their essential help at the time of the formulation of the central focus and questions of the work.

I want to thank very especially both Professor Johann Baptist Metz and Fr. Gustavo Gutiérrez. Professor Metz for having accepted me into his courses and seminars at the Katholisch-Theologische Fakultät der Universität Münster. Fr. Gutiérrez for having invited me to the Instituto Bartolomé de Las Casas in Lima and to the Curso de Verano de Teología, organized by the aforesaid Instituto and the Facultad de Teología de la Universidad Católica de Lima. Both of them for having devoted their time very generously to helping me with my work during my stay with them. My stay in Münster and Lima was made possible by a scholarship granted by the Office of International Affairs of the University of Chicago.

This work has been written in three places. The first was at the Catholic Theological Union (CTU) of Chicago, where I benefited from the support of that lively academic community. I am deeply grateful to Fr. Kenneth O'Malley, O.P., director of the library at CTU, for having proofread the first chapter and made the necessary language corrections.

More than half of the work was written at St. Procopius Benedictine Abbey in Lisle, Illinois. Fr. Abbot Hugh Anderson and the whole community of St. Procopius accepted me with truly monastic hospitality, and I found there the perfect atmosphere and the support I needed for carrying on with my work for more than a year. Taking part in the life of the community and, especially, in its prayer helped me enormously to work through all the implications of the theological issues with which I was dealing. At St. Procopius, I am especially grateful to Fr. James Flint, O.S.B., for his valuable suggestions on the manuscript and for having proofread every part of it other than the first chapter, making the necessary language corrections. Mrs. Marilyn Sherman's secretarial help has also been precious at many different stages of the work. Finally, I wrote a substantial part of this study at the Mutterhaus der Krankenschwestern des Hl. Franziskus in Münster, having benefited there from the Franciscan hospitality and the support of the community and, very especially, of Fr. Wilhelm Geelink.

My friends Joseba Segura, Ottmar John, José Antonio Zamora, Manuel Piqueras, Norbert Baumgart, and Mary Gerhart read parts of the manuscript and offered precious suggestions that have substantially improved the work. I also want to thank especially Frank Oveis for his editorial work at Continuum, his kindness, his patience, and his invaluable suggestions, and Professor Renée Schoen-René for having read the whole manuscript very carefully, editing it in ways that have improved it well beyond my expectations. I am also deeply indebted to all those who gave me their personal support during the process of writing this work, especially to Mr. and Mrs. Cengotitabengoa and their children, whose home was always mine during my time in Chicago. Finally, the present work would not have been possible at all without the support of all sorts I have received from my diocese of Bilbao. I hope this work will help me to serve better my diocesan community both as a priest and as a theologian.

Abbreviations

ABL	*The Achievement of Bernard Lonergan*, David Tracy
AI	*The Analogical Imagination*, David Tracy
BPJ	*En busca de los pobres de Jesucristo*, Gustavo Gutiérrez
BPP	*Beber en su propio pozo*, Gustavo Gutiérrez
BRO	*Blessed Rage for Order*, David Tracy
DV	*El Dios de la vida*, Gustavo Gutiérrez
DWO	*Dialogue with the Other*, David Tracy
EC	*Entre las calandrias*, Gustavo Gutiérrez
GGG	*Glaube in Geschichte und Gesellschaft*, Johann Baptist Metz
HD	*Hablar de Dios desde el sufrimiento del inocente*, Gustavo Gutiérrez
LFT	"Lonergan's Foundational Theology: an Interpretation and a Critique," David Tracy
LITA	*Lonergan's Interpretation of St. Thomas Aquinas*, David Tracy
LV	*La verdad os hará libres*, Gustavo Gutiérrez
MT	*Method in Theology*, Bernard Lonergan
ONP	*On Naming the Present*, David Tracy
PA	*Plurality and Ambiguity*, David Tracy
PPH	*The Power of the Poor in History*, Gustavo Gutiérrez
ST	*Summa Theologiae*, Thomas Aquinas
TI	*Theological Investigations*, Karl Rahner
TL	*Teología de la liberación*, Gustavo Gutiérrez
ZTW	*Zur Theologie der Welt*, Johann Baptist Metz

Chapter 1

Karl Rahner and the Turning Point in Catholic Theology

The Foundations of Rahner's Thought

As it usually happens with any thinker, it is not easy to figure out the exact original ground of Rahner's thought.[1] Therefore, it should be enough to point to those elements that make up the main pillars of his intellectual enterprise.

A crucial trait of Rahner's works was apparent from the beginning: the radicalness of his thought, that is, the search for the roots of existence. After the rise of phenomenology in Germany at the beginning of the twentieth century, a return to ontology took place among German thinkers. Martin Heidegger marks the high point in taking up the question of being, a question that for Heidegger is the most basic one, although forgotten by philosophy, and for whose analysis the whole history of ontology must be reconstructed.[2]

With *Geist in Welt*, Rahner enters his own investigation of the question of being through Joseph Maréchal and Heidegger,[3] working on Aquinas's *Summa Theologiae* I, Q.84, A.7.[4] This crucial work of a philosophical nature will remain central to all Rahner's writings. The work initiates Rahner's partnership with Aquinas, something that, despite Rahner's intellectual evolution, will continue until the end of Rahner's life. That Aquinas was always for Rahner a referential milestone can be seen not only in *Geist in Welt* but also in the later emphasis Rahner puts on the question of God as mystery. Aquinas's insight that even in the beatific vision God remains utterly incomprehensible is basic to understanding Rahner's concept of God. Moreover, Rahner was always convinced of the great importance of Aquinas for contemporary theology.[5] It would be wrong, however, to think that Rahner had an uncritical and ahistorical view of Aquinas.[6]

It is not by chance that Rahner pays attention to Aquinas. Many similarities between them can be established.[7] To begin, Aquinas, like Rahner, was a radical thinker, searching always for the bedrock of his inquiry. Both tried to rethink the Christian tradition in relation to the newness and the requirements of their own time. Aquinas, after his exposure to Aristotle and Averroes early in his life, at the time of his studies at the University of Naples,[8] faced later as theologian the challenge of reformulating "Sacred Doctrine," integrating the Neoplatonic tradition with Aristotle's philosophy. Rahner, in turn, had to deal with Kant and with the subsequent philosophical schools in his effort to show that critical inquiry and Christian faith can be brought together in a secularized society.

A further similarity between the two is the way they expand the philosophical framework on the basis of their own faith.[9] This means that for both the starting point is not merely philosophical but genuinely theological.[10] In the last analysis, the theology of both starts with prayer and ends in prayer, but in a prayer of adoration that, far from being detached from the theological enterprise, discloses the heart of the method and the gist of the content of that enterprise.[11] This intrinsic relationship between rational endeavor and religious adoration before the mystery of God marks the peak of the achievement of the theological projects of Aquinas and Rahner and can be considered a milestone in Christian theology.

Many other similarities between these two theologians can be shown. Both had problems with official censorship, and both were finally cleared. Both were accused of secularizing too much the Christian message in their effort to explore its reasonableness and its closeness to human nature. Both wrote their crucial works, Aquinas's *Summa Theologiae* and Rahner's *Grundkurs des Glaubens*, as textbooks for theology students. Both wrote extensively on questions of utmost pastoral importance in their days, and both were theologians for whom the church occupied a central role in their writings.

Rahner's reading of Aquinas followed the method of "transcendental Thomism" pioneered by Maréchal and followed by several Christian philosophers,[12] although there are differences between Rahner and Maréchal.[13] The adoption of this method allowed Rahner to confront Aquinas's doctrine with the problems of modern philosophy, and especially with the challenge of Kant's critique of knowledge. Metz, Anne Carr, and others see this Rahnerian move as his joining "the turn to the subject" that has characterized Western modern philosophy and modern culture from Descartes until the present.[14]

Geist in Welt can be defined as a Maréchalean interpretation of Aquinas's metaphysics of knowledge in an Heideggerian key that takes up the questions raised by Kant's critique of knowledge, bearing in mind Hegel's critique of Kant's position.[15] A crucial difference between Rahner and Kant is that the former's project in *Geist in Welt* is to formulate a metaphysics of knowledge, whereas Kant's work is properly described as a critique of knowledge.[16]

The critical move in Rahner is that he discusses philosophically (although his starting point is always theological, as in Aquinas) the problems raised by modernity in relation to the reasonableness of Christian faith and shows the inner link between reason and being as such. This being, finally for Rahner, must be called God. The turning point lies in the fact that far from joining the intellectual attitude of the Catholic Church of the day, suspicious of modernity, Rahner takes up the questions of modernity and confronts them on their own grounds based on a creative and innovative direct reading of Aquinas. By doing so, Rahner both renovates the tradition from within and shows that the spirit of critical inquiry characteristic of modernity not only does not contradict the tenets of revealed faith but actually points to their core. In this respect, Metz's perceptive understanding of Rahner points to the latter's "creative affirmation of tradition" and to the "salvaging trait" of Rahner's attitude, "by which he perceives the relevance and appeal of early words, concepts, and sentences of the Church's scholastic theology and seeks to 'save' them for us."[17]

Heidegger's influence on Rahner has to be assessed in order to understand Rahner's thought. Rahner himself, and also Hannah Arendt and Hans-Georg Gadamer, both Heidegger's students too, seemed to think that Heidegger did have an impact on their way of thinking through his ability to read texts closely, to make people think anew about the meaning an implications of the texts, and to question the validity of tenets taken for granted. Despite this, Rahner thought that Heidegger did not have an influence on the kind of questions he addressed, because Heidegger never addressed explicitly the question of God.[18] However, it seems safe to say that Heidegger reinforced the ontological drive already present in Rahner through Aquinas and Maréchal. In this respect, because Heidegger played a key role in making the question of Being *the* question of any philosophical inquiry, and because his whole project consisted in rethinking (he uses the German term *Destruktion,* which perhaps could currently be best translated as "deconstruction" in view of Heidegger's project) the history of ontology based on his concept of *Dasein,* or being-in-the-world, his understanding of Being and his references to the structures of Being have a great influence on Rahner's work.[19]

An important point in this sense, one that became increasingly relevant in Rahner's thought, is the existential centeredness of Being in Heidegger. For this author, the entry into the question of Being is *Dasein,* the being for which its very being is a matter of concern,[20] and that understands that being on the basis of its being-in-the-world, in a horizon of comprehension that is essentially determined by temporality.[21] This leads Rahner in the direction of "existentiell/existential" analysis,[22] following the close reading of life or existence in Heidegger, in terms both of actual determination and of structural constitution. Eventually this kind of analysis will allow Rahner to formulate his famous thesis of the supernatural existential, which can be considered the peak of his transcendental anthropology.[23]

Another crucial parallelism between Heidegger and Rahner pertains to the understanding of the transcendence of *Dasein*. Though the horizon of transcendence is radically different ("Nothing" in Heidegger's case and God in Rahner's),[24] the formal structure of transcendence is strikingly similar. Moreover, Heidegger's Nothing bears similarity with the Rahnerian God understood as an incomprehensible mystery, to the point of being a kind of "negative" of the Rahnerian picture.

The similarity becomes even greater if one realizes the importance of the *via negationis* in Rahner's understanding of God. Even in the case of the beatific vision, God's nature cannot be comprehended by the human being. Rahner confronts Heidegger's assertion that the term of human transcendence is "nothingness." That, Rahner says, makes no sense. However, Rahner seems to be aware of the problem concerning the meaning of "nothingness" in Heidegger when he qualifies his statement by saying "provided he gives the term 'nothingness' any meaning at all, and does not simply use it to signal that real and genuine existentiell anxiety that he actually experiences." This qualification is all the more significant if one bears in mind that Heidegger's analysis of the transcendence of *Dasein* in "What Is Metaphysics?" is grounded on the feeling of anxiety. How radical Rahner is in his understanding of transcendence as *via negationis* is shown by his affirmation that "it can be approached asymptotically at most, if at all, in mystical experience and perhaps in the experience of final loneliness in the face of death." One cannot but be reminded by this "final loneliness in the face of death" of the example of human anxiety at its best that Mark offers in his passion narrative, where Jesus confronts death in the midst of dreadful anguish provoked by his feeling of having been forsaken, or, in Heideggerian terms, "being held out into the nothing."[25]

Heidegger seems also to have led Rahner to analyze the basic structures of existence, helping him to give a further concreteness to the Thomistic realism. In Rahner, the question is not only that in any human act of understanding the sensible plays a central role both in providing the material upon which abstraction takes place and in the final "conversion to the phantasm."[26] Beyond that, the subject whose acts are analyzed by Rahner is a being-in-the-world for whom the historical dimension is crucial.[27]

Rahner's way of doing philosophy and theology has been called "transcendental anthropology."[28] The name of the method can vary according to the different authors that analyze Rahner's work, but the substance of their analyses remains the same: Rahner marks a turning point because he is able to show the intrinsic connection between human openness to God and human nature as the latter appears in the analysis of experience.[29] That is the reason why Rahner (although he was not alone in bringing about the change, and, therefore, the names of Yves Congar, Henri de Lubac, M.-D. Chenu, Bernard Lonergan, and others should be added to his on that score) is said to have set the agenda for the development of a Catholic theology concerned with the realities of history and contemporary society, eager to enter into dialogue with modernity, and called to be socially relevant.

The Core of Rahner's Theology

Rahner's theology can be understood as a progressive development of a systematic thought aimed at expressing a complex and multilayered experience in a meaningful and relevant way for the modern individual.[30] His whole project seems in retrospect an ongoing endeavor to disentangle all the different threads intertwined in his own human-religious experience, overcoming the pitfall of pure subjectivism by means of the transcendental method he adopted. Thus Rahner appears as a believer who engaged in theological reflection to work out the reasonableness and the implications of his faith in such a way that those elements are made publicly shareable. To that extent, his theology constitutes an example of public witness-theology at its best. In a wonderful essay on Rahner, Metz refers to Rahner's theology as "theology as biography." Metz captures the heart of Rahner's theology when he describes the latter's project as a theology that unites doxography and biography, the dogmatic and the mystic, and as "a conceptually summarized and condensed narrative of a life-story before God."[31]

Threefold Experience and Three Modes of Reflection

Three different levels or modes of reflection can be identified in Rahner's theology: the transcendental-metaphysical, the existential-historical, and the mystical.[32] Three different lines or dimensions of experience are at the base of these three projects: the transcendental experience, the historical experience of the self mediated by the historical experience of the other, and the mystical experience of the transcendent.[33] Finally, three activities derive from these three different levels: reflection, Christian practice, and prayer.[34]

It seems safe to say that Rahner progressed from a philosophical to an existential approach, and then to a mystical approach that opened itself to the confession that uncreated grace is present "always and everywhere."[35] His most comprehensive and probably best formulation of his thought, *Foundations of Christian Faith,* combines these different layers of experience and modes of reflection that span from transcendental analysis to confession. Although Rahner stressed one aspect more than the others at different stages of his life and work, the three belong together and, although distinguishable from each other, cannot be separated. Each act of the individual entails the three of them. To distinguish them in order to make explicit the whole content and complexity of human experience and yet not to separate them so as to show clearly the original unity of that experience, its ground, and its meaning is one of the peaks of Rahner's achievement.

His approach is rather philosophical at the stage of *Spirit in the World*, where the analysis focuses on the conditions of possibility of human knowledge. However, the other two elements are also present: the existential, due to the influence of Heidegger as it has been shown above, plays a role, and the mystical is inchoately present all along but is explicitly manifested in the last pages of the book. The existential dimension is clearer already at the stage of *Hearers of the Word*, where the historicity of being and the importance of that historicity in relation to revelation are explicitly stated. This existential-historical drive will become more and more important in later works, but always upon the basis of the transcendental analysis of the earlier work and with an ever growing affirmation of the mystical dimension. Finally, Rahner evolves toward a theology around the mystery of God, as it is apparent in *Foundations* and in numerous essays in his *Theological Investigations*, but without ever abandoning the insights of his earlier work.

The first level of reflection adopts a philosophical point of view to bring about what could be designated as metaphysical anthropology. As Rahner explains in *Spirit in the World* and later in *Foundations*, first of all, as far as the human reality is concerned, there is a unity in difference between being and knowing, between one's original self-possession and reflection. This, as Francis Schüssler Fiorenza says, is Rahner's basic move to overcome the premises of the Kantian position[36] and points directly to the concept of "original experience," in which everything that constitutes the human being is displayed in its original unity and whose disentanglement and analysis form the heart of Rahner's theology.[37]

Rahner's description in *Foundations* of the "original unity of reality and its own self-presence which is not *totally* mediated by the concept" and of how, nevertheless, a moment of reflection or conceptualization belongs intrinsically to that original experience is a masterful overcoming of the modern dichotomy between rationalism and romanticism. This relation between original experience and its conceptualization constitutes the backbone of Rahner's theological method, since what he wants to do is precisely to bring back the concepts of the dogmas to the fountainhead where they resound powerfully, that is, "that original experience in which what is meant and the experience of what is meant are still one."[38]

Rahner, following the transcendental-Heideggerian reading of Aquinas's metaphysics of knowledge, shows that what is understood by knowledge of an object entails several co-known elements and several underlying experiences: experience of the world, experience of the self, and unthematic or prethematic transcendental experience.

Transcendental experience is the crucial experience for Rahner. It encompasses two elements. The first element is the consciousness of the self without which no knowledge is possible. The second element is that which makes both consciousness and knowledge possible, namely, the openness of the self to being as such. It is transcendental because it appears and goes beyond what is being categorially or concretely known, while, at the same time, being the condition of possibility of knowing. It is an experience because, although unthematic and, as such, never fully captured in a reflective manner, it is the ground that constitutes the subjectivity of the subject and is present in every act of knowledge.[39]

It could be said that Rahner's thought hinges on the concept "transcendental." His is a transcendental philosophy and theology. Hence, his understanding of Christian faith is transcendentally arrived at. If one were led too easily to think that this entails a flight from experience, Rahner's project's core would be completely missed. Transcendental reflection is by no means a flight from experience but, quite the contrary, a diving into the inner mechanisms and the implications of that experience in order to unveil and make explicit its depth and breadth and, ultimately, its ground.

It is critical to understand the inner connection between "transcendental" and "categorial." Both occur together; they belong to each other; they imply and require each other. The transcendental is the condition of possibility of the categorial, while at the same time, the transcendental only can appear and be revealed through the categorial. As later will be shown in this work, this intrinsic relation between the two is crucial to understanding the importance of history and human action in Rahner's theology.[40]

The ultimate goal of Rahner's transcendental philosophy is to show that knowledge is possible only on the basis of the preapprehension of absolute being, which, in turn, implies the affirmation of that being. Hence, Rahner establishes the way for a metaphysical entry into the question of God, although God is always somehow beyond the reach of metaphysics. In other words, Rahner does not try to prove the existence of God but only to show that knowledge entails the affirmation of absolute being and, therefore, an unthematic knowledge of God.[41]

The metaphysics of knowledge is not, however, the only way Rahner deals with the meaning of human experience. Knowing is not the only activity of a person.[42] Beyond knowing, humans are subject to a whole array of feelings that manifest the way they relate to the world, to themselves, and, in general, to the whole environment in which they exist. In turn, what human beings do with their lives, that is, the way they relate to themselves and to their environment, is partially but unavoidably in their control.[43] That is the meaning of freedom and of its counterpart, the ability to make decisions.

In dealing with these questions, Rahner moves into another realm of experience where the "existentiell" and the "existential," the appropriation of existence through historical exercise of freedom and the structures of existence that make such an appropriation possible, come to the fore.

This, of course, also entails an aspect of knowledge, since anything humans experience is made conscious in and through knowledge.

The central point upon which both knowledge and freedom are built is personhood. Rahner uses different ways to show what personhood is about when he talks about the feelings of fear, hope, and love, all of which reveal the basic structures of the human being and, ultimately, human transcendence. The feeling of fear corresponds to the fact that the person is not in total control of existence, thus revealing that basic structure of dependence. Hope, in turn, unveils the movement toward liberating freedom and the inalienable personal responsibility in deciding for oneself.[44] The feeling of love is the clue to understanding the meaning of existence and the direction in which one must decide about oneself. Ultimately for Rahner, love in its transcendental dimension reveals the nature of the mystery that any human being confronts always in the depths of existence. In that case, mystery is experienced as "holy mystery."[45]

Ultimately, personhood can be described as that awareness of being related to an existence of which the self is conscious. However, this existence is experienced as not quite belonging to the self while, simultaneously, depending for its development on the decisions the self takes. Rahner pointed out from the beginning of his work that personhood, that is, the existence of a subject, is the condition for revelation and salvation. This is the main thesis of *Hearers of the Word* and the core of Rahner's approach to theology starting with the subject. Rahner always tried to show this inner connection between personhood, in all its dimensions and implications, and revelation as expressed in the formal statements of the church.[46]

Freedom as the unavoidable ability to decide ultimately about oneself despite being conditioned and not totally in control of existence is, like knowledge, subject to the twofold dimension of transcendentality and categoriality. Primarily, freedom is that transcendental human structure that makes the person heed the unavoidable responsibility of steering one's own existence. Still, this responsibility can only be exerted in and through concrete situations and actions that belong to the categorial realm of world and history.[47] If the Thomistic "sensible," widened by Rahner to the category of "world" as a result of the Heideggerian influence, was an absolute requirement for the existence of knowledge, in the case of freedom and "existentiell" self-realization, history and concrete action constitute the flesh where the transcendental responsibility of the person comes to exist.

This understanding of freedom is Rahner's entry into the question of salvation. Salvation, although always based on uncreated and created grace,[48] involves a decision about oneself before God.[49] Yet, because freedom always entails concrete decisions and actions under the specific determinations of "world, time, and history,"[50] salvation is intrinsically linked with decisions and actions in history.[51] Two consequences derive from that. First, there is an inner relationship between history of salvation and history as such, both at personal and global levels.[52] Second, salvation involves necessarily an ethical behavior in history, insofar as the decision about oneself before God must take place in and through concrete decisions and actions.[53]

The unfolding of the existential-historical experience confronts the individual with the experience of the self, but also with the experience of the other, and, finally, with the experience of the transcendent. In fact, there cannot be experience of the self without experience of the other. The former depends on the latter. As Rahner puts it, "Man experiences himself by experiencing the other *person*."[54] Equally, both require the experience of God, so that, ultimately, the three experiences form an inseparable unity and mutually condition each other.[55] Consequently, the decision about oneself is inseparable from the decision about the other, something that Rahner will express theologically by saying that the love of God and the love of the neighbor are intrinsically united.[56]

A central concern in Rahner that runs through all his theology and touches directly on the questions of history and salvation is the church. Rahner's theology cannot be separated from its understanding of the church and of the church's pastoral action. The church is that reality "in which the irreversibility of God's salvific self-expression becomes historically and institutionally tangible."[57] As such, the church is "the basic sacrament of salvation."[58]

Rahner's theology reaches its culmination in its turn to the mystery of God. This marks Rahner's third theological stage and leads to the focal point in which everything else converges.[59] At this stage Rahner makes explicit the implications of the transcendental experience, showing that the core of that experience is the experience of the transcendent that ultimately unveils itself as God understood as holy mystery.[60]

Rahner's theology, which originates in prayer and finally issues in prayer, can be seen as his effort to think and make explicit the ground and aim of that prayer in theological form. Herbert Vorgrimler expresses this basic orientation of Rahner's theology when he writes: "his theological life shows how shortsighted and foolish the distinction between seating and kneeling theologies is."[61] Using Rahner's own terminology, if prayer is the natural movement stemming from and responding to the original experience in which the self knows, however unthematically, that the loving God is the giver, sustainer, and aim of one's existence, theology is the second moment, the reflective moment, in which the self tries to establish conceptually the content of that original experience.[62]

Probably Rahner's most important contribution to the question of the experience of transcendence is his crucial insight that such an experience is always present in everyday life. Although unnoticed, it is the condition of possibility, the origin, ground, and aim of any meaningful human act such as knowing, willing, loving, deciding, and hoping.[63] From that point of view, a mystical experience is not something exceptional that only happens to a select few. On the contrary, it is present to every person, although it usually goes unnoticed because it is somehow co-natural to being a person.[64]

When, in concrete situations, the individual responds in a positive way by surrendering, without being sure and without seeing clearly, to that transcendence that appears on the horizon of those situations, then there is an experience of grace and of the presence of the Holy Spirit. This reaches its peak in the moment of the most important surrendering, namely, when death arrives and the self surrenders everything into the holy mystery with trust and hope.[65]

A Gratuitously Self-Giving God: The Supernatural Existential

If human experience leads, when understood and analyzed in all its implications, to transcendence, to being as such, to an uncharted, infinite sea in which concrete knowledge floats as an insignificant island,[66] one must ask how such an experience is possible at all. Rahner answers that it is possible only because of God's gratuitous self-communication to human beings. In other words, the subject, as a self able to experience the world, the other, itself, and, finally, being as such, and able also to decide about existence, is such a subject because it has been constituted by God's self-communication: "Man is the event of a free, unmerited and forgiving, and absolute self-communication of God."[67]

The consequences of that understanding of subjectness are theologically far-reaching. One of them is the theology of grace. For Rahner, grace cannot be reduced to a special quality somehow created by God purposely to be granted to someone in an equally special occasion. Much more radically, grace must be understood as the uncreated reality that is the very being of God.[68] It is that uncreated grace that constitutes the subject, the person, as a result of God's free self-communication. Therefore, grace is a constitutive element of personhood as such always and everywhere; that is to say, grace is the innermost and most natural reality in humanness.[69]

This understanding of grace clearly shows the radicalness of Rahner's thought and method. Rahner is not happy with a mere rethinking of the tradition. He uses the same principle Heidegger did, namely, the principle that in order to have a proper understanding of being, one must de/re-construct the history of ontology so that being can be properly understood anew once it is freed from the shackles of taken-for-granted concepts. That is exactly what Rahner does in the case of grace: to overcome the narrow limits imposed by traditional theology upon the concept of grace by tracing the reality of grace to its very origin and root, namely, God's own being.

Uncreated grace, God's own being, cannot be thought of as consisting merely in a sort of passive condition or state of being that is passed on to human beings without further consequences. On the contrary, it must be portrayed as the most, indeed as "the," active principle constitutive of the dynamics of the person. Rahner expresses this through his grounding concept of the supernatural existential, by which he wants to state that the very basis of human nature is supernatural.[70]

The pair "God's self-communication" and "supernatural existential" are probably the summit of Rahner's theology and his most valuable contribution to the rethinking of the tradition. Perhaps the most important and crucial problem theology has been wrestling with since Augustine is the relation between nature and grace. The very understanding of God, of creation, and of redemption hinges on how that relation is understood. Augustine's move to preserve the unexacted and free character of grace stressed the difference between nature and grace, thus bringing to the fore the problem of either a duality of creative principles (one of nature and the other of grace), reminiscent of Marcion's dualism, or a duality of wills in God that does not cohere with God's essential unity. In a sense, the whole development of Christian theology, with the Reformation debate at its core, can be seen as the unfolding of the implications involved in that problem.

Rahner's groundbreaking contribution lies in his unifying everything around the understanding of God as that holy mystery whose very being is the loving sharing of its being. Salvation is the becoming of that being, that is to say, of God's self-loving-sharing, in history, and it encompasses both creation and redemption. From here it follows that the act of creation is by definition a pouring out of uncreated grace and that, therefore, the duality between nature and grace is overcome.[71] Both by his understanding of grace and by his notion of the supernatural existential Rahner modifies the worldview of Christian theology both in relation to God and in relation to the work of God. At the core of that transformation is the overcoming of an extrinsicist way of looking at the relation between God and the creature. By definition, grace must be an unexacted, free gift of God. That, however, risks making grace extrinsic to nature. Rahner's achievement consists in showing that "gratuitous does not mean extrinsic."[72]

There is no such thing as a previous human nature upon which grace descends. Because God's being is grace, that is, loving sharing, the supernatural belongs to the human being right from the beginning, constituting its most important existential dimension, namely, that of being predisposed to accept God's being as a free and loving offer. Therefore, nature must be thought of as a "remainder concept" rather than a reality in itself.[73]

Rahner reaches here explicitly something that is implicit in all his theology—the intrinsic correlation between the human and the divine. God is the answer because God is also the beginning and the ground of existence: the supernatural belongs intrinsically to the human being and to creation in general. Consequently, there is no realm outside the sphere of salvation.

This means, in turn, that all reality contributes to the history of salvation. Everything is salvifically meaningful (although neither in the same degree nor in the same way) because everything is touched and encompassed by the uncreated grace of God and, hence, bears the mark of this grace, that is, is good, meaningful, and invaluably valuable. By so understanding grace, Rahner opened new ways for a comprehension of how people can be true Christians despite their ignorance of Christian faith. He expressed it with the notion of the "anonymous Christian." That affects also the way salvation and revelation are understood, with far-reaching consequences for the relationship with other religions and with secular society.[74]

This understanding of how the subject is constituted and of what grace is also gives a new and unified picture of the work of God. The traditional distinction between *de Deo creante* and *de Deo elevante* disappears to give way to a creation that is intrinsically supernaturally elevated. From here follows an integrated formulation of Christology that avoids the pitfall of depicting Christ and his redemptive work as something that did not belong to the original will of God and that came to exist only because of sin. Redemption and creation stand in unity.[75]

Christ from that perspective is not only our savior because he defeats the power of death but also and foremost the last and best being in God's creation, he in whom God's self-communication to the human being comes to its perfection, thus disclosing the eternal and unchangeable will of God, as well as the true nature and destiny of creation in general and of human beings in particular. Indeed, for Rahner, "The God-Man is the initial beginning and the definitive triumph of the movement of the world's self-transcendence into absolute closeness to the mystery of God."[76]

God as Mystery: The Incomprehensibility of God

The last, and indeed the only, word of theo-logy is about God. Every theological system must have a notion of God that coheres with all the other elements in the system. Conversely, every element in the system depends on the notion of God that sustains the whole system. In the case of Rahner, God is portrayed as "the holy mystery."[77]

For Rahner, this holy mystery is the only self-evident reality in human life. Rahner is interested in going beyond the extrinsic notion of mystery as that reality that involves a sacrifice for the intellect and uses therefore a paradoxical, but proper, language. His definition of holy mystery as the only self-evident reality in human life is based on the original transcendental experience that points to absolute being, finally identified as holy mystery, as the ground of personhood and, therefore, also of knowledge and freedom. Consequently, this holy mystery is totally near to the person and is self-evident because it is not grounded on anything other than itself.[78]

There are two, apparently contradictory, poles in Rahner's God as mystery. On the one hand, God is completely close to the creature. On the other hand, God is the absolute, incomprehensible mystery, totally beyond human reach, even in the beatific vision, or precisely in such a vision.[79] In dealing with the problems posed by these two poles, Rahner shows that this incomprehensibility is not a negative attribute of God that humans must accept of necessity in resignation, but the ultimate disclosure of the nature of human beings and, therefore, of God's self-communication. What is communicated and constitutes the human person is precisely the infinite incomprehensibility and the incomprehensible infinity of God. Therefore, the human being "shares in his own being in divine incomprehensibility," and "recognizes divine incomprehensibility as his own blessed fulfillment," and "surrenders himself unconditionally to this incomprehensibility as the true source of his own fulfillment."[80]

These reflections of Rahner are doubtless the crown of his entire ontology and theology, the cornerstone that holds all the other parts in a consistent whole. At the core of it lies Rahner's interpretation of mystery not as a deficiency of knowledge but as a constitutive ontological element. He shows that, far from being something that appears residually in the beatific vision, mystery shines forth precisely in such a vision in which the person is at the peak of its being, fully sharing in the incomprehensibility of God that constitutes the being of the person. Finally, the transcendent that manifests itself in any human act as that which is beyond reach but constitutes the ground and the horizon of such an act is fully disclosed as what it is, namely, the holy, absolute, incomprehensible mystery into which the person surrenders not out of resignation but in the most profound act of freedom, in faith, hope, and love, recognizing and embracing it as complete and blessed fulfillment.[81]

Rahner's notion of the incomprehensibility of God is completed by his theology of the Trinity, where he shows the unity between economic and immanent Trinity as an expression of the intrinsic link between the transcendence of God and God's radical closeness to the person both "in the spiritual depths of our existence as well as in the concreteness of our corporeal history. Here lies the real meaning of the doctrine of the Trinity."[82]

An interesting point to explore in relation to Rahner's theology of the Trinity is the extent to which his notion of God balances the danger of understanding God in merely christological terms. Although Christ is the last and best word or disclosure of God's will in relation to the creature, and the summit of Rahner's theological, transcendental anthropology, in the last analysis everything must be traced back to the mystery of the eternal design of God's self-communication that lies in the incomprehensible God that cannot be reduced to Christ. Christ is for Rahner the effect and not the cause of God's salvific design: "There is a knowledge of God which is not mediated completely by an encounter with Jesus Christ."[83] Rahner's position comes forth even clearer when he says "that, of course, God's will to save us is not primarily the consequence of Christ's cross, but the previous cause from which the cross and the Christ-event stem. He has loved us and, *therefore*, has sent his Son to us (Cf. Joh 3,16)." "I have been redeemed *through* Christ. Christ himself is the consequence, the effect, and not the cause, of God's will to redeem us."[84] The consequences of this understanding of the Godhead can be very promising for a development of a Christian theology of God that, although, as Christ-ian, it is and must remain christological, can avoid some of the dangers of reducing theology to Christology, a danger very real in the case of Western Christianity and apparent in post–Vatican II Catholic theology.

It is important to notice that in his last and deepest attempt to express what God is Rahner resorts to symbolic language and calls God "the holy mystery." There are two points to notice in this move. First, Rahner is once again coherent with his Thomistic epistemology according to which the imagination is needed in the last operation of knowledge, namely, the "conversion to the phantasm."[85] Any name is inadequate because God is "the nameless one" by definition.[86] That is why there must be recourse to the imagination at its highest point since what must be "named" is the totally and absolute other.

The second point is that the description of God is the limit-case of what Rahner calls the intrinsic relation between original experience and its conceptualization.[87] There is always involved in the former a tendency toward reflection, and yet the latter never captures in its totality the content of that original experience. In Rahner's reflection of God as the incomprehensible, absolute, holy mystery, the distance between original experience and concept reaches its highest expression since the concept can never reach what is precisely its very ground and its condition, and paradoxically, therefore, what is closest to it. Therefore, the only possible option is to recognize it and to surrender into it as the final and blissful coming of knowledge into its own bosom. That is also why Rahner's effort to conceptualize it issues not in a metaphysical concept but in a mythical, symbolic one.[88] In the end, reflection and prayer, "sitting and kneeling theology," come together.[89]

The Theological Enterprise

As Carr says, there is a clear match and intertwining between the content of Rahner's theology and his method. Rahner's method of theological anthropology has a strong impact on the development of the theological content of his work.[90] In relation to his method it is important to clarify how Rahner understood the relation between experience and the salvific message of Christianity; between the worldly realm and the realm disclosed by revelation; between history and eschatology. It is also important to understand how Rahner envisioned the task of theology and the relation of the latter to philosophy and science.

Anthropology and Theology: A Two-Way Path around Transcendental Reflection on Experience

It has been said above that Rahner's theology can be seen as a quest for the meaning and unfolding of the content and implications of Rahner's own multilayered yet unified experience, using transcendental reflection to unveil the ultimate, constitutive elements of that common-to-all-human-beings experience and showing the reasonableness of that reflection in order to make his findings shareable and, hence, public.

It is vital to have a clear idea of how Rahner used a double strategy to formulate his theology. On the one hand, he showed that every categorial, concrete experience pointed always as its condition of possibility to a transcendental experience that, unthematically but originally, involved the experience of the transcendent. On the other hand, he showed that that transcendent, always hinted at in any human experience, is most adequately identified with the triune God of Christian revelation.[91]

Rahner's project is none other than to make relevant and meaningful the truths of Christianity expressed by the tradition of the church in the form of dogmas. In order to avoid the danger of understanding the dogmas as cold formulas, unrelated to human experience, Rahner strives to show how they are, if understood adequately, the perfect fit for that which is already perceived, albeit dimly and inchoately, in human experience.[92] Therefore, according to Rahner, anthropocentrism and theocentrism need not oppose each other. On the contrary, they somehow require one another since both poles are intrinsically linked. He even writes that "in the deepest philosophical and theological analyses, anthropocentrism and theocentrism are the same thing."[93] Rahner uses a correlational method that links experience with revelation. According to him, there is an interlocking and complementarity between philosophical theology and theological theology, as two ways of looking at the same phenomenon from different perspectives and upon different premises.[94]

Rahner uses this method to interpret the main Christian dogmas. The prototypical example is Christology, where anthropocentrism and theocentrism fuse in the person of Christ, both the paradigmatically self-realized person that surrenders into God, accepting freely God's loving and gratuitous self-communication, and, at the same time, the very self-communication of God become flesh.[95]

An important aspect of the method is how it assesses the necessity of positive, historical revelation. It might seem that if the person can, by transcendentally analyzing experience, discover the truths of faith, at least in nuclear form, then revelation is not necessary. Rahner thinks that, on the contrary, revelation is totally necessary because the person can only arrive to an unthematic, tentative, and obscure idea of the transcendent that remains far from the content of the revealed truths. Therefore, revelation is the only way to discover and to identify what is inchoately known, namely, God's willing self-communication that is sealed forever in the Christ event. Still, historical revelation is but a categorial occurrence in time of the transcendental revelation that is embedded in any important human experience as a consequence of God's self-communication. In other words, categorial revelation is not something extrinsic to the person, but that revelation that renders explicit and concrete what the person already, although unthematically, knows in the depths of existence.[96]

Theology at Two Levels

Rahner wrote extensively on many matters, without ever producing a whole systematic account of his theology. However, his work *Foundations* can be called a synthesis of systematic theology. In fact, Rahner thought that it was impossible for any theologian to write a full-fledged scientific systematics due to the complexity of issues involved, the fragmentation of theological disciplines, and the dramatic increase in the number of sciences with which theology must enter into partnership. Yet this fact cannot preclude the formulation of a "prescientific" theology that is an honest account of hope and a justification of faith at a "first level of reflection." He gave such an account in *Foundations*.[97]

Rahner therefore distinguishes between prescientific and scientific theology; introductory and systematic theology; a theology that gives "an idea of Christianity" and a theology that gives a full account of Christianity; theology at a first level of reflection and theology at a second or further level of reflection. Rahner practiced both. Many works in his *Theological Investigations* (sixteen volumes in the German original edition, twenty-two so far in the English edition) are investigations that belong in the group of scientific, full-fledged theology. Equally, some of the works that Rahner himself edited or in which he participated belong also to the same group.[98] Rahner's distinction between prescientific and scientific theology has to do with the understanding of theology at the current stage of development of knowledge, increasingly characterized by the importance of the different sciences and by the complexities caused by the phenomenon of specialization. The crucial question becomes how, in such a situation, the whole of existence can be encompassed, thought about, and, finally, accounted for. Under current circumstances, the only way to do so for Rahner is to take a global, prescientific approach that, nevertheless, demands precision and rigorous thinking and, in that sense, is scientific in its own terms.[99]

In fact, Rahner's transcendental method is the tool he uses to give an account of faith in the form of an idea of Christianity. That method cannot claim to be able to address all the theological problems as they appear in the ever-more-fragmented and self-centered theological disciplines. On the contrary, it would be ill-suited for that purpose because the distinction among these disciplines lies, to a very important extent, precisely in the different method they must adopt to address successfully the problems that constitute their subject matter. But the transcendental method is indeed the best suited for that prescientific, yet rigorous discipline whose subject matter is the faith of the individual, both as it appears in experience and as it is proclaimed by the church, and whose aim is to show how that proclamation by the church coheres with the data that emerge from the analysis of experience if that analysis is profound enough, that is, transcendental. In that sense it can be concluded that the essence and the main motivation of Rahnerian theology, if considered from the point of view of the use of the transcendental method, are typically prescientific.

Rahner's best prescientific work is *Foundations*. As such, *Foundations* is, on the one hand, an introductory text and therefore does not and cannot deal with all the questions a full systematic theology would have to confront in order to give an exhaustive account of Christianity. However, the work assumes and uses the findings of "scientific" theology that are "commonly accepted" at the current level of theological research and that seem "reasonable" to Rahner and, without which, the work would have been impossible. On the other hand, the work wants to show the reasonableness of the main tenets of Christianity "from within human experience," which in fact means that the strong point of the work, its pillar, is more on the side of fundamental theology than on that of systematic theology. *Foundations* could be seen in that respect as a powerful fundamental theology of transcendental character that probes its claims by showing how they cohere intrinsically with the main doctrines proclaimed by the church, using the "commonly accepted" findings of systematic theology in expressing these doctrines.

That Rahner never considered himself a "scientific" theologian and that he understood his theology as revolving around only one question, namely, the inner relation between human beings and God on the basis of God's free self-communication, is clear from his own revealing words: "No, I have not practiced scientific theology, or, to be more precise, I have practiced very little scientific theology." "I have practiced theology for the sake of announcing, preaching, and working pastorally." "I am not and I do not want to be a scientist. I would like to be a Christian who takes Christianity seriously; a Christian who lives ingenuously in the present time and, on this basis, lets himself be faced with a myriad of problems, upon which then he reflects. If one wants to call this 'theology,' fine."[100]

This poses the question of whether then Rahner did produce a scientific theology and, even further, whether his transcendental method could bear fruit in relation to that theology. That, despite his own words, Rahner wrote extensively on matters of scientific theology is a fact that cannot be disputed. He worked with the tools and methods suitable for the questions analyzed, such as hermeneutics, historical criticism, critical exegesis, and so on, and he stands as a remarkable theologian on that account alone.

On the question of how fruitful his transcendental method was for scientific theology, two points are to be considered. The first is that, in writing systematic theology in collaboration with other theologians, Rahner offered a systematic contribution in the particular area of transcendental anthropology that played an important role in anchoring the foundations upon which the contributions of the other authors could be built and read.[101]

The second point is that, in developing his own systematic investigations and his contributions to common-enterprise systematic theologies in areas other than transcendental anthropology, such as God, the Trinity, grace, Christology, and so on, he combined his dealing with the different questions a systematic theology must face—and that require the adoption of different methods according to the nature of the matter analyzed[102]—with the use of transcendental method. This allowed him to refer the whole and the parts of his investigation to the core in which all of them acquire their unity, coherence, and theological relevance, namely, the only event of salvation and the only mystery of faith: God's self-communication.[103]

David Tracy's words "systematic theology with a transcendental cast" referred to Rahner's theology seem very accurate to express this in a concise and disclosive way, as well as his observation, following Rahner, that the "transcendental moment" in systematic theology has a corrective and not a constitutive character, whereas that moment is constitutive in the case of fundamental theology.[104]

A Dialogical Theology: Philosophy and Sciences as Partners

The main reason for the ever-more-complex nature of systematic theology is the increase in the number of questions that theology must face as a result of the development of the different sciences. Rahner evolved quite substantially over the years in his understanding of theology and its relation to other disciplines. In his first works, the only partner of his theology was philosophy. Moreover, in *Hearers of the Word* he claimed that philosophy must surrender to theology.[105] Later, however, he was very aware of how heavily theology borrows from philosophy. When talking about the relation between philosophy and theology, he said: "Theology necessarily entails thinking, and thinking takes place outside the realm of theology."[106]

Rahner knew from the beginning to the end of his career, because it was something implicit in his transcendental method, that theology and philosophy were intrinsically interlocked. Therefore, despite the broadening of the scope of knowledge caused by the development of the sciences, the partnership between the two was permanent and indispensable. However, over the years Rahner became increasingly aware that a new situation had arrived for theology, in which that discipline had to enter a partnership with the natural and social sciences, a partnership that had to be directly established as opposed to doing it through the mediation of philosophy.[107] Finally, theology also had to establish a dialogue with the secular, "non-scientific manifestations of the life of the spirit in art, in poetry, and in society."[108]

This manifold partnership of theology with these other domains not only shows the pluralistic nature of knowledge but also necessarily brings about a situation of pluralism within theology itself, since different philosophies and different approaches to the life of the spirit necessarily issue in different theologies. Finally, there is another dimension of plurality, namely, the fragmentation of knowledge that results from the specialization that affects all disciplines, whether scientific, philosophical, or theological.[109]

Two conclusions seem to emerge from such an analysis. First, pluralism is not something to be afraid of because it threatens unity, but a requirement of the complexity of a kaleidoscopic reality that can only be properly understood if analyzed from different perspectives and with different eyes. Second, there is for Rahner a way to relate all fragmented and pluralistic knowledge to its original unity, namely, to refer it to the conditions of its possibility, that is to say, to its ground, which is no other than the "holy mystery." However, Rahner was far from being naive and was totally aware of the challenge posed by plurality to the unity of doctrine. He always defended in that respect the necessity of the magisterium in the church, although he was careful to define the limits of that magisterium and the ways it had to be performed.[110]

A Recapitulatory Theology

Rahner's theology can be, then, justly characterized as a theology that searches for that nucleus from which everything else comes and toward which everything converges, a theology of *exitus* and *reditus* in the best tradition of Christian theology, but, as William V. Dych puts it, "in a new key." It is theology "in a new key" because it is intrinsically intertwined with experience. This experience is, on the one hand, philosophically reflected upon, especially in relation to its transcendental moment. On the other hand, it is theologically reflected upon, on the basis of lived faith. That, as already shown, is also Carr's point, as well as that of Metz, in analyzing Rahner as a theologian who successfully and intrinsically combines reflection with experience, anthropocentrism with theocentrism, and doxography with biography.[111]

Rahner recapitulates his entire work in his theology of God as the incomprehensible holy mystery. This theology of the holy mystery centers on the divine action that constitutes the only Christian mystery, that is, God's free and loving self-communication as it is unthematically affirmed in any meaningful human act (philosophical theology) and fully disclosed in Jesus Christ (theological theology).[112] The Rahner who starts with the analysis of the transcendental experience from a philosophical perspective, and who historicizes it, opening it out to existential dimensions of humanness other than knowledge and to social-political dimensions that belong to it, ends with a meditative theology based on the experience of God and centered on the mystery of God, where, finally, everything coheres. Rahner expresses this when he says: "I recognize that for me and for my theology the experience of God as the incomprehensible has come more and more powerfully to the fore of both my own existence and my theology." "I feel confronted by an incomprehensible mystery that encompasses, holds, and permeates me. We call it God."[113]

Vorgrimler describes this evolution in Rahner very perceptively as a movement toward concentration that, nevertheless, has nothing to do with reductionism.[114] In fact, this concentration or recapitulation of everything else in God as holy mystery fully coheres with Rahner's theological will and aim, namely, to give the ultimate answer to existence from within, showing that such an answer cannot be other than the incomprehensible God ever present in human existence as its innermost constitutive element and fully disclosed in Jesus Christ. In other words, although Rahner's method opened the way for new and far-reaching developments in Catholic, and in general Christian, theology, his own theological vocation and his transcendental method led him to what he always had been in search of: the foundation, the ground of existence, finally manifested as holy mystery.

Chapter 2

Johann Baptist Metz: Political Theology

Continuity and Discontinuity

This and the following chapters will analyze three different models of Catholic theology in three different parts of the world: political theology as developed by Johann Baptist Metz in Germany, liberation theology as formulated by Gustavo Gutiérrez in Peru, and public theology in North America.

Usually three authors are considered linked to political theology in Germany: Dorothee Sölle, Jürgen Moltmann, and Johann Baptist Metz.[1] Metz is chosen here because he is the only Catholic of the three, because he was Rahner's student, and the two were collaborators and friends, and because he is crucial to capture some of the potentialities and problems in the theology of Rahner. Liberation theology is a way of doing theology that originated in Latin America in the late 1960s and that currently is widespread throughout the world, present in every continent. Gustavo Gutiérrez is widely regarded as the father of that theology because he was the first who formulated it formally and has been one of its most consistent proponents.[2] Public theology in North America can be described as the effort across many denominations to formulate a theology that justifies its claims so as to make them publicly shareable and, therefore, relevant for the public realm. Such a broad description encompasses many different approaches that cannot be analyzed here. It would be a mistake to think that the concern with publicness of religion and church only takes place in North America. Many authors have analyzed the issue in different contexts.[3] There are, however, many factors that distinguish the North American context from the others. Among them are the radical pluralism of its society and the fact that the churches are multiple and have been constitutionally nonestablished since the creation of the United States of America as a nation. The present work focuses on Catholic public theology as developed by David Tracy.[4]

In the preceding chapter, Rahner was described as "the turning point in Catholic theology," with the important qualification that such a turning

point had other protagonists too.[5] Rahner's theology is central to understanding the evolution of Catholic theology in relation to the authors
analyzed in this work. This, as will become clear later, does not imply
that the three main authors examined in the remaining chapters, and the
theological currents they represent, have been equally influenced by Rahner. Far from that being the case, each of them has a different cultural and
theological background and, therefore, relates to Rahner in a different way.
Whereas Metz studied under Rahner, Gutiérrez's main exposure was to *la
nouvelle théologie* during his studies at Lyon, and Tracy studied under Lonergan in Rome. However, as Metz says, Rahner's theology plays the role
of starting or referential point in political theology, in liberation theology,
and, in general, in that kind of Catholic theology that has endeavored to
unfold the potentialities of the theological guidelines that were at the core
of Vatican II.[6]

Rahner's influence and the significance of his theology in the Catholic
realm became paramount after the doctrinal and pastoral changes that took
place in Vatican II. The main theological directions in Rahner's theology
and in the theology of the other influential theologians in the council were
officially adopted by the church, thus opening new ways for theological development and encouraging the undertaking of new theological enterprises.
In other words, Vatican II made it a central task of the church to bring
about a theological development that could work out all the implications
of the new stand of the church in crucial matters, such as its relation to
the world and to other Christian denominations and world religions. What
in the case of the theological forerunners of the council had been a matter
of personal concern and endeavor, looked upon with suspicion by Rome,
became a priority for the postconciliar church.

The council marked the beginning of a new era in the Catholic Church,
an era within which the three theological models to be analyzed must be
understood. More precisely, the new position of the church in relation to the
modern world can be considered the heart of that new era.[7] Catholic theology underwent a deep change that transformed both its underlying attitude
and its development. The main focus in attitude shifted from the previous
conservatism of neo-scholasticism to renewal. Pope John XXIII had called
the council to bring about an *aggiornamento della Chiesa,* so that, from its
inception, Vatican II was a forward-looking and a transformative council to
update the church. However, it would be wrong to think that the conciliar fathers, the theologians, and the other participants forgot about tradition. On
the contrary, the general mood and main enterprise were of "coming back to
the sources." This retrieval of the original Christian message entailed giving
up the methodological and ideological strictures of neo-scholasticism and,
in a positive way, the adoption of the new exegetical methods and the incorporation of the new research on patristics. That the Catholic Church saw

the council as an event of conversion and purification in order to be truly and fully faithful to the gospel can be clearly seen throughout the dogmatic constitution on the church, *Lumen Gentium*. The same spirit is apparent in all the other constitutions and decrees.

Methodologically, renewal meant both a rediscovery of the Christian sources and a radical openness to all the interactions affecting the understanding of Christian faith. Consequently, theology became a complex and multidisciplinary task in dialogue with other disciplines within a church that had become aware of its universal character and of the ensuing multicultural centeredness of its pastoral action. This, as Rahner had predicted, prompted a plurality of theologies. Moreover, theology became an ongoing task that, to a great extent, had to keep reformulating itself, somehow, in search of a new paradigm.[8]

In view of this structural pluralism in theology, it is easily understandable that the models of theology to be examined here present continuities and discontinuities in relation to Rahner's theology. Among the continuities, the three post-Rahnerian theologies center upon the meaning of faith and the role of theology in relation to the situation from which they stem and to which they relate. In this respect, the three follow the Rahnerian drive toward a pastoral-focused theology that is meaningful to the faithful because it deals with problems that the faithful recognize as theirs. In that sense, they are pastoral-correlational theologies.

The main thrust of Rahner's theology and of its method, as has been said in the previous chapter, is fundamental rather than systematic or practical. The same can be said of the three theologies here analyzed. However, as in the case of Rahner, such a claim must be qualified. Metz describes his theology as a practical-fundamental theology, and something similar can apply to Gutiérrez. Moreover, none of these theologies lacks totally a systematic content. In the case of public theology, several strands exist under that same rubric, with different stresses on the fundamental, systematic, and practical character of theology. However, the three models are trying to work out the core meaning of faith and the role and method of theology and, therefore, can be viewed as fundamental.

The three models also share one of Rahner's main tenets, namely, the intrinsic correlation that exists between human history and the history of salvation. In other words, what happens in human history is relevant for salvation. Therefore, salvation, although always beyond historical reach, must be acted out in history. The obvious corollary is the relevance of Christianity for public ethics and politics, something the three models emphasize, reacting strongly to the process of privatization that has developed hand in hand with modernity.

The three theologies are also, like Rahner's, apologetical. To be sure, they are not so in a defensive way, such as was the case for Catholic theology in its confrontation with "modernism." Rather, these theologies are apologetic in a positive way because they endeavor to show both the legitimacy and the relevance of Christian faith for human life.[9]

The crucial discontinuity in relation to Rahner lies in the fact that these post-Rahnerian theologies want to be anchored in the social and historical circumstances of the reality they address. In that respect, they distance themselves from the relative ahistoricity of Rahner's transcendental reflection and define both their method and their content in direct relation to the situation.

This holds for each of the three models. Political theology confronts a transcendental-idealistic view of both the human person and Christianity and affirms the inescapable primacy of concrete history(ies)-story(ies) in defining them. Both its method and its content operate within this overall framework. Liberation theology addresses a reality of oppression and defines its method as based on liberating praxis. Its contents show a reading of scriptures and tradition, and of the social situation, from the point of view of that praxis. Public theology adopts a method that enables it to put forth its claims in a context of radical pluralism in order to contribute to the public realm. Accordingly, its contents focus on issues central in public debate, whether in relation to worldviews or to practical, political stands.

Although these three models are interrelated on the grounds of their continuities and discontinuities with respect to Rahner, they represent three different views that respond to three diverse social settings, cultural traditions, concerns, and outlooks. As stated above, what is interesting in relation to Rahner is that the latter seemed to theologize in the midst of a culture that was modern but had no further specification. His theology is basically a metaphysical (transcendental, existential, and mystical) reflection somehow removed from the flux of history. The importance of concrete history and society in the other three projects becomes paramount both implicitly and explicitly, although in different ways.

It is important, however, to qualify Rahner's relation to history. On the one hand, it would be completely wrong to say that Rahner was not interested in historical developments. The clearest example to the contrary is his outright commitment to the task of transforming the church after Vatican II and his conviction of the epoch-making character of the council as "the beginning of a new beginning." On the other hand, Rahner's main theological positions are arrived at not on the basis of history-driven reflection but on the grounds of transcendental reflection. Therefore the discussion must be open in order to determine whether there is a constitutive historical-political dimension in Rahner's theology or whether, as Metz argues, such a dimension does not belong to the structuring core of that theology. The point will be discussed below.

Social, Cultural, and Ecclesial Background
of Metz's Theology

In order to understand Metz's theology, its evolution, and its main categories, it is important to know its historical, cultural, and theological background. It is equally important to define the main traits of the church within which that theology emerges and to which it relates, as well as some characteristics of the wider German society in which the church itself performs its task and works up its own identity.

Metz comes from a highly developed and organized society within what, until recently, has been called Western Europe. In fact, it would probably be more accurate to say that Metz's context is that of Mitteleuropa, especially after the deep transformation that has taken place in Europe since 1989. Metz himself refers consistently to Mitteleuropa as his cultural context throughout his work. However, in more precise terms, Metz comes from a rural, Catholic, traditional, small town, in Bavaria.[10] It is important to realize this in order to understand one of the focal points in Metz's theology, namely, the relationship between tradition and modernity.[11]

Germany belongs to the core of Mitteleuropa. To talk about Germany as a nation is obvious today, but, historically speaking, it would be more accurate to say that Germany has been a complex geographical and political reality linked to the Holy Roman Empire, a sort of over-the-centuries-decaying utopia of the lost unity of the world. In fact, this empire, created under Charlemagne, was controlled by the Hapsburgs, the heads of the Austrian Empire, from the thirteenth century until its dissolution in 1806 after the Hapsburgs were defeated by Napoleon.

During the second half of the nineteenth century, the historical power and influence of the Hapsburgs were displaced by the increasingly assertive Prussians, and the German nation was born under the Prussians in 1871, the year in which the Second Reich was proclaimed. Later, with the First World War, the Prussian Empire collapsed and Germany started a new era with the Weimar Republic. Hitler did away with the Weimar Republic and brought about the Third Reich. The situation changed again dramatically during and after World War II. A devastated Germany was divided in 1949 into two separate states, and the new, although divided, Germany was born from the ashes of the war.

Social unrest and peaceful public protests in East Germany, in which churches and Christians played an important role, led to the collapse of the East German state in autumn 1989. The fall of the Berlin Wall that year marked symbolically the end of divided Germany and the reunification of the country under the political model of the Federal Republic of Germany (West Germany until 1990). Over centuries, the borders of what today is known as Germany have varied widely, thus reflecting the instability and permanent conflict that have affected historically a great part of Mitteleuropa in general and Germany in particular.[12]

Historically, especially over the last two centuries, there has been an almost permanent quest for German identity. The complexity of the notion of *the* German, the lack of a well-grounded national political tradition, the serious conflicts and problems in which Germany has been involved, and the still relatively recent democratic experience are some of the main factors behind this quest.[13] Sociologically, and in general terms, German society is a good example of the relative homogeny of European society. The term "homogeneous" must be understood here in a strictly relative sense. To say that German society is homogeneous does not imply that there are no differences among its members. In fact, as has already been mentioned, the unification of Germany took place as late as 1871 (under Prussia), and the national language, known as High German, slowly started to gain its current primacy after Luther translated the New Testament into that particular type of German. Despite this primacy, local varieties of the German language are still common in the various regions of Germany. In general, cultural differences between the different regions (or *Länder*), as for instance between Bavaria and Westfalia, to mention but an obvious example, are clearly noticeable.

Currently, the main differences inside the reunified Germany are twofold. On the one hand, there are important cultural and ideological differences, due to the fact that each of the two former states (West and East Germany) developed a different cultural, political, and social tradition over the last forty years. On the other hand, there is an important economic difference among the former and the new *Länder*, due to the gap in wealth between West and East Germany. In 1988, the year before reunification, per capita income (technically, gross domestic product per head) was $19,743 in West Germany and $5,526 in East Germany.[14] Seven years later, in 1995, the average per capita income in the former West Germany was $26,450 and $14,706 in the former East Germany.[15] Of these two main differences, the former seems to be the most difficult to tackle. For an increasing number of people, it is crystal clear that, strictly speaking, there has been no reunification but rather a Western takeover of the former East Germany.[16]

Despite these differences, Germany and the societies of the different countries of Europe in general can be considered homogeneous societies if compared with the United States. First, the population is essentially homogeneous in terms of race and cultural background in each country, lacking (although not completely) the strong interracial and interethnic components that characterize U.S. society. Second, religious homogeneity in Europe has gone hand in hand with political and cultural homogeneity (*cuius regio, eius religio*). The historical fight against Islam to prevent it from entering Europe, and later, during the centuries-long Ottoman Empire, from crossing the border of the Holy Roman Empire, is witness to this fact. Historically, although as in the case of Islam also compounded with other political and economic factors, anti-Semitism has been present on and off in Europe since the eleventh century.[17]

Practically speaking, all Europe is Christian except certain countries of Ottoman descent like Turkey, Bosnia, and Albania. In most European countries, practically speaking, there is only one church, such as for instance in Italy (Catholic), in Sweden (Lutheran), or in Greece (Orthodox). Other churches, although existent in those countries, are an almost insignificant minority. In some countries, as for instance in Germany, there are two main churches as a result of the Reformation and of the subsequent religious and political arrangements made after many fierce and bloody religious wars. Finally, although only a few countries have officially established churches, as for instance England, the one or two churches existent in each country can be considered (with some exceptions like France) as quasi-established de facto, given their domineering position in those societies and the level of intertwining with the state in practical matters.[18]

One of the features of German society is a touch of a paradoxically efficient bureaucratic style that somewhat accompanies the sense of order and efficiency that pervades German society. Whereas in other countries bureaucracy is understood to hinder the decision-making process and the creativity of organizations, the opposite seems to have been the case in Germany up to a point (it is currently argued in Germany that bureaucracy in business has gone beyond a beneficial level).[19] However, German bureaucracy and efficiency are also viewed by many as an ambiguous feature of the nation. The main reason for this is the disastrous consequences of such a feature when applied to war and extermination, as during the Nazi period. The two world wars in the twentieth century have deeply convulsed the soul of the country. The history of the country during the Third Reich and, most especially, the Holocaust constitute a most traumatic period for German society and the German people, both at the individual level and as a whole.[20]

There are many questions involved in the issue of the Nazis and of the Holocaust. These questions can be focused by asking What? Who? and Why? On the question of What?: it is a shared belief, based on well-documented research, that, apart from the imperialistic drive of the Third Reich and its will to conquer Europe, the Nazi regime systematically persecuted all kinds of races and people that did not conform to the standards of the Aryan race. Gypsies, Slavs, homosexuals, and handicapped people are but examples of those who were the victims of their businesslike program of extermination. The Holocaust of the Jewish people, around six million of them, is the high mark of this program and one of the peaks of human madness and perversion in history.

Who? is a far more difficult and painful question than What? At stake is whether the guilt belongs only to Hitler and the small group of his top aides or, at the other extreme, to all Germans. The tendency in the first two decades after the end of the war was to blame Hitler, his aides, and his most fanatic followers for the Holocaust and the other crimes. Time, new research, and new generations started to uncover some painful truths concerning the support of the population for Hitler and his policies, the great number of people directly or indirectly involved in the program of extermination, and, most of all, the lack of protest against the laws and decrees that allowed those programs to develop or against the crimes that, too often, were being publicly committed. According to some authors, one cannot strictly speak of collective guilt, because guilt always follows from a personal decision, and it is evident that not every German supported Hitler and his policies. However, say the same authors, German society as a whole cannot avoid responsibility for what happened. Therefore, there would be a common responsibility although not a collective guilt in relation to the Holocaust and to the other atrocities.[21] In relation to this question of Who?, one frequent further question, perhaps the most painful of all, put in many different ways, is Why the Germans? The question itself, and the answer to it, are a crucial thread in the quest for German identity, mentioned above.[22]

Why? is another controversial question. Daniel Jonah Goldhagen has pointed out that many Germans were directly or indirectly involved in the killings, and ordinary people were willing to persecute and kill Jews out of a deep-seated German anti-Semitism, already present in Luther and thereafter through Hitler.[23] For many authors, however, both in Germany and elsewhere, Goldhagen's single-cause interpretation takes into account neither the complexity of the problem, its many sides and roots, nor the work done by researchers on that issue over almost fifty years.[24]

The most important controversy, however, took place in Germany in the mid-1980s and was baptized *Historikerstreit*. It involved not only historians but also other intellectuals and showed clearly the different ideological positions and interests of the people involved in it. The controversy started with an attempt by Ernst Nolte to revise the understanding of the Holocaust, questioning its uniqueness and relativizing German guilt, advancing two main theses. First, the extermination of Jews by Hitler's regime cannot be considered a unique event, since other exterminations, such as the Gulag, had already taken place before the Holocaust. Second, the Holocaust can, at least partially, be explained as triggered by fear of the threat Stalin and Soviet communism posed to Germany.[25] Several authors, on the contrary, saw Nolte's as an attempt to find an easy way to get rid of a haunting past and to accommodate to the new political start of Germany as embodied in the Federal Republic of Germany (the *Stunde Null* position). Far from accepting Nolte's theses, these authors denounced them as a neoconservative ideological manipulation of history and affirmed that the memory of the Holocaust, its uniqueness, and the responsibility of Germany in relation to it had to be an unavoidable part of German history and, as such, seriously faced by the German nation.[26] The position of both Hans Mommsen and Martin Broszat, although opposing the revision of the Holocaust and affirming its singulariry, tries to take into account a whole array of different elements and factors that include, among others, those pointed out by the defenders of the revisionist position.[27]

Economically, post–World War II Germany has been a success. Before the sweeping changes that took place in Europe in 1989, the former West Germany, a country that had to rebuild itself from the ashes after World War II, was the fourth biggest economy in the world after the United States, the Soviet Union, and Japan. For most of the 1980s and through 1990, it was leading exporter in the world, something that witnesses to its manufacturing capabilities and to the quality of its products. In terms of per capita income, Germany ranked eighth in the world at the end of 1989 (the United States ranked sixth). One of the main strengths of the country was its ability to control inflation and to maintain steady economic conditions. This stability made the German currency an important referential point in the international financial markets.[28]

From 1990 on, the German economy has been confronted with the challenge of having to transform from the ground up both the infrastructure and the productive structure of the former GDR. Such a dramatic change is not without painful economic, social, and political cost. Although final figures are still to come, reliable estimates placed the amount of money needed at more than $1 trillion, over a period leading to the year 2000. To meet this, the final figure the German people have to pay as income tax is being increased an extra 7.5 percent, something that, despite the well-known German civil consciousness and discipline, is unpopular. On the social side, unemployment in the former GDR started to come down after having peaked at 16 percent in 1994 as a result of closing down or restructuring more than eight thousand large companies. These previously state-owned companies were privatized, or disposed of, by the Treuhandanstalt, the state agency in charge of managing the privatization process until 1995. Although between 1992 and 1995 the economy grew in the new *Länder* over 6 percent annually, the rate of unemployment was still 14 percent in 1995, as opposed to 8 percent in the old *Länder*. All in all, unemployment in Germany peaked at 10.2 percent in 1996, something unheard-of in the miracle economy of Germany after World War II. The conclusion seems to be that, although the new German economic miracle is going to be more difficult to attain than the previous one that made the German economy rocket after World War II, Germany will continue playing an increasingly important role in the years to come.[29]

Despite this, the awareness of the horrors of their recent history, together with the global responsibility attached to being one of the superplayers in the economic scene, has somehow embarrassed, puzzled, and disquieted the politicians, the citizens, and the society as a whole. This was clearly the case during the 1991 Gulf War. On the one hand, Germany was aware of its international responsibility as one of the world economic superpowers. On the other hand, the memories of the past haunted the German society and its politicians, preventing them from even considering the possibility of engaging in any war. The *Friedensbewegung* (Peace Movement) during the time of the war was especially strong among the university population, but by no means reduced to it. Unable to contribute to the war with troops, the country had to pay to the United States $15 billion, a dear contribution at a time when the economic reconstruction of the former East Germany was costing the country more than $100 billion a year. Although internationally Germany has become more assertive through the 1990s,[30] it seems as if German society was at odds with itself, somehow caught in the trap of its own ethos,[31] in a way blocked by its own angst.[32]

The final cause of this angst is, doubtless, the historical events through which Germany and the German people have gone over the last 125 years, since the creation of the nation: two empires, two world wars, and the murderous madness of the Nazi period that peaked in the Holocaust. Those in Germany who incessantly review the history of their nation searching for the causes of such events point out that that history, from the Second Reich on, was built upon an inferiority complex, an overnationalistic self-assertion, a rugged anti-Semitism, a penchant for militarism, and a predisposition to follow the commands of authority.[33]

In any case, this traumatic history is the ground for people's angst, Germans' and non-Germans' alike, in respect to Germany. That translates into a primal, almost invincible, lack of confidence in the country and its people; an incapacity to face the future without anxiety, without mistrust, without defending it from the potential evil the country and its people can cause.[34]

In these circumstances, Germans are experiencing serious difficulties in trying to decide their own identity and future, both as a nation and in relation to the European Union. The most recent example of this is the ambiguity of the two main processes Germany is undergoing and the mixed feelings that those processes are generating among the population, namely, the process of German reunification after the collapse of the East German state and the process of integration in Europe following the steps established by the Treaty of Maastricht to that end. Those two processes bring back the historically famous *Deutsche Frage*.[35]

The *Frage* has always revolved around the identity and role of Germany as a nation. Strictly speaking, the *Frage* came about in 1806, when the Holy Roman Empire came to an end. The question was which kind of organization could be suitable for the German people instead of the bygone empire. The underlying question was how to bring about a unified

Germany, beyond the traditional division of the nation into different territories and powers, rooted in the feudal system, and beyond the diverging interests of the two superpowers of the time: the Prussians and the Hapsburgs. More to the point, the final question was whether the German people should have their own, and unified, state like the other main nations in Europe. The question, already debated and programmatically answered in the Paulskirche constitution of 1848, was finally answered in 1871 with the creation of the German Reich, under Prussian leadership, from which Austria was excluded.

However, the answer became a problem both for Germany and for the rest of the world, due to the hegemonic and imperialistic drive of the Kaiserreich, under the banner of the Alldeutsche program and the increasing propaganda favoring a greater *Lebensraum*. Catholics were declared enemies of the Reich, and a strong anti-Semitism started to develop. Germans, according to the feelings of the day, had, in a way, to be both Prussian and Protestant. Outside the Reich, every country with a German population became a potential enemy. Moreover, the great powers of the day also became enemies of the Reich in that they hindered the Reich's *Weltpolitik*. As a result of its defeat in World War I, Germany lost part of its territory, and the other countries started to fear a unified Germany with a population of sixty million and an impressive economy. The *Deutsche Frage* came thus to be an important question for the rest of the world.

After the difficult interregnum of the weak Weimar Republic, Hitler galvanized again the imperial spirit and sought a new answer to the *Deutsche Frage* through the proclamation of an aggressive, expansionist, race-cleansing, all-Aryan Third Reich. After the Holocaust and the catastrophe of World War II, Germany was divided again into two parts, and that division became the new center of the *Deutsche Frage*. The never-ending question was answered by the political reunification of Germany in 1989–90, on the model of the hitherto Federal Republic of Germany.

At the moment of the reunification and thereafter, the *Frage* took another old-new turn. The question being debated, not only in theoretical terms but also in relation to most relevant political decisions, was and, covertly or overtly, continues to be whether or not a reunified Germany is potentially dangerous for Europe and for the rest of the world, given the experience of the last two wars, and whether a European union can be built on the basis of such a strong nation, placed in the center of Europe, and willing to assert itself again as a *Weltmacht*. This is the main reason behind the stress politicians, and people in general, place on the importance of a strong alliance and shared goals between Germany and France as a firm ground for the European union. This is also one of the reasons for the discussion about the extent to which Europe should advance its union. While the United Kingdom defends a union that preserves a high degree of national identity and a great scope for decision making at the state level, others, especially France and Germany, have been advocating a union that takes over most state powers, thus greatly reducing the importance and role of the national state and diminishing the threat that certain nations, a reunified and powerful Germany especially, could pose to the rest.

Another important thread of the *Deutsche Frage* nowadays concerns the appropriateness of the process of reunification and the balance of power between the two former parts of Germany. The question has important ideological, cultural, and political implications. At the core of it remains the question of whether the so-called reunification has not simply been a takeover of East (economically broke) Germany by West (economic-world-power) Germany.[36] Legally, this is so because the reunification took place according to the procedure of Article 23 of the constitution of the Federal Republic (that is to say, without changing that constitution), instead of according to Article 146 of the same constitution (rewriting the constitution on the basis of the contribution of both parties and approval of it by subsequent national referendum).

From this standpoint, the reunification of Germany marks not only the triumph of capitalism over a spent socialism but also the overriding of the identity, values, and memory of the former East Germany, from which the whole nation could have benefited. Furthermore, the unification under one state, say some authors, has not taken sufficiently into account the possible benefits, both internally and in relation to the rest of the world, of other models of unification, such as different versions and degrees of a two-state federation. In any case, it is increasingly clear from a sociological point of view that more and more people in the former East Germany feel frustrated and consider that they are not sufficiently taken into account in the new reunified republic. For some authors, although the constitution and the laws are common to all Germans, there exists an important cultural difference between West and East that is more and more reaffirmed by the East as a means of protecting itself from what is perceived by the population in general as an aggressive and inconsiderate Western takeover. This fact seems to demand new ways of integrating both parts into the whole, taking into account the differences between the two. The problem, according to Jürgen Kocka and others, is that the transformation of East Germany has taken the form of a revolution from outside and from above.[37]

In the cultural realm, German thinkers set the philosophical agenda of both modernity and the critique of modernity, within a tradition more speculative than pragmatic, prone to transcendental analyses. German society has had its own prophets and critics, at least as much as, but probably more than, any other society. This is central to any analysis of Metz, because his work can be seen, on the one hand, as an ongoing dialogue with the critical spirit of modernity and, on the other hand, as a progressive intensification of the critique of Western society and of a Christianity that has accommodated itself to that society.

Kant, Hegel, Nietzsche, and Heidegger are towering figures in modern and postmodern philosophies, and all of them can be considered both modern and critical of modernity. Kant started this dual stand by criticizing the naive and triumphalistic notion of reason of Christian Wolff, while at the same time proclaiming his support of the Enlightenment. However, and this is also important in relation to Metz, the German Aufklärung (Enlightenment) was, from the beginning, different from the French Enlightenment concerning its treatment of religion and its relationship with theology. Unlike the latter, the German Aufklärung, starting with Leibniz, tried to establish a connection between revelation and reason and formed close ties between philosophy and theology and between philosophy and religion. This is not to say that those relations were uncritical of the church: witness, Kant's opposition to every kind of dogmatism. Nonetheless, revealed religion and theology, unlike the case of the French Enlightenment, continued to be central concerns of the German Aufklärung. This peculiar nature of the Aufklärung is crucial to understanding why German society never severed its ties with the churches and why the churches, one way or another, have always been respected and deeply ingrained in that society until today.

Critical social theory attained world relevance with Karl Marx and marked a turning point for the understanding of the task of philosophy and its relation to praxis and social change. The Frankfurt School developed this Marxist critical social theory, taking into account late capitalism, the tragedy and madness of Nazism, and the subsequent world war. Today, its most important representative, Jürgen Habermas, is a typical example of the attempt of the school to rescue modernity critically. His neomodern project shows the intrinsic commitment of the school to modernity, and, therefore, its radical opposition to current postmodernity.

In the field of literature, Heinrich Heine, Thomas Mann, Bertold Brecht, and Günter Grass are representative of a modern critical literature, having an artistic counterpart in the painters of German expressionism like Max Beckmann, Otto Dix, and Ernst Ludwig Kirchner, and also in more recent artists like Joseph Beuys.

An interesting case is that of the Bauhaus. The school was one of the best examples of how to bring about new ways of thinking and treating space appropriate to the new times inaugurated by industrialization and by the new utopias that were taking hold after the Russian Revolution in 1917. The project included architects, painters, sculptors, and designers, and its works, as in the case of Wassily Kandinsky and Paul Klee, show a striking similarity with the utopian Russian constructivists such as Kazimir Malevitch and Vladimir Tatlin. Just as happened with the Frankfurt School, and with the German expressionists, the members of the Bauhaus were persecuted and the school closed down under Hitler. The most prominent figures, Walter Gropius and Mies van der Rohe, took refuge in the United States and became the successful founders of the most rationalist and functionalist architecture ever made.[38]

That Germany has had its own prophets and critics is true as well for religion and theology. First of all, Luther was the father of the Reformation, reformulating the most crucial tenets of Christianity—salvation, grace, church, and the access to, and the interpretation of, the word of God—and bringing about a social revolution that changed the face of Europe and was instrumental in strengthening the German national consciousness and soul. Later, at the time of the confrontation of theology with modernity, both liberal theology and its neoorthodox critique were also born in Germany. Friedrich Schleiermacher established a dialogue with modernity from within, trying to show that, contrary to the presupposition of modernity, faith could not be rejected on the basis of modern reason but responded to the deepest longing of the self, thus inaugurating a new understanding of theology and of hermeneutics.[39]

Karl Barth, the central figure of neoorthodox theology, has been interpreted traditionally as the alternative to Schleiermacher, and in opposition to him. Barth thought that some followers of Schleiermacher, such as Ernst Troeltsch (who ended up as a philosophy professor in Berlin), led to a dead end from which theology could only be rescued if the word of God regained an uncompromisingly absolute position in any theological system. Barth, however, was far more nuanced in his appraisal of Schleiermacher than other theologians, as, for instance, Emil Brunner. Whereas the similarities of approach and content between Rahner and Schleiermacher are striking at certain points, Metz is closer to Barth in his critical spirit and in his stressing the importance of God's word understood as normative narrative.

An important point in understanding Metz concerns the status of the churches in Germany. The two main (and the only socially relevant) churches, the Evangelical and the Catholic, are semiestablished churches.[40] Although neither of them is a state church, both enjoy a special status on the basis of historical practice and of the concordats (in the case of the Catholic Church) and agreements (in the case of the Evangelical Church) with the state and the *Länder* at different moments.[41] As a result of this, the churches are recognized by the state as such; each is financed by its members through the church-tax collected by the state;[42] they are present in the state universities with chairs paid for by the *Länder*,[43] and they play an outstanding role in the realms of health and charity.[44]

A crucial point is the wealth and economic power of the churches due both to the stable and abundant income that comes through the church-tax and to the role played by the churches in the area of social services. In comparative terms, the German churches are thought to be among the wealthiest in the world. Moreover, due to their complex organization and to their impressive network of social services, they are one of the biggest employers in Germany, with all the social and political implications that this entails.

An important factor concerning both churches in recent history, although in different ways and degrees, is the traumatic time lived under National Socialism, the subsequent devastating war, and the horror of the Holocaust. In general terms, neither church opposed strongly the Nazi regime, nor did they engage in protecting Jews and other minorities from being persecuted and exterminated by the regime. However, each church must be separately assessed according to its own deeds, taking also into account those instances in which direct opposition to the regime was adopted.[45]

In relation to the Catholic Church, an important, and highly debated, point concerns the influence the concordat between the Catholic Church and the Nazi regime had in shaping the position of the Catholic Church in relation to that regime. Most authors agree that, although the Catholic hierarchy, including the Vatican, mistrusted and criticized, even condemned, the Nazi ideology up to 1933, they wanted by all means to get a good concordat from the Nazi regime. Hitler was aware of this and signed the concordat almost immediately upon his nomination as *Reichskanzler* in 1933, without arguing too much against the wishes of the hierarchy. By doing so, he secured the official recognition of his regime by the Catholic Church and its subsequent ambiguity and silence concerning his actions. The hierarchy changed its position drastically vis-à-vis the regime, became somehow tied up with the Nazi government, curtailed the ability of its organizations to set up resistance to Hitler's regime, and finally became almost a prisoner of its own decisions, fears, and wishes to avoid a greater evil.[46]

For some authors, the Catholic Church consciously pursued the concordat with a long-term view of the foreseeably disastrous consequences of the Nazi policies. For these authors both the Vatican and the German bishops knew that they would have to pay a price for the concordat but wanted, nevertheless, to have a legal instrument whereby the Catholic Church could secure its public presence in a society in which no opposition to the regime was allowed, and thus put its doctrine forward against the regime's totalitarian *Weltanschauung*, and defend its rights and the rights of the citizens.[47]

A most painful question relates to the consistent silence of both the Vatican and German hierarchy in relation to the Holocaust. Although some few bishops publicly proclaimed their anti-Semitism, thus giving the regime a moral support for the Endlösung,[48] it is a fact that both the Vatican and German bishops spoke clearly against the racist ideology of the regime. The most famous instance is Pius XI's encyclical *Mit brennender Sorge*, issued in 1937. Moreover, the Vatican included all the Third Reich's racist literature in the Index of Forbidden Books, making it clear that the racist ideology was totally contrary to Christianity. However, and this is also clear, both the Vatican and German bishops avoided a direct denunciation of the Holocaust and remained publicly silent about it. Both Pius XI and Pius XII had a draft of an encyclical condemning racism and the persecution of Jewish people. However, the former died before he could complete it, and the latter never published it, probably fearing the strong Nazi reaction to it and the possible negative consequences such a reaction could have for both Jews and Catholics.[49] The silence of the German Catholic episcopate in this question is even more surprising taking into account that there were bishops like Clemens August Graf von Galen, Joseph Godehard Machens, and Franz Rudolf Bornewasser, who, having taken a stern stance against the regime's extermination of physically or psychologically handicapped people, kept silent in relation to the persecution and extermination of six million Jews. It is clear that, among others, one important reason for this silence was the wish of the bishops to avoid the likely ensuing Nazi repression and Endlösung of the Catholic Church itself.[50]

Perhaps the clearest statement regarding the position of the Catholic Church in relation to the Nazi crimes against the Jews is the declaration contained in the final document of the synod of the German Catholic dioceses held in 1975. The document states that, with the exception of certain individual persons and groups, the Catholic Church turned its back on the Jewish tragedy, concerned itself too much with the threats to its own institutions, and remained silent with respect to the crimes perpetrated against the Jews and Judaism. The document was written by Metz and approved by the synod after minor corrections.[51]

A final point to bear in mind in relation to Metz's thought is the difficult historical relationship between Catholicism and modernity in Germany and between the Catholic community and German society around the time of the creation of the German state. In a way, Metz's ongoing rethinking of modernity and of the role of the church in a democratic and developed society is closely linked to that history.

After the Reformation, religious and civil peace were a fundamental problem in northern and central Europe in general and in the different parts of today's Germany in particular. At the time of the Reformation, religious freedom was not even conceptually envisaged. Peace, from the first social-religious peace agreement of Augsburg in 1555 on, meant a political-geographical agreement defining the boundaries of each confession, following the above-mentioned principle *cuius regio, eius religio*, thus doing away for good with the previous religious unity of the Holy Roman Empire. This circumstance has powerfully marked the subsequent history of Europe and is still reflected in the geographical and institutional boundaries of religions and churches. In 1648, the peace of Westphalia somehow stabilized the confessional boundaries and normalized the relationship among the churches. The first *Land* to admit a diversity of confessions and cults was Prussia, at the end of the eighteenth century, due to the adoption of the ideas of the Enlightenment by Friedrich II, the Great. His successors, however, tried to water down, if not to reverse, that religious freedom.[52]

The political unification of Germany brought to the fore the question of the religious identity of the country. The liberal Paulskirche constitution of 1848 established religious freedom and equality of confessions before the law and advanced the separation of church and state. This new development gave the churches, but especially the Catholic Church, all the freedom they needed to regulate themselves according to their own aims and their spiritual mission. Prior to that time, new restorative forces (periodicals, associations, formation centers, and the like) had been gaining ground in the Catholic Church, becoming increasingly vocal in opposing liberalism, affirming the importance of the papacy for the church, and defending the principle according to which the education of the youth had to be entrusted to the church and was by no means the task of the state.[53]

Liberalism won the day after 1848, and the Catholic Church found itself on the defensive. Moreover, whereas liberals favored a *kleindeutsche* territorial solution, Catholics sought a *großdeutsche* solution including Austria in the new Germany in order to secure their majority.[54] To complicate the situation further, Catholics defended the precarious situation of the pope in Italy, affirming the right of the papacy to its own state in order to guarantee the independence of the head of the church, thus opening themselves more and more to the accusation of not being true citizens of the state but loyal only to the pope. The papal *Syllabus* and, most of all, the proclamation of the dogma of the infallibility of the pope were the last straw in an increasingly tense relationship between the Catholic community and the reigning forces in Germany.

The Catholic Church, its organizations, and its political party, Zentrum, presented a well-organized body seeking to convey efficiently their principles, points of view, and public interests into the social and political realms. Such an organized body was considered a danger for the state, a power-competitor to it, and, according to Reichskanzler Bismarck, also an enemy of the state. For Bismarck it was totally wrong that the members of a church were used politically as the constituency of a confessional party, whose political pursuits were based on religious claims. Therefore, the Kulturkampf sought to bring the Catholic Church under the control of the state in order to offset its influence and social power. The Catholic Church decided to resist the pressure of the state, accepting the consequences of its resistance. In 1876, all Prussian bishops were either in prison or in exile; by 1880, over one thousand parishes were vacant, and the Catholic press was under tight political control. After the death of Pius IX, Pope Leo XIII adopted a more conciliatory stand and came to a compromise with Bismarck despite the opposition of the Zentrum Party. Although the tension of the Kulturkampf diminished, Catholics continued to be active in society through their political party, their associations of workers, their many other societies, and, after World War I, through Catholic Action. After World War II, Catholics moved further away from their separateness through the creation of an interconfessional Christian-democratic political party, led by laypeople and publicly detached from the churches.[55]

The Rahnerian Heritage and Beyond

Metz has always insisted that Rahner was for him not only the theologian from whom he received the foundations of his own theology but also the believer whose testimony reinforced his faith. "Theologian as study-and-life master" is one of the ways in which he portrays Rahner. This portrayal corresponds to the characterization of Rahner's theology as "biographical dogmatics," that is, as a theology that brings doctrine and life together in an inner interrelation.[56] To that extent, Metz's theology cannot be understood without Rahner's theology. Metz's own development is clearly a dialectical one in relation to Rahner's transcendental theology. On the one hand, he shares some of the basic tenets of that theology. On the other, his theology takes its own direction based on some central, and early, intuitions that constitute new points of departure as well as new referential points from which to dialogue critically with Rahner.

These intuitions were present in Metz at an early stage in his theological life. As early as 1959, Metz published a meditation under the title *Advent Gottes* in which he already displayed some of the main threads of his mature political theology. Although the work is closely linked to Rahner's anthropological theology and has a teleological character, many of the reflections in it signal the direction Metz's theology will later take. Themes such as memory and forgetfulness, the bourgeois society, the myth of progress, the domineering technological mind in developed societies, and, above all, the encompassing importance of history are already central to his discourse. Furthermore, the whole meditation centers around God's eschatological coming as the constitutive element of our human and Christian life. This eschatological God destroys the myths and defenses of the creatures, breaking through their manageable time-horizons and their tamed interpretation of reality, appearing suddenly before them, and totally disturbing their lives. There is always a danger of reading too much into this revealing text, but it clearly shows that Metz was already at that time standing on his own feet and willing to pursue the themes that, later on, will constitute the core of his theology.[57]

Metz cannot be explained without Rahner, but neither can he be explained as a simple development of Rahner with some critical particularities. Their theologies cannot be easily reconciled without downplaying their innermost constitutive element. In the end, the touchstone of both theologies is the way they understand God. Rahner applies his transcendental method to his multilayered experience and arrives at God as the incomprehensible mystery into whom the person freely surrenders, thus achieving fulfillment. Metz exposes the transcendental method to the painful memories of history, the prototype of which is the suffering of Christ, and makes theodicy the center of his *Gottesrede* (God-talk). From that he arrives at God as mystery, that is, the one with whom complete "reconciliation" is impossible and into whom the believer freely surrenders in the midst of the painful experience of having been forsaken by that God.[58]

Metz the student followed a clearly Rahnerian path. As Rahner did, he encountered Aquinas and Heidegger and then started to develop his own thought on the basis of Rahner's transcendental method. In fact, both his doctorate in philosophy under Emerich Coreth[59] and his doctorate in theology under Rahner can be seen as creative works of development of transcendental thought. Metz's doctoral dissertation in philosophy, "Heidegger und das Problem der Metaphysik,"[60] tries, on the one hand, to analyze Heidegger's position in relation to metaphysics through Heidegger's transcendental discussion of the ontological essence of truth. On the other hand, Metz tries (a typical move of Coreth and Rahner and the other transcendental Thomists) to appropriate and to critique Heidegger on the basis of Aquinas's thought.

In 1961 Metz finished his doctoral thesis in theology published a year later under the title *Christliche Anthropozentrik*.[61] Important to bear in mind is that Metz wrote this dissertation after reworking Rahner's *Spirit in the World* for its second edition, which appeared in 1957, and just before the publication in 1963 of the, also by Metz, reworked second edition of Rahner's *Hearers of the Word*. Those were undoubtedly the years when Metz was most exposed to Rahner's influence. However, Metz's reworking of these two books was a thorough one, deleting a substantial amount of text, reordering the material, and adding a great deal of systematization by means of footnotes and terminological additions. Rahner felt obliged to endorse Metz's work,[62] and Metz in turn felt obliged to take responsibility for the changes.[63] The freedom with which Metz undertook these revisions and their scope seem to indicate that he was not, even at that time, a mere follower of Rahner but already an interpreter of the latter, capable of reformulating Rahner's thought even through the introduction of new concepts. The pattern of the relation between the two seems to have been one of permanent dialogue and mutual influence. Rahner influenced the young Metz, but the later Metz of the political theology made Rahner turn toward a more social, ethical, and historical approach.[64]

Christliche Anthropozentrik is basic to understanding some of the permanent traits of Metz's theology. In a way, Metz's aim in this work is to pursue further Rahner's interpretation of Aquinas in a systematic manner, trying to define that which makes Aquinas a turning point in the history of Western thought. Metz's method in *Christliche Anthropozentrik* consists in going beyond the concrete points of Aquinas's thought, looking rather for its formal structure, that is to say, for Aquinas's *Denkform* (mode of thought). Therein lies Aquinas's main contribution. Basically, there are three main points in the thesis. First, Metz maintains that whereas Greek thought was anthropocentric in its contents (ontically anthropocentric) but cosmocentric in its formal structure (ontologically cosmocentric), Aquinas's thought is theocentric in content (ontic level) and anthropocentric in its formal structure (ontological level).[65] By so doing, Aquinas, according to Metz, acknowledges human subjectivity, and his correlate, human freedom, recognizes the world as something essentially linked to humanness and understands God not as an object but as the transcendent ground and horizon of human subjectivity and freedom.[66]

Second, Metz affirms that this epoch-making transformation of the way of thinking carried out by Aquinas has a biblical-Christian origin. Here Metz proceeds by steps. First, he bases his notion of *christliche Denkform* (Christian mode of thought) on the intrinsic relationship between revelation and human subjectivity (which in turn reflects the intrinsic relation between grace and nature established by God's self-communication), following Rahner's thesis in *Hearers of the Word*, a text that was being reworked by Metz at that time. Subjectivity, as that ability of human beings to be aware of and to think about themselves, is made possible by the original revelation that constitutes the horizon of human knowing and thinking. Without that horizon reflection could not exist at all.[67]

The second step follows from the basis thus established. When the way of thinking, of understanding ourselves and being in general, takes that original revelation as the horizon of understanding, then that way of thinking can be called Christian. True theology comes into being, then, when revelation becomes intrinsically constitutive of a reflectively built system of human self-understanding.[68] That, according to Metz, takes place for the first time with Aquinas.

The third step shows that it is precisely the anthropocentrism of Aquinas's paradigm that gives it its Christian character (*christliche Anthropozentrik*). Again based on Rahner, Metz argues that Christian revelation has an anthropocentric character because the human being is the only created being capable of a subjectivity that reveals the person as God's partner and as participant in the divine nature. Aquinas's anthropocentric *Denkform* is precisely the rendering in systematic thought of that originally anthropocentric character of Christian revelation that inaugurates history and has its prototypical realization in Jesus Christ. Hence, Aquinas's paradigm must properly be called *christliche Anthropozentrik*.

Finally, Metz considers that Aquinas's paradigm shift, and behind it the Logos of Christian revelation, are at the base of modernity's twofold turn to the subject and to history. In fact, Metz argues, what Aquinas started has been carried out by modern thinkers, although they have taken the wrong way in many cases. However, with respect to the anthropocentric paradigm that it adopts, modernity can be considered Christian, even if, due to its negation of those principles contained in the formal structure of its paradigm, that Christianity is anonymous.[69] Metz is totally clear in this respect when he writes that "it is necessary to learn to understand this modern, epoch-making thought in a positive way in its basic characteristics, as the process of the growing 'Incarnation' of the Christian Logos in the reflective human self-comprehension."[70]

Metz will maintain throughout his career a creative and dialectical relationship with these three points thus developed, as well as with their underlying transcendental analysis. On the one hand, he will maintain them in his later work, as for instance in the case of the intrinsic relation between Christianity and modernity. On the other hand, he will modify them, sometimes substantially but dialectically, so that his modification works more like a corrective than like a negation.

Metz has affirmed several times the corrective character of his theology in relation to the previous paradigms, especially the Rahnerian transcendental one. He has recently confirmed this character of his theology.[71] Due to this corrective character, Metz's position must be taken dialectically rather than literally in many cases. A complete negation of the position he is correctively critiquing is seldom the case. This makes his theology a tensional one, and the attempt to resolve this tension often involves misinterpreting Metz's position. At the same time, the corrective character of Metz's theology cannot be understood as a simple stressing of this or that concrete point in relation to the thought it wants to correct. This corrective character is in fact the affirmation of a new theological center point from which a new theologically powerful interpretation of Christian faith and reality emerges. This interpretation, in turn, acts as a dialectical counterweight to the theology it tries to correct, without totally denying thereby the importance of the center point in which that theology originates. That new Metzian theological center point, whose unfolding is the aim of this chapter, is anchored in an eschatologically understood history, in which Christian faith and praxis account for the whole of that history, especially for the victims and fatal failures of that history. This is possible on the basis of an anamnestic theological reason rooted in the dangerous memory of Christ's passion and resurrection and actualized by the memory of the defeated and the dead. Metz himself has explained that this corrective trait of his theology seeks to rescue and to develop the substance and intention of the position it corrects.[72]

An important point in Metz's advance toward his formulation of political theology is his early confrontation with the phenomenon of secularization. Whereas Rahner's theology was always marked by its early creative confrontation with the modern turn to the subject, Metz's theology is in some way marked by its early confrontation with the reality of a society that was becoming increasingly secularized. Secularization is for him the crisis that must be faced by Christians as a challenge and that prevents them from continuing to believe in the same way as before.[73]

As responsible for the section of fundamental theology in the international review *Concilium*, Metz edited in 1966 a volume of that review devoted to the confrontation with contemporary atheism. The contributors tried to analyze mainly the challenges that Marx, Freud, and Nietzsche pose to Christianity. In the preface, Metz points to "the task facing all Christians: the justification of faith in the face of contemporary unbelief."[74] Prior to that, in 1965, Metz also announced in *Concilium* the beginning of a section on fundamental theology, whose focal point would be the relationship between church and world, following the lines and themes of *Schema XIII* of Vatican II, the Pastoral Constitution on the Church, *Gaudium et Spes*.[75] According to Metz, fundamental theology had to confront the problems stemming from a world characterized by pluralism and secularization. In his contribution to that issue, Metz wrote an article on unbelief.[76]

The affirmation of the centrality of the phenomenon of secularization for Metz can in no way be taken as a denial of Rahner's interest in the questions of secularization and unbelief. What is meant here is that there is a difference in the *focal* interest of Rahner and Metz. Rahner's main focus was the investigation of all the implications of human experience. His transcendental analysis led him to show that God's self-communication is the founding event of the human subject and that, therefore, humans, whether they realize it or not, live always out of a grace that is "always and everywhere" because it is the original creative act of God (hence uncreated). All Rahner's theology can be seen as an unfolding and application of that central statement. In relation to unbelief, Rahner's position preempts any possibility of essential unbelief. Every categorial negation of God's existence is in fact a transcendental affirmation of that existence, because if the latter did not hold, the former could not take place.

Metz partakes in this basic Rahnerian approach early in his career, but, immediately after *Christliche Anthropozentrik*, he focuses on the questions of secularization and unbelief in a much more phenomenological way than Rahner did. Although he never rejects the principles of Rahner's transcendental theology, he realizes the problem of that theology concerning unbelief.

Strictly speaking, Rahner preempts the existence of essential unbelief insofar as a categorial or concrete denial of the existence of God involves a transcendental or formal affirmation of that existence. Therefore, Rahner's theology cannot unfold all the implications of unbelief (in its multifarious forms) for an understanding of Christian faith not based only on transcendental analysis but on historical practice.

Already in 1965, Metz had no problem in questioning the validity of Rahner's thesis of the "anonymous Christian" from the point of view of a theology that wants to tackle unbelief in its full depth and radicalness. Hence, he addressed the question of unbelief from the opposite perspective of Rahner's, namely, from the perspective of the "unbelief of the believer." In Metz's view, unbelief cannot be primarily analyzed as something external to belief but must be viewed as something that "affects the believer more basically and inescapably in his own act of faith and in the subjectivity of his own faith—as unbelief of the believer, as unbelief *intra nos.*"[77] Most interestingly, Metz makes an important move in understanding grace as the source of belief. Grace is not something that is simply there "always and everywhere" but an ever-new free gift coming from a God who does not belong to the past but who is ever again before the believer, constantly occurring in the life of this believer. Grace is an ever-happening event that belongs to an ever-happening-before-us God. This is the reason belief is always linked with human freedom and history and, therefore, contingent and threatened. Metz goes further in his confrontation with unbelief as something inherent in belief, affirming that the believer is *"simul fidelis et infidelis,"* subject to a sort of *"negative existential"* that sets off in the believer a permanent and unsolvable dialectical relationship between belief and unbelief. For Metz it is clear that faith cannot be perfect in history because it has an eschatological structure. Finally, Metz points out that, without exposing this precariousness of the belief of the believer, it is very difficult either to dialogue with the different forms of actual atheism or to address atheism simply from the perspective of the anonymous Christian.[78]

A distinct feature of this approach is Metz's radical understanding of human fallibility, of the human inescapable temptation to sin and evil. In this sense, Metz is an atypical Catholic theologian with powerful Protestant intuitions that make his anthropology close to that of Reinhold Niebuhr.[79] Witness to this are Metz's following questions: "Are there not rather forms of man's self-alienation which cannot be removed by a release from economic-social situations, however successful, and from which man will always draw the 'sorrow of his finiteness'? Are there not forms of self-alienation that cannot simply be dissolved into social-utopian expectation?"[80] This basic and central piece of Metz's intrinsically tensional anthropology was conceived at an early stage in his theological work and has powerfully marked his later political theology.[81]

These early intuitions, especially the historical-eschatological structure of the act of faith, and the understanding of grace as an ever-again-happening event that is a free gift of an ever-before-us God, are exactly what Metz tried to explain later with his tale "of the hare and the hedgehog."[82] How is it possible, asks Metz, that a transcendental analysis makes historical practice irrelevant? That, no matter the result of historical experience, the answer be "always already" there? If pure transcendental analysis is adopted, there is no room for unbelief. However, unbelief must be approached both from within historical belief itself and on its own terms, taking into account the real causes of its historical existence and the critique of religion involved in it. Since transcendental analysis places itself not in the level of history but in the level of analysis of the conditions for the possibility of history (freedom), it is a barren method to understand historical unbelief and, therefore, must be replaced by other ways of doing theology. It is easy therefore to understand why Metz starts to insist on the primacy of praxis over theory. Metz's position, which is a corrective one, does not simply try to deny Rahner's position, but does rather try to establish the actual historical-eschatological framework outside which Rahner's transcendental analysis risks being meaningless.

In the early 1960s Metz starts to analyze whether secularization can be seen in a positive light from a theological point of view. In the first essay of *Zur Theologie der Welt*,[83] he carries on the basic analysis underlying his position in *Christliche Anthropozentrik* and comes to the conclusion that the worldliness of the world, far from being anti-Christian, is in fact the consequence of the Christian principle become operative in history. Metz understands secularization as the realization in history of something that has always been present in the essence of Christianity. This realization is the main trait of modernity (*Neuzeit*). But, beyond that, Metz understands the world basically as history in the sense that history belongs to the very historically-becoming-itself of the world.[84]

The basic theological principle behind Metz's understanding of secularization is that God has accepted and assumed definitively (eschatologically) the world in Christ.[85] Christ is the historical event in which it becomes manifest, and this not only by means of Jesus' words and deeds but more originally by the very meaning of the incarnation, that God's action *upon* the world (not *in* the world) in history means God's eschatological acceptance of humankind and world in their own being. Transcendence of God and worldliness of the world do not run against each other but grow in the same direction. Since God has accepted definitively the world in its own being, God is not a competitor against the world but the guarantor of its autonomy. Since this acceptance has been manifested through the incarnation of God, it follows that the ensuing greater transcendence of God in relation to the world does not imply any greater disengagement of God with respect to creatures but, on the contrary, takes place through the Emmanuelian God-with-us event. Hence, as Metz says, "Descendence and transcendence of God grow in the same direction."[86]

Metz wants to avoid any kind of unwarranted world-optimism or incarnation-optimism, however, and distinguishes between the eschatological acceptance of the world by God and the resistance of the world to acknowledge God as its creator and liberator. Therefore, secularization is an ambiguous process that entails also secularism or rejection of God. In fact, the secularistic, God-negating aspect of secularization is intimately intertwined with the liberating dynamics of the Christian principle in history.[87] Again, this historical ambiguity of the world was manifested in Christ, since his incarnation entailed his passion as an intrinsic element. Hence, the Christian understanding of history stands always under the sign of the cross.[88]

This analysis of the ambiguity of the process of secularization runs parallel to Metz's anthropology, which in turn is founded on Aquinas's doctrine of the indissoluble relation between matter and form, and body and soul, and, beyond that, on his doctrine of the distance between essence and existence in all created beings. Metz argues that, according to Aquinas, human concupiscence cannot be interpreted simplistically and dualistically as a rejection of the spirit caused by sensuality but rather should be understood as that human, unavoidable spontaneity or indetermination that stems from the fact that the spirit only becomes human spirit through the structure of the senses.[89]

According to his interpretation of the worldliness of the world, which worldliness has its origin in the spirit of Christianity become operative in history, Metz concludes that Christians are citizens of the world in their own right and that they have to pursue the end of Christianizing the world by enhancing its worldliness. Since God has accepted the world, the church must serve the world and must not think of itself as something that God has willed as separate from the world.[90]

Some central traits of Metz's thought are already clear in his early work. One of them is his resistance to resolving tensions by splitting them into dual forces. His is an almost constitutively antidualistic approach, whose origin must be seen in the integrative character of the thought of both Aquinas and Rahner. What separates Metz, especially the later Metz, from the integrative responses of Aquinas and Rahner is that they have provided systematic answers to the problems raised by the tensions emerging in their integrative enterprise, whereas Metz is reluctant to produce any system designed to appease or reduce those tensions. To a great extent, this reluctance has its origin in Metz's critique of theology as a way of knowing too much and of providing too many responses in relation to a God who, in the end, proves to be unfathomable. There are multiple examples of this Metzian attitude, but perhaps the clearest is his analysis of the *Theodizeefrage* (theodicy question), to be reviewed later in the chapter. As a result of this, Metz's theology is purposively inconclusive in many instances, or, put in another way, positively inconclusive in order to force a negatively (insofar as God is unfathomable) conclusive response.

A second permanent trait of Metz's theology encountered at this early stage of his career is his stress on a theology of the cross over against a theology of glory. In the final analysis, the cross stands in Metz for a sign of the impossibility of reconciling those aspects that show God to be contradictory when thought of in human categories, especially in relation to the questions of evil and innocent suffering.

The third permanent trait of Metz's theology present in his early work is his concern with history. History is for Metz such a constitutively important element of the theological reason that he, already in 1961, states that "theology is man's refined understanding of himself from a historically appropriated transcendent origin," pointing out that such an understanding is "based on the address of God's free word."[91] In his reflection on the metaphysical and the theological orders, Metz is already making a point, whose further pursuit and intensification will be the centerpiece of his political theology and of his confrontation with Rahner's transcendental theology, namely, that, for theology, both the free word of God and the free human response to it occur in and through history and concreteness.[92] Metz further affirms that the historical perception by faith is "a way of actuality that is not deducible from within, that is, transcendentally" and that the enlightening of transcendental metaphysics by the theological logos "is not the product of deductive reflection. It must be learned from history."[93] In a final move that already qualifies both his understanding of history as eschatologically constituted and his understanding of transcendence, Metz affirms that "the Christian understands his relationship to transcendence itself eschatologically: he awaits the 'beyond' as something to come historically, and history itself as something to be transformed into the one kingdom of God and man."[94]

First Stages of Political Theology

After 1963, Metz becomes more eschatological and more future-oriented in his basic historical approach.[95] There are two factors that help to explain the change. On the one hand, he became that year professor of fundamental theology in Münster, thus in a better position to pursue his own project. On the other hand, that is the year he met Ernst Bloch, the thinker who both sharpened Metz's own perspectives and opened new perspectives for his theological enterprise.

Metz seems to have found in Bloch's critical, provocative, and radical thought the kind of framework he was needing in order to develop his own intuitions and theological emphasis. Metz himself gives a detailed account of his friendship with Bloch.[96] The account follows a chronological path and is most revealing with respect to the genesis of Metz's new concerns. The relation with Bloch continued until Bloch's death in 1977. During those years, according to Metz, their differences became at the same time fewer in number but more essential. To begin with, Bloch reinforced and, in certain instances, awoke Metz's interest in the categories of hope, future, utopia, and subversive eschatology, that is, Christianity's resources to oppose any kind of injustice or established order on the basis of eschatological hope. On a deeper level, he made Metz confront the issues of justice and solidarity in relation to Christianity. Hence, through Bloch, Metz came to confront Marxism, and critical theory in general, in one of its most secularly religious versions. Bloch also was instrumental in making Metz confront as early as 1967 (not without fear) the question of theodicy.

One of Bloch's works that had a considerable influence on Metz was *Atheismus in Christentum,*[97] first published in 1968. This provocative work, written by Bloch when he was eighty-three years old, reflects his latest position on the question of religion and its relation to emancipation and can help us to understand Metz's turn to political theology. Among his most provocative statements, Bloch writes that *"the best thing of religion is that it creates heretics"* and that *"where hope is, also is religion;* but the reverse, where religion is, also is hope, does not apply,*"* and also that *"only an atheist can be a good Christian; to be sure, also: only a Christian can be a good atheist."*[98]

Bloch shifted Metz's attention from philosophical to biblical categories as understood by an atheistic Jew. This marks a turning point in Metz's career. This emphasis on the Bible and the biblical religion will lead him substantially to modify his perception of what Christianity means. His position in *Christliche Anthropozentrik* was based on a philosophical interpretation of the historical realization of God's will upon the world as shown by transcendental analysis and as manifested historically in Jesus Christ. After his encounter with Bloch, Metz starts to take into account the biblical narrative, as the story of a historical relation between God and a concrete people, in order to discover the paradoxes, tensions, and contradictions that make up Christianity, biblically understood. Here one must find the source of Metz's increasing insistence on narrative, memory, and literal interpretation of the Bible. What Metz finds in Bloch's reading of the Bible is the resource he was looking for to overcome the transcendental approach of both Heidegger and Rahner. This resource allows him to understand Christianity as a dynamic way to become a subject before God in history.

Bloch is also the beginning of Metz's exposure to Jewish thinkers who, independently from being believers or nonbelievers, were all marked by the

Jewish constitutively narrative and remembering character.[99] This exposure has led Metz to insist on the essential Jewish character of Christianity and to formulate his radical eschatology.

The depth of Bloch's influence on Metz directly affects the latter's idea of God. From an ontological-transcendental Thomism for which Exodus 3:14 is understood as "I am who I am," Metz moves to a new understanding of God's identity following literally the dynamic, eschatological interpretation Bloch gives Exodus 3:14: "I will be who I will be."[100]

Bloch opened those new ways and perspectives Metz already was looking for and gave him a counterpoint in relation to which, in a critical and confrontational manner (both participated many times in Christian-Marxist dialogues), Metz started to formulate his new political theology. But, although the resemblance between the two thinkers in terms of themes, interests, categories, and even style is noteworthy, that resemblance cannot hide the substantial differences concerning both their traditions and beliefs, on the one side, and the ultimate answer each gives to the questions that conform to his thought, on the other side. As mentioned above, Metz has said that these differences diminished in number but became more important in essence over the years. As Metz puts it, referring to the relation of Christian theology to Bloch, "Christian theologians will only be able to learn from him in opposition to him. There is no other way."[101]

In his essay "Die Zukunft des Glaubens in einer hominisierten Welt,"[102] Metz points to freedom and history as the loci of God's manifestation in the world, once the traces of God in nature have lost their theophanic power as a result of the "hominization" of the world. By shifting from natural to historical theophany, Metz finds a way to oppose the atheism of Nietzsche and Marx and of the positivists like Bertrand Russell and proclaims that far from being at the end of its historical existence, Christian faith is at the beginning of its own innerworldly history. In Metz's view the hominized-historicized world is pluralistic, wonder-free, dehumanized, and an ongoingly becoming world. Using in fact a method of correlation, Metz shows that, if the hominized world is going to make sense, it requires itself to be open to the mystery of God that makes itself present when the historical experience is allowed to go to its limit. If such limit-experience is not allowed to take place, modernity dehumanizes. Therefore, in the midst of that historical experience, humans can make sense of their existence only if they transcend the blinding luminosity of the secularistic foreground and open themselves to the transcendent reality that shines in the background.[103]

There are several interesting points to notice in Metz's analysis. First, he starts to use certain social analyses to describe the situation of the modern world, so as to come closer to the historical experience of the modern person. Second, some of his later explicit criticism in relation to modernity already starts to emerge at this stage, namely, the question of privatization of the religious experience, the understanding of modern human history as the stage where manipulation reigns and the person fades away, and the critique of modernity as being in fact profoundly inhuman. (Later he will express it as the "dialectic of the Enlightenment," following Theodor Adorno and Max Horkheimer.) Third, Metz is still moving on the level of generic analysis he is going to critique later, referring to the modern person in general and as an individual, very much like Rahner. Finally, Metz continues to use Rahner's transcendental analysis to show that the experience of the modern human being only makes sense if behind and beyond the hominized, categorial experience, a transcendental one is perceived when that categorial experience is carried to its limit. Yet he begins to point to the encounter with the other in history (still generically understood as intersubjectivity) as the concrete way to make present the mystery of God in a hominized-secularized world.

Metz takes a further step toward political theology, actually using the term explicitly for the first time, in his essay "Kirche und Welt im eschatologischen Horizon."[104] Metz sharpens in this essay his concepts of world (understood as social co-world and as world of history), history (as history with an end), faith (as hope), and theology (as eschatological and social-critical). He makes clear that his new approach tries to overcome the purely transcendental, existential, and personalistic starting points in theology, but without losing the valid insights of such positions. By valid insights he means the ability of these theologies to deal with the problems that the Enlightenment poses to Christianity. Such problems cannot be tackled by scholastic theology because for that theology there exist no problems concerning the relation between religion and society. Once the unity of the two is shattered by the Enlightenment, a new theological perspective is needed.

Metz is here at pains to try to express in a positive manner the relation between Rahner's and his theology. He does not want to deny the validity of transcendental theology; he just wants to avoid its dangers. It is clear that Metz is worried by the dangers coming from a possible combination of Rudolf Bultmann and Rahner. Transcendental theology risks losing its validity if it bypasses both the historical and the social dimensions of faith by reducing the latter to a question of an existential decision of the individual. Bloch also sharply critiques Bultmann for the same reasons. If faith is merely a question of an existential decision, then faith is privatized, and history and ethical-political action are made superfluous.[105]

Metz also wrestles with Bultmann's program of demythologization. The question of how to understand the Bible will become increasingly important for Metz. Two aspects must be distinguished. On the one hand, Metz has a clearly negative understanding of myth. Convinced as he is of the liberating power of reason as formulated by the Enlightenment, he will keep throughout his career a notion of myth that equates it with a distorted interpretation of reality that leads to the concealment of truth and to alienation. From the early development of his thought, myth, for Metz, is also something opposed to history as the stage on which human beings strive to uncover the meaning of their lives and on which God's love has been manifested through the incarnation of Jesus Christ. Metz is in that respect typically modern. There is no place in his theology for a positive notion of myth (as in Eliade) connected with the final inability of reason to understand and to express the ultimate depth of reality that theology calls God. Hence, demythologization as a program is necessary for Metz, and he will consistently unmask those myths that hide the true nature of faith. On the other hand, the program of demythologization as understood by Bultmann is unacceptable for Metz because it denies faith its essential historical and social character, reducing it to a naked existential decision of the individual. The reaction to this is one of the reasons that have led Metz to pay attention to a literal reading of the Bible, despite the risks of fundamentalism that such a position entails.

Following the Blochian inspiration, Metz comes to affirm that the only way faith can make sense in the new setting of modernity is by defining itself as a transformative praxis on the horizon of an eschatological future created by the reality of a "God before us,"[106] who is at the base of Christian hope. History can only exist in relation to that eschatological end that constitutes it. In this context, the political dimension of Christianity (and hence of theology) comes to the fore, and the criterion for truth shifts from orthodoxy to orthopraxis.[107] Faith and theology thus understood have therefore an essentially critical character in relation to the world. It is interesting to notice that Metz critiques here both Rahner's anthropological theology and his own prior understanding of *christliche Anthropozentrik*. The key point is that the anthropological turn can only be legitimate if it is understood from an eschatological perspective. Only then can it have a true historical character, in which freedom plays a central role. Eschatology becomes the horizon of theology, its constitutive element, and not only a regional discipline within theology. Such an eschatology, far from being an ideology of the future, is aware of the threatened character of Christian hope and, therefore, must be formulated as a "hope against all hope."[108]

Metz's thought at this time was changing as a result of his confrontation with Marxism. In relation to the latter, Metz affirmed that transcendence must be understood rather as the confronting future than as pure beyondness and that Christians are necessarily committed to the task of transforming the world, thus overcoming the Marxist accusation that religion is a mechanism of alienation. Moreover, Marxism made Metz encounter the critical side of modernity and led him in the direction of linking truth with historical practice.[109]

Metz's confrontation with Bloch and Marx, however, far from leading him to adapt his theology to their thought, leads him to an intensification of the theological stand, to an ever-growing affirmation of the radical transcendence of a *Deus semper major.* God, being always "before us," both prevents Christians from accommodating to any given situation or ideology and is the only preserver of an ever-demanding, never-ending, ever-creative, eschatological hope that strives historically to uncover new possibilities of a reality that only God can fully disclose. These two theologically intensified elements, radical transcendence and its correlated historical orthopraxis, will become crucial in Metz's political theology and in his critique of Rahner's transcendental theology.

Metz was thus rapidly evolving from a philosophical-transcendental theology to a biblical theology aware of the uniqueness of the God-in-history of the Bible, the God of Abraham, Isaac and Jacob, and, most of all, Jesus. At the same time, the *Gottesrede,* the very notion of God, was changing. The God already emerging in Metz's early political theology is an ungraspable God, a truly one-and-multifarious God that is always beyond while at the same time always "before us" in history, a God that cannot be controlled in any way, a provocative and radically unsettling God.

Finally, Metz's theology was becoming a "negative theology," an intrinsically critical theology, increasingly aware of the provocative power of a *Deus semper major* who cannot be either deductively grasped or properly described through *via eminentiae.* This new theological perspective is intimately intertwined with a new perception of the world and its history from the "other side," from the side of the victims, the oppressed, and the injured. This perception is critical of the ideology of progress and needs to be related theologically to the scandal of the cross and to the christological-eschatological hope against all hope.

The last two essays of *Zur Theologie der Welt* show again how Metz's theology was rapidly evolving towards political theology through the 1960s.[110] Metz is trying to define exactly where his theology, which he already calls "political theology," stands. He formulates the twofold character of political theology: its negative aspect, as a corrective of the dangerous tendency toward privatization in contemporary theology, and its positive side, as an attempt to formulate the eschatological Christian message under the circumstances of modern society. Deprivatization of theology is the primary aim of political theology.

Metz here presents transcendental theology more critically than before, implying that God's self-communication, the cornerstone of Rahner's theology, seems to be understood by transcendental theology in a personal way that precludes its social dimension as liberating promise. Metz is basically saying that transcendental theology could be formulated in any political-historical situation, precisely because it does not take into account that situation to reach its conclusions. Socially, transcendental theology is blind. Since the person is analyzed as an abstraction, as a "type" of all and every person, the essential and original relatedness of this person to other persons in a particular situation is not taken into account. Therefore, transcendental theology, Metz concludes, moves within the precinct of the private and has, originally, no social-political dimension. Although this critique touches Rahner's theology, it seems to be directed especially to a Bultmannian, existential interpretation of transcendental theology when he writes that this theology "practices demythologization at the price of another myth: that of worldless existence and private subjectivity."[111]

Metz affirms also that his political theology responds to the situation created by the Enlightenment. He takes an important step toward his characteristic emphasis on practical reason in relation to Kant's philosophy. Enlightenment, that is, the liberation of humanity on the basis of reason, is not primarily a theoretical enterprise. It is only possible if it includes a political dimension that takes into account that reason can be emancipatory only if it is aware of the social and political factors that condition that reason. Those social-political conditions must be transformed to make the use of public reason possible. Hence, the Enlightenment is intrinsically political.[112] Metz's understanding of the Enlightenment, therefore, incorporates the social critique of Marxism, according to which theoretical reason can only play a correct role within the framework of practical reason.[113]

The Enlightenment, so understood, is the partner of political theology, and the only way of responding to it adequately is by retrieving into the core of theology the intrinsic practical-political dimension of Jesus' eschatological message. A critical understanding of the Enlightenment is correlated with a critical-political interpretation of Christianity. For Metz, the importance of the social-political input in theology does not depend only on the Enlightenment but is directly given by the biblical message. Jesus' story is a social-political one according to the gospels. In this respect Metz thinks that John's is the gospel that best describes both the transcendence and the political dimension of Jesus. This political dimension has an eschatological anchoring. Later on in his theological development, Metz will put the emphasis on the interruptive character of this eschatological attribute of the gospel, stressing the importance of the gospel of Mark.

Metz points out that freedom, peace, justice, and reconciliation (almost the same as the symbolic motto of the French Revolution, "Liberté, egalité, fraternité") are the eschatological promises of the biblical tradition,[114] thus following his initial (and subsequent) strategy of affirming that the Enlightenment has a biblical-Christian origin. However, Metz's appropriation of the Enlightenment has shifted substantially to take on an eschatological-political character. As he himself acknowledges, whereas his previous theological interpretations of the worldliness of the world had a christological and anthropological character, much like Rahner's theological anthropology best disclosed in Jesus Christ, this time the Enlightenment is understood as a future-oriented enterprise, which, if it is going to be rightly understood, must be related to the eschatological dimension of the Christian message. Nevertheless, Metz goes on to say that these different ways of understanding the worldliness of the world, far from excluding each other, are intrinsically related, thus giving a clue to the dialectical nature of his own theology and of the way his theology relates to that of Rahner.[115]

The crucial point is that the Christian eschatological message is the only way to maintain the universality of Christianity. This is so because, insofar as its fulfillment is eschatological, at the end of the times, it prevents Christianity from identifying itself with any historical achievement, making it the fountain of the permanent critical resource needed to guarantee a never-ending transformation of history. This eschatological character is to be understood not as a negation of the world and its history but as a critical-dialectical counterpoint to them. Metz wants always to make clear that his approach is different from the premodern, precritical one in that the latter denies the world in its worldliness, whereas his has a positive, albeit critical, confrontation with it. In other words, theology for Metz must relate positively to the Enlightenment, trying to rescue the Enlightenment from its own pitfalls on the basis of both critical theory and, most of all, biblical religion.

In the fifth edition of *Zur Theologie der Welt* there are some footnotes that did not exist in the first edition of 1968. The additions are revealing because they include references to Adorno and Walter Benjamin with respect to the crucial issues of practical reason and eschatology. These authors did not become relevant to Metz until the 1970s. However, some typical issues of the Frankfurt School were present in Metz's thought already in the 1960s, such as, for instance, the hegemony of technical reason and technical manipulation of the world and the need for reinterpreting the Enlightenment to avoid its dangers and to lead it in the right direction.[116]

On these bases, Metz comes to the conclusion that political theology is not a regional theology but a basic approach that must characterize any theology.[117] It is the formal expression of faith of a church that understands itself as an "institution of the critical freedom of faith." Metz had already affirmed that eschatology was not simply a part of theology but its focal point. Now, this stress on eschatology is subsumed under the wider political dimension theology must have if it wants to respond to the problems posed by a world that is neither cosmos nor pure existential or personal reality. In his later writings, after 1980, Metz comes to the conclusion that theodicy is *the* question theology must address. This shifting emphasis shows clearly the evolving character of Metz's theology and his constant attempt to formulate his political theology more appropriately.

As in the case of Rahner, the church occupies a central position in Metz's thought: this reveals the pastoral and practical character of Metz's theology. His final aim is not to understand the modern world and to interpret it theologically, but to transform it. This is another trait of his thought that totally squares with the modern spirit, for which the transformation of the world is not only possible but has become the distinctive calling of the modern person. Here can be found some (but not all) of the roots of the strong ethical drive of Metz, something that happens also in the case of liberation theology. On the other hand, Metz tests his theology against the real church, asking himself whether the church has historically been an institution of critical freedom. His answer is in the negative, but he affirms that a change can and must take place. In other words, he advocates a church that becomes fully aware of the eschatological and political content of the Christian message and understands itself as the effective, historical institutionalization of that critical and liberating message. The truth the church proclaims cannot be only theoretical but must be "done" by the practice of the church. The central principle of love must become a revolutionary power against a society that lives under the threat of irrationality, injustice, war, and lack of freedom. This is radical, but Metz does not advocate anarchy. It has always been his point that institutional mediation is necessary for any sustained, transformative practice.[118]

Metz has always been aware of the distance between the type of church he envisions and the actual one. In the 1960s and 1970s his position was hopeful in relation to the possibility of transforming the actual church. In the 1960s, that hope was grounded in the search for renewal that swept the church as a result of Vatican II and was expressed in some documents of the Council and in some papal encyclicals, such as *Populorum Progressio* (Paul VI, 1967). In this, his position is similar to that of Rahner. Both took a very active role in the synod of the Catholic Church in Germany that tried to define the program of the transformation of the church in that country. Metz was assigned the writing of the final document of the Synod, *Unsere Hoffnung,* approved with few changes. In the late 1970s and most of the 1980s Metz pointed to the Latin American church and its grassroots communities as the sign the church was really changing, affirming that some of the same spirit was appearing among Christians in Germany and in other developed countries. Lately, this emphasis has somehow faded, and it is not clear where Metz stands in relation to the real possibilities for the existence of the transformed church he advocates.

Political Theology as Practical Fundamental Theology

Metz's political theology matured substantially in the 1970s as a result of its own organic growth, fostered to an important extent by its exposure to the critique of Metz's own students and of theologians in general and by its confrontation with the Frankfurt School, especially with Adorno and Benjamin. It is not an exaggeration to say that political theology became one of the most important contributions to the Catholic (and Evangelical) theological scene after the Rahnerian theology that Vatican II backed. Metz's works were widely translated (into more than ten foreign languages), and Metz was invited to conferences and symposiums all over the world, but especially in Europe and North America. That ensured an important exposure of Metz's political theology to the theological community, giving Metz the opportunity to rethink his positions and to advance toward a more rounded and systematic presentation of his thought. By the middle of the 1970s, Metz's theology had been widely analyzed and many important studies had been published about it.[119]

One of the things that Metz tried to clarify was the meaning of the term "political theology."[120] Metz wants to make clear that such a term has nothing to do with a "neo-politicizing of faith" or a "neo-clericalizing of politics." Far from being so, "political theology" relates in a positive way to the Enlightenment, acknowledging it as an important development on the road to emancipation. Metz goes on to say that a critical relationship between politics and theology has been made possible by the Enlightenment's distinction between state and society. If that distinction is borne in mind and respected, theology can contribute to a critical political discourse in the social-public realm on the basis of the social implications and tasks of the Christian message. Moreover, a political theology can make an important contribution to something that is most needed, namely, establishing a positive relationship between church and modern, democratic society. This political realm in that society, according to the Enlightenment, is a realm of freedom—not a previously given and unchangeable reality, but a reality continually shaped and reshaped by the free action of the citizens.

A theology that, accepting this, reflects on the political implications of the Christian message brings new resources to the task of relating the church and its function to that realm of freedom in which the political reality is shaped. In so doing, political theology can go beyond the simple discourse on the secularization of modern society, establishing new and meaningful links between the Christian message and modern society. In relation to society and political discourse, Metz thinks that a political theology can bring to that discourse the implications of the coming Kingdom of God. Since this kingdom is eschatological, it places all the possibilities of political discourse under a double light: on the one hand it makes them all relative and subject to critique; on the other hand, it places them in the realm of freedom.[121]

In order to understand Metz's evolution it has to be born in mind that, at the end of the 1960s and during the 1970s, Metz widened the scope of his intellectual partners to include those of the Frankfurt School. Most of the new partners were both atheist-Marxist and Jewish, something that distinguishes Metz dramatically from Rahner and that has had a decisive impact on his theology. Adorno and Benjamin are among the five authors that Metz quotes more than ten times in *Glaube in Geschichte und Gesellschaft,* the others being Bloch, Kant, and Rahner. Interestingly, Heidegger is only mentioned twice (and one is indirect) and Aquinas four times. This alone gives an idea of the transformation undergone by Metz since the early 1960s. Metz's exposure to the Frankfurt School awoke in him new potential ways to confirm and to develop his own basic intuitions. Most of all, Adorno and Horkheimer lent him a systemic critical view of modern society, in which the famous "dialectic of the Enlightenment" plays a central role. This interpretive clue will be extensively and consistently used by Metz throughout his work.

From Benjamin, himself intuitive and Metzian-like, Metz has received powerful intuitions and clues (among others the standardization in modern society and the lack of power and creativity of the subject, the myth of endless progress in history, the apocalyptic emphasis, the importance of memory and narrative) that have helped him to deepen his own thought. Ottmar John in his analysis of the importance of Benjamin for theology in general and for political theology in particular[122] perceptively writes that it is not relevant whether Benjamin can be considered a theologian or whether—if viewed as a theologian—he can be seen as close to Catholic theology. John goes on to say that, on the contrary, what makes Benjamin relevant and fruitful for theology is his independent, close-distant, confronting, nonidentical use of theological issues and concepts that stem from a concrete biographical-historical, tragic situation to which Benjamin sought to respond. Benjamin is relevant and can and must be theologically interpreted by Christianity only on the basis of his otherness and distance, indeed radical nonidentity, in relation to Christianity and theology: on the basis of his Marxism and Judaism; of his being persecuted as Jew and Marxist; of his fleeing; of his having killed himself. Therefore, the theological reception of Benjamin's work must be "a reception in opposition."[123]

In relation to the content of Benjamin's thought, John points out several questions that are and have been especially important and influential with regard to theology in general and to political theology in particular. One of these questions is Benjamin's critique of the reigning ideology of progress, especially as formulated in Benjamin's thirteenth thesis about the concept of history. Such an ideology, which pervades the historical imagination of the modern mind, is grounded in an empty and homogeneous notion of time—a time in which history and progress go always forward hand in hand, endlessly and unstoppably. This notion of time as an empty and homogeneous forward-stream must be debunked in order to unmask that reigning ideology of progress. To do so, first, the destructive power of the amoral, empty, endless time must be disclosed through the acknowledgment of the victims of that destruction, and, second, the stream of this endless and catastrophic time must be interrupted. The Holocaust stands out as the most important example of destruction, but other victims include the destitute and the marginalized by the never-ending stream of progress. Finally, John brings to the fore the importance of Benjamin's category of memory as a means to reconstitute both history and the consciousness of the subject on the grounds of remembering the massive suffering in history.[124]

Not only with Benjamin but also with Adorno, Horkheimer, and Habermas, Metz has held an ongoing dialogue through which he has been able to go further into his understanding not only of society and of the modern subject but also of religion and its liberating role in a society rooted in a "dialectical Enlightenment."[125] In relation to Metz's understanding of the Enlightenment and of modern society, his exposure to the Frankfurt School is paramount. Important to bear in mind is that Metz belongs to a current of thought in Germany that somehow moves around similar interests in relation to the analysis of modernity and Christianity.[126] Metz has also worked out his understanding of the Enlightenment through the confrontation of his thought with the interpretation of other thinkers. In that respect the works of Hans Blumemberg, for whom the Enlightenment not only does not come from Christianity but represents an emancipatory break from it, and of Hermann Lübbe could serve as example.[127]

In 1977 Metz published his most systematic account of political theology, *Glaube in Geschichte und Gesellschaft*.[128] The book included revised versions of various key works Metz published in the 1970s, works in which he defines the categories of "memory" and "narrative." The work is divided into three sections ("Concepts," "Themes," and "Categories"), of which the first, and especially its fourth chapter, gives the whole coherence and systematization. To this date, *Glaube in Geschichte und Gesellschaft* is the most complete account of Metz's political theology, although he has developed it further in the 1980s and 1990s, especially in relation to the questions of postmodernity, poverty, and theodicy.

He defines political theology as a practical fundamental theology. By practical fundamental theology, he means a fundamental theology that is practical in two ways: on the one hand, it is intimately related with the concrete history and stories of the church(es), of society(ies), and of the different groups within those church(es) and society(ies).[129] This plurality is crucial for Metz, since theology cannot be just an abstract reflection on "humankind" or "society" or "church" but is intimately linked with the concreteness of people, church(es), and society(ies). On the other hand, and consequently, political theology is practical because it comes to understand the situation of people, church(es), and society(ies) on the one side, and the Christian message on the other side, in and through a praxis that, based on the concrete biblical narrative, takes sides to favor always the subject, especially the oppressed, the destitute, the conquered, and the dead.

Political theology is also for Metz the formal, fundamental structure of a dogmatics that must be understood, in its own narrative and concreteness, as, so to speak, the categorial side of fundamental theology. In this respect, he writes that "fundamental theology is in a way formal dogmatics, and dogmatics only is meaningful if it becomes material fundamental theology."[130] As in Rahner, the content of dogmatics must be articulated and reflected upon in relation to the problems of human beings.[131] However, Metz and Rahner, although in agreement in relation to the intertwining of fundamental theology and dogmatics, do not address the same questions and do not have the same anthropological and theological perspectives. Metz insists on the practical character of his theology (thus the name *"political* theology") precisely to differentiate it from Rahner's transcendental theology. Trying to explain the nexus and the difference between the two, he writes that "Rahner's basic thesis of theology as anthropology cannot be directly adopted by a political theology of the subject, but this political theology could give Rahner's thesis a mediated historical and social evidence."[132]

Metz's endeavor must be understood as a reaction against a society that lives under the complete dominion of a distorted Enlightenment that pursues power and wealth and that has an ahistorical discourse about liberal values. Metz believes that both theology and the church have adapted themselves to this domineering social model. His aim is to unmask the situation and to rescue the transforming power of Christianity. This is, in Metz's understanding, the only way to liberate the subject and society from their current enslavement. It is easy to realize how far this Metz is from the Metz of *Christliche Anthropozentrik*. In fact, there still are some similar underlying threads, like the basic attempt to come to grips with the Enlightenment and the attempt to do so on the basis of Christianity's own resources. However, a crucial refocusing has taken place in-between. The new focus separates Metz from Rahner and makes political theology a real alternative concerning the way of understanding both Christianity and the mission of the church in the modern era.

Rahner showed that, by following to the last consequences the modern "turn to the subject," transcendence appears as the final horizon and the condition of possibility of both knowledge and freedom. Metz values Rahner's insight but is not happy with it. What he observes is the pervading existence of practical unbelief, the existence of a domineering culture based on power and control, and the loss of relevance of the church in developed societies and of its capacity to react against such a situation. As Metz sees it, modernity has taken over the range of values traditionally assigned to Christianity and has dismissed the church as a backward institution opposed to those values. The church, in turn, has reacted showing that, far from that being the case, the new emancipatory thrust of modernity and the values the latter defends are ultimately of Christian origin, thus legitimating its own existence as church in contemporary society. The problem for Metz is that the church has in fact disempowered itself in its effort to prove its modernity. Both theology and the church have accepted the premises of the domineering forces (most of all privatization) and have betrayed their own identity. In a later book, Metz writes that "the messianic religion of the Bible has become a bourgeois religion in today's Christianity."[133] To reverse this situation and to retrieve the liberating power of Christianity (most needed to rescue also the true spirit of the Enlightenment) are Metz's main focuses and the ground of his political theology.

Following the analysis of the Frankfurt School, Metz confronts the Enlightenment, becoming increasingly critical in relation to it. From *Christliche Anthropozentrik* to his discourse on the *Gotteskrise* (God crisis), his development can be seen as an intensification of the critical-disclosive power of Christian theology in relation to modernity. For him, modernity, although emancipatory in principle, has lost track of its own memory and historical anchoring and has fallen prey to a colonizing instrumental reason, that is to say, a reason that, as Habermas puts it, is centered on the system-world that has colonized the life-world. However, it always must be borne in mind that modernity is never seen by Metz as something negative in itself. Quite the contrary, the Enlightenment is a positive historical development that must be criticized in order to preserve and to promote further its most important values and historical longings. Therefore, "theology must prove its ability to take the Enlightenment seriously as an epoch-making event and to review it critically."[134]

To say that Metz has had an increasingly critical approach to modernity does not imply that he has ever had an acritical, sanguine approach to modernity and its social outcome. Metz is very aware of the inability of Catholic theology and Catholicism in general to face the challenges of modernity during the nineteenth century. It is clear that he is keeping in mind the problems at the time of the Kulturkampf, the political activities of the Catholic Zentrumspartei, and the cultural front of the Catholic Vereine when he refers to that inability.[135] So important is this for Metz that, in relation to theology, he speaks of a *Tragödie der Theologiegeschichte* (tragedy of the history of theology) when referring to the isolation and purely defensive attitude of theology in confronting modernity.

His previous *Säkularisierungsthese* (secularization thesis) is substantially qualified in *Glaube in Geschichte und Gesellschaft*. Metz reviews the theological strategy used to "Christianize" the secularization process through a historical-incarnational theology according to which the autonomy of the world, of the secular, stems from the inner dynamics of the relationship between God and creation. Metz acknowledges that he himself made this thesis his in his previous work *Zur Theologie der Welt*. The problem with the thesis is that, although it shows that the freedom of the world has an inner Christian origin, in setting the world free, Christian faith has to pay the price of its own "worldlessness."

For Metz, to admit such a secularization without any qualification risks separating the world from Christianity, accepting the privatization of religion typical of modernity, and, therefore, cutting off the historical and social-ethical implications of the Christian message. Metz also criticizes the Protestant-liberal secularization thesis, according to which modernity is the historical realization of the Christian values of freedom and emancipation. Such strategies lead in the end to the self-destruction of theological reason; theology, in its attempt to explain, and to come to terms with, modernity, throws itself into the arms of modernity and loses its own identity.[136]

Theology has in his opinion deceived itself with respect to the Enlightenment. Far from adopting a critical-constructive attitude in relation to it on the basis of the Christian message, theology has simply adapted itself to the premises and implications of the historical realization of the Enlightenment, thus losing its own identity and power. Metz speaks of a "triumph of the Enlightenment over the Christianity of the church." Instead of confronting modernity on the grounds of theological reason, theology, reacting somehow ashamedly against its earlier consideration of the Enlightenment as *the* enemy of Christianity, has surrendered to it and has made the Enlightenment the *locus theologicus* in which theology finds its own character and finds the realization of the Christian values. The Enlightenment, far from being confronted by theology, has made the latter its home.[137] An interesting parallel critique can be found, from the perspective of the United States, in H. Richard Niebuhr's famous sentence about the Protestant-liberal interpretation of Christianity: "A God without wrath brought men without sin into a kingdom without judgment through the ministrations of a Christ without a cross."[138]

At the end of the 1970s, Metz wrote an especially clear and provocative essay in which the question at stake is whether religion must adapt always to the spirit of the time, to remain, so to speak, always updated, always at the very edge of the times in a culture that calls itself progressive and is marked by its orientation toward the future. Must Christianity adapt always to new times, or may it under certain conditions remain noncontemporaneous? In order to explain his thought, Metz gives a short account of how religion and theology have confronted the Enlightenment.[139]

The first response to modernity was the neo-scholastic, antimodernist response. Instead of a real response, both the Catholic Church and Catholic theology built walls around and isolated themselves from the new emancipatory thrust of modernity on the basis of the atemporal eternity of their teaching. That was a clearly *ungleichzeitige* (noncontemporaneous) response, a response that refused to be adapted to the spirit of the time. The second response, mainly Protestant earlier on, although also Catholic after

Vatican II, was the "progressive," "critical," *gleichzeitige* response of liberal theology—a response that, obsessed with being absolutely modern and re-sponsive to the spirit of the time, was but a simple adaptation to that spirit; a response, therefore, in which the Christian identity is completely lost and the church becomes the provider of services needed by a *bürgerliche Religion.* The third response—and here Metz includes Rahner's theology and political and liberation theologies—seeks to bring to the fore the creative character of the noncontemporaneousness of Christianity and make it fruitful for so-ciety and for every subject in it. It takes seriously the spirit of the time, the emancipatory drive of modernity, but criticizes it on messianic grounds, on the grounds of a *messianische Religion der Nachfolge* (messianic religion of discipleship). This response is both irritant and provocative and is linked to that liberating-cognitive praxis of following Jesus and seeing reality with the eyes of the victims.

The task of Christian theology is to react, denouncing the premises of the Enlightenment and especially its subtle destruction of the subject it affirms to enlighten. This is a central issue in *Glaube in Geschichte und Gesell-schaft.* The subject has been sacrificed to the power of technical rationality. The latter has taken over the Enlightenment, bestowing all the power on those systems (mainly capitalism and bureaucracy) that, instead of promot-ing the freedom and the creativity of the individual, reduce them to a pure instrument. Metz follows here Adorno and Horkheimer's diagnosis of the Enlightenment, as well as Habermas's development of this diagnosis. The-ology, whether Protestant liberal or Catholic progressive, has fallen into the trap of modernity. Although in practice making the subject a mere instru-ment of systemic forces, modernity has developed a brilliant discourse about the subject and the enhancement of its freedom. Theology has appropriated this discourse as its own and has followed an idealistic path turning its back on reality and on practice. It talks about the subject, about freedom, history, and justice, as if such realities were independent of the actual subjects and of the actual conditions of history.

Metz analyzes the main features of the Enlightenment that theology must critically confront. These features, which are interrelated, include:

1. privatization as the life-form of the modern citizen, totally adapted to the rule of exchange as the rule of social life;

2. the crisis of tradition, which deprives society of the liberating force of historical memory and reduces the scope of reason to discursive rationality;

3. the crisis of authority that follows from that of tradition and deprives society and reason of the accusing authority of suffering;

4. the crisis of metaphysical reason, replaced by an enlightened reason whose logic entails not a liberating praxis but a domination-praxis controlled by the elite of the enlightened;

5. the crisis of religion as a result of the crisis of metaphysics and of the falling apart of the unity of society and religion; and the appearance of an elitist rational and ahistorical religion that disempowers the critical stand of Christianity.

Theology must rescue the subject from the forces of this culture of privatization and subtle domination. The only way to accomplish this is to reinterpret, to create anew, a self-awareness of the subject by placing it before God. The Christian God calls each person to become a self-aware subject that assumes a solidary existence in society.[140]

To achieve its aim, theology must be practical, i.e., must retrieve the practical constitution of its own logos and bring it to the core of its enterprise. If in *Christliche Anthropozentrik* Metz had pointed to the anthropocentric turn as the key to understanding modernity, in *Glaube in Geschichte und Gesellschaft* he affirms that the crucial turn is from a theoretical to a practical reason as represented by the Kant of the second critique and by the Marxian primacy of praxis. Metz identifies Rahner's enterprise mainly (but never in a simplistic way) as a confrontation with the Kant of the first critique, whereas political theology wants to bring into the inner part of theology the noetic principle of the primacy of practical reason. Only that way can idealism be overcome.

In considering his theology a practical hermeneutics of Christianity, Metz distinguishes his position from that of Wolfhart Pannenberg (universal-historical hermeneutics in which negativity and praxis do not play an important role), Jürgen Moltmann (eschatological hermeneutics that risks reducing the suffering of Christ to an innertrinitarian reality), and Rahner (transcendental hermeneutics that risks running into an ahistorical and idealistic Christianity).[141] On the one hand, theology must be intrinsically linked to a social-historical praxis that illumines the meaning of Christianity. On the other, such a praxis is not free from determination but must be based on the scriptural narrative. In other words, the way God saves in history and the demands and tensions stemming from God's claims upon the subject (individual and as a people) are constitutive elements of the theological reason and the only anchors of its true identity. Therefore, theology has an essentially anamnestic and narrative structure.[142] The introduction of the notion of memory into the core of political theology (mainly due to the influence of Adorno and Benjamin) is one of its milestones, since it allows Metz to establish a nexus between the eschatological future and the historical praxis of becoming a subject before God according to the scriptures. It is, in this sense, the nexus between tradition (and the praxis it discloses) and eschatology.

The interrelated categories of memory and narrative have a constitutive character in Metz. They refer not only to the concreteness of the Christian message or theology but, much more generally, to reason and understanding themselves. Briefly said, either the modern, emancipatory reason realizes its memory-based-narrative inner structure and grounds itself in it or that reason, abandoned to itself, becomes a monster, an erratic and dangerous, even deathly, monster. First of all, narrative must be understood as a reenactment of a concrete story (memory) that refers to a founding experience. A narrative, then, does not primarily aim at passing on some historical, objective information, but at reviving a concrete and relevant experience in those who hear the narrative of the story that captures that experience.

Metz refers both to Benjamin's explanation of the features and role of the narrator and the difficulty of transmitting an experience in modern, technical society and to Adorno,[143] and he concludes with the latter that a reason that cannot, or does not want to, refer back to and take into account the experience transmitted by a concrete narrative remains a technical reason. A narrative has also a practical effect because its content relates to the interest of those who hear it, because the reenactment of the original experience becomes a liberating, relevant experience for them. What is being told is happening anew. In relation to this, Metz refers to the sacraments as "macrosigns of salvation narratives." Narrative memory is crucial for theology, and not only for the kerygmatic proclamation, because only that way can theology really be based on the narrative structure of that proclamation and on this proclamation's invitation (and demand) to act out that narrative in history: "The logos of the cross and of the resurrection has an indispensable narrative structure."[144]

The notions of praxis and subject and the categories of memory and narrative complement the previous emphasis on eschatological hope and bring political theology almost to completion. Through the use of these elements of his thought, Metz accomplishes most of his aim of confronting modernity in a positive manner while rescuing it on the basis of Christian identity. More precisely, Metz

1. appropriates the program of the Enlightenment through the notion of the subject and through the radical understanding of history as emancipation-process lent by eschatology;

2. appropriates the Marxian critique of both religion and bourgeois modernity (one of the several meanings of the term *bürgerlich* widely used by Metz) and critiques the idealism of theology with his notion of praxis and its cognitive primacy;

3. secures the identity of Christianity, strengthens the notion of praxis, criticizes the rationalism and the ahistoricism of modernity, reinforces the positive meaning of tradition and authority, and shows the social-historical dimension of knowledge through the categories of memory and narrative;

4. overcomes the evolutionism of liberal ideology, the dialectical utopianism of Marxism, and the technocratic factualism, and gains a critical vantage point through his understanding of subject as becoming-subject-before-God.

That the logos of theology has a practical core is particularly the case in Christology. Any talk about Christ must be primarily based on the practice of following Christ. Central to Metz's view of the *Nachfolge* (discipleship) is that following Christ is not only a moral act of the individual; on the contrary, the *Nachfolge* has a constitutive social-political structure.[145]

The praxis of following Christ is the basic motif of Metz's book *Zeit der Orden?*[146] based on a series of talks Metz delivered at the annual meeting of the superiors of religious orders in Germany that took place in Würzburg in 1976. The main thesis of the book is that the religious orders are especially called in this time to follow Christ in a radical way that can be prophetic and transformative for the whole church. If the orders represent historically the expression of resistance and reform in the life of the church, that same spirit must be actualized in the current German church. This church is, according to Metz, being divided into two halves: a service-church for *bürgerliches Lebensfeiern* (bourgeois life celebration: a typically Metzian integrative term, very difficult to translate into English because of the multivalence of meanings it entails) and a church that becomes more and more a social sect. The church is reacting with angst to the new powers and processes, and that leads "to a backwards stabilization." The book is revealing of Metz's view of the German church and of his strategy to rescue it from the situation of lack of identity in which, mostly inadvertently, the church finds itself.

Anamnesis provides not only a means to give the church and theology the necessary material to discover its identity and the criteria for their discourse but also a way to resist and to overcome the culturally hegemonic model of reason based on domination and victory. The core of Christian anamnesis is a story of passion, that of Christ, that unmasks the victors' understanding of history and culture. This memory of suffering and passion is also an anticipatory memory of resurrection and eschatological hope. This enables Christianity to be wholly solidary, that is, to account for those who have died and have been defeated and destroyed and to act in history for the liberation of all under the pressure of the apocalyptic end of that history. Christianity then becomes religion understood as sociohistorical praxis struggling to constitute and to rescue the subject on the basis of faith and eschatological hope in the God of the living and the dead before whom all are called to become subjects.[147] This is actually the thesis of *Glaube in Geschichte und Gesellschaft*. Christianity has, therefore, in Metz's theology, a clear historical mission in our days: to rescue the subject from its modern alienation, rescuing at the same time modernity from its own self-destructive power. The Christian principle of individuation must overcome the *bürgerliche* principle of individuation.[148] The future of human beings depends on this mission of Christianity whose historical agent is the church. So does the future of Christianity. Metz has dealt several times with this issue of the future of Christianity and church, which for him is indissolubly related to the future of society and of the subject. A church adapted to the currently domineering modernity (the bad side of modernity Metz would say) has no future because it has lost its identity and transformative power. Equally, the future of the subject and of society is endangered by the self-destructive power of a domination-driven modernity.[149]

Metz points out that Christian praxis has a special pathos because it is made up not only of action but also (and essentially) of passion, not only of joy but also of suffering.[150] He explains that he does not want to curtail the importance of historical action but to correct and qualify it so that it is able to account for the whole of reality, and not only for a part of it, namely, that which belongs to the victors.[151] More specifically, Metz is addressing here one of the deepest traits of modern reason. Understanding and action oriented to achieve a goal are the weapons by which progress is attained. Science, whether natural or human, has an essentially explicative character in modernity. It is meant to be the basis for a transformative action that, in the end, aims at liberating the world from all kinds of limitations. This is the myth that Metz, like Reinhold Niebuhr in the context of the United States, wants to unmask. For Metz, transformative-emancipatory action is not the whole story. Human history is also unavoidably made of passion, of suffering for which reason must also account.

The influence of the Lutheran theology of the cross is clear here. Moltmann develops this theology explicitly in his book *The Crucified God*.[152] Metz, however, wants to warn about what, in his opinion, is Moltmann's focus on (although not only) the suffering of Christ within the Trinity, as an inner aspect of the trinitarian dynamics. Metz makes it clear that he is more interested in the suffering of Christ as prototypical of what happens in society, especially to the poor and the defeated. For Metz, the suffering of Christ shows the true depth of suffering in the world and, therefore, becomes prophetic and denouncing, empowered to criticize the triumphant ideology of a society that talks about freedom, success, and bounty while oppressing the poor and destroying every resistance to its own advance.

There can be no real future if the dead and the victims have no place in it. Metz masterly calls the Christian understanding of the future a "future based on the memory of suffering."[153] Because Christian memory includes passion, suffering, and victims, it becomes a dangerous memory in that it confronts and unmasks a triumphant society by making present the injustice and the victims that society has created. It is, therefore, a subversive memory and, as such, an active presence in history of God's interruptive act of salvation at the end of history, when God will rescue those whom history has destroyed and forgotten, namely the defeated, the oppressed, and the dead. Metz analyzes this crucial connection between future and past suffering in his article "The Future in the Memory of Suffering."[154] For him, a *memoria resurrectionis* that does not include as an essential element the *memoria passionis* is pure mythology (in the pejorative sense Metz gives this term).

Metz critiques three ideologies typical of modernity. In general, the *Homo emancipator* has divided his responsibility in history into two halves. The modern subject does not want to take responsibility for that half of history that is made of suffering and of guilt, but only for the other half, namely, progress and success. This, according to Metz, must be applied to the idealistic-liberal, to the Marxist, and to the positivist ideologies of history. The idealistic-liberal ideology of the victors goes hand in hand with the evolutionistic view of history. The second one, utopian Marxism, is also touched by the same modern orientation to a better future in history, promises a paradise to future generations, but is unable to account for or to rescue the victims of history. The third ideology Metz wants to unmask is the positivist-technocratic version of history in which the laws of the economy mark the path and pace of progress in a history in which, as in the other cases, the responsible subject has vanished. In this respect, the three partake in the "exculpatory mechanism" that characterizes the ideology of modern emancipation, as Metz writes in his powerful essay "Erlösung und Emanzipation."[155]

In this essay, Metz clearly identifies the specificity of the Christian message of redemption, neither as a mere religious version of modern emancipation nor as an easy idealistic supplement to solve the mistakes and contradictions of the historical, dialectical emancipation. In this sense, "Emancipation is by no means simply the immanent side of redemption, neither is redemption simply the transcendent side of emancipation."[156] Redemption stands on its own feet as a message that takes into account both the reality of guilt in history and the dead and defeated of that history. Without the history of redemption, the history of emancipation becomes a dangerous and banal history of a freedom without responsible subject. In order to correct it, theology must develop a soteriology that is a political theology of redemption.[157]

In Metz's understanding of history, the victims are not an exception, something due to a mistake, to a mechanical, occasional failure, so to speak. On the contrary, the victims are systemic in history. That is the reason the victims must be taken into account and must come to the fore in history to interrupt and to unmask it. In this understanding of history resounds powerfully Benjamin's sentence, "The tradition of the oppressed teaches us that the 'state of exception,' in which we live, is the rule."[158]

If *memoria resurrectionis* can become a dangerously victorious ideology without *memoria passionis*, the latter can become completely defeatist and hopeless without the former. Those two belong intrinsically together. This in turn implies that the move from one to the other is not a simple, mechanical, mythologically miraculous one. On the contrary, it is a move full of meaning. That the dead resurrect means that they are an indispensable and meaningful part of the present and of the future. It means that the meaning of the present and of the future does not depend only on the living and the powerful, but also, and especially, on those who have died, who have been vanquished, who have been defeated.[159]

Because Christian hope is universal, Christianity is truly solidary. Therefore, solidarity is one of the three categories Metz develops, the other two being memory and narrative. Loyal to his understanding of the universality of the Christian message, Metz understands solidarity not only as a category of the present but also as a category of the future and, most importantly, of the past (*nach rückwarts*). Solidarity means basically the affirmation and support of the subject as such under any historical circumstances, especially under the threat of suffering and destruction of that subject. It is a practical category, a category that affirms its truth in action and that, in so doing, brings into existence the power of memory and narrative through mystical-political praxis. Whereas the mystical dimension is the universal one, the political refers to the particular, to the historical. Only when solidarity takes sides in and through the political-historical can the universality of the mystical be validated. Conversely, only the mystical-universal can validate the political-historical, freeing it from forgetfulness and hatred. So conceived, solidarity is the category that rescues the subject from all that threatens that subject: forgetfulness, oppression, and death. It is also a category of practical reason—a reason that comes to know and to understand neither on the basis of purely discursive reason nor on the basis of scientifically competent reason, but in and through a nonneutral, solidary praxis based on a narrative memory. In other words, the solidary praxis of the church that follows Christ and always takes sides in favor of the poor, the oppressed, the suppressed, and, in general, *the* other, recognizing this other as a subject, becomes a practical way of understanding and making history.[160]

Closely following Benjamin, Metz makes it clear that a history that is not lived under the pressure of the essentiality and unavoidable identity of a *now* that always threatens to die is not history at all. It is only empty, meaningless time in which the subject is lost, dissolved, systemically alienated. In a continuum time, in which the flow of indiscriminate information is inflationary, events cease to be unique and become just more of the same.[161] Religion must necessarily mean interruption of this continuum in which everything looks the same and loses its identity. It must be a rebellion that affirms the end of time, thus confronting the myth of development and evolution and constituting time anew in the uniqueness of the *now* and the responsibility of the subject in a history understood from an eschatological perspective. In order to achieve this, religion must rescue its apocalyptic sting most of all in relation to so many utopias that far from interrupting the ideological evolutionary discourse extend it to its limits.

Contrary to Bultmannian demythologizing, Metz points out that the apocalypsis is so intertwined with history that it founds and constitutes it. No real, historically and ethically active hope is possible without the tension between the dangerous memories of the past and the apocalyptic interruption of history. In this sense, "Christology without apocalyptical dimension becomes a conqueror's ideology."[162] Christians follow Christ waiting for the near, apocalyptic coming of his kingdom. Each second and each act become relevant in that perspective, and the follower of Christ must take responsibility for them. Therefore, apocalyptic expectation, far from being an empty or emptying myth, means historical, solidary action against all kinds of injustice, taking sides with the poor and the dispossessed. Such an apocalyptic expectation is the firm ground of a hope that knows that it is not its own master and origin—a hope that is real and, therefore, provoking and dynamic in a history that is full of meaning and that has become humane. This is the hope in which prayer can be grounded; a prayer that, according to Metz, makes it possible for Christians to rescue their identity by finding out who they truly are precisely in and through prayer. "Praying to God we remember that we are ourselves. Prayer is the oldest form of the struggle of human beings to keep their own self and their identity before the highest danger."[163]

The Intensification of Political Theology

The 1980s led political theology onto two different paths.[164] On the one hand, political theology must respond to the important ideological, cultural, and ethical changes taking place in society and also to the changes taking place in the church. On the other hand, in so doing, it must continue its effort to make its own theological position more explicit, both formally and in content, dealing more explicitly and directly with the question of God.

The 1980s were a complex decade in which profound changes took place. Economically, the decade opened with the second "oil shock," which triggered a worldwide recession characterized by high inflation, high unemployment, and, more deeply, a lack of solutions for the new situation. At the same time, the conditions of the world market changed dramatically as a result of the rocketing economic growth of Japan and, to a less but nevertheless significant extent, other Asian countries, based on technological and cultural factors. That shocked the foundations of the preexistent economic and financial world status quo. The United States and Europe, unable to cope with the new conditions of the market, were forced to restructure in depth not only their industry but also their traditional economic policies. Keynesian policies (almost a dogma until then) were over, inflation and the budget deficit became the number one enemies, and monetarism rose in importance in order to control them. Latin America collapsed economically, entering a period of economic catastrophe that only at the end of the decade and the beginning of the 1990s started to be reversed. So did sub-Saharan Africa, whose weak and tentative recovery had to wait until the mid-1990s. The World Bank, in its 1990 report, affirms that "for the poor in these countries, the 1980s was a lost decade."[165] The myth of continuous growth and bounty for everybody (the economic utopia) was also over. A huge foreign debt accumulated by African and Latin American countries witnessed to the fact that something had changed radically and that operating under the previous premises was not possible any longer.

Politically, the new situation brought conservatives back to power in Europe and in the United States. Social policies were dramatically altered, and all governments (included surviving socialist governments in countries like France and Spain) put market-oriented economic policies in place, which they then enforced with strict orthodoxy. Countries unable to adopt the measures of this new economic orthodoxy crashed, and the socialist-communist bloc disappeared as a real alternative by the end of the decade. That signaled a profound crisis for social and political utopias.

It is not by chance that the movement called postmodernism grew significantly in the 1980s, fostered by this collapse of social and economic utopias. Underlying postmodernism there is a rejection of the macro (and rigidly universalistic) worldviews typical of modernity, of the ideologies that had a solution for humankind (understood too uniformly) and that thought there was an enlightened (or critical) way of getting there. Those illusions broke into pieces and a new kaleidoscopic, fragmented reality took its place: one that has no solutions and in which there is no such thing as humankind and universal concepts but just different persons and realities.

Neither is it by chance that fundamentalism grew in the 1980s in part as a reaction against the frustration caused by Western modernity, its instrumental (and tyrannical) rationality, and its inability to understand and to enter into dialogue with cultures other than the development-obsessed one and with dimensions of existence other than the positivistic and efficient one.[166]

Changes in the Catholic Church are especially important in relation to Metz. The 1980s represented, on the one hand, a period of reassessment of

Vatican II. This reassessment, both pastoral and theological, was prompted by a certain tiredness and disappointment in respect to the enthusiasm and great hope that followed the council. It also reassessed the rather optimistic view taken by the council on the possibilities of human progress (although a close analysis of the texts of the council shows that they never lack an awareness of the dangers and contradictions surrounding that progress). On the other hand, the change of popes brought to Rome different pastoral and theological attitudes. The new policy was oriented to reinforcing the power of the pope in the church as a means of ensuring the unity of Catholicism and of affirming Christian identity, preserving it from its social and cultural dissolution. Reevangelization became the new key word.

Also with respect to the theological orientation of the Roman magisterium, a new direction was taken. In a simplistic manner this can be illustrated by saying that if Rahner was the official theological hero of the 1960s and the 1970s, Hans Urs von Balthasar came to occupy his place in the 1980s. In practical terms, tensions arose between theologians and the magisterium. Such tensions became explicit on the occasion of the various processes conducted by the Vatican Congregation of the Doctrine of Faith to judge the orthodoxy of several theologians and to adopt disciplinary measures against them if their theology was deemed inappropriate.

The point to stress is that, far from retreating to calmer waters, Metz's theological development in the 1980s and beyond can be best characterized as a process of intensification of the basic intuitions of political theology, dealing more directly with the question of God and of God's mystery in terms that can systemically account for the experience of radical nonidentity. Intensification belongs to Metzian hermeneutics. Theology cannot know the truth by means of a strategy that tries to follow a middle course in which, in principle, everything has the same weight and must be subject to the test of reasoning and global perspective. Metz thinks that radical and concrete monotheism with all its practical and also painful consequences is rather the way to theological truth when he writes that "a moment of excess and of risk belongs to truth finding."[167]

Confrontation with Postmodernity

Metz is still concerned with the interpretation of the Enlightenment and its relation to Christianity, but this time his analysis is prompted by the crisis of modernity and its utopias that explodes in the 1980s, and by the ensuing postmodern movement.[168] In general terms, Metz's position concerning postmodernity could be summarized by saying that postmodernity confirms Metz's diagnosis of the enlightened, liberal, *bürgerliche* society.[169] His announcement of the dissolution of the subject in a culture dominated and controlled by the evolutionary ideology of progress, without a sense of real history and of responsibility for it, is now proclaimed and explained by the postmodern philosophers.

The importance of the self had been a central piece of the Enlightenment. Kant's idea of the Enlightenment as a process of emancipation of the self, Locke's and Rousseau's understanding of society and government as directly linked to the needs and free will of the subjects, and Marx's emancipatory dialectical materialism centered around the self-consciousness of the oppressed and the historical, liberating role of the enlightened working class were all based on the capacity of the self to understand and to act responsibly and, hence, to be the master of history.

Postmodernity, with its linguistic turn, its radical critique of knowing and of the distinct concept, its dissemination of meaning (in Jacques Derrida, for example), and its investigation into the archaeology of the self and of knowledge (in Michel Foucault), sets off a radical crisis of the self-conscious and responsible self. Every metatheory or understanding of history is deeply questioned and replaced by a *pensiero debole* (weak thought; so Gianni Vattimo) or by a tentative, pragmatic, almost cynical thought (as, in a way, by Richard Rorty). Revealing both the tensions and intentions of postmodernity and Metz's concerns and own tensional, dialectical thought, Metz quotes Derrida and Foucault as both critics and prophets in relation to the role of Christianity and theology.[170]

The disappearance of the subject and the end of ideology bring about a deep ethical crisis that risks accepting everything uncritically, issuing in eclecticism, sheer plurality, enthronement of facticity, and radical suspicion of any norm based on an overarching interpretation of reality and history. Metz describes the ethical situation in postmodern Europe as a situation between the ethical suspension and the *kleine Moral*. The features of this *kleine Moral* (small morality) are, among others: renunciation of long-term loyalty, insistence on exchange-rights concerning any engagement, and suspicion of any universal concepts. Metz concludes that such a *kleine Moral* is the guiding ethics of the "liberated majority," a majority that has no regard whatsoever either for the nonliberated minorities or for the suffering of the other.[171]

In the religious domain, sociologists and religious analysts announce a postmodern religious revival, a new quest for religious experience, especially of a free and noninstitutionalized sort. This postmodern religious quest is a quest for the informal, for the unknown, and, in a way, for the otherworldly. Westerners have become fascinated by Eastern philosophies and religious movements, and the sects are having a high time in developed countries. Postmodern religious quests, however, have also taken another direction toward fundamentalism across the different religions and confessions, partly due to a reaction against a colonizing modernity, partly to the fears and insecurity of the current time.[172]

For Metz, this postmodern era is the confirmation of the "apotheosis of banality" and, in a way, its logical consequence. It is also a time when myth, once again, comes to take the place of truth. Myth-friendly postmodernity is the ultimate negation of the biblical God. Whereas, according to Metz, the motto of the 1970s was "Jesus, yes—church, no!" that of the 1980s is "Religion, yes—God, no!" Religion, says Metz, plays in postmodern society an aesthetic and compensatory role but is void of any transcendent, historical, ethical, or liberating content. It is just another myth created by society to satisfy its own needs. Metz calls this a situation of "religion-friendly Godlessness."[173] Also playing with words, which refer to the fall of real socialism in eastern Europe, Metz seeks to encompass the postmodern ethos and crisis. Whereas a minister of the former West Germany referred to that fall with the phrase "Marx is dead. Jesus lives," Metz refers to the new situation with the phrase "Marx is dead. Nietzsche lives." By that he means that nihilism and sheer "will to power," and not biblical Christianity, are the doctrinal referent of postmodernity.[174]

Metz thinks that God and the subject fall or stand together. If the former does, so does the latter and vice versa. Nietzsche is for Metz the prophet of the current situation who declares both God and the subject dead.[175] Metz agrees with, and praises, Nietzsche's linkage of God's and the subject's death. For Metz, since the subject has been eliminated by the systemic forces controlling society, it follows that God has no place in that society either. The postmodern love for religion is in fact the last expression of its underlying atheism and the apotheosis of a culture that has killed values, the possibility of universality, and ethical criteria. Indeed, for Metz, if God disappears, everything loses its final root and anchoring and becomes lost, destructive, and self-destructive. If God is dead, then so is modernity as a project of emancipation, so is universal reason, and so are universal values and ethics.

If modern thinkers, like Kant, understood the Enlightenment as a coming of age of both the subject and society, Metz refers to the process taking place in modern society as a process toward a second *Unmündigkeit* (minority), that is to say, a reversal of the emancipation the Enlightenment promised, as a result of an Enlightenment that has fallen prey to pure instrumental reason and therefore to domination and Nietzschean "will to power." A humankind that was supposed to be of age is in fact undergoing a second period of underage and tutelage. The process of secularization-emancipation has much to do with this second underage. This process of secularization not only has undermined traditional religion but has finally disempowered and dissolved the subject. The subject is less and less its own memory and more and more the result of its own, empty experiment. For Metz, following Benjamin, this subject seems to be, in the era of technical reproduction, just the reproduction and repetition of the society-modeled subject, instead of the emancipated self promised by the Enlightenment. This second minority is far more dangerous and difficult to overcome than the first one because it is experienced as something positive and good. Lack of consciousness, privatization, retreat from politics, and, most of all, the replacement of history by a mere collage of facts are the symptoms of this situation. Because reason has been cut off from its essentially narrative-remembering structure, the subject is helplessly lost "between an abstract historicism concerning understanding and a thoroughly aestheticizing conversion of history into posthistory."[176]

A proof of this second minority of humankind is the process of remythologization that is taking place to compensate for this second *Unmündigkeit*, a remythologization that entails giving up the unity of reason in the name of the dissemination and plurality of life and its history, through a sheer polymythology. Postmodernity is in this reading not only the logical consequence and the expression of self-destructive modernity but also its own self-realization. Its clear-sighted prophet was Nietzsche, who, from the perspective of God's death, already considered the self dead and any talk about the "I" a pure anthropomorphism. For Metz, current postmoderns are unable to realize their own situation. They believe they have something new to announce, when what they are is simply a grotesque mask of the consequences of a self-destructive modernity. They are not prophets but simple epigones.

The only solution for Metz is to rescue the subject (and identity, and epistemology, and universal ethics) on the basis of the memory of God.[177] This becoming a subject on the basis of the memory of God has a social-political character. There is no way the individual can become a subject in isolation. The subject comes to itself through and with others, including the dead, the vanquished, and the victims. Metz claims that this inner connection between God, the subject, and the other belongs to the core of the biblical message and distinguishes his "I" from the "I" of idealistic theology, of interpersonal theology, and of depth psychology (*Tiefenpsychologie*). Postmodern mystification and mythologization of history and reality are no solution for the problems of modernity. The mythological narrative is merely compensatory. It does not cure, it does not heal. It only furthers the problem by placing it in the alienating sphere of the myth. Metz, in a way following something that Heidegger said, "Only a God can rescue us,"[178] argues that the only cure for both the subject and society is the biblical God, the uncompromising God, the one who neither consoles nor compensates but liberates,[179] or, otherwise said, the alternative between alienation and liberation in postmodernity is itself dependent on the alternative of "either the polytheistic-aesthetic gods of postmodernity or the biblical God, either Dionysus or the God of Abraham, Isaac, and Jacob, who is also Jesus' God."[180]

With respect to the biblical God, Metz stresses the one-sidedness of Israel in relation to the surrounding high cultures, expressed in its incapacity to distance itself, mythologically or compensatorily, from the terror of reality.

Israel remains an example for Christianity as the people who do not allow themselves to be consoled by myths, as a people, hence, "poor in the spirit," prepared to pay the price for their radical monotheism, remaining always a "land of screams," unconsoled, always going back to their God, like Job, and asking, Why? There is always an eschatological hope in Israel, a hope based not on a rescuing God beyond history but, in all historical radicalness, on a God who comes to bring history to its end and who, therefore, constitutes history, time-consciousness, and historical responsibility.[181]

Metz stresses the importance of history and responsibility through the "apocalyptic expectation." Christianity and the church must retrieve that tensional, dramatic expectation in order to be meaningful in the postmodern time. In the apostolic era, Christians lived in and by the near expectation of the definitive coming of the Lord. Christology and apocalyptic, interruptive eschatology belonged together at that time. Christian theology, however, has too often left aside the historical, eschatological, imminent aspect of salvation, mainly due to having partially accepted the influence of the Gnostics, through a notion of universal eschatology, later assimilated and passed on by the Neoplatonists.[182]

The Metz who confronts postmodernity is a Metz who intensifies his theology of history and makes the very concept of history and time dependent on the radicality of "the end of history" and of "the end of time." Metz confronts both a mythical understanding of history and what, in his opinion, is a triumphalist crowning of the ideology of capitalism, as the ultimate solution and the historical realization of the modern promise of freedom, after the resounding failure of real socialism in eastern Europe.[183] He does so by unmasking the ideology of unending time, of self-moving history, of subjectless society, of memory-void reason, of mass-media-controlled public opinion, void of imagination. He concludes that the death of God is also the death of consciousness, of history, and of ethical responsibility.[184]

Metz's thought comes back, so to speak, to its base, after having gone all the way around. Modernity as emancipatory enterprise is, on the one hand, for Metz, a historical, political expression of the biblical promises of freedom, justice, and peace. This enterprise has been instrumental not only in promoting those values in society but also in carrying out a necessary critique of religion and church in history. On the other hand, modernity has lost its own roots, its own memory, its own narrative of suffering and death and has become a one-sided, technocratic, domineering, destructive force without regard for its political-liberating other half. Now, again, is the turn of biblical, radical, nonideological Christianity to carry out a critique of that modernity and to rescue it by bringing it back to its memory and narrative. This thesis that the enlightened reason and the modern subject can only be rescued by going back to their historical origin and, ultimately, to the biblical God is far from being, despite certain resemblances, a restorative thesis against the emancipatory thrust of modernity. Quite the contrary, Metz presses the issue of that thrust, demands it be brought to completion, probes its consistency and practical-historical coherence, and, after pointing out its pitfalls and deathly deviations stemming from its uprootedness, asks for that emancipatory thrust to be anchored back in the roots of biblical monotheism.[185]

An important question for the recent Metz, linked to the postmodern dissemination, concerns unity and diversity as a response to the postmodern insistence on plurality. In accordance with his radical approach, Metz questions the depth of the currently assumed cultural plurality of the world. For him the Western-exported technological rationality and its mental presuppositions have been deeply ingrained, not only in fact but, most of all, as an incontrovertible assumption of the reigning progress-led culture and policies, all over the world. If such is the case, then the alleged plurality remains, in the end, a peripheral, mostly compensatory and aesthetic facade, behind which people's way of thinking and imagination have already been standardized.[186]

There are two main threads in Metz's thought in this respect. First, plurality cannot be so radical as to deny universality. Metz's understanding of universality is supported by both the universal ideal of the Enlightenment and Christianity. There is in Metz always a double approach to his historically centered theology. One is the philosophical, historical, social-scientific approach. The crux of this approach is a self-conscious and self-critical Enlightenment grounded in a reason that is not mainly theoretical (first Kant) but practical (second Kant). The second approach is strictly theological, based on Metz's understanding of biblical Christianity. His notion of universality is based on both. In the last analysis, this notion is directly related to Metz's understanding of God and history. Metz's God is a radical God: the God of radical monotheism, the God of radical creation, the God of the radical, apocalyptic end of history, the only one who can rescue the dead and the defeated in that history and, therefore, account for the whole of it. Such a radical God is the origin, the support, and the guarantor of equality and universality. Conversely, only universality can befit the God of radical monotheism.

Second, Metz thinks that universality can and must be defended as one of the values of the genuine Enlightenment. Following Adorno and Horkheimer's *Dialektik der Aufklärung,* Metz talks about "the halving of the Enlightenment." What he means is that from the two halves of the essentially ambiguous modernity, that of an instrumental reason and that of an universally solidary, practical reason, only the first half has been developed and exported by Europe (later by the United States too) everywhere in the world via technology and mass media. This has created what Metz calls a bad colonializing Eurocentrism (as culture of domination) that cannot be overcome by withdrawing now under the excuse of plurality. Europe must repair the damage it has caused and fight for the other half of the Enlightenment to take the lead, so that a universality based on justice and on the recognition of the other can finally take place. Only, so to speak, by this second Europeanization can a true polycentric world become a reality. Moreover, in recognizing not only the other but mainly itself in the tragic result of its colonizing, domineering, historical behavior, Europe must see and judge itself with the eyes of its victims[187]

Given the fact that the Enlightenment originated in Europe, universal values have a concrete, geographical origin, and, in this respect, there can be a positive form of Europeanism. In his confrontation with postmodernity, Metz has also intensified concreteness and geographical-historical determination as opposed to sheer, idealistic, abstract universalism. Ideas and ideals have a concrete origin and must be always related to it. Any inculturation, whether political or religious, must bear this in mind. Otherwise, inculturation becomes a rootless and uprooting process that leads necessarily to ideological manipulation and to oppression. In referring to Eurocentrism, there must be taken into account that there is a "European spirit," which, despite being European, is intrinsically anti-Eurocentric in its pursuit of freedom and justice for all. Europe, says Metz, is the cradle of the ideals of universal reason, freedom, and emancipation, and no postmodern talk about plurality and multiculturalism must interrupt the pursuit of this ideal. For Metz, this ideal of the "European spirit" is, indeed, the only guarantee of plurality.[188]

Christianity is directly affected by the possibility of combining universality with plurality and constitutes the touchstone in relation to that possibility. Consistently with his thought, Metz rejects the possibility of a "naked Christianity" and calls for a Christianity based on the memories of the biblical tradition. By "naked Christianity" he means a Christianity that has no social and cultural anchorage and determinations. This is the wrong path toward universalism and is a denial of reality. Here Metz applies to Christianity his intensification of concreteness and geographical-historical determination. Christianity was born of Judaism and was based on traditions and memories that were culturally determined. To ignore this is to miss the point on which Christianity hinges and to open the door to deceitful forms of domination under the pretext of undetermined universalism. Concrete biblical memories are the only element that can make universality possible in the midst of particularity. This is so because those memories present the God of Israel as a transcendent God, and only before a transcendent God can the subject be constituted and come to itself through and with others and be recognized as truly other and different.[189]

Concerning his idea of a biblical Christianity, Metz strongly emphasizes "the halving of the spirit of Christianity," by which he means the opposition between Greek thought and biblical tradition in constituting Christianity and its theology. Metz defends a Jewish Christianity that truly incorporates the spirit as well as the faith of Israel. Christianity is not the end result of a happy combination of the tradition of Israel with Greek logic. The Hellenization of Christianity undermines its very nature, since essential to it is not the discursive Greek reason but the Jewish anamnestic one. Either the faith of Israel is understood on the basis of its anamnestic logos or it loses its inner nature when interpreted through Greek discursive categories. This development in political theology is to a great extent a consequence of Metz's "discovery" of Auschwitz and of Judaism, an issue that will be discussed later in the chapter.[190]

Christianity as Solidarity

Both the Enlightenment and Christianity must review themselves and confront their own responsibility in relation to a world torn by scandalous differences between the First and the Third Worlds, by a history of colonization, racism, and domination, and by the unwillingness to take into account *the* other, especially the dead, the oppressed, and the defeated. In its irrationality, racism is one of the clearest ways in which the human fear and horror before the unknown and the different express themselves. Racism is for Metz not primarily an experience that refers to other countries or to conquest and colonization but a painful home experience that, although traumatically and most brutally and inhumanly expressed in the Holocaust, continues, for him, to be present in current Germany.[191]

Metz's political theology had long established the principle of the necessity of "global thinking" for a meaningful theology.[192] One important part of this global perspective is the realization of the situation of the world—a world that is more united than ever before, but also a world in which there are outrageous differences between rich and poor countries grounded in unjust political, cultural, and economic structures. In this respect, the Third World has always been present in Metz's thought. However, he has undergone a twofold process of getting closer to Third World realities and perspectives. On the one hand, he has held an ongoing dialogue with liberation theology, a dialogue that underwent a particularly intense period in the 1980s. On the other hand, he has also intensified his direct experience of that reality through personal visits to some countries that have allowed him to discover the centrality of "the eyes of theology," that is, of a theology capable of "seeing," of directly experiencing the reality of this world and of integrating this direct experience into theological discourse.[193]

The Third World, both as society(ies) and church(es), poses a great challenge to Christianity. Its very existence, with its misery, its abandonment, and its more than problematic future, is a frontal, practical denial of the Christian message. Metz calls a reality that so contradicts the assumptions and the core of the Christian message a nonidentity reality in relation to Christianity. Together with the other two nonidentity elements in modern history, the Enlightenment and Auschwitz, the Third World demands from theology something that transcendental theology, with its lack of practical and social-historical dimensions, is unable to deliver, namely, a fully inner-theological assumption of the experience of nonidentity in theological discourse. This assumption is the constitutive ground and the final aim of political theology.[194]

The example of the "discovery" of America and the subsequent process of military, religious, economic, and cultural conquest remains as a typical example of the way European countries have behaved in relation to those who were culturally and technologically weaker than them. Although justified in many different ways, America's and every other colonization is an act by which a civilization with a cultural and technological advantage takes over another, weaker civilization. The process of colonization, historically justified in terms of being in itself good for the colonized, is a practical denial of the values represented both by the "European spirit" and by Christianity.[195] Colonization, however, although it has centuries-long roots, is not confined to the past. There is a "secondary colonization" of a cultural sort that has taken place in recent times through the invasion of the Western *Kulturindustrie* and mass media. This colonization is all the more dangerous because it robs the colonized people of their own historical memories and therefore of their identity.[196]

Pressing on with his analysis concerning plurality, Metz concludes that the conditions for such a plurality are the recognition of the other as other, as nonidentical, and the pursuit of political-historical solidarity as the practical realization of the liberating power of the memory of suffering. The crucial factor in acknowledging the other is precisely the recognition and acceptance of the nonidentical otherness of that other. Only when such otherness is recognized and accepted is the other acknowledged. Plotinus's famous principle of knowledge, "Like is always known by like," is in Metz's opinion a perversion of the original, biblical-based principle of knowledge, "Unlike alone can know unlike," and marks a most dangerous turning point in Christian theology.[197] In stressing the need for the recognition of the other in his or her otherness as a central trait of the biblical love commandment, Metz has, somehow, integrated in his theological thought what he calls Emmanuel Levinas's "alterity theorem."[198] The experience of the other in her or his otherness is an unavoidable path to the experience of the radical otherness of God. Both experiences, in this respect, belong together.[199]

Biblical Christianity alone can become truly solidary and be, through the responsible mystical and political action of a church that also seeks conversion and radical change, the element of transformation of the domination-oriented half of modernity into its political, solidary, liberating, justice-for-all-oriented other half.[200] The church must be a real community of disciples that follow Jesus and give witness to his liberating message in a practical way. Christianity's inculturation hinges on the same point: an ecclesial and social praxis of solidarity and recognition of the other on the basis of the biblical, subversive memory of suffering.[201] This practice of the church, by which it discovers the full meaning of the gospel, is a historical-political praxis guided by an anamnestic reason grounded in the *memoria passionis et resurrectionis Jesu Christi*. This practice of the church is mystical inasmuch as it entails a complete surrender to God and to that memory of Christ that is also the memory of the suffering of the biblical tradition. It will be political in a double sense. First, as a matter of fact, it will be political because the action of the church always is a public action with some covert or overt presuppositions and options. Second, and more important, because Christianity has a historical and public character centered in that memory, it must accept the consequences of that character and align itself with the poor, the destitute, and the defeated and show that the Kingdom of God is near. In this sense, Christian practice is not a practice of political power and domination but, most of all, a practice of "open eyes," a practice capable of seeing more than what is normally seen, especially in relation to the unseen, unnoticed suffering in the world—a practice capable of bringing that suffering to the awareness of all and of making that suffering meaningful on the political scene.[202] Metz has consistently defended the double structure (in unity) of Christianity: the mystical and the political. Both are required in following Christ in true "poverty in spirit."[203]

Metz is deeply concerned about the conversion and transformation the church must undergo to be faithful to this kind of Christianity. The church must change in three ways in order to be loyal to its true mission. The three of them are interrelated. First, in relation to its deeds and action, the church must turn from being a religious-services-oriented church to a socially critical-prophetic church through a solidary praxis.

Second, in relation to its inner dynamics and organization, the church must turn from being a church guided from above to a church of active, self-responsible members who, within the community of the church and together with the other members, personally respond to their Christian callings. The church must turn "from a controlling church for the people to a church of the people."[204] Metz sees this change taking place in the base communities of the Catholic Church in Latin America, which aim at building up a church from below. This emerging, from-down-up church is not the result of applying to the church the model of civil democracy but stems from inner Christian roots, indeed from a radicalization of the Christian life in every member of the church as a Christian-member-of-the-church. In other words, every Christian must become a responsible self both in society and in the church, building thus together church identity and social, civil identity.

A church so understood is also a church in which the one-sided hierarchical authority of the church must be criticized and reinterpreted, to include also the notion of the faith-life-linking authority of the faithful.[205]

Finally, in relation to the question of universality and inculturation, the church must turn from being a Eurocentric church to a universal, truly Catholic church. Only a church that has a conscious Christian-political, mystical-political character, only a church made of active, responsive members, can be a universal church, a church in which the inculturation of the gospel becomes not a theoretical problem that must be solved but a practical task being carried on by the praxis of that church. That universal church will be such to the extent it is capable of acknowledging others in their otherness through the actualization of the biblical, Christian, Gentile-oriented charisma of the church. This actualization requires that a truly universal church be understood as a church that, in and through its praxis, adopts a twofold option: an option for the poor and an option for the other in his or her otherness.[206]

The crisis of Christianity will only be overcome by this kind of church and church practice. As Metz insists time and again, that crisis is neither, primarily, a cognitive crisis nor a crisis of lack of message-content. This is a crisis triggered by the inability of the church to show how that message relates to concrete history and to the experiences of nonidentity in it and how such a message can be the practical response to those experiences.

One important problem concerning the political responsibility of Christians in relation to situations of injustice and oppression is the problem of how a political struggle can be fought on behalf of the Christian commandment of love, especially in those situations in which violence, both structural and physical, plays an important role. First, says Metz, the love of the enemy cannot justify Christians, in the name of this love, refraining from fighting against situations of oppression and scandalous injustices. Second, Christians must try to fight violence with firmness but without violence, because means, and not only aims, matter. It is by using other means than the usual ones, especially the violent ones, that Christians set a new, prophetic standard in the political scene. Christians must play a crucial political role, yet their position in relation to politics is a peculiar one. What most characterizes the political role of the Christians is their ability to see more, to see with the eyes of their faith, of the Christian message, the invisible, unnoticed, inopportune suffering in every society and in the destitute countries in the world. Christians contribute to the transformation of society by making known what they see, by bringing it to the public eye, especially through their own solidary praxis. In this respect, Christianity is for Metz a *Schule des Sehens* (school of seeing), a seeing capable of discovering both the suffering of the world and, in it and through it, capable of discovering God.[207]

The relationship between politics and Christianity belongs to the core of Metz's understanding of both theology and reason as constitutively narrative and historically anchored. In his ongoing dialogue with modernity and democratic, citizen-centered society, Metz is always suspicious of a merely discursive, civil-values-based, ethical discourse. He is convinced that the Western discourse on human values risks being a purely nominal, conventional discourse that, although rooted in Christianity, has lost its own memory and its firm bedrock thereby. For that reason, he is convinced that the universal dignity and value of every human being is rooted in the biblical narrative of the universality of suffering that claims the attention and the resistance of every person. For that reason, he insists on the public, political import of Christianity and on the contribution of Christians to the public realm through a concrete praxis of solidarity based on the biblical narrative.[208] It is important to notice that Metz speaks always as a theologian, that is to say, when he speaks of politics, he does so not from the point of view of the civil realm of politics and of political pragmatism but strictly from a theological perspective that wants to take seriously into account the historical-practical dimension of the Christian message.

The task of theology is precisely to disclose that inner nexus between historical-political praxis and biblical message and to do so in a way that responds to the challenge of the poor and the destitute. Political and liberation theologies, although from different perspectives and circumstances, represent very similar attempts to fulfill that task. The most important similarity between the two, mentioned above, is that both must be understood as postidealistic theologies. Whereas idealistic, transcendental-universal theology seeks to respond to the challenges of modernity with a theological reason that seeks to disclose a universal, structural identity (although in difference) of being, political and liberation theologies try to respond to those challenges with a theological reason structurally constituted by the historical, concrete experiences of nonidentity.

Liberation theology, however, cannot be simply described as the political theology of the Third World. It is, on the contrary, a theology with its own origin and identity. Its origin is the nonidentity experience of the scandalous and crying-out-to-heaven situation of the poor in Latin America. In relation to this particular experience of the church in Latin America, Metz sees in liberation theology a concrete realization of the inculturation of the gospel in a multicultural world and church. Liberation theology is a practical affirmation of the fact that in the church there are different faces, different experiences of nonidentity that defy the common understanding both of the world and of Christianity. Through liberation theology, Christian theology becomes polycentric and the church becomes a truly universal-polycentric church. Moreover, Metz sees in liberation theology an overcoming of what, in his opinion, has been the historical dilemma between grace and freedom in the church—a dilemma that has made the church reluctant to accept modernity's drive to emancipation. For him, liberation theology grounds freedom in grace and comes up not with a merely static concept of freedom but with a dynamic notion of liberation on the very basis of the Christian message.[209]

Theology as Theodicy

The existence of the poor and destitute brings to the fore the question of the suffering of the innocent. The ultimate form of suffering and destitution of the innocent is their death and extermination, a fact in human history that represents a challenge to the understanding of God, or *Gottesrede*. Such a challenge becomes a touchstone of Metz's theology, compelling it to confront the question of theodicy.

In the late 1980s and beyond, Metz has also intensified his discourse about the nature and the constitutive logos of Christian theology as regards both the logos of the Enlightenment and what he interprets as the present epistemological crisis of the different sciences. Metz probes whether the logos of the enlightened reason can be merely discursive or, as he pleads, needs the compass of memory and narrative to take both direction and stock.

Metz's main partner is modern, critical philosophy, from the "masters of suspicion" on. Loyal to his apologetical approach, Metz aims at giving a reason for the Christian message and, most of all, for Christian hope; however, he aims so not *ex-ante* but *ex-post,* after having exposed that faith and that hope to the questions coming from the practical-historical experiences of nonidentity, of contradiction, and, in a way, of denial of that message and faith. Those experiences are also the concrete ground from which critical philosophy stems. Metz's enterprise, however, does not end just there. Its response is not merely an articulated defense of Christianity. Beyond it, that response includes a "firing back," a critical contribution to the understanding of the central categories of that philosophy, namely, critical reason, truth, emancipation, freedom, justice, solidarity, and history, from a strictly theological field. In that sense, Metz's theology discloses to that philosophy something new that is not obvious given the limited horizon of philosophy. Metz brings new resources to the discourse, and, therefore, his theology is, not despite, but in and through its theological peculiarity and its biblical-monotheistic radicality and intensification, a public theology.

In the sense that Metz understands the theological enterprise as a reflection on God that is responsive to those historical situations and events that make it difficult to talk about God, his is a theology that exposes the Christian God to those experiences of nonidentity that cannot be easily reconciled with an idealistic understanding of God, experiences that directly contradict the values of the biblical message and central attributes of the idea of God. In this respect, Metz calls his theology a postidealistic theology. His is a theology that lets itself be questioned by history and praxis and does not arrive at its understanding of human beings, history, and God only on the basis of transcendental, idealistic, or universalist reflection.

Metz, as pointed out above, identifies three main historical, concrete challenges or experiences of nonidentity that theology must confront: critical, practical-reason-based Enlightenment; the Holocaust, as represented by and in Auschwitz; and the Third World, marked by poverty, structural injustice, colonization, and destitution. The first challenge takes away the intellectual impartiality of theological thought. Theology must make clear the interests that lead its interpretation of reality and its reasoning. The second challenge takes away the possibility of reasoning theologically beyond history. Historical catastrophes must constitutively inform theological discourse. The third challenge takes away the possibility of reasoning theologically beyond cultural and ethnic determinations. Theology must be aware of the different cultural settings and must be informed by a culture of acknowledging the other in their otherness and alterity. As a result, idealism and universalism, understood as transcendental reflections beyond ethical, historical, and cultural determinations, must be declared insufficient and must be dialectically confronted by a theology whose discourse is suffused with those determinations.

Has a theology so understood something new to say to philosophers and critical-social analysts and thinkers that directly affects and challenges their discourse and makes them take into account theology as a disclosive discourse? In answering this question, Metz has established a dialectical, fruitful tension between determination and radical openness, between concrete, remembrance-based narrative and negative discourse, between historical determination and eschatological apocalypse. In other words, Metz arrives at his radically negative theology not by reflecting, like classical philosophers and theologians, about God as such, realizing that nothing proper can be said about the radical other, the absolutely transcendent, and concluding that, at its best, theology must remain a negative discourse. Without denying either the validity of the conclusion or the legitimacy of that kind of discourse, Metz takes a completely different approach. The starting point of his reflection is the concrete, painful, catastrophic experience of nonidentity, and he brings that experience to the core of theological discourse so as to make it not the last word but the radical question about and to God. This theology is, in the last resort, rather prayer than discourse, or, otherwise said, issues in a negative, challenging, disquieting discourse whose best and paradigmatic language is prayer. On these grounds, Metz comes to say that theology must be radically understood as theodicy.

The question runs basically as follows: if the memory of suffering is crucial to rescue the subject and to make sense out of Christianity; if that memory is paradigmatically expressed in the passion narratives of the gospels; if God must interrupt history eschatologically to rescue the dead and the defeated; if the church must be the institution that witnesses to that eschatological interruption in history on the grounds of a social-political praxis based on those subversive memories of suffering and injustice, then who is that God whose work is so pervaded by suffering and injustice? This is what Metz calls the *Theodizeefrage*. For him the real question about God is the theodicy question. Any theology that does not face that question is inauthentic; there is no other way of penetrating the mystery of God.[210]

It is not surprising that political theology, which stresses the theology of the cross and understands theology primarily as negative theology, comes up with the question of theodicy. However, such a question only acquired centrality in Metz's theology after his "discovery" of Auschwitz. This "discovery" took place around 1978. Metz has acknowledged that it happened "late (too late?)" in his theology.[211] This, however, does not mean that Metz did not know about Auschwitz before. Auschwitz appears for the first time in *Unsere Hoffnung*, and before that Metz recalls an encounter he and Rahner had with the Czech Marxist philosopher Milan Machoveč in 1968 in which Machoveč confronted Metz with the question of how Christians can pray after Auschwitz.[212] Metz develops the implications of "after Auschwitz" in four theses:

1. Christian theology and Christian identity after Auschwitz can only exist in the face of the Jews.

2. Because of Auschwitz, Christians can protect their identity in front of and together with the history of beliefs of the Jews.

3. The Jewish dimension of Christianity must be stressed anew.

4. Christian theology after Auschwitz must regain the biblical-messianic concepts for its ecumenical endeavors.[213]

Obviously, Auschwitz stands as a powerful symbol of the Holocaust. When Metz speaks of Auschwitz he means it in this symbolic sense, hence encompassing the whole tragedy of the Holocaust, that is, the systematic extermination of the Jews by the Nazi regime that led to the killing of six million Jews.

Auschwitz is an event that unites several threads of political theology. First, it is a catastrophe that interrupts violently any discourse about progress and about emancipation. With Adorno and Horkheimer, Metz thinks that Nazism and Auschwitz are not historical events due to isolated or particular factors but the consequence of systemic factors stemming from an Enlightenment that has become self-destructive. Sheer madness follows from a reason that has lost its references. Metz has referred many times to something the Spanish painter Goya wrote on one of his paintings: "El sueño de la razón produce monstruos."[214] Auschwitz is one of these monsters. In this respect, Metz, following Adorno and Horkheimer, has also a systemic explanation of the Why? of the Holocaust that directly relates to his political theology: the lack of an anamnestic anchoring leaves reason in the hands of all kinds of ideological manipulations, out of which madness and death follow.

Second, and more important theologically, Auschwitz interrupts any discourse about God and forces theology to think about how it is possible to talk about God after such a tremendous catastrophe in history. This is the core of the *Theodizeefrage*. Theodicy comes to the theological fore and becomes *the* theological question. It is important to notice that Metz distances himself from a rationalist understanding of theodicy. For him, theodicy is not the rational justification of God in front of the evil in the world but the question of how it is possible to talk about God taking into account the history of suffering of a world that is God's.[215]

The relationship between theology and theodicy becomes crucial for Metz. As Adorno said, metaphysics was fatally wounded after Auschwitz,[216] so Metz questions the possibility of theology after Auschwitz. For him, a theology that is unmoved by Auschwitz (as Rahner's) is spent. Theodicy is *the* question of theology. Theology has no final, solving answer to this question, simply because that question is also *the* eschatological question. Theology seeks just to take the problem of theodicy in all its depth and to find a new language in order to make that question unforgettable.[217]

For Metz all the attempts to give an answer to the question posed by theodicy are doomed to failure. According to his view, Augustine's attempt to overcome the dualism of Marcion by blaming the human being for the existence of evil in the world entailed important problems that have hindered a right theological understanding of the question of the existence of evil and suffering in history and of how to understand God in relation to it. The problems Metz sees in Augustine's paradigm are:

1. The dualism of deities in Marcion changed to a dualism of people in Augustine: the elected and the *massa damnata,* the latter being responsible for the evil in the world.

2. If the freedom of the human person is grounded in God, then it is not possible to disassociate God from the consequences of that freedom as Augustine claims.

3. Augustine reduces God's rescuing or salvation to redemption of sins, hence not accounting for the suffering in history that cannot be traced back to sin. The eschatological question concerning the justice of God is dissolved by reducing it to a mere anthropological question about human sin.

Metz thinks that Augustine justified God by condemning human beings, thus opening the door to the modern atheism that is rooted in the question

of theodicy. Also, because Augustine's doctrine proclaims a sort of absolutism of sin in history, Christianity has always cast suspicion upon human
freedom. Hence, the secular reaction has been to oppose freedom to guilt,
making the contemporary person reluctant (if not unable) to acknowledge
and to accept guilt in human action.[218]

Augustine, in Metz's view, ignored the biblical paradigm. Metz claims that
this was caused by "the halving of the spirit of Christianity" that occurred
when the Greek spirit took over biblical faith.[219] Although the Pauline and
Johannine writings are influenced by the Greek spirit, an original Jewish
spirit belongs to the constitutive core of the New Testament. This Jewish
spirit is, above all, anamnestic. It understands thought as remembrance, a
remembrance of stories in which suffering and crises play a crucial role.[220]
Israel always turns the question of suffering to God, as is clearly the case
in Job, in the prophets, in the Psalms, in Exodus, and finally in Jesus. The
"*Mystik* of suffering because of God (*des leidens an Gott*)"[221] is the core
of Israel's poverty in spirit. The question then is whether God made the
Israelites or Jesus happy, whether God consoles or brings about an unsolvable crisis that constitutes the main characteristic of Christianity. Metz is
clearly favorable to the latter. Christianity for him is not a religion of happiness and easy answers (something postmodernism tries to reach with its
"myth-friendly and religion-friendly Godlessness") but a religion of crisis
and agonistic hope; it is a religion that disquiets, interrupts, contradicts, en-
dangers, and forces one to have hope against all hope in an unending praxis
of universal justice, solidarity, and peace that is always suspended by the
catastrophes of history.[222]

The God of Christianity is the God of the Bible, the incomprehensible God
that must be trusted and into whom the believer must surrender precisely
when experiencing being forsaken, as does Jesus on the cross, and without
having answers to such a contradiction.[223] That is why, in the end, the only
attitude toward God is a prayerful *leiden an Gott*,[224] and, consequently,
the only theology possible out of that prayer is a negative theology. The
theodicy question in Metz, therefore, must be seen not as a follow-up of
the nineteenth-century theodical furor but as the question that holds the
key to unveiling God's true and paradoxical nature in relation to human
beings. In other words, theodicy for Metz is not a problem in relation to the
traditional understanding of God (that is the reason why he does not accept
traditional interpretations of the theodicy question either) but the only way
to understand what is meant by the reality of God.

Metz expresses his understanding of the attitude of the believer toward
God with the term *Gottespassion* (God-passion). This term has two meanings. The first meaning manifests the believer's *Leidenschaft für Gott,* or
passion for God. The second meaning, *leiden an Gott,* shows that human
suffering is finally referred to God by the believer as the only one who ul-

timately must account for it. In this sense, Metz opposes *leiden in Gott* to *leiden an Gott*. He maintains that theology has tried to understand the problem of suffering in history by developing the idea of suffering as a divine reality, as an inner-trinitarian trait (*leiden in Gott*). In principle, Metz does not oppose that, but he fears that a theology of the divine suffering will be an *Ästhetisierung* (aestheticizing) of suffering, especially in a postmodern, aesthetics-prone society, while forgetting about the reality of concrete suffering in the world. It is the latter that must be faced by theology following the biblical faith. The only answer the Bible has is to suffer, referring that suffering to God, and accepting the lack of divine answers. Such a nonanswering answer is a constitutive part of that core of Christian spirituality that Metz calls the *"Mystik des Leidens an Gott."* Commenting on Jesus' prayer on the cross, he writes that "his suffering was a *Leiden an Gott*. His praying scream on the cross is the scream of the one who, having been forsaken by God, had never himself forsaken God."[225]

With respect to Metz's emphasis on negative theology, it has to be noted that the relationship between theology and prayer is not new in Metz.[226] However, in this regard Metz has also intensified his discourse. Theology begins in prayer and ends in prayer. Prayer, says Metz, in its flexibility and complete freedom is a limitless language, a language that knows no barriers, a language that goes, at least inchoately, well beyond what is being explicitly expressed and into the inexpressible. In this sense, everything can be said to God in prayer, from rage, frustration, and accusation, to downright denial of God's existence. Beyond being such an all-flexible language, prayer is a discourse suffused with experience and with concreteness; it is a living discourse and, hence, the very matrix, the natural setting, of a biographical theology. In the last analysis, theology stems from prayer, talk about God from talk to God. Negative theology is also a result of intensification. The language of prayer is more suffused with negative theology than the official language of theology itself. Theology is nothing other than reflexive prayer-language.

Negative theology cannot be understood as a negation of positive theology; rather, it should be seen as the necessary setting for a proper understanding of anything being predicated of God. In this respect, negative theology does not aim at denying the possibility of affirming that, as in John, God is love. It does not aim at denying the all-mightiness of the creating God. It aims at relating any and every positive statement about God to the radical experience of nonidentity, of the radical, unexplainable otherness of God. It aims at relating all these divine attributes or predicates to their eschatological, end-of-time character. In that sense, resurrection must be affirmed and yet related to the second, interruptive, history-constitutive coming of Christ. It is necessary to stress, so to speak, a Christology of Holy Saturday (*Karsamstagschristologie*) before jumping into the Christology of

Easter. Jesus' scream on the cross cannot be forgotten after the resurrection. It still belongs to the resurrected Christ. The one who does not hear that scream any longer "does not hear theology but mythology, does not hear the gospel but a conqueror's myth."[227]

Eschatology, the second coming of Christ, belongs in the center of Christology. There cannot be a triumphant, realized soteriology, but only a soteriology that lets itself be questioned and interpreted by the actual, historical, massive presence of evil and of innocent suffering, past and present, in the world. That past, present, and future memory must regain its central place in the Christian community. Christianity is, originally, a narrative-and-memory-based community that, as a result of the process of developing a theology, became an argumentation-based community. Only by retrieving that dangerous memory and living by it will theology not forget in its responses all its questions and cries. Thus, the radical and true experience of missing God (*Gottesvermissenserfahrung*) will be again at the center of the theological talk about God.[228]

Chapter 3

Gustavo Gutiérrez:
Liberation Theology

Liberation theology is a theological development that cannot be properly understood except in relation to the characteristics of the society and the church where it emerged as a way of understanding both Christian faith and theological reflection. In the case of Gustavo Gutiérrez, this context is mainly the Peruvian one, although the broader Latin American society(ies) and church(es) must be also taken into account to understand his theology.

Social, Cultural, and Ecclesial Background
of Gutiérrez's Theology

The Peruvian society is in sharp contrast with the German. Its per capita income was a bare 9.5 percent of the German one as of 1998, and its wealth and economic structure have deteriorated over the last thirty years; only about 10 percent of the working population had a proper job in 1992, thus reflecting the deep crisis in the country as a whole during the 1980s. According to the World Bank, Peru's per capita income (technically gross national product per capita) had a 0.2 percent negative average annual growth between 1965 and 1989 and, even worse, a negative 0.9 percent average annual growth between 1985 and 1992. The national economic results of the years 1990–92 were almost catastrophic, with a negative growth of 5 percent per year on average. Only from 1993 on did the economy start to recover, with a gross domestic product growth record of 12.9 percent in 1994 and a 5.9 percent positive average annual growth between 1990 and 1998. In analyzing these data it must be borne in mind that whereas the total gross national product grew by 56 percent from 1965 to 1989, the population grew by 90 percent in the same period, so that economic growth did not keep pace with population growth. Population has more than tripled since 1950, increasing from 7.6 to 25 million in 1998.[1]

One of the recent problems of Peru has been its international isolation, a paradoxical phenomenon in a country that has traditionally based its economy on exporting its products (guano, sugar, cotton, fish, oil) and that has struggled to liberate itself from external dependence. If the dependent situation was dramatic, the marginalized situation has been somewhat tragic. The last straw in the process of isolation of the country (the marginalization of the country is a complex fact that has to do with many Peruvian and international factors) was the policy of Alan García, constitutional president between 1985 and 1990. President García decided not to pay the foreign debt of the country, taking an attitude of confrontation in relation to international organizations like the World Bank and the International Monetary Fund. Links with developed countries were cut off, and Peru lost its access to international financing. This, united to the internal crisis, meant an almost complete lack of investment, which fueled the pace of economic deterioration.

Alberto Fujimori, elected president in 1990, attempted to reverse the situation, starting to service foreign debt and trying to reach an agreement with the International Monetary Fund in order to have access to international funding. His economic policy pursued the adjustment of the economy, fighting against inflation and public deficit, liberalizing prices, drastically reducing tariffs to open the economy to foreign competition, and increasing public income. In other words, Fujimori followed an orthodox policy of stabilization and liberalization according to the recommendations of the International Monetary Fund. Such measures were devastating for the poor majority of the citizens, including the middle classes, especially in the years 1990–92, although there were signs that new jobs were created in the 1993–95 period. In October 1995, the government reached an agreement with its international creditors, by which foreign debt, unserved for ten years, was reduced by 45 percent. However, the financial situation of the country continued to show unsolved structural problems, with a swelling national budget deficit that increased by 100 percent in 1995 in relation to the previous year.[2]

Peru is a classic example of a colonial country whose expectations of emancipation and economic development have not come to fulfillment. After some decades of industrial and economic growth, the country followed, especially in the 1980s, a dangerous path of progressive deterioration of almost all the crucial aspects that make up its life. It is not an exaggeration to say that the country was in shambles at the beginning of the 1990s. The economic deterioration of the country during the 1980s went hand in hand with its social and political decay. In Lima, the capital of the country, with a population well over six million people, only 5.3 percent of the people who wanted to work had a proper job in 1990; 8.3 percent were officially unemployed, whereas the rest, 86.4 percent, were thought to be underemployed—that is, they pursued some kind of activity in order to survive.[3] Most of the latter were self-employed in a very broad sense. They did whatever they could in a completely flexible and informal manner outside the legal framework and the formal economy. They are called in Peru *informales*—a group of people who have to survive on their own because the state can do nothing or little to help them, a group whose ranks have increased dramatically.

About 60 percent of the population of Lima live in shantytowns with deficient, or outright lack of, basic services like running water, electricity, and sewage. Most of their inhabitants have emigrated from the Sierra, the mountainous part of the country, looking for opportunities for themselves and their children. Although the situation of these urban poor is dramatic, they still think that the future can be better in the city than in the Sierra.

Because people know that they can expect almost nothing from the government (Fujimori promised to create a $500 million emergency social program in 1990 to compensate for the hardship of the adjustment, but only $68 million were actually allotted to that end), they find their own way to survive. This, however, gravely erodes confidence in the institutions of the country, and the citizens become more and more *informales,* that is to say, living increasingly with their back to the system, including the law.[4] In 1990 people showed their frustration with formal politics and parties when they turned down those parties and elected the relatively unknown Fujimori, an outsider, to be their president. In 1992, with the support of the army and of more than 70 percent of the population, President Fujimori suspended the constitution, fired the judiciary, disbanded the parliament, and decided to govern by decree, claiming that such a move was necessary to overcome corruption and to defeat terrorism. In October 1993, the country approved a Fujimori-tailor-made new constitution that, among other things, allowed the president to be reelected. Fujimori's claim to get his will accepted was that the changes he proposed were indispensable to eradicate corruption at all levels. However, his critics pointed out that such a discourse remained mainly rhetoric since he could achieve his aim only because the army, which seems to be at the center of the institutional corruption, supported him. The international community, although it officially reacted against Fujimori's self-coup in 1992, accepted in practice his move and reinforced his power. After the approval of the new constitution and the victory of Fujimori in the 1994 presidential election against former United Nations Secretary General Javier Pérez de Cuéllar, Fujimori's legitimacy went undisputed until June 2000. During and after the presidential elections in 2000, he was accused of manipulating both the campaign and the results of the election, and the competing candidate, Mr. Toledo, declined to take part in the run-off election. The international community refused to acknowledge the legitimacy of the process, and public protest and riots ensued. Thereafter, several scandals have ruined Fujimori's public image, and he has announced his retreat from the presidency and a new election. This marks the end of the Fujimori era.

Peruvians today are caught up in reflecting upon the causes of the current generalized crisis of state and society in the country. The answers are by no means simple, and they seek to integrate an increasing number of factors usually forgotten by the traditional analyses of political ideologies and parties. There seems to be a consensus that the current institutional and economic collapse has causes that are structural and historically rooted— one of its traits is the cleavage between the formal Peru and the real Peru. At the base of that structural collapse lie the conquest and the colonization of the country.[5]

The four main problems of the country—poverty, corruption, drugs, and terrorism—are interrelated, and, despite some improvements, no solution seems to be at hand to put the country back on track. This lack of solutions becomes tragic in some cases and poses the question of whether some countries have a viable future. In South America, Peru, Bolivia, and most of the Andean countries find themselves in such a situation. In Central America, Honduras, Nicaragua, Guatemala, and El Salvador face similar circumstances. Other countries in the world, especially in sub-Saharan Africa, have the same problem.[6]

This desperate situation in countries in which the hope to solve structural problems is fading away questions once again the adequacy of the international economic order, especially after three decades in which the poor countries have become poorer while the rich ones have become richer. According to the United Nations, in 1960 the richest 20 percent of the world's population enjoyed 70.2 percent of the gross world product. In 1989, their share had grown to 82.7 percent, and to 86 percent by 1997. In the other extreme, the poorest 20 percent got only 2.3 percent of the gross world product in 1960. By 1989, their share had decreased to 1.4 percent, and to a mere 1 percent by 1997. In 1960, they were 30 times poorer than the rich. In 1989, 60 times poorer. In 1997, 74 times poorer.[7] Although generalized and massive poverty is characteristic in most countries in the Third World, it would be a mistake to think that poverty is not a reality also in highly developed countries. The United States, the most powerful country in the world, is a painful example of a rich country that contains a vast minority of poor persons who live in inhuman conditions and whose situation got alarmingly worse through the 1980s and the first half of the 1990s.

In Peru, poverty also got much worse during the 1980s and part of the 1990s. The trend toward development between 1950 and 1975, when per capita income almost doubled, stagnated after 1975, and started a free fall after 1987. In 1992, per capita income (at constant prices) was about the same level as in 1950, but unlike forty years earlier, the prospect for development was depressingly dim. In Lima, the "critical poverty index" almost tripled from December 1987 to March 1991, and, accordingly, the percentage of households below the poverty line grew from 16.9 percent to 44.3 percent between 1986 and 1990. The average governmental monthly salary (measured in constant 1985 dollars) fell from $231 in 1980 to $39 in 1990. Although the situation has improved between 1992 and 1999, the underlying conditions remain precarious and structurally weak.

Although corruption is a social disease from which no country in the world is free (witness the wave of scandals in Japan, Italy, France, Spain, and Belgium in the 1990s), some claim that it is a structural evil in Peru due to the politics of clientelism and favoritism that has characterized the country because of its colonial history. Besides, poverty promotes public corruption in Peru, thus dramatically undermining the morale of the population. Corruption is painfully present in the different institutions of the state and in the business community and is especially widespread among the police and the army. Apart from moral, historical, and structural considerations, corruption is also due to the inability of the government to stay on top of the situation, to pay its public employees a salary good enough to keep a family going, and to make them abide by the law. Many public employees abuse their authority to get the extra money they need to survive. In the case of the army, corruption is thought to have reached dangerous levels, with members of the army getting money from drug barons in exchange for protection.

If structural problems gave it its ground, poverty and corruption strengthened the cause of the deadly Partido Comunista del Perú (the Sendero Luminoso). Although its strength has decisively declined since the arrest of its leader, Abimael Guzmán, in 1992, Sendero has been one of the worst plagues of the country between 1985 and 1992 and continues to be a problem. The group, today not as firmly united as in the 1980s and the beginning of the 1990s, has always portrayed itself as an uncompromising revolutionary political party (of radical Maoist character) with a strategy of liberation that uses violence to destroy the system to its base. Any other solution is pure reformism for Sendero. Its discourse has been almost religious: current society must be totally overhauled in order to give birth to a completely different society free from any trace of injustice or exploitation. In practice, this means that among the main targets of Sendero have been not only the army and the police but also those institutions and realities that pursue the development of the country. Up to a point, the church and the committed Christians have been more dangerous to Sendero than the army, because the more their success in changing the situation, the less possible has been it for Sendero to appear as the only group that has a solution for the country. This is the reason why Sendero started to kill foreign clergy, affirming that they will wipe out the church once they take power. In the areas controlled by Sendero or threatened by them, mainly rural areas in the Sierra, the situation of violence and terror has had a heavy impact on the population, creating desperate situations that will mark the life of the people for decades to come.

Drugs are another difficult problem intertwined with the other three. The country has traditionally grown coca for health and nutritional purposes. Over the last two decades, but especially in the 1980s, coca plantations attracted drug traffickers, making coca growing one of the few profitable activities in the country. Peru was assigned to produce coca paste that was then taken to Colombia, where cocaine was made. The importance of the economy of coca in Peru is thought to be rather high. Although an accurate determination of how important it is does not exist due to the clandestine nature of the activity, analysts agree that it is not exaggerated to think that it amounts to 10 percent of the gross national product. Such a source of wealth in the midst of dire poverty explains why coca growers are not willing to give up their plantations simply for moral reasons; why both Sendero and the army seem to have reached agreements with drug traffickers by which the latter give money to the former in exchange for protection; why, therefore, corruption makes it difficult to fight against the traffickers.[8]

Peruvian society is marked by discrimination and division.[9] In the cultural domain, Peru is a partially unblended mixture of different pre-Columbian and post-Columbian cultures and traditions with diverse worldviews. In the middle of the two cultures and traditions stands the trauma of the Spanish conquest and of the subsequent colonization. Such a trauma has been operative since the conquest and still affects the natives. Although at the time of the Spanish conquest the Incas were the ruling people in Peru, with Cusco as the center of an empire, called Tahuantinsuyo or Tawantinsuyu, extending from southern Colombia to northern Chile, it would be a mistake to think that their culture, dominant at that moment, was the only native culture. In fact, there were other cultures and peoples. Some of them had been subjugated and even destroyed by the Incas' imperialist policy during the fifteenth century. Peru, in that respect, as many if not most other countries, is a succession of cultures and peoples that eliminated or dominated the previous one, and no romantic view of the Incas (and the danger of such a view is still real today) can resist the historical data.[10]

An interesting testimony regarding the situation of the natives after the conquest is given by Huamán Poma de Ayala (ca. 1530–1620), a native who became Christian and who wrote a report on the exploitation of the Indians by the colonial system, as well as recommendations to overcome such a situation. His intention was to present the report to the Spanish king. The importance of the chronicle lies in three points: first, it is written by a native who loves his people and sees the situation from the perspective of the natives; second, it transcends the mere account of facts, looking for the systemic causes; third, to a great extent, the author writes from a theological point of view. Huamán denounces the systemic oppression of the Indians, pointing to the fact that all the officials of the Spanish administration together with the clergy (the Jesuits are highly praised though) plot to exploit the natives and help and cover each other for that purpose. Hence, he comes to the conclusion that the system is completely rotten and that it is not possible to change it from within. The conquerors have subverted in their practice the values they preach. Instead of announcing the true salvation to the natives, they are corrupting them with their example. In short, the world is upside down. The only hope is the intervention of the king to overhaul the system. Huamán is important theologically because he has a clear understanding of Christianity as a religion in which poverty plays a crucial role in following Christ and for which the poor are "the poor of Jesus Christ."[11]

A thorough assessment of the European colonization of America is a difficult task, not least because of the emotions and passions that such an event arouses. On the occasion of the fifth centennial of the "discovery" of the new continent by the Europeans (the continent had already been "discovered" for ages by the natives), celebrated in 1992, many studies were published from different angles. Beyond the two extreme positions (European positive appraisal on the basis of culturization and evangelization and native rejection because of the destruction and oppression), many of those studies try to adopt the more pragmatic approach of considering the event a historical fact that must be analytically understood in order to assess it more evenly. Gutiérrez is one of the authors who has tried to progress in the understanding of the colonization of America through his historical-theological study on the Spanish Dominican Bartolomé de Las Casas (1484–1566). The study coheres with the previous theological enterprise of Gutiérrez, since the conquest and the subsequent colonization and evangelization of America are central to understanding the current situation of its countries and the role of the church in them.[12]

One of the immediate consequences of the conquest was the dramatic near extermination of the native population, which in 1570 was a mere 12 percent of the population existing in 1520.[13] Gutiérrez points out both the existence of several, diverging estimates and the difficulty of adjudicating among them. Favoring a middle position, it would be relatively safe to estimate that, in the case of Peru, the figures for the native population were 9 million in 1520 and 1 million in 1570. In the case of Spanish America in general, the population would have been 57 million in 1492 and 9 million in 1570. Gutiérrez mentions in *En busca de los pobres de Jesucristo* four main causes (there were others too) of such a genocide: first, malnutrition and change in food habits; second, the diseases brought by the Europeans to the "New World," against which the Indians were not immunologically prepared; third, war mortality; fourth, the inhuman conditions under which the natives were forced to work, especially in the mines.

In general terms, the indigenous majority of the population has been prevented from sharing in the full rights of citizenry until very recently. The independence of countries from the Spanish kingdom did not solve this problem of discrimination. According to some, who basically follow

José Carlos Mariátegui's interpretation of independence,[14] the natives were even more oppressed after independence because the movement of independence had its roots in an Enlightenment brought from Europe, unable to integrate the political and cultural reality of the natives in its programs and ideals. Indians were simply a problem and a hindrance.[15] The problem is, according to Mariátegui, a structural one, based on the system of land tenure. Like Huamán Poma de Ayala, who complained that the situation of the Indians had no solution because all the social forces (that is, *corregidor, encomenderos,* priests, soldiers, etc.) supported each other to rob them,[16] Mariátegui claims also that "the judge, the subprefect, the commissary, the teacher, the tax collector, all are in bondage to the landed state. The law cannot prevail against the *gamonales.*" Consequently, the solution must also be structural, social, economic, and not purely altruistic or humanitarian.[17]

One way the political system prevented, in fact, the natives from taking part in elections was to grant voting rights only to males who knew how to read and write (from 1896 on). In 1956, people with voting rights amounted only to 30 percent of those who could have voted on the basis of age against less than 15 percent in 1931.[18] The rest could not vote because they could not read and write. In other words, the majority of the population was excluded from the political life of the country and from any possibility of exerting power or raising its voice other than rebelling against the system with the consequent repression.[19] The inertia of considering the natives not quite as full citizens is still a reality, although the situation has substantially changed after the people from the Sierra started to migrate massively to the coastal cities in the 1940s. This migration, which still continues, has been described as an assertive action on the side of the native population in order to fully share in the benefits of the other citizens and to make effective their theoretical political rights.

Many authors have come to the conclusion that the marginalization of the natives in Peru allowed them to resist better the cultural imposition of the conquerors and to keep their own traditions. In fact, the persistence of the Quechua language is a sign of the native cultural resistance for these authors.[20] Quechua was made co-official language of Peru, together with Spanish, by Velasco Alvarado in 1975, but later, in the constitution of 1979, its status as co-official language was restricted to the areas where it was spoken. In 1972, between 3 and 4 million Peruvians out of a total population of 14 million spoke Quechua. They were concentrated in the Andean Sierra, and half of them, about 2 million, were monolingual. Quechua disappeared from the coastal region in the sixteenth century as a result of the conquest. In the Andes, natives became increasingly bilingual under Spanish pressure, especially after Quechua was forbidden due to the rebellion of Tupac Amaru and after the Jesuits, defenders and spreaders of the native language, were expelled in the eighteenth century. Since then, Quechua has been receding slowly but steadily and is limited to rural-domestic use.[21]

Traditionally, the excluded Indian has been the nonperson, ignored and abused by the ruling white minority. Between the two, the mestizo has been left in an ambiguous position.[22] One of the most compelling descriptions of the Indian as a nonperson is given by José María Arguedas in his book *Los ríos profundos*. In his opening chapter, Arguedas presents us with two characters: el Viejo, who represents the postcolonial landowner who owns not only the land but also the lives of those who serve him, and el Pongo, the Indian who works for the landowner on the estate, who also serves him also at home, and who is treated as a serf without rights ("like a worm asking to be stepped on"). For Arguedas, el Viejo is the Antichrist, whereas the face of el Señor de los Temblores (the Christ of the cathedral of Cusco) looks like that of el Pongo.[23]

The racial structure of Peru is not as simple as natives, whites, and mestizos. After blacks were brought as slaves, multiple combinations were possible from the three basic races of natives, blacks, and whites: from natives and whites came the mestizos; from blacks and whites, the mulattos; from natives and blacks, the *zambos*.[24] In turn, from those basic combinations many others came into existence, creating a very complex racial mix. Gutiérrez has repeatedly affirmed that in Peru (and in many other Latin American countries) racism reigns. He is also fully aware that, in Latin America, not only the natives but also the blacks must be counted among the nonpeople.[25] Although legally blacks were below natives, in fact the lowest level in the social scale was that of the common Indians, with blacks miming their Spanish owners' treatment of and attitude toward the natives. Only the leaders among the natives were superior to the blacks in the social scale. Another important difference between blacks and natives was that the former, unlike the latter, sought to integrate themselves into the Spanish society.[26]

In the second half of the nineteenth century, when the 1856 law abolishing both slavery and the tribute of the natives caused a retraction of labor, one hundred thousand Chinese were brought into the country as a new source of cheap labor to work in the coastal guano deposits and on the plantations of sugar and cotton.[27] Still later, about eighteen thousand Japanese arrived in Peru (hence the Japanese descent of current president Fujimori) between 1899 and 1924, to work in the cotton and sugar plantations. It seems that their working conditions were better than those of the Chinese. Later, more Japanese came to Peru, called by those relatives or friends who had come first.[28]

For some authors, like Mariátegui and Julio Cotler, the division of Peruvian society has been so deeply and systemically rooted that it has made impossible the constitution of a nation.[29] Around 1920, a new generation of intellectuals and politicians came to the fore in the life of the country. One of the aims of these post-Enlightenment Peruvian thinkers was to overcome the division and to formulate a project of an inclusive society able to allow the different cultures to contribute to the creation of a commonly shared multifaceted identity.[30] They represented the most serious attempt at rethinking the nation and at changing its structures, becoming a milestone for later generations. Politically, the towering figures of this generation were Víctor Raúl Haya de la Torre (1895–1979), founder of the political party Alianza Popular Revolucionaria Americana (APRA), and José Carlos Mariátegui (1894–1930), founder of the Partido Socialista Peruano (later Comunista) and of the Confederación General de Trabajadores del Perú. Other figures of that outstanding generation include the poet César Vallejo (1892–1938) and the anthropologist and writer José María Arguedas (1906–69). The influence of this generation on Gutiérrez can hardly be overemphasized. He is clearly heir to them and the one who has established a most fruitful theological dialogue with that generation.

For Carlos Milla, the aim of this generation was "peruanizar el Perú."[31] Haya de la Torre and Mariátegui inaugurated the Peruvian anti-imperialist and socialist tradition in the 1920s, and both collaborated for a while until their differing views on the issue of whether or not to accept the decisions of the Third International Socialist (only the tip of the iceberg in their debate on how to understand and to put into practice anti-imperialism and socialism in Peru) led them to different positions and political strategies: Haya followed a multiclassist path based on his interpretation of the particular characteristics of "Indo-America," whereas Mariátegui decided to stick to the principle of class struggle, but understanding class as a reality broader than just the working class, encompassing all deprived classes, especially the native peasants. Mariátegui died at thirty-five, just when he was directing the foundation of the party and the union, and thus his political activity never fully matured.[32]

A socio-demographic revolution started to take place after 1940, due to the massive migration from the Sierra and the Selva to the cities. This is a crucial development in recent Peruvian history and constitutes the immediate referential point (but not the only one to be sure) for Gutiérrez's notion of "the irruption of the poor in history." The fact is that from 1930 on, the rural masses in Peru started to move to the cities looking for the opportunities that the urban centers offered in terms of jobs, services, and social mobility. The current population of Lima is almost nine times greater than in 1940. Whereas the rural population grew from 4.5 million in 1940 to 6.7 million in 1990, the urban population grew from 1.7 to 15.6 million over the same period.[33] Bearing in mind that Peru in 1990 was not richer than it was in 1950, in terms of per capita income, it is easy to understand that such a massive migration has created grave dysfunctions in a system that cannot provide services for the newcomers. Yet migration continues, thus subverting the social structure of the colonial system in which the native population did not belong to the cities of the ruling minority.[34]

In the 1960s, this new social presence of the hitherto excluded masses, together with an increasing awareness of the need for structural changes and a growing antidependence (mainly from the United States) movement, led to the crisis of the old state and to an attempt to form new political bases for the nation. After the disappointing results of the democratic government during the period 1963–68, the army took over the country in what was to be another milestone for the future history of Peru: the military government of the General Velasco Alvarado, which declared itself to be revolutionary, and lasted from 1968 to 1975.[35] The government of Velasco tried to bring into existence a structural reform of the country in order to overcome the endemic evils that had prevented Peru from being an integrated nation. This is another widely analyzed period of the history of Peru that still is being debated. For different reasons, almost everybody is critical of it, but also almost everybody acknowledges its importance in the history of the country.[36]

In general, the military revolution was considered almost outright communism by those whose companies were nationalized. Carlos Iván Degregori thinks that the left was disoriented and confused with respect to the Velasco regime.[37] Although many on the left were sympathetic with the project of Velasco, only some of them collaborated with him. The others always distrusted the regime due to its military character and the ambiguity of its leaders. They mostly agreed on the necessity of the reforms undertaken by the government, but, in the end, they thought that these reforms were both not thorough enough and too directed from above because the regime did not want to empower the masses too much. Cotler, for instance, thinks that Velasco tried a top-down revolution that sought to integrate politically the masses while taking away their political autonomy. In other words, for Cotler the military regime sought in the end to disempower politically the masses of their potential to act as a class.[38] Carlos Franco (who was fully committed to the cause of Velasco) has a different view: the revolution was socially democratizing in content but politically authoritarian in form. He contends that the former would have been impossible without the latter, because the grassroots movement and the political forces had proved over the previous fifty years their inability to bring about structural changes.[39] Rolando Ames thinks that although Velasco's regime was a military dictatorship, it also opened new spaces of democratization and participation.[40]

Velasco undertook a series of wide-ranging measures (expropriation of U.S. companies, nationalization of basic industries and of the banking system, land expropriation and reform, nationalization of the main mass media, educational reform, creation of companies owned by workers, promotion of social participation at all levels) that showed his determination both to change the situation and to be in command of the change, but his regime paid the price of its military nature and always lacked coherence and consistency. His project was, in principle, both global (it affected all the segments and levels of society, aiming to change individual and social behaviors in order to make the existence of an integrated nation possible) and interventionist, including promoting and regulating participation. However, in practice, the regime was internally incoherent due to the opposed political interests and ideologies inside it, and, therefore, the implementation of its program was patchy and ambiguous.

Concerning the relation of the Peruvian church to the Velasco regime, Jeffrey Klaiber claims that the church never legitimized the military regime but approved of its reforms and closely collaborated with it to bring about social change. He also claims that the regime sought the advice and support of the church and based many of its policies on Catholic social teaching. He further argues that the Velasco regime somehow forced the church to adopt a clearer social stand, and, in that sense, it quickened the evolution of the church toward an open and active role in favor of the poor. However, says Klaiber, there were moments of tension, and the church started to confront the regime when, in its last phase, it expropriated the main mass media and adopted a more authoritarian style of government.[41] There were in fact various positions within the church. A somewhat different position from that of the hierarchy regarding the military regime was taken by a group of priests close to the views of liberation theology and organized under the name ONIS (Oficina Nacional de Información Social). Generally speaking, this group, although sympathetic with the transformative measures implemented by the government (one of its founders, Luna Victoria, later held an important job in the ministry of education), kept a critical distance with respect to the regime in order to force it to take more daring steps in changing the structures of the country.[42]

The role of the Catholic Church in Peru has been crucial since the conquest. Already in the fifteenth century, the church played a decisive role. Isabella I of Castille and Ferdinand V of Aragon sought to legitimize internationally their possession of the conquered lands by getting the pope to support their claim. As early as 1493, Pope Alexander VI acknowledged in five bulls the right of the Spanish crown to the territories in America under the condition of evangelizing them. The papal bulls were one of the main elements used by the crown to justify its possessions and the legitimacy of its policies, arguing that the crown had fulfilled the condition of evangelizing those possessions.[43]

This role of the church also has been ambiguous from the outset, marked by the fact that the church came hand in hand with the conquerors, playing a crucial role in Europeanizing the native population in the name of Christ.

The main point is the intimate relationship between conquest and evangelization that has its roots in the previously mentioned bulls of Alexander VI of 1493. These bulls legitimize the possessions of Spain in America insofar as Spain Christianizes their inhabitants. In 1508 and 1529 new bulls established the patronage of the Spanish crown over the church in the American territories, meaning that the administration of missionary work (such as the sending of missionaries and the appointment of bishops) was directly under the crown. That determined that the role of the church in America was intrinsic to the advance of the conquest, that the administration of the task of evangelization was in the hands of the crown, and that the roles of church and crown were not clearly separated. Hence, it is easy to understand why, on the one hand, the role of the church was in many cases one of oppression on the part of many greedy members of the clergy for whom evangelization and conquest belonged together, and why, on the other hand, the fight for the rights of the natives was led by missionaries who came in conflict with the crown.

In analyzing the attitude of either the church or the Spanish authorities toward the natives no simplification can be warranted. Basically, both institutions acknowledged the freedom of the natives, and they never gave up this principle. In the case of the Spanish crown, the freedom of the natives, who from a legal standpoint were considered free vassals of the king, was crucial to prevent the colonizers from getting control of the native people. This ensured the crown the ultimate control of the land and of the people. At the same time, the law favored, almost always, the existence of mechanisms to give the conquerors compensations at the expense of the natives and to make the latter work in public works and in the mines for the benefit of the crown. This led in practice to a situation of real exploitation of the native population.

Gustavo Gutiérrez has examined this difficult issue in his historical-theological work on the Spanish missionary Bartolomé de Las Casas. His work makes it clear that, despite the flaws of the church, many of its members also played a crucial role in denouncing the colonial exploitation and in defending the right of the Indians to be considered of equal dignity with the white ruling minority, also in the name of Christ. One difficulty in judging the role of the church in the conquest and colonization is, on the one hand, the difference between principles and practice and, on the other hand, the diversity of attitudes and actual behaviors inside the church with respect to that practice.

In the domain of principles, papal legislation was crucial. This legislation proclaimed the principle of the equal human dignity of the natives and that of their freedom to accept Christian faith. An example of this is the papal bull *Sublimi Deus* of 1537. However, the papacy accommodated in practice to the requirements and pressures of the royal powers, partly because the alliance of Rome with Charles V was precious for the Catholic Church at the time of the Reformation. Thus, the efficacy of *Sublimi Deus* (not the bull itself) was suspended one year after its promulgation due to the pressure of Charles V on Pope Paul III.[44]

As for the different attitudes and behaviors in the actual practice of the missionaries, one reason for these differences was the existence of various religious orders in charge of the evangelization of the natives. Although far from being completely consistent (witness the general of the Dominican order Cardinal García de Loaísa, who became archbishop of Seville, president of the powerful Consejo de Indias, and general governor of the West Indies, but who was also instrumental in nullifying the efficacy of *Sublimi Deus*), the behavior of the mendicant orders, Franciscan and Dominican, and more specifically the behavior of the missionaries belonging to them, and later that of the Jesuits, can be considered sensitive to the cause of the Indians and oriented by a truly pastoral interest. The members of the Mercedarian order (not the order itself) and the secular clergy, in contrast, seem to have been more concerned with their own benefit, taking part in abuses and exploitations, and lacking discipline, although there were important exceptions to the rule also among them.[45]

The exploitation of the natives was given a philosophical and theological justification already in the sixteenth century.[46] For Gutiérrez, who has explored this issue at length, it is clear that the philosophical and theological justification of the wars waged against the Indians and of the ensuing system of *encomiendas* (the "entrusting" of land and of the natives living in it, usually to soldiers as a reward for their military services), dispossessing the Indians of all their rights and property and obliging them in practice to work both for the crown and for the *encomenderos,* was crucial to legitimize the conquest and the oppression of the Indians. However, always trying to avoid any type of simplification, Gutiérrez points out that Spain was the only European country where a debate over the legitimacy of the colonization took place. All the others, Portugal, France, England, and Holland, took that legitimacy for granted.[47]

The justification was necessary to stem the protests of some Spaniards who cried out against the colonial practices and also to justify the conquest and the exploitation of the natives. The protests started in 1511 with a sermon given by the Dominican Antón de Montesinos on the island of La Española (Hispaniola, Greater Antilles), in which he denounced and condemned the exploitation of the natives and disputed any right to the occupation of their land and any treatment of them other than as human persons.[48] After a hard fight, in which the Dominican missionary Bartolomé de Las Casas was the key figure in the defense of the natives, the colonial practice was justified and carried out in a more consistent and harsher manner under Philip II.

The work of Las Casas (1484–1566), although outstanding in denouncing the abuses and the illegality of the conquest and in trying to alter the civil and ecclesiastical laws that regulated the process of colonization, was by no means the only such effort. Las Casas awoke relatively late in his life (in 1514) to the oppressive situation in which the natives lived. At eighteen, he sailed to America to make his own career, fought against the natives, was given a part in one *encomienda,* and later, after being ordained a priest in Rome between 1506 and 1508, he continued the administration of his *encomienda,* combining it with pastoral work. In other words, Las Casas took an active role in the system of oppression, which he later would criticize, before converting to the cause of the natives.[49]

Las Casas fought unceasingly, from 1515 on, a titanic battle to alter the laws regulating the life of the natives. From his visit to Ferdinand V in 1515 to his memorandum to Philip II and to the Consejo de Indias just a few days before his death in 1566, he never gave up his aim: not only to denounce the unjust situation of the natives, and to change the laws to make that situation impossible, but also more radically to deny the right of the Spanish people to rule over the natives against the will of the latter and to demand the restitution to the natives of all that had been stolen from them.

Las Casas never achieved his goal, but he scored some points. His greatest triumph was the promulgation of Las Leyes Nuevas in 1542 by Charles V, which forbade the existence of the *encomiendas.* However, the spirit of the new laws was against the interest of the crown in getting as much wealth as possible from the colonies and contradicted the real foundations of the Spanish conquest. Their enforcement caused numerous conflicts, and finally the *encomiendas* and the other mechanisms of domination were fully restored in 1545. Since the missionaries continued their denunciations of the situation, Philip II ended the debate with the so-called Junta Magna of 1568, a meeting of rulers and theologians that declared the Spanish presence in America to be just and that approved of the mechanisms of colonization. The decisions of this meeting were put into practice by the Viceroy Francisco de Toledo in Peru from 1569 to 1581. He ordered a theological justification of the right of Spain to the American territories (*El Parecer de Yucay*) and made sure that the ideas of Las Casas were firmly countered in theory and in practice. Finally, Toledo and Philip II ordered the confiscation of all the works by Las Casas, signaling the end of the controversy.

The first and probably most influential book by Las Casas, written in 1534, in which he laid down the main tenets he would defend for the rest of his life, was *De unico vocationis modo omnium gentium ad veram religionem.* The theses of the book were assumed by Paul III's bull *Sublimi Deus* of 1537 and served later for the promulgation of Las Leyes Nuevas in 1542 by Charles V.[50] Following Isacio Pérez, it seems right to distinguish between the *espíritu lascasiano* (after Las Casas) and the *espíritu filipino* (after

Philip II) to reflect the different policies in relation to the Indians. Whereas part of Las Casas's spirit was taken up and brought into law by Charles V, Philip II undid what Las Casas had achieved.[51] Isacio Pérez claims that part of the spirit of Las Casas was definitely incorporated into the Philipian practice and into the *Código ovandino* (never promulgated) and that Philip II, moved again by the denunciations of the missionaries, later changed his attitude toward the situation of the natives.[52] The facts seem to prove, though, that although some of the spirit of Las Casas could have been still operative after his death, the main tenets of his doctrine and the practical aims he pursued were completely rejected both in theory and in practice.

Gutiérrez's work on Las Casas, especially his *En busca de los pobres de Jesucristo,* is very important in relation to the present chapter. Las Casas is Gutiérrez's theological and ecclesial hero. Although Gutiérrez makes it clear that he does not want to make Las Casas a "liberation theologian," it is crystal clear that he is for Gutiérrez a model both in perspective and in content for liberation theology. The basic thesis of the book is that Las Casas brought completely new insights and approaches into the theological discussion, as regards the understanding of human nature, history, and God. His positions and insights were far more advanced than those of the most enlightened minds of his time, such as the other Dominicans Francisco de Vitoria and Domingo de Soto. For Gutiérrez, Las Casas's innovative, groundbreaking theological insights were made possible by three interconnected factors: his direct knowledge of the reality (conquest, behavior of the Spaniards in the conquered territories, Indian institutions, culture, and religion), his radical defense of the Indians, who, for Las Casas, were the image of the suffering "Christ of las Indias," and his liberation-and-praxis-oriented and liberation-and-praxis-based theology. This unique combination allowed Las Casas both to gain insights in the domains of the understanding of universal salvation, of religious freedom, and of human rights, and to gather the strength and the determination needed to confront the majority and to defend the rights of the Indians from the oppressing practices of both the Spanish crown and the *encomenderos.*

Pope Pius V and Philip II struggled between them to ensure the control over the church in America, but neither of them achieved his aim. Whereas Pius V never approved of the demand of the Spanish king to create an "Indian patriarchate" that would have operated as an autonomous church parallel to Rome, neither could he control the actions of Philip II over the Spanish American church, nor subordinate that church to papal supremacy. Philip II decided to take a practical path after 1568, enforcing the royal patronage of the overseas church through the action of the viceroy and through the factual powers of the Consejo de Indias. Thus the colonial church in Peru fell increasingly under the control of royal patronage, especially after the Bourbons came to power in Spain in 1700. The royal control became so strong that the norms and condemnations coming from Rome were completely neutralized and made void by the Consejo de Indias.[53] That severed in practice the links between the nascent church and Rome, prevented the creation of a truly native church, and constituted a serious obstacle "to the missionary development of the American Church in the seventeenth and eighteenth century."[54] Among other things, the royal patronage made the Peruvian church dependent on the interests of Spain, making that church subservient to the Spanish crown. The Bourbons sought to empower the secular clergy at the expense of the religious orders in order to strengthen the position of the crown: whereas in the sixteenth century 63.16 percent of the appointed bishops were from religious orders, only 24.25 percent of them belonged to religious orders in the eighteenth century. The conflict between religious orders and state produced, among other things, the expulsion of the Jesuits from the American colonies in 1767.[55] After independence in 1821, the new Peruvian state inherited the former royal patronage over the church and exerted it until the patronage was given up in 1979.[56] Until very recently, the church has been seen in Peru as subordinated to the state and as an institution that, far from questioning the status quo, took that status quo for granted.[57]

Together with the changes in the life of the country, the church also started to change and to become critical with respect to the social situation in Peru in the 1950s. Some authors point to certain events as characteristics of the change: the creation of the Christian Democrat Party in 1955, the new current of thought around the social teaching of the church inaugurated by Leo XIII in 1891, and the celebration of the first Semana Social de la Iglesia in 1959, during the closure of which the archbishop of Lima, Cardinal Landázuri, advocated greater social justice for workers and governmental measures leading to a redistribution of wealth.[58]

In the wider Latin American context, the different churches of that continent came together for the first time in the first general conference of Latin American bishops, held in Río de Janeiro in 1955. Although that first conference did not have the direct social, justice-related approach subsequent conferences had, it was clearly an attempt to interpret the new social challenges the church had to confront in a society that was becoming more complex and increasingly touched by the transformations of modernity. In a sense, it might be said that Río was an attempt to respond to those challenges from the perspective of the social teaching of the Catholic Church and to stress the presence of Catholics in society, especially those organized around Catholic Action. Although focused primarily on other concerns, such as the lack of clergy, the Río Conference did not fail to point out the dire social problems of the region, devoting a chapter to them. The conference demanded special actions to be developed by the church, aimed at the very root of the unjust situation, and already used the metaphor of the "loud cry" for justice later taken up and developed by Medellín, Puebla, and Santo Domingo. Río also spoke of the need to pay special attention to Indians and African Americans and to their cultures. The seeds of incultura- tion are also already visible in the conference.[59] After Vatican II, the church deepens its process of internal and external changes in a climate of increas- ing consciousness of the need for emancipation widespread throughout the Latin American continent. According to Klaiber, two strands seem to mix within the church in Peru. On the one hand, the period 1955–68 is the opening of the church to the modern world, along the lines of the Vatican II constitution *Gaudium et Spes,* and of the theologies of "secularity" born of a similar matrix to the conciliar constitution. On the other hand, this process of modernization opened itself to the social problems of the country and to the expectations for emancipation raised by the Cuban Revolution and by other political and social developments. By the end of the period, the reality of generalized poverty had challenged the basic presuppositions of the "modern" and optimistic view of the world.[60]

An important element to take into account in examining this period is the widespread influence of the model of analysis of the social-economic situation of Latin America called the "theory of dependency." Arthur F. Mc- Govern claims that this theory, which was first formulated in 1969, adopted two different modalities: a radical version given by André Gunder Frank, a thinker raised in the United States who studied economics at the Univer- sity of Chicago, and a modest and nuanced version given by the Brazilian Fernando Henrique Cardoso. The kernel of the theory was that developing countries were dependent upon the developed ones and that the latter estab- lished a relational framework that made impossible the development of the former. The obvious consequence was that the relation of dependency had to be cut off. This theory of dependency was influential on the social analy- sis of Gustavo Gutiérrez when he first formulated his liberation theology at the end of the 1960s: "Dependencia y liberación son términos correlativos" (Dependency and liberation are correlative terms), he wrote in 1971.[61] The theory of dependency spread throughout Latin America in the late 1960s, but its spirit was already active before it came to be formulated theoretically. The military in Peru, for instance, had come to the conclusion that the coun- try was under foreign (mainly U.S.) control and that the basic industries had to be nationalized.[62] That is exactly what they did once they took over the government in 1968.[63]

In 1968, two crucial events took place. On the one hand, the military, as has been said, took over the government in Peru, and General Velasco de- clared his determination to deploy revolutionary measures aimed at solving the structural problems of the country regarding justice and social inte- gration. On the other hand, the bishops of Latin America celebrated their second general conference in Medellín, Colombia, with the global aim of interpreting Vatican II from their own regional perspective. The results of the conference were epoch-making for the Latin American churches. In Peru, the church took a decided stand against the unjust social structures and demanded radical changes to eradicate all kinds of injustice.[64] The theme of the conference was "The Church in the Current Transformation of Latin America in the Light of Vatican II." The conference approved important conclusions concerning three main areas: human promotion, evangelization, and the church. Especially important were the conclusions related to the issues of justice, peace, and the church, which, according to the conference, should embrace poverty in its own life.[65] Medellín is a milestone not only in the life of the Latin American Catholic Church but in the life of the Catholic Church at large.

According to Gutiérrez, Medellín is crucial because it was a reading of Vatican II from the perspective of a church that wanted to understand itself as the council did, namely, as a "universal sacrament of salvation" for its own world: Latin America. That entailed taking into account the misery of the Latin American countries. That misery, says the Medellín document on justice, "cries out to heaven."[66] Gutiérrez has analyzed in depth the relationship between Medellín and Vatican II. According to him, Vatican II had three main challenges to respond to: modernity, ecumenism, and the world of the poor. Although both Pope John XXIII and Cardinal Lercaro brought the issue of poverty to the forefront, the council did not take that issue up. John XXIII not only spoke of the situation of the poor as an important issue to which the church must respond but made it clear that the church had to be, especially, the church of the poor. Even though Lercaro insisted on the same point, the council did not finally deal with that issue. In his analysis, Gutiérrez argues that Vatican II did a great job in relation to both the dialogue with modernity and the ecumenical dialogue but that it was not until Medellín that the church dealt centrally with the issue of poverty and its causes. Medellín is for Gutiérrez a prophetic voice that makes the entire Catholic Church face that issue and respond to it.[67]

For Gutiérrez, the coming of age of the Latin American church occurred when Medellín took a route that clearly defined the identity of the Latin American church: the preferential option for the poor. Gutiérrez repeats here that such an identity is not for the Latin American church alone but that, through it, Medellín challenged the universal church by affirming that the identity of the church as such entails today solidarity with the poor.[68] The decisive point for Gutiérrez is that the Latin American church was in the position to unmask the ambiguities of modernity that had mostly gone unnoticed by the council. Whereas Vatican II read modernity basically in a positive and optimistic way (though there are some critical remarks), Medellín reflected the experience of those peoples and countries for whom modernity had meant oppression and exploitation.[69] In Gutiérrez's view, although Medellín had been conceived as a meeting to analyze Latin America in the light of the Vatican II, the concrete knowledge of what was happening in that continent reversed the theme, and Medellín became an analysis of Vatican II in the light of the Latin American reality.[70]

The relationship between Vatican II and Medellín can be summarized by saying that, on the one hand, Medellín was a consequence of the council and adopted the main theological tenets of the conciliar documents. These tenets are the universality of salvation, the profound unity between creation and salvation and between salvation history and human history, and the church as the sacrament of salvation in the world. From these principles derived the positive approach to other religions and to society at large and the overall missionary and pastoral impulse and orientation of the council. On the other hand, Medellín, by reading these principles from the perspective of the impoverished and oppressed, discovered a new focal point from which to reinterpret those theological tenets: the intrinsic link between Christianity and the poor based on God's will and manifested in Jesus Christ. In offering back that discovery to the universal church, Medellín became a catholic event, well beyond the boundaries of Latin America. One of the main contributions of Medellín to the universal church took place when the synod of bishops gathered in Rome in 1971 approved the document "Justice in the World." In the document, the bishops affirmed the constitutive importance of social justice in relation to Christian faith. Besides this, two other contributions deserve mentioning: the importance of commitment to justice in discovering all the dimensions of faith and the awareness concerning the renewal of the church brought about by the grassroots communities.[71]

That same year of 1968, just before Medellín, Gustavo Gutiérrez presented the guidelines of what was to be known as the theology of liberation.[72] Such a theology represented a new way of doing theology from "the underside of history"[73] and anticipated the spirit and the themes of Medellín. It also was crucial in the development of the third conference of the Latin American bishops, celebrated in Puebla, Mexico, in 1979. Puebla proclaimed the preferential option for the poor of the Latin American church.[74]

Between Medellín and Puebla, the church in Peru lived an intense period in which, besides its contribution to the policies of the military government promoting structural change, it took with all seriousness its commitment to the poor and initiated a new program of evangelization to fulfill it. According to Catalina Romero, the church, out of faithfulness to the Christian message, discovered that the poor were the locus and the main addressees of that message and set out to make the poor the center of its pastoral activity, encouraging them to become subjects of their own liberation. That, in turn, converted the church and Christian faith into elements of identity that gave spiritual strength and a religious dimension to the process of liberation of the people.[75] After General Velasco was ousted in 1975, his successor, General Morales Bermúdez, adopted a restorative program, undoing most of the achievements of the Velasco regime. That made the church take a critical distance from the government and identify itself more clearly with the cause of the people, especially the poor.[76]

Puebla, however, also showed the growing tensions within the Latin American churches, including the Peruvian, that led to important divisions in the 1980s. In the final message of the bishops in Puebla, the bishops themselves acknowledged their differences in opinion and thinking, although they denied being divided among themselves.[77] An example of the tensions within the Peruvian church are the difficulties that the Peruvian Bishops Conference encountered when, in 1983, the Congregation for the Doctrine of the Faith asked the Peruvian bishops to produce an official statement on liberation theology. After a year, the bishops, unable to reconcile their positions, came up with two different texts. Finally, called to Rome to find a solution, they approved a common text.[78] In the Catholic Church, these years were marked by John Paul II's insistence on the "new evangelization," a theme the pope himself chose as the central theme for the Fourth General Conference of the Latin American Bishops. This conference took place in Santo Domingo in 1992, coinciding with the celebrations of the fifth centennial of the coming of the Europeans to America.

The term "new evangelization" brought about an important debate. For John Paul II, the meaning of the term is closely linked with his central conviction that a "new," truly Christian, truly religious evangelization is most needed in the world. As far as Latin America is concerned, as early as 1983, he announced the celebration of the Santo Domingo Conference, and he set its agenda around the theme of the "new evangelization." The term has been highly problematic in Latin America because what was at stake was the Latin American reception and rendering of Vatican II, namely, Medellín, the Second General Conference of Latin American Bishops, which had taken place in 1968. For many bishops and theologians, as well as for the most dynamic groups of Catholic people in the region, Medellín meant the beginning of the conversion of the Catholic Church to the ways of God in that continent, aligning itself with the poor and the destitute and announcing by words and deeds their liberation and salvation. Medellín was, therefore, the core of the "new evangelization," and not only for the Catholic Church in Latin America but for the entire Catholic Church, called thereby to convert itself, to make a preferential option for the poor, and to read, and act in, history from the side of the poor. For these people, John Paul II's message had to mean deepening the conversion and the ways brought about by Medellín.[79]

Santo Domingo mirrored two different, although intrinsically interrelated, intrachurch tensions: on the one hand, the growing differences among the Latin American bishops concerning the role and the mission of the Catholic Church in the region; on the other hand, the struggle between Rome and the Latin American bishops to set the agenda and the procedures of the conference. Both tensions can be brought together around the struggle to set the terms of the identity and the mission of the Catholic Church in Latin America. Evidently, Medellín and liberation theology were at stake.[80]

In the end, and despite all difficulties, Santo Domingo produced a reasonably good, albeit neither as prophetic as Medellín's nor as theologically dense as Puebla's, final document. There is wide consensus that this document reaffirms the basic intuitions and statements of both Medellín and Puebla, most crucially the preferential option for the poor, and breaks new ground in the recognition of Indian and African American cultures and the inculturation of Christian faith in those cultures. However, the tensions around and in Santo Domingo made many fear that the Latin American church, as envisioned by Medellín, was being, in practice, watered down. Jon Sobrino was especially critical in his assessment of the conference. For him, Rome was trying to undo what Latin American Catholics had done over the last twenty-five years since Medellín, and he feared that nominally radical and clear statements in favor of the poor may in practice bear no fruit. He, among others, noted that, in Santo Domingo, the traditional way of pastorally approaching an issue following the method seeing-judging-acting, officially inaugurated in Medellín, was altered and replaced by the sequence judging-seeing-acting. Very perceptively, he noted that such a subtle change reveals an attempt to subvert the incarnate, bottom-up approach to theology of Medellín that has been characteristic of the Latin American Catholic Church ever since. Gustavo Gutiérrez and Francisco Chamberlain were also far from being sanguine about Santo Domingo but tried to get the best they could out of it. The three authors, Sobrino, Gutiérrez, and Chamberlain, profoundly lamented the forgetfulness of the conference with respect to the recent martyrs of the Catholic Church (Archbishop Romero, Ignacio Ellacuría, his companions, and the two housekeepers, and many other, mostly lay and common, officially unimportant, people) killed as a result of their commitment to the cause of the poor and of justice in their pursuit of the Kingdom of God.[81]

The future of the Latin American Catholic Church is closely linked to the changing social and economic conditions on the continent. Coming out of a dramatic crisis that devastated the region in the 1980s, every Latin American government confronts new challenges to reach a threefold and interrelated objective: to balance the budget, to renew the productive structure of the country, and to regain international recognition and competitiveness. The frail situation of democracy in several Latin American countries and the persisting poverty of the masses make it difficult to achieve those goals and pose new challenges to the church.

First Steps of Gutiérrez's Theology

Gutiérrez was in Europe between 1951 and 1960. During these years, he studied philosophy and psychology in Louvain (1951–55) and theology in Lyon (1955–59) and Rome (1959–60). In Lyon, he was mainly exposed to *la nouvelle théologie*. Strictly speaking, the movement appeared in the French-speaking world in the 1940s and was led by some Jesuits at their French theological school of Fourvière. However, in a broader sense, it has come to encompass also the theological enterprise of some Dominicans at their theological school of Le Saulchoir. In both cases, it was an effort to dig in the sources of scripture, patristic tradition, medieval history, and Thomism in order to present an alternative to the reigning neo-scholasticism and to face openly the challenges posed by modernity and social-cultural transformations to Christianity and to the Catholic Church. The main representatives of this movement, among whom M.-D. Chenu, Yves Congar, Henri de Lubac, and Jean Daniélou were outstanding, were looked upon with suspicion by other theologians and by ecclesiastical censorship until their work was finally recognized at Vatican II. The movement partakes in a characteristic of all important reforms, namely, to bring about a breakthrough by going back to the original sources.[82]

Gutiérrez also was exposed to other theological currents that became decisive at Vatican II. Overall, he was able during his European stage to assimilate those attempts to come up with new ways of being Christian and of developing a Christian thought that were so characteristic of the French-speaking world at that time. By the mid-1950s, both the praxis of the church and theology in France had been able to process the trauma of the Enlightenment and of the French Revolution and the social changes brought about by industrialization, as well as their response to them. Gutiérrez's exposure to this outstanding renewal has marked his pastoral strategy and his theological thought.

The issue of the relation between Gutiérrez's theology and his exposure to the theology and the pastoral praxis of the church in the French-speaking world during the 1950s deserves to be the topic of a dissertation. Such an analysis would clarify the relationship between European and Latin American experiences and traditions in the work of Gutiérrez, thus helping to understand all the richness of his intuitions and the importance of his contribution to the theology of a church that wants to be catholic, that is, universal. The analysis (and similar ones regarding other liberation theologians) would also contribute to deepening and making more fruitful the dialogue between liberation theology and other theologies in the different regions of the world, particularly European and U.S. theologies.

Some basic aspects of how his European years have influenced Gutiérrez's theology deserve especial attention.[83] One is the development of *les mouve-*

ments spécialisés d'Action Catholique (Catholic Action's specialized movements) in the French-speaking world, specialized movements, each made of many small groups working with a common methodology called *la révision de vie*. Important traits of this pastoral work were that it was performed by laypeople belonging to the pastorally targeted milieu (workers, students, rural population, and so on) assisted by a priest; its members considered themselves committed Christian militants; and it aimed at publicly witnessing to Christian faith by transforming society on the basis of Christian principles. The method used by these specialized movements is vital to understanding Gutiérrez's theology. That method is clearly oriented toward action and divided into three parts: to see, to judge, and to act. To see involves knowing the facts and analyzing their causes. To judge entails looking critically at them from the point of view of the word of God. To act aims at transforming the situation according to the will of God. This framework is crucial to understanding the role of the social sciences in Gutiérrez's theology, realizing at the same time that the second step is the theologically central one for him, while the third one is the way to validate the truth of the word of God in practice.

A second aspect concerns the theological developments of *la nouvelle théologie*, a pastorally driven theology for which the life of the church became a central theological source. This theology came up with important developments in content and method, among which were the overcoming of the duality nature-supernature by de Lubac, the formulation of the role of the laity in church and society by Congar, the link between pastoral practice and theology, and the use of social sciences (including Marxism) as partners reclaimed by Chenu and Daniélou. These developments are important to Gutiérrez's theology. Equally important in that regard is the pastoral consequence that derives from these theological developments, namely, that Christians must give witness to their faith in society, becoming "incarnated" in the different social milieus. It is not difficult to see the connection between this pastoral principle and the commitment to the poor demanded by Gutiérrez.

The relationship between European theology and liberation theology has been the object of controversy and has been very often analyzed either in polemic terms or from the point of view of what makes them different from each other.[84] However, in Gutiérrez's theology, that relationship also entails important commonalities. As Medellín cannot be explained without Vatican II, neither can Gutiérrez's theology be understood without the important theological breakthroughs that took place in Europe from the 1940s on and that became officially adopted by the council in the 1960s. At the same time, as Medellín cannot be interpreted as a simple application of Vatican II to Latin America, neither can Gutiérrez's theology be seen as a Latin American adaptation of the new European theology. Medellín and Gutiérrez's theology represent a critical appropriation of Vatican II and of its underlying theological tenets from a Latin American point of view marked by the massive presence of poverty, injustice, and death. Finally, both Medellín and Gutiérrez's theology are truly catholic in that both bring forth important claims that affect the way the mission and the praxis of the universal church are to be understood.[85]

One of the first works by Gutiérrez after coming back from Europe is *Líneas pastorales de la iglesia en América Latina*.[86] This work analyzes the four main models of pastoral activity adopted by the Catholic Church in Latin America through its history, thus setting the agenda for Gutiérrez's theology as intrinsically related to the church. After the description of those models, most of the book is devoted to the theological analysis of them. Revealingly, there is an introduction about the nature of theology and a final reflection on Vatican II.

In analyzing the work of Gutiérrez it must be kept in mind that, since he came back from Europe, he has always devoted a part of his pastoral activity to the formation of Catholic leaders in both the university and the professional milieus. Many of his works have developed from talks that were first aimed at those groups. This trait of Gutiérrez's works shows the important linkage between pastoral practice and reflection that pervades all his theology. This linkage has much to do with the spirit of Vatican II. This council was, according to Rahner, a council of the church about the church, a pastoral council, and the beginning of a new era marked by a new understanding of what being a Christian means. Gutiérrez seems to be fully influenced by these conciliar traits in his theology. First, because of the primacy of pastoral action in his reflection. Second, because one of his central interests consists in defining what the church is and should be in Latin America. Third, because he is convinced that a new way of being Christian has started in his continent. (In that sense, he considers that the new evangelization of Latin America began with Medellín and has been theologically fleshed out in liberation theology.) Finally, because for Gutiérrez theology reaches its fullness only in relation to the church, and as a service to the life of the church and to its insertion in the world.[87]

Like Aquinas in the *Summa Theologiae*,[88] Gutiérrez begins by situating theology among the other forms of knowledge, making clear, following Jacques Maritain, that theology, although related to the sciences and to philosophy, is another form of knowledge.[89] Then he moves on to define the different functions theology has performed in the church's history: monastic-spiritual theology, scholastic-scientific theology, and, finally, theology as critical reflection on the praxis of the church. Praxis comes first; theology comes later as a second act.[90]

Gutiérrez already puts forward his later definition in *Teología de la liberación*. Theology is understood as the critical reflection on the church's action in the light of the revealed word.[91] Pure pastoral activity is not enough. That activity must be reflected upon and assessed on the basis of God's word. There already appear here some characteristic elements of Gutiérrez's work. On the one hand, his theology has a practical intention. What he wants is to define the kind of pastoral action the church must conduct in Latin America to respond to the historical realities in which such an action takes place. Gutiérrez is, therefore, looking for a program of transformative action. In relation to other theologies, Gutiérrez's entails a transformative program. Following Marx's dictum, Gutiérrez is mainly interested not in analyzing reality but in changing it, in liberating it.[92] That, in turn, means that Gutiérrez's theology (inasmuch as it wants to continue to be a transformative program) is dependent upon both a right social analysis and a viable plan of social transformation. But, on the other hand, his is not a theology based on pure activism. Theology has at its center the word of God that always judges any historical practice. For Gutiérrez, then, both poles must be kept in tension. Only through transformative praxis can the truth be discovered and done, but this truth, in turn, will always judge that transformative praxis. This constitutes for Gutiérrez the hermeneutical circle.[93]

The relationship between church and world is the perspective from which that theology is thought out, and its presuppositions are the church as event and the historicity of theological knowledge.[94] These are basic tenets of *la nouvelle théologie,* later taken up by Vatican II in its dogmatic constitution on the church, *Lumen Gentium,* and in its pastoral constitution on the church, *Gaudium et Spes.* The close relationship between the dogmatic and the pastoral constitutions on the church shows the will of the council to talk about the church not only on the level of dogmatic principles but also from the point of view of how the church becomes in practice "the universal sacrament of salvation."[95] Theologically speaking, that is one of the foundations of Gutiérrez's work. As Vatican II thought it necessary to spell out how the church was going to be that sacrament of salvation in the modern world, Gutiérrez's work accepts that definition of church as "universal sacrament of salvation"[96] and then sets out the task of defining how that can be realized in the concrete case of Latin America. His theology is therefore intrinsically ecclesiological. This is also one of the bases for Gutiérrez's insistence on praxis. It is in the task of transforming the world that the church "does the truth," discovers it, and announces it to everybody.

The final trait of Gutiérrez's theology already present in his first work is that his field of analysis is Latin America. In *Líneas pastorales,* Gutiérrez wants to analyze how the church relates to the world in the particular case of Latin America. His focus on Latin America shows Gutiérrez's commitment to his own people. One of his aims has always been to think theologically about the situation, the life, the problems, and the hopes of the Latin American people, with a particular focus on the Peruvian reality. Other than his main interest in changing that reality, he also has always wanted to shape a new theological voice from a different perspective that challenges the other theological voices and the praxis of the church. In that sense his is a Catholic-universal theology from the perspective of Latin America.

The four pastoral models described by Gutiérrez are: Christendom, New Christendom, Mature Faith, and the Prophetic Pastoral model. In introducing the four models, Gutiérrez claims that a reflection on them is necessary to orient correctly the direction the Catholic Church must take in Latin America, because the church risks losing its direction due to the anguish and anxiety derived from the "very fast process of 'dechristianization.' "[97] It seems then that, at that time, Gutiérrez was reading the situation in terms of dechristianization rather than in terms of the coexistence of faith and poverty, as he does in his later works. To see Latin America as a continent in the process of dechristianization presupposes in a way that the global analysis of that society is made from the perspective of its transformation toward modernization.[98] This approach will later be relegated to a noncentral position. At the beginning of the 1960s, however, Gutiérrez was interested in the dialogue between faith and contemporary thought.[99]

The first model, the pastoral approach of Christendom, presupposes Christian unanimity in society, as in medieval times, and gives the primacy to the religious order over the secular order in their somehow common task. Its lasting presence in Latin America is clearly a legacy of the Spanish rule. Gutiérrez is interested in showing that this traditional approach has involved a lack of clear separation between church and state. He also points out that the church continues to practice this approach.[100] Gutiérrez seems to be combining his Peruvian experience with his French-European experience. That enables him to see that one of the reasons for the persistence of the Christendom approach in Latin America is that neither Spain nor Portugal, the evangelizers of the continent, were shaken up by the social and religious crises that took place in other European countries, like Germany with the Reformation and France with the French Revolution. That circumstance, however, had already been pointed out by the Peruvian Marxist thinker José Carlos Mariátegui, whose influence on Gutiérrez is manifest.

The second model, New Christendom, is the response to social dechristianization and focuses on the creation of Christian institutions that make Christianity present in society and endeavor to transform that society on the basis of Christian principles. This approach began to appear in Latin America in the 1940s and appealed especially to intellectual and professional cadres that pursued the social and political transformation of the continent. For Gutiérrez, its main value lies in its pursuit of the incarnation of Christianity in culture. Its main danger is to reduce Christianity to one ideology.[101]

The name New Christendom is taken from the title of Maritain's book *Humanism intégral: Problèmes temporels et spirituels d'une nouvelle chrétienté*. For Gutiérrez, the best definition of this model is found in that book.[102] Gutiérrez also thinks that Maritain was the most influential Catholic thinker in shaping the New Christendom model in Latin America.[103] It seems safe to say that Gutiérrez learned from Maritain, while at the same time evolving toward a different understanding of the relation between salvation and social order.[104]

The third pastoral line of the church in Latin America analyzed by Gutiérrez seeks the formation of Christian militants, helping them to attain a mature faith, that is, a faith personally appropriated and not only received from tradition, and that, therefore, becomes an encompassing and dynamic principle that constitutes the central drive of the person. In this sense, the believer must always act according to the requirements of those who follow Christ as disciples. "Mature faith" means, therefore, an operative faith lived out in the ongoing Christian praxis of discipleship.[105] That aim is difficult to achieve in the case of the masses, and, therefore, it remains restricted to small groups around the specialized movements of Catholic Action. Unlike the previous model, this one does not pursue the creation of Christian institutions in the temporal order but maintains that Christians must participate in the various secular institutions existent in their society. Its main problem for Gutiérrez is that the mature faith sought by this line of action, besides being aimed at a minority, is impossible to attain by the nonperson masses of Latin America.[106]

Gutiérrez embraced this pastoral model at the beginning of the 1960s. In 1960, he was appointed national ecclesiastical assistant to the UNEC, the Peruvian organization of Catholic students created in 1943 (but initiated in 1941) that functions like a specialized movement of Catholic Action. That same year, 1960, the UNEC adopted the method of *révision de vie* that had started to be introduced and used in 1958 and that the UNEC continues to practice today. At the same time, a new theology started to ground the work of the movement, namely, the theology of the distinction of planes promoted by Gutiérrez through talks to the different groups of the UNEC also in 1960.

According to Cecilia Tovar, Gutiérrez followed Congar and other innovative European theologians in distinguishing between the natural plane, that of society and politics, and the supernatural plane, to which evangelization, the church, and the UNEC belong. Tovar also points out that Gutiérrez developed little by little, at seminars he organized and led at the UNEC, the themes from which liberation theology would arise: pastoral models of the church (1964 and 1965), human history and the history of salvation (1966), faith and commitment, faith and ideology, and poverty in the Bible (1967). By 1970, the UNEC embraced the option for the oppressed and a line of action aimed at liberating evangelization with the poor.[107] Tovar's account gives a clear idea of how Gutiérrez has evolved from a position more linked to *la nouvelle théologie* at the beginning of the 1960s toward a more Rahnerian (also present in the conciliar constitution *Gaudium et Spes*) theology by the end of the 1960s. It also helps us to understand the close link between Gutiérrez's theology and his pastoral work, because it is in his work with the UNEC and with the Movimiento de Profesionales Católicos that he developed his theology.

The fourth and last model analyzed by Gutiérrez, the Prophetic Pastoral model, is not a reaction against, but a deepening of, the third one. It seeks a reorientation of pastoral action taking into account those who are outside the church, and it pursues a living out of the social requirements of the gospel in a radical manner that entails denouncing the church's backing of the unjust social order and supporting instead the revolutionary processes in Latin America. The model, according to Gutiérrez, is still tentative, and reductionism and loss of Christian identity are its dangers.[108] This fourth model is clearly the one Gutiérrez thinks the Latin American Catholic Church must embrace. Between 1960 and 1967, he shifted from the third to the fourth model, reflecting his theological evolution, as well as his greater experience of the Latin American reality after his return from Europe. In this fourth model a radical struggle for justice comes to the fore, something that will occupy a central place in Gutiérrez's later development of the model in *Teología de la liberación*.

From a theological point of view, this fourth model is based on an understanding of salvation and grace that makes room for those who are not members of the church. Salvation does not depend on explicit faith but has been offered to all in Jesus Christ and depends on the response to that offer through the practice of true charity. Faith works through charity. Salvific grace has been offered to everybody and not only to those who are members of the visible church. The mission of the church is both to announce, through God's word, that salvific grace in history and to judge that history. That makes its pastoral work prophetic, which, in turn, requires the church to be poor in spirit.[109]

Gutiérrez thinks that the crucial breakthrough lies in Rahner's notion of the supernatural existential,[110] according to which everything is touched by grace and autonomy before God is not possible. And because grace is already at work in history, eschatology is also present in history, moving it from within. Therefore, the church can and must learn from human history and also from nature.[111] Following Teilhard de Chardin, Gutiérrez explains that the church must learn from nature because nature is evolving as if preparing for the encounter of God with the creature. It is a cosmic evolution. Gutiérrez adopts here Teilhard's optimism in relation to the good direction toward which history and nature are evolving. Later, Gutiérrez will substantially qualify this optimism with his critique of history and his reflections on the existence of massive innocent suffering.

A most interesting point concerns the relation between the insistence on the importance of personal faith for this prophetic pastoral work and the condition of the masses in Latin America. In order to confront the problem posed by secularization, Gutiérrez, following Karl Barth and Dietrich Bonhoeffer, distinguishes between religion and faith and calls Christianity a faith. That allows him to overcome that problem, since secularization, he claims, makes religion problematic but does not oppose faith.[112] In his later work, however, Gutiérrez will adopt a different perspective, devoting considerable thought to the subject of popular religion. Moreover, he will not be much interested in the question of secularization, coming to the conclusion that the problem in Latin America does not consist in lack of belief but in the conditions of poverty that degrade the poor to the condition of nonperson.

Gutiérrez debates the question of whether Christianity is going to be possible only for a minority able to come to a mature, personal faith, with exclusion of the masses, unable to come to that stage.[113] Whereas at this point the question is how the masses can be integrated in a pastoral action that seeks mature Christians with personal faith, in Gutiérrez's later work the masses of the poor will be considered the bearers of salvation and revelation,[114] and, therefore, to work with them and for them means also to be evangelized by them.

In the final part of *Líneas pastorales* Gutiérrez reflects on Vatican II and stresses the importance of the new pastoral drive of the church and the theological innovations that make it possible for the church to take with all seriousness the reality of the human being and history, as well as that of nonbelievers and other religions.[115] Clearly, Gutiérrez had not yet arrived at his later view of the council from a truly Latin American perspective.

In July 1968, Gutiérrez delivered his groundbreaking talk, "Hacia una teología de la liberación."[116] The talk, delivered in the Peruvian city of Chimbote, is historical because it marks the beginning of liberation theology. The talk was also the occasion for a personal encounter of Gutiérrez with the Peruvian writer José María Arguedas. This writer read the text of Gutiérrez's talk at Chimbote and felt that they had many things in common. Shortly afterward they met for the first time and initiated a short but deep friendship.[117] The text is divided into three points, with an introduction and a conclusion.[118] The introduction deals again with the nature of theology and its relation to faith and committed action. To have faith is to respond positively to God's offer of salvation through active charity. Although faith implies the affirmation of truths, Christian truth is a truth that must be done first and then thought and formulated. Theology is a second, but completely necessary, act that accompanies the pastoral activity of the church.[119]

The newness of "Hacia una teología de la liberación" in relation to *Líneas pastorales* is the introduction of the notion of a "theology of human liberation." For Gutiérrez, the process of liberation is a "sign of the times."[120] As such, it constitutes a call to action for Christians and, therefore, also a matter for reflection. To have faith entails commitment to that process of liberation. However, theology, in order to reflect adequately on that sign of the times, needs to open itself to the human sciences that provide a precise knowledge of the Latin American reality. The conclusion is that "a genuine theology of liberation can only be a team effort, a task which has not yet been attempted."[121]

The body of the talk revolves around the relationship between human work and the Kingdom of God, between human liberation and salvation. Traditionally, points out Gutiérrez, the church had understood itself as an agent of divine salvation related to the hereafter, leading in practice to a conformism with the reigning social situation that converted the church into a supporter of that situation. Modernity, and here Gutiérrez mentions Descartes, Kant, Hegel, and Marx, has made human beings aware of their role as active subjects of their own history, bringing the issue of human emancipation to the fore. The profound social changes and revolutionary processes brought about by modernity are a sign of the times to which Christians must commit themselves on the basis of their faith.[122]

The responsibility of human beings to control their destiny and to be the agents of history is a typical theme of modernity that runs throughout the entire work of Gutiérrez. Themes like emancipation, liberation, and controlling one's own destiny are central to his enterprise. In that sense, Gutiérrez belongs to modernity. The points to explore are, however, whether his understanding of these notions is somewhat critical of modernity and whether he has evolved in that understanding. The issue is important and will be taken up at several points in this and in the remaining chapters.

In discussing the issue theologically, Gutiérrez draws on two main documents, Paul VI's *Populorum Progressio*[123] and Vatican II's *Gaudium et Spes*.[124] For Gutiérrez, "the theology of liberation means establishing the relationship that exists between human emancipation—in the social, political, and economic orders—and the kingdom of God."[125] Human development is an integral part of one's vocation and of one's communion with God. Evangelization and salvation include it. The latter "affects the whole human being."[126] Therefore, human work and human history acquire a substantive value in themselves, and a growth in humanness means a step toward salvation: "Integral development is salvation."[127] Hence, to create a just and fraternal society is to work for the cause of salvation. Theologically, there is a unity between creation and salvation insofar as creation is the first act of salvation. The other stage of salvation, the coming of the Kingdom of God, brings with it the requirements for justice and the elimination of misery and exploitation.[128] It follows, then, that politics also relates to salvation. The underlying theological issue is that of the relationship between nature and grace, and, despite the apparent distance, Gutiérrez's affirmation that politics relates to salvation is made possible by Rahner's intrinsic link between nature and the supernatural.

God is encountered in history because God is irreversibly committed to human history in Christ.[129] Christ is the point of encounter of God and the creature and the expression of the utter importance of human reality and history within the divine plan. It follows then that to believe in God and to encounter God in history through the other are intrinsically linked.[130] In reaction to the Marxist accusation that Christianity is the opiate of the people, Gutiérrez responds that faith energizes the action of Christians in society and makes them commit themselves to liberation. At the same time though, faith always relativizes human work, pointing to a stage beyond the one already attained.[131]

A Theology of Liberation

The important pastoral question here—and, therefore, also the theological one—is how to say to the poor, who are subject to life conditions that mean a love denial, that God loves them?
                    —Gustavo Gutiérrez, *A Theology of Liberation*

Roughly speaking, the 1950s are the European years of Gutiérrez, during which he is exposed to *la nouvelle théologie;* the 1960s are the years of his applying his European theological foundations to the Latin American situation; the 1970s mark his formulation of liberation theology; the 1980s are the decade in which he develops the themes of spirituality and God as intrinsic elements of his theology, as well as a period of reformulation of certain crucial aspects of liberation theology. To be sure, all these divisions are profoundly interrelated, and, rather than changes in direction, they signal different steps within the same enterprise, namely, that of liberation theology. Naturally, along with the basic continuity of that enterprise, some discontinuities or changes in emphasis take place. The Latin American years of Gutiérrez can also be divided into pre-Medellín (the 1960s), between Medellín and Puebla (the 1970s), between Puebla and Santo Domingo (the 1980s), and post–Santo Domingo. This division has the advantage of linking Gutiérrez's theological evolution to the two doctrinal milestones of the Catholic Church in Latin America (Medellín and Puebla) and to the later developments at Santo Domingo.[132]

Within this overall framework, whereas in the 1960s Gutiérrez evolved toward a greater awareness of the real situation in Latin America and moved increasingly in the direction of connecting human action in history with salvation, in the 1970s he will proceed to apply that connection to the concrete case of the church in Latin America. Thus, he comes to formulate his own theological position, known as liberation theology. Due to the ecclesial character of Gutiérrez's theology, Medellín can be seen as an important milestone in the process of defining it. Several traits of Medellín deserve mentioning.

First, the challenge of Vatican II to the Latin American church. That challenge was particularly important after the council but already occurred before it. In 1962, several Latin American theologians were called to a meeting by Bishop Manuel Larraín of Talca (Chile), who was president of CELAM (Latin American Bishops' Conference) at that time, shortly before the beginning of the council, "to reflect together on how to relate the church's message more relevantly to the particular circumstances of Latin America."[133] During the council, several meetings of Latin American theologians took place, setting the foundations for the later developments. The common thread was to reflect on the situation of the church in Latin America, to analyze the social changes that were taking place at the time, and to try to devise the role the church had to play to respond to those changes. Between the end of Vatican II in 1965 and Medellín in 1968, the Latin American church was clearly in the process of defining how to relate creatively the doctrine defined by the conciliar constitution *Gaudium et Spes* to the world in Latin America. Momentum was gained when Paul VI published his encyclical *Populorum Progressio* in 1967 and eighteen bishops from ten nations of the Third World wrote "A Letter to the Peoples of the Third World" that, on the grounds of the encyclical, was a clear denunciation of the exploitation of the poor countries by the rich ones and a call for the church to align itself with the poor.[134] This process led to Medellín as a mature formulation of how the Latin American Catholic Church saw its identity and role when confronting its faith with the reality of its continent.

Second, Medellín was crucial in promoting the new theological thought represented by liberation theology. As Gutiérrez puts it, "it was the texts of the Episcopal Conference of Medellín which brought to public attention the theme of liberation as the pivot for apprehending faith."[135] Medellín wanted to respond to the needs of the poor and oppressed in Latin America, thus shifting the center of the theological discussion with regard to Vatican II and promoting a new line of thought that would come to be known as liberation theology.

Third, Medellín was an ecclesial event in which Gutiérrez played a key role as a theological expert. There is no doubt that his influence at Medellín was decisive to establish the overall orientation and the theological framework of the assembly[136] and that, in turn, he was confirmed and encouraged by the spirit and the result of the conference in his search for a theology of liberation.

By 1969, Gutiérrez already had the outline of his groundbreaking work, *Teología de la liberación*, published in 1971. On the occasion of a Sode-pax[137] conference, he presented his "Notes for a Theology of Liberation," from which he later developed his major work.[138] *Teología de la liberación* must be understood as Gutiérrez's central statement, whose implications he has continued to develop ever since. Broadly speaking, that book is a creative working out of the significance of the central tenets of Rahnerian theology—namely, the pervasive presence of grace in all created reality and the inner connection between the history of salvation and history at large—for the reality of a Latin American continent mired in poverty and starting to rebel against it and against its causes. In this sense, Gutiérrez does not simply apply Rahner's theology to Latin America. In adopting a new perspective, he opens new avenues that both challenge and transform the theology of Rahner, revealing aspects of it that were neither discovered nor suspected by Rahner.

Gutiérrez's crucial move is the adoption of a new perspective. His program is to reinterpret the central dogmas and themes of the Christian faith from a new standpoint and viewpoint, namely, that of the dispossessed. In this respect, it is worth noting the similarity in difference between Rahner and Gutiérrez. Formally, both of them reinterpret the dogmas and themes of Christian faith from a new position in relation to previous theologies. Rahner overcame the barrenness of scholasticism by turning to the subject and looking into it to show that it was intrinsically related to God. From that new perspective he could develop his theological anthropology that had in Christ its center and its illuminating paradigm. Gutiérrez builds upon the Rahnerian findings and adopts Rahner's anthropological perspective. However, he both transcends and critiques Rahner in two directions. First, Gutiérrez does not accept the Rahnerian subject in general but looks for the concrete and historical subject in his own society.[139] That subject is recognized as the poor, the dispossessed, the oppressed in its various versions. Gutiérrez, therefore, does not "turn to the subject," as Rahner did, but his is a "turn to the nonsubjects," who, unlike the Rahnerian subject, are both profoundly religious and utterly poor. The problem then is not to show how this subject relates to God, or that God is the horizon and ground of existence, but to show who God is from the perspective of the poor and to encounter God's mystery in a situation marked by pervasive injustice and innocent suffering.

Second, Gutiérrez takes up the Rahnerian theme of the unity of history in general and history of salvation and applies it to the task of liberating the poor in history. This, in turn, entails that rather than accepting Rahner's notion of history as such, Gutiérrez wants to remake and reread concrete history from the perspective of the poor and for the poor. Finally, his method is not transcendental but practical, because it is not possible either to adopt the perspective of the poor or to discover what God's preference for them means without a previous commitment to them.

Gutiérrez's program entails also a rereading and remaking of both history and Christian life.[140] Gutiérrez's work is in itself a rereading of the main themes of Christianity from "the underside of history," but his program of rereading history goes well beyond the boundaries of theology. The heart of that program is to proceed systematically to reinterpret all crucial moments in history from the new perspective.[141] Gutiérrez's work on Las Casas is a contribution to this program, which also includes a rereading of the great theologians in the new key.[142]

This new perspective of Gutiérrez's theology and overall program has its origin in three different, yet interrelated, factors: a critical understanding of the Latin American situation, the changes that had taken place in Catholic theology and in the church's understanding of its relation to the world as manifested in Vatican II, and the clear position advocating a radical transformation of the structurally unjust Latin American situation taken by the Latin American church at Medellín.[143] The last two factors have already been discussed. The first one constitutes a centerpiece in Gutiérrez's theology and is worth analyzing.

Understanding the Latin American Situation

The critical understanding of the Latin American situation is an incorporation of the social sciences into the theological enterprise. This element did not appear in his "Hacia una teología de la liberación." In that work, Gutiérrez had already affirmed that theology had to open itself to the human sciences in order to get to know the concrete situation of Latin America.[144] In taking this new step in *Teología de la liberación,* Gutiérrez applies to his theological reasoning the principle already set forth by Chenu and Daniélou that theology needs the help of the social sciences for its own purpose, including the help of Marxism. The two theories Gutiérrez uses for understanding the Latin American situation are the theory of dependency and some elements of Marxist social analysis, especially that of class struggle.[145]

The theory of dependency[146] allows Gutiérrez to formulate the crucial move from development to liberation. A central point in this shift lies in the question of conflict. This category runs throughout Gutiérrez's whole understanding of history and of liberation theology. Whereas developmental theories did not unmask the underlying conflict of interests between developed and underdeveloped countries, dependency theory shows that the situation of the latter has its cause in that of the former, thus unmasking the conflict between the two and also showing the need for a radical break from such a state of affairs.[147] Because history is conflictual, and because there is a situation of injustice at the root of the conflict, taking sides is unavoidable.

Siding with the poor is the only honest possibility according to Gutiérrez's interpretation of both history and Christian faith.

One of the things to bear in mind in assessing Gutiérrez's appropriation of the theory of dependency is that, in the 1960s, Latin America was undergoing a process of deep change in which the critique of international capitalism and the drive toward political and economic independence played an increasingly important role. The Cuban Revolution was a symbol of the aspirations of Latin America as a whole, and, in fact, it played an outstanding role during the 1960s in spreading the model of revolution throughout Latin America.[148] Besides, the theory of dependency was a Latin American product, born around the group of theoreticians working for the UNO (United Nations Organization) at the Chilean see of the Economic Commission for Latin America (ECLA).[149] Because of its Latin American roots, the theory was more reliable for Latin Americans than the theories of development coming from the centers of thought and power of the rich countries. This was certainly the case for Gutiérrez. As Robert McAfee Brown points out, during the 1960s, Gutiérrez underwent a process of change from his European views, acquired during his previous studies in Europe in the preceding decade, to a new theoretical framework that could help him understand the reality of Latin America.[150] Gutiérrez himself acknowledges that developmental theories and policies, although also defended by the ECLA at some point, were hailed by international organizations, whereas the theory of dependency was developed in Latin America in order to explain the situation of the continent from the point of view of the dominated countries and to offer an alternative to the failure of developmentalism.[151] For Gutiérrez, any effort to develop a poor country is doomed to failure if the situation of dependency is not overcome first. Gutiérrez comes then to say that liberation is the natural answer to such a dependency.[152]

Although Gutiérrez accepts the dependency theory, and concludes that Latin American countries are structurally dependent, he is fully aware of the limitations and lack of maturity of such a theory. From that awareness he concludes that the theory of dependency has to place its analysis within the framework of the class struggle that is going on worldwide if it really wants to unveil what is at stake in the rich-against-poor-countries confrontation.[153] This opinion gets stronger over the years. In 1976, Gutiérrez argues that "the primary confrontation is not between powerful ('developed') nations or continents and weak ('underdeveloped') ones, but between different social classes."[154] As several of his critics have pointed out, though, he offers no thorough justification for holding such an opinion. It is clear, however, that, at the time of these assertions, he was convinced that a true Marxist analysis that takes into account a revolutionary praxis to bring about a socialist regime was the only way ahead. In reaching such a conclusion, the thought of José Carlos Mariátegui was decisive.

Liberation of the poor countries from their dependence on the rich countries that cripple their development, however, is but a concrete step within the human march toward emancipation that characterizes modern human history. Human beings fight to gain control over their own history, thus becoming agents of their own destiny. Therefore, history is a process of human liberation in which, through struggle, humankind achieves freedom and opens the way toward its never ending process of re-creation.[155]

This, according to Gutiérrez, is already taking place in Latin America under the form of a spreading revolutionary ferment that seeks economic, social, and political liberation as a first step toward a new society. Socialism is the most fruitful way ahead, but, as in the case of Mariátegui, Gutiérrez argues it must be a Latin American socialism, able to take into account the complex reality of the continent. Ultimately, Gutiérrez is pursuing a new society and a new human being. Gutiérrez does not aim simply at overcoming poverty at any cost, but at bringing about a new social organization that is an alternative to the prevailing capitalist model and that fits the profound human longing for freedom and fulfillment. For him, the interest of the poor countries is not to repeat the model of the rich ones, based on coercion and injustice, but to come up with an alternative model that enables them to reach a more humane society.[156] One of the problems that such a utopian view poses, and to be sure Gutiérrez is fully aware of it, is the trade-off between utopia and the overcoming of poverty. Given the fact that it is not easy to achieve both at the same time or in the right proportion, a decision about which one of the two, and to what extent, takes precedence must be made at every important point in history. This question became far more prominent at the beginning of the 1990s—given the dire situation of Peru, the precariousness of its institutions, and the changes that had taken place recently in the world economic sphere and in the former socialist countries—than it was at the beginning of the 1970s, when the presupposition was that creating an alternative order was the best and only path to overcoming poverty.

In order to bring about a new society and a new human being, the oppressed must be fully involved in bringing about their own liberation. Hence, a policy of conscientization of the oppressed along the pedagogy of Paulo Freire is most needed.[157] It is once again evident that Gutiérrez seeks a complete liberation for Latin America. That entails in the first place that Latin America be capable of understanding itself on its own terms. Hence, Gutiérrez's insistence on Latin American thinkers such those of the ECLA, Mariátegui, and Freire.

The influence of the Brazilian thinker Freire on Gutiérrez lies essentially in his understanding of a pedagogy of liberation for the poor, a tool that Gutiérrez deemed invaluable to carry out the task of helping the poor to become aware of their own situation and to assume the role of liberators of themselves. It is noteworthy that both Freire and Gutiérrez view society as divided into oppressed and oppressors and aim at liberating the oppressed from their situation by helping them to understand it. The term "conscientization" was coined by Freire to express the process of becoming conscious of what reality is and how it works.[158]

The Role of the Church

For Gutiérrez, the struggle for liberation in Latin America is a "sign of the times" that challenges the church and demands a response from it. The church must read politically those signs and commit itself to liberation, taking sides with the oppressed. This, according to Gutiérrez, was already happening after Vatican II among certain groups of lay apostolic movements, among important parts of the clergy, and among the members of religious orders. Medellín, says Gutiérrez, made this new orientation a task for the future for the whole Latin American church.[159]

Liberation requires the active participation of the oppressed themselves. Since that participation is hindered by oppressive social structures, the historical mission of the church is to activate all the mechanisms that favor liberation. This implies understanding the conflict between oppressed and oppressors that characterizes the Latin American social reality, to conscientize the poor so that they become aware of the situation and of the role they must play to overturn it, to support their demands, and to be ready to be their voice. In other words, following Medellín, Gutiérrez thinks that the church must embrace a program of social transformation of Latin America, taking concrete measures to make it happen and using its social power and influence to that end.[160]

Despite the similarities, there are also important differences between Medellín and Gutiérrez. First, if one analyzes the Medellín documents on justice and peace, whereas the latter adopts from the outset an analysis of the situation based on the tensions between classes and on the international structures of dependency, the former tries to walk a middle course explicitly rejecting both liberal capitalism and Marxism as the only possibilities of economic organization and making an appeal to the economic agents to follow the social teaching of the church.[161] Second, although both Gutiérrez and Medellín make it clear that the church must support the poor in their attempt to change the unjust social structures that characterize the Latin American societies, Gutiérrez is bold in affirming that such an action involves conflict and fierce struggle, something Medellín is reluctant to do.[162]

The resemblance between Medellín and Gutiérrez, though, is outstanding in the way both envision the role of the church in denouncing and opposing the unjust structures reigning in Latin America and in helping the poor to become aware of their situation and to gain social presence. In that respect, Medellín not only offers a blueprint for a just social and political organization[163] but makes the church a most active agent of social transformation, assigning to it the tasks of conscientization and of becoming a "catalyst in the temporal realm."[164] Medellín's document on poverty also bears great similarity to Gutiérrez's views on the matter, notably concerning the analysis of the different meanings of poverty and the call to the church to become poor with the poor as a sign of solidarity and protest.[165]

Faith, Utopia, and Social Program

One of the most common accusations Gutiérrez has had to face is that he reduces the content of Christian faith to a mere political program based on Marxist analysis. No attentive reader of his works can ever come to such a conclusion. However, Gutiérrez himself seems to be aware of the complexity of his thought and has tried to explain the interrelatedness of the different levels of rationality he uses in his analyses, especially in the section entitled "Fe, utopía y acción política," in *Teología de la liberación*.[166] This section is important to assess both whether Gutiérrez's claims in relation to his proposals regarding social transformation are scientific, philosophical, or theological, and how he grounds them.[167]

His understanding of liberation is helpful for this purpose. Liberation must be integral, and to that end, it must occur in three interrelated realms: the socioeconomic, the realm of human realization, and the realm of sin. Liberation from sin, that is, redemption, is the only way to uproot the cause of every evil and injustice in the world. It has its origin in God's gratuitousness and has been granted to humankind in Christ. In that sense, Christ is the only way to integral liberation. On the second level of liberation, history itself is defined by Gutiérrez as a process in and through which humankind conquers new levels of freedom and continually pushes itself toward higher levels of realization, whose final aim is the creation of a new humanity in a new society of solidarity. This, in turn, implies, on the third level of liberation, that the socioeconomic structures that hinder that human movement toward fulfillment must be radically changed to put them at the service of human realization.[168]

A crucial point is the interrelatedness of these three dimensions of liberation and how human and God's agencies play necessary, albeit different, roles in making them possible and in bringing them to their fulfillment. To these three dimensions of liberation correspond, in turn, three ways of knowing in the epistemological sphere: the scientific, the utopian-philosophical, and the way of faith, similar to those defined by Maritain in his work *Les degrés du savoir*. Finally, those ways of knowing themselves develop and are validated by and through concrete praxis. The question, then, of how Gutiérrez grounds his claims concerning liberation must pay attention to how he combines these different dimensions of knowing and acting.

The scientific level concerns the knowledge of the situation and requires the use of social sciences to describe and to explain the causes of the underdeveloped Latin American situation.[169] As stated above, Gutiérrez uses the theory of dependency and Marxist social theory, although, to be sure, only the scientific aspects of Marxist theory, rejecting the philosophical ones that proclaim intrahistorical salvation and deny the validity of religion.[170] Class struggle seems to be for Gutiérrez a reliable explanation of the situation that meets the requirements of scientific rationality, although he is aware that there still are many elements concerning that theory that await final clarification. Gutiérrez claims that class struggle is a fact that has been clearly established by social analysis. Its existence is not debatable and has nothing to do with ethical or religious options. The questions open to scientific research concern only how the struggle takes place in a specific situation, but not its existence and central place in contemporary society.[171] More puzzling is Gutiérrez's bold assertion that the undertaking of a social revolution actually in progress in Latin America is "based on studies of the most rigorous exactitude."[172] Such a statement contradicts the usual cautiousness with which Gutiérrez deals with social sciences and does not find support in his work as a whole. It was made in 1974, in the period that perhaps could be characterized as the most radical and belligerent of Gutiérrez's theology. A far cry from that statement is Gutiérrez's later assessment of the social sciences.[173]

In any case, Gutiérrez's acknowledgment of the existence of class struggle does not entail his embracing all the tenets attached to the Marxist explanation of history based on the dynamics of class struggle. Gutiérrez's interest is to show that the existence of poverty is structural and that its causes lie in the oppression of some classes by others. The element he wants to stress is that conflict is embedded in current social relations and that any talk about Christian love must reckon with such a conflict and must lead, on purely Christian ethical grounds, to taking sides with the oppressed. In no way does he accept Marxist elements of the class-struggle analysis such as historical determinism or the dictatorship of the proletariat. Further, Gutiérrez remains more vague than Marxist theory does as to how the struggle of the oppressed class is going to lead to a triumph of the socialist society and what stages it must go through in order to reach the "new society" toward which economic, social, and political liberation is but one step.[174]

Ultimately, Gutiérrez affirms the necessity of a Latin American version of socialism, along the lines opened by Mariátegui. Again, Gutiérrez is consistent with his permanent idea that dependency must be overcome at all levels, including the use of Marxist theory. An adequate use of it requires its adaptation to the particular conditions of Latin America. Mariátegui himself thought the same way, combining the main contributions of Marxist theory with an investigation of the Latin American reality. As Alberto Flores Galindo says, Mariátegui keeps a tension between the world horizon of his thought and its national anchorage.[175] What Gutiérrez values most in Mariátegui is the creative loyalty to Marxist principles that enabled him to supersede the dogmatism of the mainstream Latin American Marxist thinkers, while, unlike Haya de la Torre, maintaining the core of the Marxist analysis concerning the interpretation of social reality. Mariátegui proved his independence by creating a socialist party in Peru based on the principle of the leadership of the working class but open to the middle classes and the masses, instead of creating an orthodox communist party.[176]

The scientific knowledge of reality is not enough. There is a second, utopian level of knowing in Gutiérrez's analysis. Gutiérrez's understanding of utopia[177] can be considered from different angles. First, concerning its sources, Gutiérrez's notion of utopia is made up of four strands: the Enlightenment's vision of humankind and of history, the Marxist version of the Enlightenment's vision as formulated in the new humanity based on a classless society, Bloch's future-oriented reflection on hope,[178] and recent discourse on utopia emphasizing its rationality (Blanquart) and its ability to transform history (Ricoeur, Freire), a discourse that has worked to reinterpret the meaning of Thomas More's *Utopia*.[179] The first two strands, the Enlightenment and Marxism, deserve a further analysis.

Concerning the Enlightenment, Gutiérrez's construal of it has become more critical over the years because individualistic rationalism and liberalism were its offshoots. However, the Enlightenment is, to an important extent, the matrix of Gutiérrez's utopia with its emphasis upon freedom, emancipation, and self-realization. Gutiérrez reads history as humankind's long and never ending conquest of new, qualitatively different ways of being a person, on its way toward a new society based on those values.[180] The pace of that march has increased over the last decades, becoming a theological "sign of the times" that must be properly construed by the church in order to play a correct role in the advent of that society.

Gutiérrez's late-1970s paradigm, opposing "liberal" to "liberating," has obscured the fact that those two opposed models of action and thought are actually grounded on the same basic paradigm, namely, that of the Enlightenment. The liberating model takes up the values of the other one (freedom, equality, and brotherhood) and purports to make them true in society. In that sense, Gutiérrez changes perspectives rather than paradigms, critiquing the liberal model from the perspective of the oppressed and claiming that the utopia of the Enlightenment can only succeed within the liberating model.

Finally, Gutiérrez, although fully aware of the presence of conflict in history and of the need for revolution in order to bring about a new order, still partakes of the evolutionistic optimism of modernity for a new humanity. Thus, for example, he sees history, from the Reformation and the Renaissance to the cultural, personal, and social criticism of Marx and Freud, as a progression toward new achievements in the domains of freedom and emancipation. This optimism is confirmed by his citations of Teilhard de

Chardin. Most of all, in the Gutiérrez of *Teología de la liberación,* human agency plays a crucial role in shaping history and in bringing about human emancipation and self-realization. This same approach runs through all the history of modernity and is key to Marx's doctrines.

The second strand of Gutiérrez's notion of utopia, Marxism, lends Gutiérrez, as mentioned above, the analytical tools to unmask liberal ideology and to unveil the basic class struggle going on in society. Marxism, for Gutiérrez, is both science and utopia. He wants to preserve both, because the two are important to ground his claims. With Louis Althusser, he claims that Marxism is a science for understanding history and society. That scientific element distinguishes Marxism from utopian socialism and enables it to be practical. With Benedetto Croce, Antonio Gramsci, and Mariátegui, though, he opposes Althusser's construal of Marxism as science alone and asserts its utopian, ethical dimension. This ethical-utopian element is the force behind Marxism as a politically transformative praxis to overturn the status quo and to bring about a new classless society in which a new humankind can dawn. For Gutiérrez, the basis for a concrete and realistic program of social transformation stems from science, whereas the motivational drive for actual political action comes from utopia. Hence, both elements are necessary for a transformative political action.[181]

Gramsci's work has been important in shaping Gutiérrez's understanding of Marxism. It is not always easy to interpret Gramsci's thought. Most of his works, his famous *Quaderni del carcere,* were written in prison, under the fear and constraints of censorship and smuggled away after his death without being edited or published by Gramsci himself. However, although his thoughts and terminology are often puzzling, his influence can be traced in Gutiérrez's work, especially in relation to Gramsci's formulation of a nondogmatic Marxism, his important notion of a "philosophy of praxis," his very famous understanding of the formation and role of intellectuals as "organic intellectuals," and his theory of transformation of society not centered only in a party but closely connected with the people, who, seeking their own liberation, must play a crucial role in achieving it. Gramsci, like Mariátegui and Gutiérrez, was both a social activist and an intellectual. On the one hand, he was a member of the communist section of the Partito Socialista Italiano and a founder, with Amadeo Bordiga and others, of the Partito Comunista Italiano in 1921, of which he became secretary general in 1924. On the other hand, Gramsci was also founder and soul of the papers *Ordine Nuovo* and *Unità,* in which he first formulated the importance of the transformation of society from below, creating *commissioni interne* in every factory and also among the peasants, and came to be the best theoretician of Marxism in Italy. Gramsci was critical of both Croce and Georges Sorel, two very influential thinkers in Mariátegui.[182]

Concerning the notion of utopia, it is necessary to distinguish utopia as the formal principle that propels an ongoing and never ending transformation of history from utopia as formulation of the historical plan to achieve the final aim in history, namely, the new society grounded in freedom and solidarity, in which people will truly be the agents of their own destiny. These two aspects, the formal and the material, are deeply interrelated. In fact, there is a tension between the two, because any specific formulation of utopia seems to run counter to the very essence of it, namely, its ability to transcend any given state of affairs by pointing toward endless unrealized possibilities. This tension is present in Gutiérrez's discussion of utopia. On the one hand, he characterizes it at times as the source of a permanent cultural revolution, that is, more as a principle of transformation than as a concrete program.[183] On the other hand, he envisions it as a new state of affairs in which human freedom, self-realization, and self-control in solidarity will be finally real for everybody. Furthermore, it can be argued that this formulation stems from the drive to emancipation of the Enlightenment, corrected by the Marxist critique of liberalism. Therefore, it involves clear Marxian traits as the creation of a new social consciousness and the social appropriation both of the means of production and of the political process. The crux is that there must be both a vision and a connection with the actual circumstances of history for the formal principle of utopia to become operative. The former, according to Gutiérrez, is the arena for the latter.[184]

Finally, from the point of view of its adequacy, utopia for Gutiérrez fulfills the three criteria required to make it a principle of historical dynamism and radical transformation: it is related to historical reality, it is verified in praxis, and, lastly, it is rational.[185] These three criteria separate true utopia from mere dream. Following Freire, Gutiérrez asserts that the connection with historical reality means that utopia must entail a denunciation of the existing order and an annunciation of a new one. The verification through praxis implies that the denunciation must be translated into concrete transformative action toward the creation of the new, announced state of affairs. In that sense, Gutiérrez agrees with Paul Ricoeur that utopia must be concretely related to the possibilities offered at each point in history. Finally, following Blanquart, utopia must be rational; that is, it must be able to unveil those nonapparent but existent possibilities that represent a quantum leap in the development of sciences and of the understanding of reality in general. In that sense, utopia, unlike ideology, does not mask reality but unveils its true nature and hidden potentialities.

After science and utopia, the third way of knowing reality is the knowledge based on faith and interpreted and made explicit in theology. In this theological regard, two different levels of assertions are found in Gutiérrez. On the one hand, his formal basic tenets, inherited from *la nouvelle théologie* and from Rahner, and assumed by Vatican II, are the intrinsic unity between nature and grace, between the history of salvation and history at large, and between the love of God and the love of the neighbor.[186] On the other hand, he develops some more positive theological positions that, although intimately connected to the basic ones, represent his own reading of the Bible and of Christian doctrines from the point of view of the poor and are the result of the application of his theological method. The central point of that method is that theology must be done from a position of active commitment to the cause of the poor in history and consists in a critical reflection on praxis in the light of the word of God.[187]

The most important of these theological stands are the understanding of God's salvific action in history as liberation of the oppressed, the emphasis on commitment to the poor and on the practice of justice in interpreting the meaning of the love of God and of the neighbor, and the centrality of spirituality understood as the practice of discipleship that entails political action to liberate the poor. Within these themes, the story of Exodus is paradigmatic of how God acts in history by liberating from political oppression. Christ is interpreted as the full expression of God's liberating power. The promises are also construed in the same direction. However, Gutiérrez never reduces salvation to political liberation. His point is rather to counter the prevailing reductionism coming from a spiritualization of salvation that bears no connection with human history and that denies the essential unity of history. In order to avoid reductionism, Gutiérrez uses a twofold strategy. On the one hand, he places the foundation of any liberating act in Christ's liberation from sin, which transcends political liberation although includes it. On the other hand, he makes clear that the fulfillment of the promises is eschatological, and every single historical realization can and must be criticized in the light of those eschatological promises. This second set of theological tenets implies a circularity within the method. On the one hand, they represent an interpretation of the word of God based on the commitment to the poor and from the perspective of the poor. On the other hand, according to Gutiérrez, theology is always done from a concrete social location, whether it is recognized or not. For him, that social location must be that of the oppressed and of the poor.

In understanding these three ways Gutiérrez has of approaching reality (science, utopia, and faith), it is worth analyzing Mariátegui's influence on him. This influence can hardly be exaggerated. Gutiérrez was a pioneer in studying Mariátegui's thought although he never published his notes,[188] and he taught a course on Mariátegui for several years.[189] Although Mariátegui's influence on Gutiérrez has been noticed and analyzed by several authors such as Robert McAfee Brown, Curt Cadorette, Jeffrey Klaiber, Arthur F. McGovern, and Michael R. Candelaria, the extent of that influence deserves to be the object of another study. Its findings would be helpful to understanding Gutiérrez's adoption of three of the main tenets of his liberation theology, namely, the need for independence concerning action and thought in Latin

America, the adoption of a critical social theory based on Marxist analysis as the best scientific tool to know the Latin American social situation of poverty and oppression, and the pursuit of a socialist society as a first step toward a new human order.

Some biographical resemblances between Mariátegui and Gutiérrez help to understand the relationship between the two. Mariátegui was born, like Gutiérrez, to a mestizo family. Also like Gutiérrez, he suffered early in his life from a problem in one of his legs that kept him in bed for a long time and that remained a problem for the rest of his life. A third common element is that Mariátegui also spent several years in Europe (from 1919 to 1923) that marked a turning point in his career, from his "stone age" to his mature work. During these years, he lived mainly in Italy, but also in France, Germany, Switzerland, and other countries. As Gutiérrez assimilated in Europe *la nouvelle théologie*, which brought sweeping changes to Catholic theology at that time, Mariátegui assimilated the new currents that were transforming social and political thought in those days.

Upon his return to Peru—the fourth common thread—Mariátegui turned to the national and Latin American realities in order to understand them better and with the final purpose of building a new society based on the recognition of all people as equal human beings with equally real rights. In so doing, Mariátegui, like Gutiérrez, permanently combined action with thought, fully aware that the latter was necessary to bring the former to its articulation in what he called "organic thought." To that end, he provided the socialist movement with institutions that acted like think tanks. A similar move is Gutiérrez's creation of the Instituto Bartolomé de Las Casas and of the periodicals *Signos* and *Páginas*. Finally, Mariátegui was a widely respected thinker and leader who became an integral part of the intellectual and political Peruvian tradition, with influence on the whole Latin American continent. His main contribution was the formulation of an indigenous socialism. Gutiérrez, in turn, is a highly respected thinker not only in the Peruvian, Latin American, and world Catholic Church but also on the theological scene in general and in the larger realm of society as the founder of liberation theology. Something Mariátegui wrote discloses the heart of both his ethical ground and his work method: "My thought and my life are one process. . . . I have written with my blood."[190] The same applies to Gutiérrez.

Another aid to understanding Gutiérrez is Mariátegui's view of religion, utopia, and myth. Mariátegui thought that the narrow notion of religion held by the atheist freethinker was definitely spent. In fact, his thought has far-reaching implications for the notion of reason and rationality. Although without formulating it explicitly, Mariátegui left behind the rationalism of classical atheism and positivism and came to acknowledge the special status of religion and myths within human reason. For him, religion had made a clear contribution to the task of advancing human culture and civilization. He, therefore, talks of the religious factor as somehow decisive in the development of countries and peoples.[191] The examples he uses are the classic examples of Catholicism and Protestantism, somewhat along Weberian lines, although without citing Max Weber. For Mariátegui, Catholicism lacks the drive toward economic development that characterizes Protestantism. In that sense, Spanish Catholicism separated Latin America from progress.[192]

The element that makes religion a powerful cultural device is the transforming myth that it involves, especially when religion is lived with mysticism and passion, that is to say, as a force that leads to envisioning new realities that are somehow beyond the obvious boundaries of reality. Mariátegui valued that utopian, transformative power of religion, something that, in his opinion, was completely missing in the case of science. He asserts that the latter kills the power of symbol and of myth[193] and that the strength of revolutionaries does not lie in their scientific knowledge but in their faith, passion, and will. Theirs is a religious, mystical, and spiritual strength. In relation to Gutiérrez's understanding of "the power of the poor in history," and to his view of theology as second act, it is interesting to notice that for Mariátegui that revolutionary faith will be found not in intellectuals but in the masses. The function of the intellectual will be to interpret and formulate the thought that emerges from the action of the masses. Finally, Mariátegui thought that religion was definitely spent as a cultural device. Revolutionary and social myths have taken the place of the old religious myths.[194] The divergence from Gutiérrez's understanding of religion is substantive, but both authors share the belief that faith can powerfully fuel a utopian vision to transform reality radically. Both are convinced that scientific analysis, although necessary, is clearly insufficient to propel politically transformative action. Such an action requires a vision, and vision, in turn, must be supported by eschatological transcendence (Gutiérrez) or myth (Mariátegui).

Coming back to the initial question of whether Gutiérrez's claims regarding social transformation are scientific, philosophical, or theological, it is again necessary to distinguish between the formal and material nature of those proposals. Formally, the proposals have their origin in the basic theological view of the unity of nature and grace and of the history of salvation and history at large. To that extent, to propose the transformation of reality as a constitutive element of the Christian doctrine of salvation is definitely a theological claim. Furthermore, to argue for a radical transformation of structures that oppress the poor and exclude them from society and to call Christians to assume responsibility in that task are also theological claims based on the unity of the love of God and the love of the neighbor and on the intrinsic relation between love and justice. However, to propose the radical overturning of the existing economic system, denying the possibility of reforming it, and its replacement by a socialist economic system are not theological claims but concrete applications of theological claims to historical and social circumstances. As analyzed above, such concrete proposals result from the combination of some social analyses whose adequacy is open to discussion[195] and of a certain understanding of utopia that entails one view, but not the only possible one, of history and humankind. Gutiérrez establishes a notable link between faith, political action, and utopia. Gutiérrez, consistent with his unitary understanding of history, claims that salvation and political action are interrelated. In explaining how they relate to each other, he contends that utopia operates as the linkage between political action and faith because it sets the stage for the creation of a new human being in a society that is truly solidary. In order to bring that new society into being, utopia sets political action in motion. In that respect, utopia both causes political action and illumines it. But, since, from the point of view of faith, the new society envisioned by utopia is a human version of the communion of all human beings with God, the true meaning and direction of political action are finally revealed in the encounter with the perspective of the gospel that takes place through utopia.[196] A final element to bear in mind in relation to utopia, and crucial in Gutiérrez's thought, is the, so to speak, Christian version of utopia, represented by the Kingdom of God. That kingdom is already present in history, although its full realization is eschatological. This eschatological actuality ("already but not yet") of the Kingdom of God is the tensional element that both moves the Christian to act toward the actualization of that kingdom in history and critiques any actual realization in that direction.

The conclusion of this section is that Gutiérrez's main point is the intrinsic link between the realm of salvation and the realm of liberating human agency in history. The two imply each other. However, although intrinsically united, the two realms are different. Radical liberation can only stem from salvation insofar as salvation abolishes the ultimate root of evil that is sin. Furthermore, salvation is an eschatological reality that, as such, is already present in history but only in a germinal way. On the other hand, the determination of the concrete shape liberating human agency must take cannot be established only on the basis of the principles that derive from faith but needs mediations that belong to the autonomous sphere of the social sciences. Finally, no concrete historical determination of liberating human practice can be fully identified with Christian practice as such. Faith remains always a critical yardstick of every historical realization on the basis of its constitutive eschatological dimension.

The Subject of Liberation and Evangelization

During the 1970s, liberation theology in general shifted toward a major emphasis on the role of the poor as direct subjects of both liberation and evangelization. Juan Luis Segundo claims that depending on the importance of that emphasis, two different models of liberation theology can be identified.[197] He sees in Gutiérrez a clear shift from the first model represented by his *Teología de la liberación* to the second one as expressed in *The Power of the Poor in History.* Moreover, he sees the former work as far more solid than the second in intellectual terms. Finally, he asserts that the second model is more capable than the first one of integrating popular religion and cultures in the theological reflection. Segundo also claims, however, that this second model has lost some of the strength the first one had to generate critical thought, due to its programmatic identification with the leadership of the masses both in bringing about liberation and in evangelizing. The theologian, as "organic intellectual" of the masses, is more prone to defend and to justify the positions of the latter than to criticize them.[198]

Gutiérrez's theology changed in its perception of what he calls "the major fact" of the Latin American church and society, and, related to that perception, it also changed the understanding of the identity and historical role of the poor and the view on the relationship between the poor and liberation theology. Roughly speaking, three periods can be distinguished in Gutiérrez's treatment of those issues. The first one corresponds to his analysis of *Las líneas pastorales de la iglesia en America Latina,* in the mid-1960s. At that time, Gutiérrez perceived that certain political, intellectual, and Christian minorities in Latin America were becoming aware of the need for radical change and that some revolutionary processes were already on the move. In that context, Gutiérrez stresses the importance of a mature faith in those militant Christian minorities and of a prophetic pastoral action by the church. Gutiérrez knows that it is not easy to integrate the masses under those parameters, although he is convinced of the necessity of their integration. Two main points stand out: a comprehension of Christian faith that separates it from the popular religion of the masses and the view that some conscious minorities lead the process of transformation of the continent.

At the time Gutiérrez wrote *Teología de la liberación,* those views had already altered. First, he perceived that the most important fact in the life of Latin American society and of its church was the quest for liberation and the progressive awareness in the different sectors of the church of the role to play in relation to that quest.[199] Second, Gutiérrez adopted the interpretive class-struggle analysis, stressing the importance of conflict in social relations and the role that the oppressed class was called to play in bringing about its own liberation. However, that class is not yet at that stage, and, therefore, a policy of conscientization of the oppressed must be developed. The church is called to align itself with the poor and to contribute to their conscientization.[200] Third, the poor are mainly understood as a social class, but Gutiérrez already introduces a distinction between the oppressed peoples and the exploited social classes.[201] Fourth, Gutiérrez sees Christian faith as becoming more pure through the process of the "disenchantment of the world," called secularization. However, he already points out that such a process takes on a different twist in Latin America. The purification of Christian faith in that continent does not spring from secularization, as in Europe, but from the overcoming of an alienating understanding of religion that is subservient to the reigning status quo. Moreover, Gutiérrez acknowledges that the process will be complex and original also due to the characteristics of popular religion in Latin America.[202] Lastly, evangelization is understood as a Christian praxis based on commitment to the liberation of the poor. That praxis has to be adopted by all the sectors of the church.[203]

The progression from secularization to deideologization marks the shift from a progressive to a liberating approach. However, both partake of the common aim of purifying religion and of replacing it by adult faith, through a process of enlightenment. The shift from pure and adult faith to the consideration of the nature and values of popular religion marks a challenge to the ideological framework of modernity (both classical and critical) that is at the core of liberation theology. It, therefore, introduces a tensional element in that theology whose far-reaching consequences, both methodological and in content, are still being explored in several directions.[204]

The third step signals a more overt move to emphasize the role of the poor as agents both of their liberation and of evangelization. The formulation of this step took place during the mid- and late 1970s and was reinforced in the 1980s. A representative work of that period is *The Power of the Poor in History*, a collection of essays that show Gutiérrez's progressive attention to the nature and role of the poor.[205]

The perception of the "major fact" in Latin American society and church evolves through the period, increasingly emphasizing the leadership of the poor in liberating themselves. Eventually, that "major fact" is identified as "the irruption of the poor in history."[206] The expression denotes that those who had been absent in history have become present in it in a sudden, powerful, and bursting manner. Gutiérrez is so convinced of the depth of the awakening of the masses that he even identifies their movement toward liberation as a fact that includes the whole people.[207] The important point is that in terms of elite-versus-masses as leaders of the liberating process, the role of the latter becomes increasingly decisive for Gutiérrez.

He states that whereas the work of the elite for liberation could vanish at some point, the pursuit of liberation by the masses would hold firm because "we have documentary evidence that it is and ever shall be the poor who are the makers of history."[208] It would be wrong, however, to conclude that the elites are not important for the liberation struggle. In fact, Gutiérrez is totally aware of the support the poor need for carrying on their struggle. Such support is multifarious. Two aspects of it must be stressed. The first concerns the articulation of the praxis. To that purpose, intellectuals are needed, but those intellectuals are not members of a self-standing elite that conducts the revolution but interpreters and articulators of the movement of the poor as fully committed members of that movement and of its liberating praxis. They are called, therefore, to be "organic intellectuals." Theology, concretely, must be understood as the "second act" of the "organic intellectual," whose first act is the liberating praxis itself.[209] The second aspect relates to the vast array of services and functions needed by the liberating process that can only be delivered by professionals qualified for it and that require method, resources, and program. Gutiérrez has always been aware of this need and has devoted much time and energy to promoting committed professionals.[210]

The poor are identified not only as the main subjects of transformation but also as subjects of evangelization. The relation between the poor and evangelization and the understanding of evangelization itself take, therefore, a new twist. If before, evangelization had to be essentially conscientization of the poor, now the poor themselves are acknowledged to be evangelizers of those who wanted to evangelize them, because they are the historical subject-bearer of the kingdom.[211] The perception of who the poor are also widens throughout this period. In general, the poor are defined as those not recognized as persons by the established order. What initially was the oppressed class, and later the exploited classes and oppressed peoples, becomes in the third period exploited classes, despised ethnic groups, marginalized cultures, and women.[212] As later comments by Gutiérrez himself reveal,[213] this shift responds to a progressive appreciation of the breadth and complexity of the world of the poor. Gutiérrez, however, is persistent in his original affirmation that the socioeconomic aspect is basic, although it does not include all the dimensions of the poor. The introduction of marginalized cultures and despised races signals a progressive integration of the indigenous people in the analyses of liberation theology. This introduction, however, complicates the analysis of the factors that cause poverty and conflict in society, a complication to which liberation theology is still trying to respond adequately.[214] The same applies to the inclusion of women among the poor.

The awareness of popular religion and its relation to liberating faith also changes in this period. Popular religion is acknowledged as one of the constitutive dimensions of the world of the poor. In that sense, Gutiérrez starts to define the poor of Latin America as both "believers" and "oppressed."[215] Their religion must be analyzed to see how it contributes to or hinders the liberation struggle. The conclusion is that, on the one hand, popular religion is a stumbling block on the road to liberation insofar as it is not itself liberated from the elements imbued in it by the ruling classes to protect their position. On the other hand, popular religion is acknowledged as entailing a profound liberating power once that religion is made part of the awareness of the poor concerning their situation and liberating role.[216]

Spirituality and God

After Puebla, Gutiérrez devotes most of his theological effort to deepening the insights of liberation theology concerning spirituality and the notion of God.[217] Before starting to analyze these two subjects, some observations are needed. First, this new period represents a change in the issues on which Gutiérrez focuses his reflection. Those issues become explicitly theological or, in technical terminology, more related to systematic theology than to the fundamental theology emblematic of the previous period.[218] Second, the sources used for theological reflection also change. Instead of the recourse to the social sciences characteristic, although by no means exclusive, of the 1970s, Gutiérrez uses the Bible as the main source of the work that will be examined in this section, accompanied by theological works and religious and secular poetry.[219] Finally, these changes do not represent an overturn of the previous project but a concentration on some of the theological themes that were already crucial in the preceding phase. The basic presuppositions that underpin Gutiérrez's theological enterprise remain unchanged, namely, the primacy of Christian praxis as "first act" and the understanding of theology as a "second act," the adoption of the perspective of the poor in order to interpret both the situation and faith, and the pursuit of liberation as the necessary praxis that verifies the truth of the theological positions.

A Spirituality of Liberation

Gutiérrez's discourse on spirituality is the cornerstone of his theology and, possibly, his main contribution to the theological enterprise. Gutiérrez's achievement consists in showing that spirituality is the interlocking piece that welds together God's mystery as manifested to the creature and the response of the creature as the only means to penetrate the depths of that mystery. Thus spirituality becomes the key that unlocks the access to God's "well," a well that is the only and true place from which theology can develop.

Spirituality has been a constitutive element of liberation theology from its inception.[220] Liberation itself as a Christian task is a way to follow Christ, a way of living in the Spirit, and, hence, concrete spirituality.[221] This inner connection between liberation and spirituality makes liberation theology a true Christian theology, that is, a true reflection on God that naturally springs from the actual experience of following Christ, God incarnate.[222] From the point of view of Gutiérrez, there is no true liberation without sharing in the fruits of salvation. Those fruits have been provided gratuitously by God in Christ and are accepted by the believer in loving response to Christ, materialized in the practice of discipleship that constitutes the essence of spirituality. That practice of discipleship, in turn, leads to the other and, especially, to that other who is the poor, the nonperson. That is so not because that other is vested with special moral qualities but because the poor are the special object of the gratuitous love of God and the main bearers of the values of the kingdom. These are the decisive traits of the mystical-prophetic liberating spirituality that constitutes the source of liberation theology.

Every work by Gutiérrez on liberation theology deals with the question of spirituality not marginally but centrally, yet the work in which he has systematized his thought on that issue is *Beber en su propio pozo*.[223] This work can be characterized as Gutiérrez's *Invitación a la vida heroica*[224] because, as was the case in Mariátegui's book, Gutiérrez shows in it that the radical transformation of Latin America must be, first and foremost, anchored in a personal disposition to carry out a heroic practice. In Gutiérrez, that heroic practice means to follow Christ into his death in order to rise with him.

The main thesis of the book is that a new spirituality is being born in Latin America that consists in a different form of following Jesus. That new way of discipleship, in turn, originates in the special circumstances and events taking place in the Latin American society and church.[225] In that respect, Latin American emergent spirituality "drinks from its own wells."[226] Those special circumstances are what in other works Gutiérrez calls "the major fact" happening in Latin America. In the light of the word of God, that is to say, theologically, those circumstances are interpreted as a kairos, a special time of solidarity, prayer, martyrdom, judgment, and grace, but, most of all, of hope. From that new spirituality in Latin America comes liberation theology, as the reflective moment on the practice of following Christ in a kairotic time.[227] Thus, Gutiérrez closes the circle around the question of independence: liberation theology is a theology that has broken free of First World domineering theology not just on the basis of pure will or intellectual exercise but because a new way of being Christian has emerged in Latin America under the guidance of the Spirit. And because that is so, Latin American spirituality and theology are both a contribution and a challenge to the spirituality and theology of First World countries.

Gutiérrez's definition of spirituality contains its defining traits: spirituality is a global and communitarian itinerary in search of God that stems from an encounter with the Lord and consists in following Christ by living according to the Spirit.[228] First, the trinitarian structure of spirituality reflects both the mystery of God and the fact that an encounter with the triune God is the goal of every Christian spirituality. Second, spirituality is a global itinerary, in the sense that it encompasses all aspects of human existence, not only the so-called religious dimension of that existence.[229] Gutiérrez is a staunch opponent of any reductionism or dualism. His view of Christian vocation is overarching in the sense of involving every aspect and moment of human existence. The call to be holy as the Father is holy affects every act of the Christian. This coheres with his Rahnerian views concerning the intrinsic unity of grace and nature and of the history of salvation and history at large.

It equally coheres with his integral notion of salvation. Third, spirituality is a communitarian itinerary, the way of a whole people and not only of individuals. It is not possible to be Christian by oneself. Spirituality is always collective and ecclesial. Like the people called by God that walked through the desert in Exodus, the church, as the new messianic people, is also on its way in search of God. Fourth, spirituality is always an itinerary in search of God. It entails an apprenticeship along the way in order to get to know God. It is, in that sense, a historical project always in the process of becoming.[230] Fifth, it springs from an encounter with the Lord that has its origins in God's initiative.[231] Finally, it consists in a new way of being, namely, the way of those who live according to the Spirit,[232] that is to say, following Christ along the paths of freedom and love that are the signs of the Kingdom of God. It entails a creative practice, because no road has been previously built for a Christian.

In Latin America, spirituality as praxis of discipleship has its own traits. It consists in the acceptance of God's irruption in the life of the Christian community manifested in the irruption of the poor. It means to take sides with life in the dialectic of death-life that is continually at play in that continent. Neutrality is not possible. Finally, it can only take place through the incorporation into the spiritual experience of a people, the poor. That, in turn, involves identification with the world of the poor in all its dimensions. In Latin America, finally, the spiritual journey flourishes with the blood of the martyrs who, like Christ, have accepted death as a pascal event, as the pass to resurrection.[233] Gutiérrez underlines often the importance of the martyrs. The Latin American martyrs are all those who, following Christ in the special social, political, and economic conditions of that subcontinent, have been murdered because of their praxis in favor of the poor. Although symbolically represented by Archbishop Romero, they are many, most of them lay, socially unimportant, people. For Gutiérrez, they represent the confirmation of the renewal of the church in its commitment to the poor, the very basis of its liberating strength, and a permanent spring for the life of this church.[234]

A Journey into the Mystery of God

God has increasingly become the summit of Gutiérrez's theology, and, in that sense, he bears a striking resemblance to Rahner and Metz. If at the time he wrote *Teología de la liberación* Gutiérrez defined theology as a critical reflection on historical praxis in the light of the word of God, in the 1980s theology will become for him a talk about God.[235] That does not annul the validity of the original definition but, as Gutiérrez likes to say, places that definition in its proper context and relates it to its final aim: in essence, theology is nothing but a word about God. This, in turn, fully coheres with Gutiérrez's view of spirituality. The latter is a pilgrimage in search of God, and it is in the ongoing unveiling of the word of God through that pilgrimage that the Christian community finds its words to talk about God. Gutiérrez stresses two points. First, God, out of sheerly free and gratuitous love, makes revelation available to the poor, while hiding it from the sages and powerful. Second, in the itinerary in search of God, there are two moments: the moment of silence, which includes both contemplation and committed praxis, and the moment of speech, of the word of theology, in which that which has been contemplated and practiced first is reflected upon and formulated.[236]

The particular journey of the people of God in Latin America, the poor and all the others who identify themselves with the poor, has led to a progressive discovery of God and of the face of that God vis-à-vis the poor. Two main and interrelated features define that face: God is the God of life; and God most especially loves and cares for the poor[237] in a gratuitous and free way that can never be fully predicted or even comprehended.[238]

El Dios de la vida is the title of the book in which Gutiérrez deals systematically with the question of God. The book is a treatise on both *De Deo uno* and *De Deo trino*, divided into three parts, each of them focusing mainly on a different person of the Trinity but within a continuous discourse on God.[239] Gutiérrez, however, does not say explicitly that he is dealing with the Trinity, possibly because his theological discourse owes its nature and strength not to a systematic way of thinking but to the experience of the people on their way to God. It is noteworthy, though, that Gutiérrez practices what Rahner said, namely, that the original discourse about God knows nothing about separating the two treatises just mentioned but is and must be a unified discourse. Also implicitly, Gutiérrez takes somehow for granted the other great Rahnerian insight concerning the Trinity, namely, that of the intrinsic unity between the "economic" and "immanent" Trinity.[240]

In Latin America, the burning theological question is how to speak about the God of love in the midst of the poverty and oppression that cause the innocent to suffer.[241] Gutiérrez contends that this is what separates liberation theology from progressivist theology. Whereas the latter asks about the possibility of talking about God in a secular world that has come of age, the former asks the same question but refers to a religious world that lives in poverty and oppression.[242] This does not deny that liberation theology is related to other theologies, especially to the groundbreaking European theologies around Vatican II. Neither does it deny that Gutiérrez, like other theologians, is a professional, learned, and modern theologian who asks questions that reflect a modern and learned mind. The point here is rather that liberation theology has its own perspective and concerns. Moreover, from this perspective and concerns, liberation theology shows new insights in relation to the question of God. From that question, as it is formulated by liberation theology, flow several other questions that deserve analyzing: the relationship between the understanding of God and the social position from which that understanding is effected; the dialectic of life-death; the relationship between justice and gratuitousness.

For Gutiérrez the first question when talking about God is not whether or not God exists but rather which God is the object of discourse. The underlying issue is the critique of religion, what Segundo calls the deideologization of theology.[243] Gutiérrez distinguishes clearly between God and the idols. The latter are manipulations of God generated by those for whom the absolute value in the practice of their lives is not the God of the Bible but a created reality, especially wealth.[244] In this respect both Metz and Gutiérrez stress the necessity of unmasking false gods, that is to say, idols. For Metz, as discussed in the preceding chapter, modern society, especially in the 1980s and beyond, tries to compensate for the hardship of life by aesthetics and consoling myths, while rejecting the uncompromising God of Israel. Gutiérrez sees idolatry mainly in the unrelenting pursuit of wealth that characterizes modern culture.

In the pursuit of an idolatrous practice, human life is destroyed. The result of idolatry is death, completely opposed to the search for the true God that leads to life.[245] The most grave sin in Latin America since the time of the conquest has been the sin of idolatry, by which the peoples of the continent have suffered enslavement, oppression, marginalization, exploitation, and, in the last analysis, death. This is an important element in the theological interpretation of the situation of massive poverty that affects the peoples of Latin America. The root of it lies in the sin of idolatry. Liberation, according to Gutiérrez, cannot take place unless sin is definitively uprooted from human hearts, something that exceeds human power and is the work of God alone.

Gutiérrez's investigation on the work of Las Casas focuses on the analysis and consequences of the idolatry of money. Las Casas himself had pointed out that the greatest obstacle to the evangelization of the Indians was the idolatry of the Christians who were trying to justify their exploitative practices under the cover of their missionary work.[246] Gutiérrez shows that some theologians of the time, like García de Toledo, even tried to justify those practices theologically by asserting that God made the gospel available to the Indians by enticing the evangelizers with the gold and other riches of the Indians.[247] Idolaters, moreover, purposefully misconstrue the God of the Bible as a God who justifies their idolatrous practices. This is the worst thing for Gutiérrez, and it is the reason why behind every theology there is always a concrete social practice and an economic system. The difference between progressivist and liberation theologies lies not in intratheological arguments but in the social position from which these two theologies emerge. Progressivist theology is born in the countries that exploit the poor countries, whereas liberation theology springs from those poor countries that are becoming aware of the exploitation they suffer.[248] One of the tragedies of the church in Latin America is that its members are on both sides of the struggle. The church is divided along the lines of social position. From those lines, different theologies derive. For that reason, the present time is a time of judgment for the church. Neutrality is impossible. Either God or the idols, either the oppressed or the oppressors, either life or death.

Idolatrous practices are the cause of the racism and of the internal divisions that prevent the Latin American countries from becoming viable societies. This is an issue where Mariátegui, Arguedas, and Gutiérrez fully coincide. Very accurately, Cadorette argues that there is a deep unity between Mariátegui's "social analysis, Arguedas's novels, and Gutiérrez's theology. Each has incorporated the viewpoint of the poor as a key methodological principle."[249]

Arguedas and Gutiérrez enjoyed a short but intense friendship that began in 1968 just after Gutiérrez's first presentation of his sketch of liberation theology. Arguedas, who had abandoned his allegiance to the church, saw in Gutiérrez's talk the theological expression of his own ideals and values, as well as a picture of God with which he could identify himself. Gutiérrez, in turn, discovered the depth of the theological insights of Arguedas's work and the inner tragedy that, mainly as a result of a deep depression, was tearing him apart until he finally took his life at the end of 1969. The encounter was short but very deep at the intellectual, personal, and religious levels. In a letter to Gutiérrez, Arguedas wrote, "How well do we understand each other and see together, joyfully, the light nobody shall extinguish."[250]

Arguedas, like Mariátegui and Gutiérrez, was mestizo, and his childhood experiences with an Indian family that took care of him marked his views on Peru, his work, and his project for Peru. His most well-known novel, *Todas las sangres,* is a description of, and a reflection on, the profound divisions that have made Peru an impossible national enterprise and the presentation of his view of how, in solidarity and mutual respect, a new Peru must be built where *todas las sangres* are called to participate.

What separated Arguedas from Mariátegui was his religious sensibility. Mariátegui was interested in the religious factor but mainly as the conveyor of the myth that empowered people to dare to transform reality radically. As Washington Delgado argues, although Arguedas had cut off his links with the church, he remained always a religious author.[251] The striking thing is the depth of his theological insights. Furthermore, as in the case of César Vallejo—whom Delgado considers also a religious writer despite his complete distance from the church—the fact that these insights are conveyed in literary language makes them more penetrating and compelling. Their expression in a creative language gives them a closeness to human experience and a sharp accuracy that profoundly resounds in the reader and makes it possible for them to carry an existential content and meaning that goes well beyond the limits of scientific language. Gutiérrez, as a person of exquisite aesthetic sensibility and an admirer of literary language and of the sublimity of poetry as a quasi-supernatural language, has been influenced by Arguedas to an extent still not fully analyzed.

As has been said, Gutiérrez's breathtaking work *Entre las calandrias* is an analysis of the religious dimensions of Arguedas's works. In it, Gutiérrez unveils many of Arguedas's views that appear in the work of Gutiérrez himself. To begin with, there is in Arguedas, according to Gutiérrez, a project of liberation.[252] One formulation of his utopia was the construction of "the fraternity of the wretched," that is, a fraternity born for and of the liberation of the oppressed by the oppressed themselves.[253] Gutiérrez acknowledges that Arguedas and Mariátegui shared views on the role of myths and on socialism as analysis and as a project, but that Arguedas had besides a sense of "the magic." Arguedas himself thought that his appreciation for Mariátegui and Lenin never did away with "the magic" in him.[254] That sense of the magic pervades all his works, a characteristic that is present in most Latin American writers, and enables his narrative to convey those elements of reality that cannot be captured within the limits of scientific rationality but that, nevertheless, are deeply immersed in human nature and powerfully present in history.

The combination of the mythical and the magic gives the work of Arguedas a breadth and a depth that unlock new possibilities of cultural realization or rehabilitation of modern society. That is possible because Arguedas's utopia reawakens and legitimizes those dimensions that, although doubly forgotten in the Eliadean sense, still haunt the modern mind. Arguedas retrieves those dimensions, among which the dimension of the cosmological communion is crucial, and reintegrates them into the realm of culture and human ethos. Thus he bridges some of the breaches that modern culture, driven by an instrumental rationality, has created between cosmos and person and within the human soul. To be sure, Arguedas himself saw the limitations of his intuitions, realizing the somewhat idealized and simplistic version of his Andean universe, and fought to reconcile them with the tensions and dislocations of the modern Peru that he discovered in amazement and shock in the coastal city of Chimbote.

Arguedas's views evolved over the years, as his literary works show. His primordial world was unquestionably the world of rural Peru, the Peru of the Sierra where the native culture was still powerful and where social relationships between the destitute and subjugated natives and a white, or mestizo, ruling minority were fully in place. Arguedas discovered coastal Peru later in his life, especially the newly industrialized places where, as in Chimbote, new social and cultural processes were taking place.[255] His early literary work, represented by his short stories "Agua" and "Yawar (Fiesta),"[256] describes the world of the *ayllu* and of the tensions between *comuneros* and *mistis*, between the poor and the powerful. Arguedas shows in his stories his interests as an anthropologist and researcher of the culture, myths, and ways of life of the native population of the Andean Sierra. The universe of those stories is the small universe of the rural villages. The city is a far-away reality, an ambiguous one for the natives. From those stories to his last novel, *El zorro de arriba y el zorro de abajo,* Arguedas moves from the rural world to the world of the town (Abancay in his novel *Los ríos profundos*) and, finally, to the environment of the new realities in Peru: the challenges of industrialization and the crisis of the old regime described in *Todas las sangres* and the disjointed world of the industrial Chimbote, the world that in his novel *El zorro de arriba y el zorro de abajo* Arguedas tried to understand and to interpret. His utopia was defined in *Todas las sangres,* a utopia that somehow seems to him impossible to realize in the environment of the new Peru of Chimbote.

The religious theme runs through all those works, playing an important role in them. Arguedas, besides being a superb writer and a friend at heart of the destitute natives, was a man of principles and values, a man who had to face the religious question, among other things, because he knew that religiosity in general and Christianity in particular were decisive in the life of Peru. In relation to the notion of God, Arguedas explores the double function of religion, its taming power at the service of the powerful (the "padre grande de Abancay" in *Los ríos profundos*) and its liberating and revolutionary power (the "padre Cardozo" in *El zorro de arriba y el zorro de abajo,* perhaps a character based on Arguedas's view of Gutiérrez). Arguedas's main point is to determine which God is the object of belief rather than whether or not God exists. The poor do not have the same God as the rich. The God of the latter is a killer God: money; the God of the poor liberates and gives joy and hope.[257]

Arguedas is so religiously intense that Rendon Wilka, the hero of his best-known novel, *Todas las sangres,* is like a personification of Christ in the Indian milieu, somebody who speaks with true authority, who is completely clear in ethical terms and never wavers, who announces a new state of affairs, who enlightens all the others with his words and deeds, and who unleashes the liberating power latent in the soul of his people. Finally, he is also killed because of the danger he poses for the established order, although no fault has been committed by him. Immediately after he is shot, telluric movements take place, "as if the mountains started to walk," so as to express that, as in the case of Christ, an irreversible new time had begun.[258]

Whereas literary characters lend Arguedas the opportunity to analyze the dire situation in Peru, the experience of Job provides Gutiérrez with the material to deal with one of the most difficult questions for liberation theology, namely, the relationship between God's justice and God's sovereignty. Such a question stems from the existence of innocent suffering, and involved in it lies the most challenging problem of the coincidence and divergence between human liberating action and God's liberating power.[259] Job personifies the just, the innocent who is subjected to suffering and dejection. Job knows that his friends are wrong and that their theological views concerning the doctrine of the retribution have nothing to do with God and God's behavior toward creatures.[260] He, therefore, seeks an answer, an answer that he deems possible only if he can see God face to face. For Gutiérrez, Job's friends have the wrong answer because they use the wrong theological method. Instead of reasoning on the basis of experience, an experience of destitution and suffering, as in Job's case, they reason on the basis of principles; their theology is abstract and takes into account neither the concrete situation, the suffering and hope of human beings, nor the limitless love and compassion of God. They are technically skillful yet utterly wrong.

Along the way, Job realizes that his suffering is not an isolated case but just an instance of the pain and injustice suffered by the poor. In that respect he discovers that to be a man of God entails being just to the poor and solidary with them. This is what Gutiérrez calls the first broadening of Job's comprehension of his religious views prompted by his own situation. It is, for Gutiérrez, the prophetic moment in Job's discovery.[261] This prophetic moment is basic to purify popular religion of its potentially alienating elements. It is the moment of the analysis of the situation, to discover its causes and to act accordingly, but not on the basis of purely social reasoning, not even on ethical or utopian grounds, but out of strictly religious reasons: the prophetic language springs from the justice of God, from a God who cares for the poor and condemns the oppressor, from a God who acts out of sheer gratuitous love and wants that love to pervade every human relation. But that is not enough. Justice is necessary, but God is beyond that realm.

Job, contrary to the popular image about him, was not a patient character but somebody who knew he was right and, therefore, sought to confront the God who was responsible for his tragedy. That, says Gutiérrez, helped him purify his faith instead of adopting a purely passive attitude that would have paralyzed him. In his face to face with God,[262] Job will realize that God's gratuitousness neither can be reduced to the human understanding of justice nor can be fully comprehended by the human mind. Before God, only the language of contemplation suffices. The prophet must remain silent because the mystery of God surpasses the limits of history. Job understands it through his personal encounter with God. He gets no answer to the precise questions he was addressing, but the answers he gets through that personal encounter with God, to which his spiritual itinerary has led him, are deeper and more final than the ones he was seeking. Job widens his perspectives. Now, he recognizes that the fact that he is innocent does not imply that God is guilty.[263] The encounter, finally, empowers him to abandon himself into God's unfathomable love, a love beyond justice[264] that manifests God's greatness, freedom, but, most of all, gratuitousness.

Gutiérrez's interpretation of Job shows several things. First, it shows that prayer and contemplation are paramount in Gutiérrez. Silence, prayer, and listening to what God has to say are central pieces of liberation theology because they intrinsically belong to it; they belong to the very method of that theology. Furthermore, prayer and contemplation are not separate moments from practice, but an inner element of that practice.[265]

Second, Gutiérrez's analysis of Job places the problem beyond what Metz calls Augustine's way of explaining the existence of evil in the world. Whereas, according to Metz's interpretation, Augustine's explanation blames human beings in order to exculpate God, in Gutiérrez's Job, the latter, claiming his innocence, starts blaming God for his dire situation and ends up discovering that his innocence does not entail that God is guilty.

Third, the question of Job's self-abandonment into the hands of God becomes the decisive term in this discussion. It suggests that Job comes to accept God, even if he has not the answers he was pursuing from his perspective. This self-abandonment means that a risk is accepted in taking such a step. The problem is not solved, but it is put into another perspective that changes the logical framework. Although there are some differences between Gutiérrez's and Metz's treatment of the theodicy question, the point of surrendering to God despite the lack of full comprehension plays in both authors a key role. Metz's *leiden an Gott*, though, is more tragic than in Gutiérrez. The final self-abandonment into God's hands takes place not in the final joy of Gutiérrez's Job but in the midst of an *unversöhnheit* (irreconcilability) that persists in the very act of self-abandonment.

Finally, Gutiérrez's intuition that God's unfathomable love is beyond justice does not mean a suspension of the ethical (the prophetic language is indispensable in Gutiérrez) but rather means placing the ethical within the broader scope of God's gratuitousness.

Gutiérrez's reflection on Job is somehow a breakthrough in his theology. The work on Job helps Gutiérrez to formulate in a more complex and nuanced manner his doctrine of salvation, making explicit some of the aspects implicit in his previous insistence on the gratuitousness of salvation. In *Teología de la liberación,* he had already identified three interrelated levels of salvation within a unified process: the political, the human-utopian, and the religious, asserting that the latter was the only fountain of the other two levels of salvation.[266] His work on Job represents a new step in the same direction because it helps Gutiérrez to clarify the deep meaning of the religious level of salvation. On the one hand, the dimension of gratuitousness is enhanced. On the other hand, that gratuitousness appears now in a different logical order than the logical order that rules the other two levels of salvation. God does not act gratuitously in the same way as humans do. God's justice cannot be equated with human justice because God's has its origin in God's utter freedom and greatness. God's loving and absolute care for the creature (immanence) has its origin and salvific nature in God's utter freedom and greatness as the absolutely other (transcendence). This is the central point in the dialogue between Job and the Lord. Job has many difficulties in his attempt to understand what the Lord is saying. The dialogue is asymmetrical: whereas Job is asking for a straightforward and logical answer to his claims, according to human logic, the Lord's discourse decenters the dialogue and, somehow obliquely, places the dialogue in a totally different domain, the domain of God's love, freedom, and cosmological care in God's own terms. Job's conversion and acceptance of the Lord hinge on his discovery that he simply cannot envision God in purely human terms. What Gutiérrez names "the mysterious encounter of two freedoms" is made possible only once he discovers and accepts that he and human beings in general are not the measure of God's creation; only when he realizes and accepts that the Lord's freedom and unencompassable greatness are the only measure of everything that has been created; only when, despite his own rage and pain, he accepts that everything is gratuitous because it has been created out of the limitless gratuitousness of the Lord.

Gutiérrez's reflection on Job also opens new avenues in liberation theology due to its stress on the discontinuity between human agency and God's agency. God's action and God's reasons for acting cannot be simply subsumed to the way humans act and reason. This was precisely the point Job had to understand and to accept. Both the God liberator of Exodus and the understanding of Christ as liberator are presented from a different perspective. The interpretation of these terms in *Teología de la liberación* was almost straightforward and could lead to the danger of suggesting that God's liberation in history was somehow continuous with the way humans liberate themselves. To be sure, Gutiérrez never affirmed in that work that there were a continuity, but neither did he stress the discontinuity in the same way and with the same insistence he does in his work on Job. Therefore, this latter work can be considered a new development or, at least, a new explicitness in Gutiérrez's theology.

After his work on Job, Gutiérrez keeps his permanent insistence both on the liberating power of God in history and on the importance of human responsibility concerning the creation of a just and liberated society. At the same time, though, by making it explicit that God's action cannot be reduced to human terms and that God's work happens to be sometimes incomprehensible to human beings, Gutiérrez is implying not only that any historical effort on the road to liberation falls under eschatological judgment but also that it must be relativized vis-à-vis the absolute freedom of God's gratuitousness.[267] Such a relativization of human agency does not imply in any way that humans are discharged of their unrelenting search for justice. It entails, though, that, theologically speaking, that human agency must be rethought in the broader perspective of the gratuitousness that encompasses the practice of justice. The working out of the implications involved in such a rethinking is a fruitful and promising path in the development of liberation theology.[268]

New Challenges and Developments

Gutiérrez has made it clear that liberation theology cannot be conceived as a finished project. Quite the contrary, it is a theology that, on the basis of a new perspective and praxis, tries to develop new answers to the questions brought up by new circumstances.[269]

Among others, three main developments have prompted Gutiérrez to clarify some of his views: the sociopolitical changes that have taken place in Latin America and in the world, the changes within the Catholic Church, and the experience of the struggle for liberation. Among the sociopolitical changes, the return of Latin American countries to democracy, the sweeping changes that have occurred and are still taking place in the former socialist countries and in the remaining socialist countries, and the new economic global situation deserve mentioning.[270]

The changes in the Catholic Church involve a doctrinal interpretation of Vatican II somewhat different from the one that formed the ground for liberation theology. Besides, more and more members of the hierarchy are adopting a critical approach to the theses and the practice of liberation theology. Finally, several authors of liberation theology, among them Gutiérrez, have been subject to a process of doctrinal discernment by the Vatican and asked to clarify the meaning of some of their theological tenets.[271]

The experience of the struggle for liberation, in turn, has increased both in terms of the number of people committed to it and in terms of the number of projects undertaken. The late 1980s and most of the 1990s have been extremely difficult from a social and political point of view, and new forms of solidarity have been developed to overcome a dire situation. There is no doubt that this solidary practice, which has importantly involved a high degree of self-organization of the poor themselves, marks a new achievement in the ongoing task of making the church responsive to the reality of the poor.[272] However, the possibilities of bringing about an overall social, cultural, economic, and political transformation of society, in line with the utopian dimension of liberation theology, have been severely curtailed both ideologically, by the triumph of the *pensée unique,* and politically, by the success of proposals that, like Fujimori's in Peru in the 1990s, have nothing to do with that utopian vision.

Although liberation theology in general and Gutiérrez in particular are still in the process of reacting to some of the new circumstances, some work has already been done in that direction. In 1986, Gutiérrez published one important new work in which he reviewed and clarified some of his basic tenets.[273] In 1990, he also wrote a new introduction to his *Teología de la liberación* and altered a section of that book with the same purpose.[274] In these works, Gutiérrez affirms that both praxis and theological reflection are open processes that make it possible and necessary to review them continually. He writes that, in fact, his most important works after *Teología de la liberación*, such as *El Dios de la vida, Beber en su propio pozo, Hablar de Dios desde el sufrimiento del inocente,* and *La verdad os hará libres,* have been part of that ongoing effort, "causing the essential to appear more clearly and the accessory elements to lose the relevance they once seemed to have." For Gutiérrez there are three basic tenets of liberation theology that shine even more as time goes by: "The point of view of the poor, the theological task, and the proclamation of the Kingdom of life."[275] Gutiérrez discusses at length the most central theological and pastoral point made by liberation theology, namely, the preferential option for the poor. His central claim is that such an option is absolutely theocentric. It is not the case that Christians must make a preferential option for the poor on the basis of social analyses or human compassion, but they must do so because "God's predilection for the poor, the hungry, and for all who suffer is based on God's gratuitous goodness." He further writes that such an option "is a theocentric and prophetic option, rooted in the gratuitousness of God's love and required by this gratuitousness."[276]

He also reviews in these works another three important points. First, on a formal level, Gutiérrez is insistent on the auxiliary role played by social sciences in his theological reflection.[277] Gutiérrez is increasingly aware of the lack of maturity of those sciences. That, in turn, means that, for Gutiérrez, the use of social sciences must be cautious. He also categorically affirms that his theology is grounded not on social sciences but on the sources that are specific to the theological task, namely, scripture and the experience of the Christian community.[278] Second, Gutiérrez acknowledges explicitly the limitations of the theory of dependency and the need for improving the understanding both of the full extent of poverty in Latin America and of its causes.[279] More important still, he clarifies his use of class-struggle analysis. He gives it the meaning of a social fact consisting in the confrontation of interests that is present in common life, while downplaying the technical meaning of the term as a Marxist tool of social analysis.[280] Gutiérrez's third move consists in expanding his notion of the poor, acknowledging the complexity of the world of the poor, stressing the existence of many kind of oppressions, and making it clear that all those oppressions are not reducible to class conflict.[281]

All in all, Gutiérrez's later developments signal the evolution of his thought toward an increasing emphasis on the theological sources, a clarification, although by no means elimination, of the use of social sciences in his theology, and a substantial expansion of the universe of the poor and of the complexities that it involves.

Chapter 4

David Tracy:
Public Theology

David Tracy's theology is a paradigmatic example of how post–Vatican II Catholic theology has evolved in the United States.[1] Although some elements of that theology are similar to the central traits of the theology of Metz and Gutiérrez, Tracy's program has an identity of its own. To show that identity is the central aim of this chapter. An important factor in shaping that identity is the context in which Tracy has developed his theology, namely, U.S. society. Therefore, before analyzing that theology, a view of its context is necessary.

Social, Cultural, and Ecclesial Background
of Tracy's Theology

U.S. society is a complex reality not rarely understood and often oversimplified when examined by those who are foreign to it.[2] Due to a series of factors that will be analyzed throughout the chapter, it became a singular society with a peculiar mixture of enlightened politics and strong moral and religious values. The awareness of being something new and powerful and the feeling of having been entrusted with a historical, worldwide mission are decisive features of what is usually called "the American experiment."[3]

The American Experiment

North America was an outlet for the colonial enterprise of Spain, France, and England.[4] Whereas the Spaniards were strong in the South and in the West, and the French were mainly interested in the fur trade and had their stronghold in Quebec, the English colonizers occupied initially the East Coast.[5] For those English colonizers, the new land offered the possibility of a new beginning—for some of them, a new religious beginning; for others, a new social beginning. In both cases, America was seen as a promised land.[6] Many authors point to reasons for seeing America as a new beginning. Among them, the lack of constraints characteristic of Europe and the vastness and richness of the land were paramount. Thus were set the bases for a new culture, for a new political system, and for the forging of the new person the American was called to be.[7]

The eastern colonists adopted a form of government that ultimately led to today's U.S. democracy. Several factors were conjoined to bring this about, including the parliamentary experience of England, the private character of many of the expeditions, the religious motivation, the distance from England, the autonomous character of the different settlements, the ideas of the Enlightenment thinkers, and the conditions attached to the colonizing enterprise.

Contrary to the imperial character of the Spanish conquest and colonization, tightly organized, developed, and centralized under the Spanish crown, the English settlers in America were private groups that came at their own risk, each with different purposes and programs. Although most of them based the organization of their settlements on English traditions and forms of government, they enjoyed a great deal of autonomy in devising the concrete rules of their political system. Moreover, the various groups settled in different territories, and each of them developed its own organization, hence giving birth to the system of independent states. Not until the Confederation was formed in 1777, which later became a Union under the Constitution of 1787, did the different states have institutional links with one another. A plurality of settlements, interests, and conditions, later coordinated under the Confederation and under the Union, therefore, made up at that early stage the constitutive plurality and pluralism of U.S. society and culture. The passage from plurality to pluralism took place with the Union, since such a step entailed that the different states had to convene in order to discuss their different ways and to choose common rules, while leaving adequate space for keeping their peculiarities at the state level. An example of this is that, according to the Bill of Rights of 1791, no church could be the established church of the Union, but the states were free to have their own established churches if they wished to do so.

Religious motivation was paramount in the case of the Puritans and the Quakers, and these two groups gave themselves a political system in accordance with their religious views. These religious groups were highly communitarian, and hence they had a clear awareness that, although always under the supreme will of God, they were giving themselves a political organization. Some of these communities developed a covenant or compact, a truly social contract by which all the members agreed to their religious enterprise and to the form of their government. A classic in that respect is *The Mayflower Compact* of 1620, by which the Pilgrims gave themselves a form of democratic government before they arrived on the shore of what is now Provincetown Harbor.[8] In the case of the Virginia settlers, the political organization had a more secular character, but the consciousness of self-government was equally high, since the basic equality of the settlers and the private character of the settlement were characteristics common to almost all groups in the colony.

Different authors have diverging views concerning the influence of the Enlightenment on the adoption of democracy in the United States. A radical Americanist position is adopted by Daniel J. Boorstin, for whom the influence of the European thinkers was negligible. Although he does not deny that the Founding Fathers knew the thought of the theorists of the Enlightenment, his view is that the conditions of the settlements and the adaptation to the American environment were the reasons why a government of the people was adopted. Moreover, the republicanism of Jefferson and Washington was for Boorstin clearly aristocratic. For Richard D. Heffner, however, although adaptation to the American environment played a crucial role in the emergence of the new nation and of its system of government, the ideological framework of the American Revolution was provided by the Enlightenment.[9]

The end result was that when the Union emerged in 1787, the fathers of the nation based the legitimacy of the government on the will of the people and devised a political system that clearly contained the seeds of the tripartite division of powers characteristic of the current democratic system. To be sure, the Founding Fathers did not have in mind all the elements that characterize the current U.S. political system. The Declaration of Independence of 1776, the Constitution of 1787, and the Bill of Rights of 1791 must be seen as foundational documents of a nascent democracy. The history of interpretation and fulfillment of those foundational documents has included crucial episodes of strife, division, tragedy, oppression, and war. Along the way, some important, inner contradictions of the system were progressively dispelled and overcome. The task still continues, and, in that respect, American democracy must be understood as an ongoing enterprise whose definitive orientation and development have been and continue to be in the hands of the American people. Clear examples of such dynamics are offered by the history of slavery in the country, by the amendments to the Constitution, by the civil rights movements, and by the never ending interpretive activity of the courts, and especially of the Supreme Court, in relation to the Constitution.

The citizens of the new nation not only sensed that they were beginning a new life and inaugurating a new era in history but also clearly felt that they were a chosen people that had to accomplish the historic mission of being a beacon of liberty and democracy to all the peoples on earth, eventually transforming or helping to transform the way people conducted their political business all over the world.[10]

From its very inception, the new nation grounded its quest for freedom and democracy, as well as its sense of having been entrusted with a historic mission, on ethical and, ultimately, religious values. In that sense, it presents an original and almost unique combination of the secular values of the Enlightenment with the religious values of Christian faith. The United States is, therefore, a nation marked by the combination of modernity and tradition.[11] Many people have noticed and analyzed these two components of U.S. society. Tracy not only sees those two components at work in the "American experiment" but also points out that this circumstance shows that a proper understanding of both reason and the public realm includes not only argument but also conversation, not only the Enlightenment but also religious traditions. The implication, somehow Metzian, is that, without the anchoring of the covenantal tradition, the Enlightenment lacks the resources to disclose the nature and transformative possibilities of reality and ends up being oppressive.[12]

Another central feature of the United States is its pluralism. Contrary to the traditional uniformity of the European societies, usually arranged along ethnic, cultural, and religious lines, American society sprang from an original plurality of interests, beliefs, and cultural mores that, far from decreasing, continued to multiply with the massive waves of immigrants that have unceasingly flooded the new nation over its two hundred years of history. Plurality is a constitutive element of the American political system, of its culture, and of its religious life. Although this plurality has created a culture of pluralism to a great extent, it has also experienced great failures, of which the two gravest have been the destruction of the Indians and the enslavement of the black people.

The American experiment, with the traits that have just been described, was the end result of the combination of several threads, among which three stand out: the biblical tradition, the republican tradition, and the dynamics of the modern state with its emphasis on economic development and bureaucracy.[13] These three original threads, still operative, have informed the American soul. However, their combination, although successful in many respects, entails tensions and contradictions that deserve close scrutiny.

Among the inner contradictions of the system, the treatment given to the Indians and the enslavement of the black people must be singled out in the first place because they constitute the gravest examples of the ambiguities and systemic wrongdoings embedded in the American experiment. For the U.S. Catholic bishops, "Our nation was born in the face of injustice to Native Americans," and "Slavery stained the commercial life of the land through its first two hundred and fifty years." Robert Bellah writes that the deprivation of land and livelihood suffered by the Indians at the hands of the settlers "was the primal crime on which America society is based." That "primal crime was compounded with another enormity," namely, "the forcible transportation of the African Negro out of his own land and his enslavement in America. Thus at the very beginning of American society there was a double crime, the incalculable consequences of which still stalk the land."[14] Both facts stand in clear contradiction to the biblical strand that proclaims the equality of all human beings before God and to the doctrines of universal citizenship and of equal rights that characterize the republican tradition. They blatantly contradict the grounding principles of the new nation proclaimed by Jefferson in the foundational charter of that nation: the Declaration of Independence. That document states: "We hold these truths to be self-evident, that all men are created equal, that they are endowed by their Creator with certain unalienable rights, that among these are life, liberty and the pursuit of happiness."[15] Finally, they constitute painfully clear examples of the dark side of "Western civilization" that prevents it from dealing adequately with "the other" and "the different." That dark side is made up of aggressive and self-righteous Christianity, blinding Eurocentric anthropology, and the dictatorship of the ruthless rationalism of the Enlightenment.[16]

The arrival of the Europeans and their unrelenting thirst to take over and to exploit the lands traditionally owned by the Native American peoples[17] wreaked havoc on those peoples. The diseases brought in by the Europeans, the wars of extermination, and the displacements of entire peoples from their traditional territories to the reservations caused a tragic decimation of the native population. By 1887, four hundred years after Columbus, the Native American population had been expelled from their territories, and that population was about 15 percent of what it had been when the whites came to North America.[18] Those who survived had to face inhuman conditions, total uprootedness, and social dejection on the reservations.

According to William Hagan, the pattern of white behavior in relation to Native Americans was consistent:

1. Whites come and interact in a quite friendly manner with the native population, which, on more than one occasion, helped them to survive under difficult circumstances.

2. Whites start to grab land from the natives. The latter resist the invasion, and fighting breaks out. Both parties suffer material and personal losses.

3. Natives are termed "savages," lawless people that must be punished for their crimes. Militias to fight them are organized. Later, in the westward expansion, the federal army is called upon to protect the "defenseless settlers" from the "savages."

4. Native people are defeated and a treaty is signed, by which they agree to retreat to a part of their former territory, leaving the rest to the whites.

5. The unremitting process of settlement puts pressure on native people, and new settlers invade the natives' territory despite the treaties, very often coveting the land or its mineral resources. Fighting breaks out again. Native people retreat further. A new treaty is signed.

6. Finally, after treaties are blatantly disregarded by the white settlers, proving the lack of determination and capacity of the federal government to stem the illegal actions of the states, the local governments, and private individuals, the natives are forced to take "the trail of tears" that leads them to a reservation escorted by the federal army.[19]

Life on the reservations was very hard in most cases and did not prevent the continuation of the process of systematically dispossessing the natives of their lands, now their reservation lands. The Dawes Act served to transfer ninety million acres of native land to whites. Since 1887, the reservation lands that by different means have passed to white ownership amount to two-thirds of the total reservation lands at that date. As late as 1960, the Tuscarora lost a case in the Supreme Court and had to yield part of their reservation for the Niagara Power Project despite the dissenting opinion of three justices who, appalled by the ruling, wrote, referring to the U.S. nation, that "Great nations like great men, should keep their word." Unfortunately, although treaties were originally signed between two independent nations, their force was always contingent upon white interests. The Supreme Court decided in 1903 that hypocrisy was not needed any longer when it ruled with good conscience that the U.S. Congress could violate the treaties at will. Since then, the destiny of the natives has been not only de facto, as was previously the case, but also de iure in the hands of the white people. The actual policy followed by the government has swung according to the particular views of each government. Whereas during the 1920s Indians suffered a policy of "integration," the new policy of the Roosevelt administration in the 1930s and 1940s changed completely toward empowerment of the natives, including the extension of welfare policies to the native nations and the payment of indemnities for losses incurred by those nations as a result of previous measures. Eisenhower's government, however, shifted again and adopted a policy of "termination." The 1960s and 1970s saw again a reversal of policy, thus starting a new trend that basically has been followed since.[20]

The point to notice is that for most whites, for the settlers that were pushing the "frontier" westward, the natives were a nuisance that had to be eliminated at any price.[21] For most of the best of the ruling elite, of the intellectuals, and of the reformers, they were lawless "savages" living in the "wilderness" who had to be Christianized and transformed into true members of the new society that had brought civilization and progress. Some of the Founding Fathers, like Jefferson, thought that way. They accepted that the natives were human beings but believed that they were living in a primitive state from which they had to be rescued. From that point of view the white expansion westward was understood as the fight of civilization against "savagery."[22] Besides, because the natives, pursuing their own interests, cooperated with each side during the American Revolution, but mainly helped the British, the new nation considered them untrustworthy. The conclusion was drawn that, because they had helped the unjust enemies, they also had been defeated along with the British and, therefore, had lost their just claim to their lands. The subsequent conflicts, painful for both parties led to the policy of treaties.[23]

In principle, those treaties were understood by both parties as permanent, and the doctrine commonly accepted was that the natives could not be dispossessed of their lands except by their own consent. A treaty, therefore, expressed the consent of both parties, and was equally binding for both. However, from the point of view of the whites, natives were an inferior and backward people, and, in a paternalistic way, it was the mission of the white people to look after the welfare of the natives. In practice, the "white father" treated the entrusted children in a completely despotic and unfair way mostly based on military superiority. On the occasion of the ruling of the Supreme Court in the *Cherokee Nation versus Georgia* case in 1831, Chief Justice Marshall gave an official rubber stamp to the paternalistic approach by defining the status of the native nations as "domestic dependent nations" and by affirming that "Their relation to the United States resembles that of a ward to his guardian." That opened the door to treating the natives as subjects rather than as citizens, as was clearly the case under Theodore Roosevelt, and, therefore, to applying to them a policy of colonization that finally put them entirely in the hands of the whites and dependent on whichever policy was followed by the government in office.[24]

One of the best examples of how a paternalistic policy can be destructive even if guided by good intentions is the case of the reformers. Very active at the end of the last century, their point of departure was that natives had to be assimilated into the white society. Therefore, the reformers, following the principle of taking care of the welfare of the natives, were prevented from understanding the point of those whose welfare they sought and, rather than affirming their identity, pursued a policy that caused extraordinary damage to the native nations. One of the cornerstones of their policies was the Dawes Act of 1887, which, by allotting the communal land of the reservations to each individual, thus disregarding the tradition of communal property in which the native culture was rooted, ultimately caused the native nations to lose two-thirds of their lands to white owners.[25]

Although Native Americans were able to advance their cause during the 1970s, unfortunately they still constitute a reality that current U.S. society is at pains to understand and to deal with appropriately. In that sense, the situation of the Native Americans continues to test the spirit and the limits of the American experiment. Alfonso Ortiz diagnoses in a clear-sighted way the depth of the problem. Apart from the initial complete inability of the newcomers to place themselves in the position of the native, compounded with the economic interest involved in the colonization, he shows how a series of terms deeply embedded in American culture display a bias that has pervaded the attitude toward the natives and set the stage for their actual elimination: "Western civilization," "frontier," "wilderness," "civilization versus savagism," "Christianity versus heathens," "law versus lawlessness," "Manifest Destiny," and "history naming." Due to that bias, American written history has been for him "the handmaiden of conquest and assimilation." That has made history so distorted that it is irrelevant. Furthermore, claims Ortiz, the cultural differences result also in a distinct mental framework that involves different comprehension of basic notions like that of place, time, religion, and leadership. For him, the problems still persist in U.S. society, and overcoming them involves a series of changes, among which telling a history from the other side is crucial to the task of changing the view about the natives ingrained in American culture.[26]

The history of African Americans is perhaps more tragic and complex than that of the Native Americans. In the case of the former, the negation of personhood was even greater. There are at least three reasons for making such an assertion. First, they never had any chance to secure their position with treaties. In that respect, natives were better off, because at least they were recognized as "independent domestic nations." Second, it was always acknowledged that Native Americans had a right to the land because they were the original inhabitants of the continent, a condition that did not apply to African Americans. Finally, the latter were enslaved also by the natives at some times, which clearly shows their inferior position.

Apart from this, they were compelled by force to leave their countries and to be brought to America, with the consequent destruction of their roots and identity. Although slavery has very ancient roots,[27] over the four hundred years and more that the Europeans, and later the Americans, traded slaves, starting in 1444, "Africa lost an estimated forty million people. Some twenty million of these men and women came to the New World. Millions more died in Africa during and after their capture or on the ships and plantations."[28] In fact, the trade did not rocket until the Europeans "discovered" the "New World." After that event, systematic slave trading was organized by the Portuguese and later by almost every western European nation, particularly Holland, France, and England. Slaves came from all social strata, and most of them came from the west coast of Africa, where the merchants organized a whole system of supplies with the collaboration of Africans. In the eighteenth century, the annual number of slaves forced over the Atlantic ranged between fifty thousand and one hundred thousand.

The "discovery" of the "New World," therefore, marked the beginning of a historical turning point in the relationship between Europe and Africa. The latter was tragically forced to provide the slaves needed to exploit the riches of America, thus opening the era of the most abject episode concerning human relations in the whole history of humankind. Utter human dejection and death, destruction of cultures, complete disregard for human dignity, and high levels of ideological justification that combined pure cynicism with the loftiest religious principles characterized this era of human history in which "Western civilization" became the hegemonic power in the world. That civilization and that power, including Christianity, were thus tainted forever with a most horrendous crime that was systemic, that lasted more than four centuries, and whose consequences have haunted, haunt, and will haunt the Western world and the African continent and poison international relations.

It was not until 1619 that the first black people stepped on what is now U.S. soil. Those people were Africans who had been first brought to Spain, who bore Spanish names, and who were being transported to a different destiny, probably the West Indies. Their status on American soil was not that of slaves, but, as many other white people at the time who had come from Europe, black people of African origin were indentured servants who, after having completed the stipulated time working as servants for their masters, regained their free status. It was not until forty years later that the institution of slavery started in the British colonies of North America, under the leadership of Virginia and Maryland. Still, black people kept their right to vote for a long while. In the case of Georgia they kept it until the middle of the eighteenth century.[29]

Slavery came about as a result of economic conditions and of the forced character of black immigration. Since Africans did not come voluntarily to America, Southerners did not have to attract them and, finally, took advantage of that to pass laws that made black people slaves—at first, for their lifetime if they were not Christians; later, even if they were so; finally, the condition of bondage was extended to their offspring. The Founding Fathers, among them famous Virginians like Washington and Jefferson, had vested interests in slavery. As slaveowners, they made sure that the Constitution did not outlaw slavery, thus contradicting the spirit of the Declaration of Independence.[30]

Slavery, however, was always a thorny problem. By the end of the eighteenth century, after independence brought to the fore the notion of natural rights and the question of the equality of human beings, the justification of slavery was much harder than before. In the fervor of the revolutionary period, the northern states, starting with Vermont in 1777, abolished slavery. In the South, the economy, which was the underlying foundation of slavery, entered a period of depression. Moreover, by the end of the eighteenth century, many in American society had come to see black people as inassimilable, even if they were free. At the same time, some of the Founding Fathers, like Jefferson, did finally see that slavery could not be squared with the spirit and the proclamations of the American democracy.[31] That underlying tension between principles and reality, compounded with the feeling that blacks were not assimilable to a white society, led to certain practical proposals about freeing slaves and sending them away as colonists to some islands of the West Indies or to Africa.[32] The foundation of Liberia in 1821 by the American Colonization Society can be seen as a partial, and not very successful, realization of those proposals.

According to Heffner, the invention of the cotton gin did away with the abolitionist trend in the South. The new machine so increased productivity that between 1790 and 1810, the production of cotton bales was up from 4,000 to 175,000 a year; by 1860 annual production approached 4 million bales. That entailed a strengthening of the "peculiar institution," as slavery was called in the South. Demand for new slaves and for land rocketed. Between 1820 and 1860 the slave population increased from 1.5 to 4 million. That, in turn, gave birth to two opposed trends: in the South, a full-fledged ideology developed to justify slavery ethically; in the North, the abolitionist movement (by no means supported by the majority of citizens) got increasingly stronger.[33] However, even at that time, the movement to find a solution to slavery was alive in the South. In 1832, the Virginia legislature discussed the possibility of a solution based on freeing slaves and sending them overseas as colonists. Although a majority favored abolition of some kind, in the end, the proslavery arguments, mostly offered by the slaveowners (a powerful minority), and the difficulties of devising and financing a coherent plan of freeing slaves and sending them away produced a final proslavery vote.[34] As a result, the situation of the slaves, if anything, got worse, and the ideology to justify slavery became more blunt, giving way to one of the most ruthless systems of slavery ever known. For Lerone Bennett Jr., although any form of slavery was hell, "there were gradations of hell," and, according to his opinion, "By all accounts, the British-Protestant colonies were the deepest pit. The French and Spanish could be cruel, and often were. But they did not seem to be driven by the same demons that pursued the Puritans."[35]

Both despite and because of the harsh conditions of slavery in the eighteenth century, which made it progressively harder to balance the increasing numbers of slaves (in some states more numerous than the white population) and to curtail their possibilities of organizing themselves, African Americans developed their own identity. That will to self-affirmation in the midst of negation has pervaded the history of resistance of the African American community from the creation of the Free African Society in 1787 to more recent leaders such as Martin Luther King Jr. and Malcolm X. Two strands unite in configuring the movement for liberation of the African American community. The first thread concerns the cultural, religious, and political identity of that community, whose roots were African; the second refers to the identity of the American experiment itself, its values, aims, and the utopian vision involved therein. Consequently, two different aims, which in some respect create an inner tension, pervade that liberation struggle. On the one hand, the affirmation and deepening of the original identity of the African American community constitute a permanent trait of the struggle. That trait stresses the retrieval of the roots of that community, making it different from the rest of American society. On the other hand, the struggle has always sought to make American society play according to its original rules as defined by the Declaration of Independence, the Constitution, and the subsequent amendments, thus vindicating the right of African Americans to be full citizens of that society. This second aim stresses the right of the African American community to be American.

According to Bennett, African Americans created a distinct identity when, their hopes shattered of being free after the American Revolution, they reacted to the social oppression they experienced by turning inward and creating their own social institutions. The people who led the creation of such institutions must be considered the Founding Fathers and Mothers of African America. The emerging structure of African America involved four steps, all taken in the last two decades of the eighteenth century: the creation of the Free African Society in 1787; the increasing spreading out of the black church movement, with the creation of new churches starting in 1794; the founding and expansion of social and fraternal organizations; finally, the beginning and progressive strengthening of the movement for equal rights.[36]

While these institutions were being created mainly in the North by free blacks, other structures of identity and resistance were developed in the South, where the conditions of life of the slave population reached unimaginably inhuman peaks.[37] Most slaves lived on plantations. There, they "transcended their environment, creating a new structure of meaning" that was the foundation of their hope. This structure was based on "concentric circles of community" that gave birth to the soul of "Black America." According to Bennett, the energies flowing from that soul "organized themselves around three axial forces."[38] The first was the axis of the spirit, around a Christianity reinterpreted according to the African past and to the conditions of suffering of slavery—a Christianity of deliverance that was opposed to the white Christianity whose main obsession was how to teach the slaves to accept their condition as natural. The religious communities, although outlawed, were extremely lively and had a communal and spontaneous character with natural leaders acting mainly as preachers. The other two axes were that of music and rhythm and that of the family. The latter developed despite all the truly inhuman measures taken by the slaveowners to prevent its formation.[39]

After their legal enfranchisement, the situation of African Americans remained difficult, having to overcome the real barriers to full social integration that were not done away with by the legal enfranchisement. The Thirteenth Amendment abolished slavery in 1865. The Fourteenth Amendment made blacks citizens in 1868. The Fifteenth Amendment enfranchised them in 1870. All those measures were taken in the aftermath of the Civil War. Prior to the war, and during the war, all kinds of attempts were made to find a compromise between the North and South in all matters, including slavery. Lincoln, contrary to common opinion and to his later image of being the Great Emancipator, was prepared to compromise with the South on the issue of slavery if the South showed its readiness to accept the Union and the principle of no extension of slavery to the new territories. For him, the question of principles concerning the condition of the slaves took a second place; his first concern was to come to an agreement with the South.[40] Lincoln's pattern of behavior, like Jefferson's before him, is but an example of how volatile matters of principle have been in American history. The same volatility, together with American pragmatism and the lack of real power among African Americans, determined that the implementation of the rights defined by the Thirteenth, Fourteenth, and Fifteenth Amendments would be a tricky business whose disentanglement is still in process.

After a short period of grace once the Civil War ended, during which black people voted and held public offices,[41] the policy of segregation continued to be practiced in the South.[42] Social hostility to full equality brought about movements like the Ku Klux Klan, founded in 1866 to prevent equality by creating a situation of terror. Finally, in 1896, the Supreme Court blessed segregation by formulating the doctrine of "separate but equal," which had nefarious consequences. This doctrine asserted that the existence of separate facilities for blacks and whites "was constitutional, as long as both races had equal facilities."[43] A system of castes that pervaded all the aspects of life developed under the umbrella of that doctrine. The end result was hatred toward, segregation of, and discrimination against African Americans, which translated into thorough social inequality.[44] Not until 1954 was this doctrine abandoned by the Supreme Court.

One of the ways African Americans took in order to improve their condition was to migrate to the cities of the North, such as New York and Chicago. Far from being accepted on equal footing, black people had to endure harsh conditions in those cities, including social and geographical segregation. The result was the creation of racial ghettos that deteriorated over the years, in which crime and human dejection are common currency, and that, therefore, constitute nowadays one of the main reminders of the shortcomings and failures of the American experiment. However, the migration to the North opened new opportunities for the formation of a middle class among African Americans. Besides the market, welfare policies and the governmental antipoverty program of the 1960s and 1970s were instrumental in achieving this result.[45]

The civil rights movement was a powerful instrument to stir the awareness of the American population concerning the contradiction and injustice involved in the segregation practiced against the African American community. The movement developed in different directions and was embraced by both black and white leaders. However, black leaders were more appealing to the black community and exerted a crucial role in gathering support for the causes they defended. Two of the most powerful leaders of this movement in the 1960s were Martin Luther King Jr. and Malcolm X. Religion played a most important role for both of them. Whereas the former made his Christian principles and faith the basis for his nonviolent struggle against discrimination and for true equality, the latter broke with Christianity and sought to find a more solid ground for African American identity and liberation in Islam. Both were assassinated. Many of the principles and ideas developed by King bear a strong similarity to liberation theology.[46]

From a theological point of view, the struggle of African Americans for their dignity and rights has developed into a full-fledged black theology, which has in James H. Cone its best known, but by no means its only, representative. It is interesting to see the similarities between liberation theology and black theology. As the former seeks to interpret and to change reality, history, and theology from the perspective of the poor and the oppressed, the latter seeks the same from the perspective of black people, who also are oppressed. Cone establishes theologically the legitimacy and need of being black, with full identity, in a hostile and racist society dominated by whites. It is precisely based on black identity that he reinterprets Christian faith. In that sense, he comes closer to Malcolm X, at least the post-Mecca-trip Malcolm X, than to the theses of King seeking integration. However, he is able to value both these leaders and to integrate the position of both in his theology.[47]

The economic factor was an important, although not the only, element in the discrimination against both Native Americans and African Americans. In fact, the United States cannot be understood apart from the economic ideas that, from the beginning of the nation, glorified the values of wealth, private property and initiative, and self-reliance. In other words, for better or for worse, the American experiment has always been founded and developed along the lines of liberal capitalism.[48] Therein lies part of the strength of the experiment, as well as an important number of its contradictions.

The tension between utopian democracy and the constraints of economic development, with its bureaucratic model of government, was already present at the very inception of the nation. Madison and Hamilton came to represent very early two visions of the new American democracy. After collaborating in the writing of *The Federalist Papers* in order to foster support for the new federalist constitution whose cornerstone was the Union, these politicians parted ways. Whereas the Virginian Madison took a more decentralizing approach in the administration of power and fought against organizing national institutions of economic power, Hamilton, a truly enlightened thinker in political and economic terms, realized that the future of the nation depended on its ability to develop economically. On that basis, he defended the creation of a central bank as the cornerstone of a national economic policy in financial and commercial matters. In that sense, he was the forerunner of the current industrial and financial power of the United States. Washington, the power broker of the time in his office of president, took the Hamiltonian side, thus favoring the formation of a modern capitalistic nation based on industry, finance, and trade. The Federalists, as Hamilton, Adams, and their party were known, lost their political power as early as 1800 and disappeared as a party. Nevertheless, their model of society, involving both economic development and bureaucratic governmental power, finally won the day. Jefferson, and later the populist Jackson, tried to fight against the forces of the market but were finally defeated.[49]

By the early nineteenth century, capitalism, mainly represented by the cities of the North, was the powerful engine of the nation that was going to condition its future. That, in turn, determined the reinforcement of the Union at the expense of the autonomy of the states. By the second half of the nineteenth century, the agrarian South felt the supremacy of the modern capitalistic North and tried to restore the old balance of power. This effort, compounded with the related issue of slavery, finally led to the Civil War, whose result determined the type of society the United States was going to be: a capitalistic democracy powered by economic development. Thus "the American dream" became a symbol not only for achieving personal freedom in a democratic society but, most of all, for achieving personal advancement in the economic sphere.[50]

From an economic point of view, success has been spectacular. The United States is the most powerful country in the world, economically speaking. Its income per capita, measured in internationally compared terms, is, with that of Switzerland, the highest in the world, and its gross domestic product is bigger than that of Japan, Germany, and France together. Historically, the United States has been the solution for many people escaping from poverty in Europe and in other regions of the world. Its current population is almost fifty times larger than in 1800. At the same time, this outstanding leap in population has been accompanied by increasing wealth. Today, the gross national product per capita is almost ten times greater than in 1869. Especially since World War II, the United States has been the flagship of liberal capitalism and the leader of the Western capitalist world. Since the Breton Woods Conference, the dollar has been the worldwide referential currency, even though new strong currencies have increased their international position over the last twenty years. To this day, the United States, although its political and economic leadership in the world are not as strong as forty years ago, remains the international power broker and the force with which all other forces must reckon. Some of the keys to that success are the size of the country, both in terms of population and natural resources, the flexibility for change, and the never ending process of creation (and destruction in the Schumpeterian sense of the term) of wealth made possible by the mobility of people and capital in permanent pursuit of better conditions and results.[51]

The historical praxis of the country united in fact the development of democracy and economic progress. Despite the success of the experiment, both in political and economic terms, its shortcomings and tensions are also undeniable. Politically, the United States has had and still has problems at home and abroad. At home, apart from the problems concerning the Native Americans and the African Americans, other important historical problems also rooted in discrimination have concerned the political rights of women and those of the ethnic minorities, some of which have been unjustly treated.[52] As some authors have pointed out, the principles underlying the Constitution and the Bill of Rights have not been applied to everybody in the course of history. In fact, a double ethical standard has operated depending on whether or not people were accorded their full humanhood. Racial, cultural, religious, and gender prejudices, combined with powerful economic interests, have caused the system to contradict its own principles, thus generating crises still unsolved.

Abroad, the United States has also been accused of using a double standard, applying the principle of defense of "national interest" in dealing with other nations while claiming officially to defend the values of democracy, freedom, equality, and justice. Early in the life of the new nation, the pursuit of national interest caused problems with those nations, such as Spain and Mexico, that resisted the U.S. attempt to take over their territories.[53] Despite the Monroe Doctrine, which advocated full respect and defense of Latin American democracies, U.S. nationalism led to an aggressive foreign policy that created much enmity abroad. Later, nationalism evolved into imperialism under the cover of fulfilling the historical mission of carrying the seeds of religion, civilization, progress, and freedom to conquered countries like the Philippines. The Monroe Doctrine was replaced by Theodore Roosevelt's policy of "speak softly and carry a big stick," and aggressions and interferences in Central and South America became frequent, thus creating a powerful anti-Yankee feeling in those regions that persists today.[54] More recently, economic expansion through American multinational companies, together with the role that the United States came to play in the two world wars and in the subsequent Cold War, made the United States the policeman of the world with naval and air bases deployed in all continents. As Heffner puts it, "the flag followed the dollar," thus making it difficult to avoid the suspicion that U.S. international policy has more to do with the defense of economic "national interests" than with the preservation of peace and freedom in the world.

From an economic point of view, one of the worst plagues of the U.S. economy has been its cyclical nature, which, together with phases of expansion, has created deep depressions, among which that of 1929 is prototypical. A permanent problem has been that, despite its richness, U.S. society has been haunted by its inability to eliminate persistent poverty. In general terms, the United States has 60 percent more poor people than other developed countries. About 13 percent of the U.S. population lived under the official poverty line in 1990, but whereas about 10 percent of the white population fell below that line, 32 percent of black people did so, thus showing the huge gap in wealth and social conditions existing between races in the country. Between 25 percent and 50 percent of the poor (depending on how they are measured) are people who, due to structural, cultural, and institutional circumstances, cannot get out of their situation of misery and live under inhuman conditions that seem to be permanent for them. This part of the population has been called by some the "underclass," and although the term has been contested, it serves the purpose of underlining the existence of specially destitute people in the middle of the most affluent society in the world.[55]

Poverty is the flip side of the inequality coin. The United States is the nation with the highest percentage of poor, and with the highest level of inequality in terms of income, among the highly industrialized countries. In 1999, the net income of the richest 1 percent of the population was equal to that of the poorest 37 percent, a ratio that had doubled since 1977.[56] One of the causes of this situation is the American system of values that, without denying the importance of social solidarity, stresses the significance of self-reliance and of free play in the market more than other developed countries do. At the same time, the United States, unlike most of the other developed countries, is a very plural and complex society where many races and cultures intermingle, thus creating difficulties of integration that do not exist, at least to the same extent, in other societies. Such difficulties are an important factor in determining the economic and social differences within U.S. society. The integration of differences in a common society has always been, and still remains, one of the permanent challenges such a society has had to face throughout its history. Although the issue is much broader than its economic implications, its adequate solution is crucial to solve the problems related to poverty and inequality.

Religion and the Public Realm in U.S. Society

Religion is an important feature of U.S. society. Washington, Madison, Adams, Franklin, and Jefferson held views on religion heavily influenced by the Enlightenment. For example, they clearly leaned toward deism, referring to God as Architect, Supreme Being, Providence, and similar names, thus completely avoiding any personal reference to God. Moreover, although the three Virginians had personal links with their Anglican parish churches, in which they took turns as vestrymen, and Franklin always helped churches financially, they also, somehow contradictorily, were suspicious of historically revealed faiths. Finally, much like Rousseau, they all were convinced that a sort of civil religion was needed to sustain society and guarantee peace and progress in it.[57]

Contrary to the enlightened deism professed by the Founders, according to which historically revealed religions were to be looked upon with suspicion, U.S. society has been a most favorable soil for the creation and growth of multiple religions and denominations—a soil, moreover, where religious dissent always sought to establish its home, finally doing so.[58] The majority of the citizens have not shared and do not share the deistic principles that informed the nation.[59] U.S. society stands out as a combination of a strongly secular process and a not less strongly religious soul. In that sense, it is a challenge to the secularization thesis. U.S. society is a rare case among developed nations with regard to the religiosity of its citizens. The acceptance of the secularization thesis has been customary in Europe among social analysts and religious thinkers. According to that thesis, advances in the scientific and technological domains entail a progressive differentiation and autonomization of realms as a result of which the importance of religion decreases both in the life of the individuals and in society. Privatization and secularization are taken for granted under this scenario. The United States challenges such an equation. Being the richest country in the world, and having a cutting technological edge, it remains nevertheless a very religious society both in itself and in comparison to other developed societies. More than 90 percent of the population believes in God; 60 percent are members of some church (27 percent in 1865, 48 percent in 1940, 64 percent in 1960); and almost 40 percent attend religious services once a week.[60] Moreover, its high level of religious practice and church membership, practically stable over the last twenty years, defies all the predictions of the secularists.

A related and important issue for the purpose of this chapter concerns the different positions pertaining to the public role of religion and theology in U.S. society. In this sense, it is important to pay attention to the significance of civil religion. The term "civil religion" has recently been used by Bellah, but its roots go back to those crucial moments in history when the nature of the "republic," and its substantive foundation, had to be established. Briefly and formally expressed, "civil religion" in the United States refers to those elements that constitute the foundation of the nation and of its ethos and that, therefore, share somehow in the sacredness that characterizes religion.

The discussion around civil religion is important because it raises a foundational question in a society that has a marked tendency to be pragmatic, procedural, and expedient and where critics contend that politics has become the field of power-brokering rather than the realm in which policies are decided on substantive grounds. The atomization of interests that results from individualistic behavior thins out the social fabric and erodes the foundations of the national experiment.[61] To raise the question about civil religion is an attempt to reflect on the problems of the current situation and to go back to the foundations of the nation in order to revamp the national experiment.

Martin E. Marty is helpful in discerning the different uses of civil religion. He distinguishes between two main lines of interpretation of civil religion. The first one admits that the nation is "under God," that is to say, that its ultimate foundation is a transcendent deity. The second one finds in the nation itself, or in its social process, the sources of quasi-transcendent values. Furthermore, he identifies two varieties within each kind: the "priestly" and the "prophetic." The former is "celebrative, affirmative, culture-building," whereas the latter is "dialectical." Civil religion carries within itself the seeds of idolatry insofar as one of its components is the nation itself. When the nation or elements of it, such as democracy or capitalism, are exalted to the point of becoming an absolute, idolatry occurs, and with it absolutism, injustice, and terror in social life. But even in the case of considering God the absolute, it is possible to utilize the religious symbols and principles to justify ideological and political stands. Consequently, the prophetic or unmasking dimension is necessary in order to overcome these dangers and to establish new goals that ensure the future and the health of the experiment.[62]

There are various strands making up these kinds and varieties of civil religion. One is the strand of biblical tradition, embraced by the different Christian denominations. A second strand is the deistic faith of the enlightened Founding Fathers. A third strand is represented by a secular set of humanistic values that emerge from the life of the social and democratic national process, as it appears, for instance, in John Dewey's thought.[63] Sidney E. Mead clearly identified the first strand and a mixture of the other two when he wrote that "the United States, in effect, had two religions, or at least two different forms of the same religion, and that the prevailing Protestant ideology represented a syncretistic mingling of the two. The first was the religion of the denominations.... The second was the religion of the democratic society and nation." That second religion was for him "articulated in terms of the destiny of America, under God, to be fulfilled by perfecting the democratic way of life for the example and betterment of all mankind."[64] All three strands are truly American, and all three belong in the experiment. The emerging picture is a kaleidoscopic one in which transcendent values and human processes merge in a unique American way. The conclusion then is that rather than a strict civil religion, whose ambiguity, dangers, and pitfalls are obvious, there is a particular, albeit not univocal, way in which religion,[65] philosophy, and Enlightenment culture have played a public role in the life of the nation. In Marty's words, all of them have claimed their right to be present at the "Republican Banquet."[66]

Another set of questions is related not to whether or not religion belongs in the public realm but, more radically, to whether the public realm itself has not all but vanished in a society dominated by technical rationality. Already in 1927, Dewey discussed the issue in a most interesting way, asking, among other things, "Is not the problem at the present time that of securing experts to manage administrative matters, other than the framing of policies?" and affirming thereupon that "It may be urged that the present confusion and apathy are due to the fact that the real energy of society is now directed in all nonpolitical matters by trained specialists who manage things, while politics are carried on with a machinery and ideas formed in the past to deal with quite another kind of situation."[67] Briefly, if reason has become purely instrumental, then technocratic problem-solving has taken over moral-practical reasoning, and the public realm has been reduced to a simply technical domain. Questions about principles, ends, and values have been, therefore, pushed to the private sphere. The retrieval of the public realm is, hence, linked to the recovery of practical reason. Within this set of questions concerning the nature and problems of public reason and public realm, Tracy's work can be understood as an ongoing task exploring how to understand and interpret traditions and, more precisely, how those traditions, and his own Catholic tradition in particular, relate to the questions that are or should be debated in the public realm.

Tracy's work is also directly related to another set of questions, namely, those concerning the public nature of theology. The questions in discussion are whether there can be a public theology and how a public theology can make a religion-originated claim shareable by people who do not partake in the religious faith and tradition from which the claim stems. The term "public theology" is by no means univocal, and, therefore, it is open to different interpretations. In chapter 2, it was described "as the effort across many denominations to formulate a theology that justifies its claims so as to make them publicly shareable and therefore relevant for the public realm." By calling it an effort, two points were stressed. On the one hand, it was emphasized that "public theology" is an ongoing enterprise rather than a finished product, although some specific formulations of it already exist. On the other hand, the term "effort" suggested that "public theology" refers more to a methodological stand in doing theology than to a concrete theology, such as political theology and liberation theology. Marty, to whom Robert W. McElroy attributes the coinage of the term "public theology,"[68] has a far more concrete understanding of "public theology." He uses that term in relation to "the work of various figures who have interpreted the nation's religious experience, practice, and behavior in the light of some sort of transcendent reference." For him, the classic public theologian of the twentieth century is Reinhold Niebuhr.[69] According to McElroy, the term "public theology" "has come to apply to an effort by non-Evangelical Christian theologians to steer a course between the fundamentalist approach to social reconstruction and the secular notion that spiritual values should not influence public policy or the constitution of society."[70]

Three positions can be distinguished on the U.S. scene. The first position is related to the political activism of fundamentalists and radical evangelicals in recent times. According to most authors, this activism has substituted purely political advancing of its views for the discussion and defense of those views in the public arena.[71] Underlying that first position is the belief that entering the arena of public discourse entails accepting the epistemological and ideological tenets of liberalism and that, consequently, such a move would involve the negation of what is being defended, namely, that private morality must be also public and that the only foundation of both morality and society in the United States is the Bible.

A second position, somewhat based on MacIntyre, emphasizes the importance of tradition, and more concretely of Christianity, in order to build up a social and moral order; opposes the liberal-secular discourse as both barren and prejudiced against tradition and religion; opposes also the fundamentalist approach on both theological and civil grounds; and involves different opinions concerning the extent and nature of theology's engagement in public discourse.[72]

The third position, in which Tracy can be placed, has a more positive, although not uncritical, appraisal of the Enlightenment, and it clearly favors the engagement of theology in the public realm. A central tenet of those favoring this position is the acknowledgment of the importance of particular traditions, while at the same time affirming the possibility of making public claims from tradition, based on publicly shareable arguments and dialogue. However, also within this group opinions differ in their criticisms of the Enlightenment, in their views of reason, and in the theological understanding of the Christian tradition. John Courtney Murray is a clear example of this third position from a Catholic perspective. More generally, the social teaching of the Catholic Church has consistently defended the publicness of Christian moral claims on the basis of its understanding of natural law and its belief that human reason, although fallen, is not totally perverted. From a different perspective, Reinhold Niebuhr represents a public theologian with an Augustinian anthropology.[73]

Catholicism and the Public Realm in the United States

It is a common opinion among church historians that the history of the Catholic Church in the United States has been marked by the attempt both to keep its Catholic identity and to be loyal to the American experiment.[74] This attempt continues to define, to some extent, the relationship between the Catholic Church and the nation, and the tensions involved thereby have been and continue to be an indication of the truly innovative character of what can be termed as the Catholic experiment in the United States.[75] It is important to examine some of the difficulties that made the life of the Catholic Church in the United States an experiment. The first was the Protestant character of the nation.[76] The important point in regard to Catholicism, something different authors almost unanimously hold, is not that Catholics were a minority but rather that the new nation had a Protestant character. How to be both a Catholic and a member of a nation with a character forged by those who were fierce enemies back in Europe was a challenge to Catholicism that compelled the Catholic Church to experiment beyond the obvious boundaries of its doctrinal strictures.

The second difficulty that fueled the experiment was the combination of the spiritual allegiance to Rome with the civil allegiance to the democratic principles of the American experiment. For most of their history in the United States, Catholics have been suspected of being "papist." The fact that they proclaimed their spiritual allegiance to the pope was interpreted by many Protestants as a severe limitation of Catholics' loyalty to the country and of their patriotism. Those who attacked Catholics on that score held that in case of conflict between the two recipients of this dual allegiance, Catholics would disregard their Americanness and would follow the dictates of Rome. Although Catholics were politically involved at all levels, the depth of the prejudice concerning the limits of their patriotism surfaced on the two occasions a Catholic candidate was a party nominee to contend for the presidency of the nation. In the first case, Alfred E. Smith, New York's governor for four terms, had to face, besides the normal criticism to which every candidate is exposed, intense opposition based on pure prejudice against his being Catholic, before being defeated in the election of 1928.[77] John F. Kennedy's election in 1960 has been normally interpreted as the sign of Catholics' full sharing in the life of the nation. Religion again became a major issue in Kennedy's campaign, and the candidate met the fears raised by his detractors, who doubted his patriotism in case conflict between the interest of the nation and the criteria of the Catholic hierarchy should arise, by firmly stating, "I do not accept the right of any ecclesiastical official to tell me what to do in the sphere of my public responsibility as an elected official."[78]

A third hindrance that compelled the Catholic Church to experiment was the tension between the democratic character of the American experiment and the hierarchical character of the Catholic Church. In U.S. society at large, that hierarchical character has being perceived as a clear sign of authoritarianism. As a result, public opinion has tended to view Catholics in general as authoritarian, dogmatic, and antidemocratic. The accusation often directed at Catholics at different points in the history of the country is that they want to control the nation and make everybody act as a Catholic, regardless of the different opinions of the citizens. In other terms, in regard to the discussion about the public role of the Roman Catholic Church in the United States, its detractors have historically contended that the Catholic Church lacks the willingness to be truly and sincerely public and to accept the pluralism that characterizes the country. Although those detractors were always a minority, often seen as bigots by most citizens, the main consequence of their actions was to create a powerful and lasting anti-Catholic image in the public mind.[79]

Finally, the tension between the principle of religious freedom enshrined in the U.S. Constitution, on the one hand, and the traditional Catholic tenet, until Vatican II, of there being no legitimate religious option but Catholicism, on the other hand, has also compelled the Catholic Church to experiment. Also on this score the situation in Europe was very different. Rather than religious freedom, Europeans had a bloody tradition of religious wars and of religious persecutions. Although the French Revolution introduced the principle of religious freedom in the French Constitution, the real situation during the revolutionary period was one of fierce confrontation between church and state and of religious persecution, even, in the end, against the followers of the constitutional church of L'abbé Gregoire. The situation of the Catholic Church in Europe, therefore, after the religious wars and the trauma of the French Revolution, was either one of establishment (Italy, Spain, Austria) or one of persecuted resistance (England, Scandinavia), according to the current political status of each country. In the case of those countries divided by the religious wars, the final peace did not bring in religious pluralism but delimitation of religious borders within the country (Germany, Switzerland). In the ideological realm, the Catholic Church opposed the ideas of the Enlightenment concerning religious freedom until Vatican II.[80] On the contrary, the United States was created as an experiment based on the liberal ideas of the Enlightenment. Freedom, democracy, disestablishment of the church, grass rootism at all levels, and economic liberalism have been the natural traits of the experiment. In turn, the Catholic Church at its highest level opposed the Enlightenment, supported absolute monarchies, denied the principle of religious freedom, defended church establishment, proclaimed the infallibility of the pope, and condemned modernism. Naturally, these moves did not benefit the image of U.S. Catholics and caused continuous suspicion about their capability to embrace the democratic character of the nation.

In that sense, the pontificates of Gregory XVI (1831–46), Pius IX (1846–78), and Pius X (1903–14) dealt a severe blow to the efforts of U.S. Catholics to show their fellow citizens their utter acceptance of the American experiment. Their encyclicals *Mirari Vos* (1832), *Quanta Cura* (1864), and *Pascendi Dominici Gregis* (1907) opposed religious freedom, separation of church and state, liberty of conscience, and, in general, most of the basic tenets held dear in the United States.[81] Leo XIII (1878–1903) and Pius XI (1922–39) confronted the challenges of modernity in a far more positive way. Rather than just condemning modernism in a purely defensive manner, both adopted a more analytical and descriptive approach in regard to the new realities of the times and retrieved the Thomistic tradition as a device that, while allowing them to value human reason and nature in general, established a relation between them and the order of grace. Especially important for the Catholic Church in the United States were their social encyclicals *Rerum Novarum* (1891) and *Quadragesimo Anno* (1931).[82] The positive influence of these popes on the U.S. Catholic Church and on establishing a progressive social policy in the nation has been amply acknowledged. In particular, the work of John Ryan was crucial in translating the social thought of the popes into the U.S. situation and in applying it to the particular circumstances of the country.[83]

It could be said that when the U.S. bishops launched their Program of Social Reconstruction in 1919,[84] just after World War I, a new era was inaugurated that powerfully changed the image of the Catholic Church in the country. From then on, the Catholic Church was perceived as a progressive body in social matters, despite its doctrinal conservatism. Thus, the Catholic Church fully backed the welfare programs of Roosevelt in the 1930s and 1940s and adopted Keynesianism as its central economic theory. As Jay P. Dolan points out, what Leo XIII gave the U.S. Catholic Church was a set of principles around which a full doctrine was articulated to defend the position of workers, to empower the poor, and to offer alternatives to the domineering laissez-faire capitalism of the late nineteenth century and the early twentieth century. Such a move was a big step toward making the Catholic Church a public religion.[85]

The novelty of "public Catholicism" was that it elaborated a doctrine that, based on the Catholic tradition, gave the church a tool to analyze and to judge the social processes that were taking place in the country and offered elements of public reasoning that could be shared and discussed by non-Catholics. In this sense, it inaugurated a tradition of public thought in the U.S. Catholic Church that runs through the work of Murray and is apparent in the major pastoral letters issued by the bishops over the last decades. Under these endeavors the Catholic Church is trying to develop a church identity that, following in the steps of the republican tradition and of a more biblical understanding of religion, defines and expresses its Catholicity in ways that, once again, want to be both religiously relevant within the Catholic tradition and unambiguously American. It would be naive to think that because Catholics are already full U.S. citizens, all problems concerning Catholicism in the country are solved. If anything, social and cultural equal footing with mainstream citizens poses the problem of discovering what Catholic identity means in such a situation and how Catholics can contribute to U.S. society on the basis of their tradition. Such a task has been and continues to be all the more pressing in view of the process that the nation has had to face in order to rethink itself in the wake of the crisis of the 1960s.[86]

Before Vatican II, three main lines can be identified in building a Catholic public discourse and action in the United States, according to David O'Brien. One follows the dialogical republican tradition; a second one is a reflection of the institutional church and of the grassroots practice of the immigrant period; and the third follows a more radical interpretation of Christianity on a biblical basis, placing the emphasis on uncompromising discipleship with a social commitment to transform sinful personal and communal realities. He identifies these three styles of public Catholicism as republican (Murray), immigrant (Catholic mobilization in political matters), and evangelical (Dorothy Day, Thomas Merton).[87] The last one, according to Joseph P. Chinnici, was born in the generation before Vatican II and planted in the United States the seeds of most of the changes that, at the liturgical, ecclesiological, theological, and spiritual levels, the council introduced in the life of the church and in the understanding of Christianity. The forerunners, according to Chinnici, sought, each one in a different way but all of them focusing on the transformation of the person in Christ, to bridge the gap between nature and grace, faith and reason, structure and spirit, Catholicity and Americanness, church and society, action and contemplation, and hierarchy and laity.[88]

The public character of Catholic theologians has increased dramatically since Vatican II. Two models of public theology have come to the fore: the republican and the prophetic. The republican, in the tradition of Ryan, was represented by John Courtney Murray at the time of the council and has been lately retrieved and developed, certainly not in a mimetic but in a critical way, by David Hollenbach and also, to some extent, by John Coleman. The prophetic has been exemplified by the work of Matthew Lamb, by the German-Canadian Gregory Baum, and, in a different direction, by the Catholic feminist theologians Rosemary Radford Ruether and Elisabeth Schüssler Fiorenza, among others. The republican model seeks a dialogue between the Catholic tradition and U.S. society; accepts, although not uncritically, the framework of the American experiment and of Vatican II; uses mainly modes of discourse that can be publicly shared; and is addressed both to the Catholic community and to society at large. The prophetic model challenges the existing framework both in the Catholic Church and in U.S. society, criticizes both church and society on the basis of a radical-biblical interpretation of the Catholic tradition and of a critical social theory, emphasizes the Christian-identity pole in its dialogue with society, and seeks the transformation of both church and society.[89]

David Tracy and Catholic Public Theology in the United States

For myself...there is no more central demand for theology than its demand for publicness.   —DAVID TRACY

Tracy's work represents an original contribution to the ongoing task of formulating a dialogical theology that is loyally rooted in its own Catholic tradition and that, at the same time, relates to the wider society. There are several elements that justify calling his contribution original. To begin with, Tracy's theological foundations are intrinsically linked to the relatively recent Catholic project that seeks to respond to the challenge of modernity while, at the same time, retrieving the best of premodern theology in the process. Tracy experienced firsthand how one of the figures that has influenced him most, Bernard Lonergan, wrestled through the difficulties of that crucial passage from premodernity to modernity until he finally arrived at the formulation of a new way of doing theology.[90]

Provided with the transcendental foundations he inherited from Lonergan, Tracy himself formulated his own theological project. There are certain foundational elements of the project that have remained, albeit not completely unchanged, throughout the years. Besides the ultimate recourse to transcendental thinking, Tracy has been seeking from the beginning to come up with a theological formulation of Christianity that, while being faithful to scripture and tradition, could make sense to the contemporary mind and, furthermore, could also claim validity in the realm of public discourse. Thus his constant endeavor to formulate a theological method suitable to that end and his emphasis on critical correlation.

Also a permanent trait of Tracy's project is his search for a global view, both in theological and in cultural terms. Theologically, Tracy's aim is to conceive and develop an inner coherent theology capable of embracing the three basic theological steps: the fundamental, the systematic, and the practical. But, as he learned from Lonergan, Rahner, and others, such a theological enterprise has to be for him intrinsically linked to the very way human beings think about and envision themselves; that is to say, it has to be aware of the different interpretive disciplines or modes of thought and expression claiming validity in the wider cultural context, such as science, philosophy, and art. For Tracy, a public theology deserves such an appellation only when it is capable of taking into account and of responding to the different claims concerning directly or indirectly the sort of questions with which theology deals. In fact, that has led Tracy to establish an ongoing dialogue with the competing philosophical and metascientific theories that come from modernity, critical modernity, and postmodernity.

In developing his own theology, hermeneutics has played a crucial role in Tracy's case from the beginning, precisely because the core of the Lonerganian enterprise is clearly hermeneutic.[91] But, throughout the years, not only has Tracy's enterprise become increasingly hermeneutic, but the hermeneutical tool itself has been progressively sharpened, both theoretically and critically, thus making hermeneutics a refined and self-conscious centerpiece of his whole project. He has come to understand the hermeneutical task in quite different terms from Lonergan. Roughly speaking, whereas Lonergan uses "psychologizing hermeneutics," Tracy disclaims it and uses "objective hermeneutics" as defined by Ricoeur's interpretation theory.[92]

Other elements, however, have receded more and more into the background. One of these elements is method itself, about which Tracy says he has "spent a great deal of time (perhaps too much)."[93] Method has decreased in importance not only because, in the last analysis, there is no suitable method unless there is a substantive theology that uses it but also, more radically, because Tracy has become increasingly aware of the limitations of modern theology, of which method is but a part. That means that Tracy has been able to realize the limitations of the theological turn to modernity, whether such a turn comes from Whitehead, from Rahner, from Lonergan, or, more recently, from Schubert Ogden or from Hans Küng. Furthermore, Tracy has become almost convinced that modernity, whether theological or philosophical (as in the case of Habermas, for instance), has to be rescued through a dramatic widening of scope that does away with its stricture, arguing that "there are good reasons to understand our period and our needs as more postmodern than modern."[94]

Correlatively, a notion of reason that is not only suspicious but also decentered has gained substantial ground over the last years in Tracy's work. And that, in turn, has decentered, but not derailed, his program. Crucial in this recent development has been his dialogue with postmodernity and his realization that a public theology in a time that cannot name itself has to go back to its own tradition. Theology can retrieve from tradition symbolic modes of naming God and reality, like the mystical-prophetic, that, by using patterns of thought totally neglected and marginalized by logical and methodical modernity, have a shocking and liberating disclosive power. For Tracy, "Modernity's pervasive lack of interest in traditional forms for naming God and thinking God has become an unacknowledged part of the present malaise of modern theologies and philosophies of religion."[95] In other words, it could be said that Tracy is foundationally a Thomist[96] who, in order to find an alternative to the powerlessness of a modernity that has reached its limits, is trying to retrieve other paradigms that, although overcome in a sense by Aquinas's paradigm shift from *lectio* to *quaestio*, entail nevertheless modes of understanding reality, and therefore of naming God, potentially more disclosive than Aquinas's mode of thought. Tracy is becoming more and more convinced of the insufficiency, despite its indispensability, of the Aristotelian-Thomistic-modern paradigm in order to get to the heart of reality, including in it human beings and, most of all, God. Therefore, he is exploring new ways, trying, for instance, to retrieve hermeneutically Plato's evolution from mythology to critical reason, and then from self-critical reason to rediscovered and reinterpreted mythology (*Timaeus*), or interpreting the sublime Johannine mode of naming God, bearing in mind Mark's tragic rendering of the passion. In short, the critical enterprise is necessary but not sufficient to disclose the nature of reality. However, Tracy seeks not a pre-modernity comeback but an overcoming of the strictures and blind alleys of modernity, while keeping its critical-emancipatory potential.

Tracy's theological evolution can be clearly traced through his main works. *The Achievement of Bernard Lonergan* shows Tracy's modern and critical appropriation of his own Catholic tradition. *Blessed Rage for Order* marks the intensification of the modern-theology moment in Tracy's theology. *The Analogical Imagination* signals a first enrichment and questioning of that modern moment brought about by the use of a hermeneutics that includes a critical-dialectical moment within itself. *Plurality and Ambiguity* marks the intensification of that questioning through a critical and constructive discussion of the radical, all-encompassing, decentering stance of postmodernity. Finally, his current work on God, still in process and exemplified in his books *Dialogue with the Other* and *On Naming the Present*, indicates his attempt to name that most crucial theological category, God, using a decentered, yet ultimately substantive, strategy. The rest of this chapter will be a more detailed analysis of what has been briefly sketched here.[97]

Lonergan: From Conceptualism to Method

Tracy's mind or thinking framework was, to a great extent, wrought in Lonergan's forge, as a consequence both of the latter's original retrieval of Aquinas and of his subsequent confrontation with modernity and with the rise of a culture in which science and human action in history play a central role.[98] The parallelism between Lonergan and Rahner is noteworthy. Both Rahner and Lonergan sought a way out of the barrenness of neo-scholasticism by going back to the sources, namely, to the works of Aquinas. Moreover, in taking up the Kantian challenge, both of them followed the path of transcendental Thomism developed by Maréchal, and, for both, "the turn to the subject" was a crucial move. Finally, they realized that "historical consciousness" and the emergence of pluralism were central traits in the contemporary situation, and they tried to respond to them. Something especially worth noting is that both authors reinterpret and revive theology on the basis of their rescuing metaphysics from the Kantian challenge and, particularly in Rahner's case, from the Heideggerian assault on the possibility of the metaphysical enterprise. Their foundational works, Rahner's *Geist in Welt* and Lonergan's *Insight*, are precisely characterized by a retrieval of being, or a positing of being, through the transcendental structure of knowing. Both end up "proving" the existence of God as the ultimate condition of possibility of the knower. However, both authors evolved from the foundational "cold" of their philosophical work to the "warmer" and more complex world of history and human existence, where meaning and existential responsibility come to the foreground.[99]

The differences between the two authors are also important. Briefly put, Rahner's enterprise, although methodologically based on "the turn to the subject," centered around theologically substantive matters and resulted in the emergence of a new theological paradigm. At the heart of that paradigm lay a reinterpretation of the mystery of a self-communicating yet incomprehensible God and the correlative theological notion of the supernatural existential. In the case of Lonergan, although his work on theologically substantive matters is significant, his major contribution lies "in the reflective attitude and structural forms which ground all his individual achievements."[100] In other words, Lonergan's main achievement is of a formal-methodological nature and concerns the unveiling of the structural framework that underlies, in general, every thinking operation and, in particular, the theological enterprise. Michael O'Callaghan has expressed in a very succinct manner the main difference between Lonergan and Rahner when he writes that "Rahner is a theologian concerned with working out the general and special categories of foundational theology. Lonergan is a methodologist concerned with how these categories are to be worked out."[101]

This tension between Rahner and Lonergan, or, in other words, between substantive theological thought and theological method, is very apparent throughout Tracy's whole career. Having initially concerned himself mainly with methodological issues, trying to go beyond Lonergan, Tracy has increasingly realized the importance of actually discussing the central questions of Christian theology. Consequently, his two main works over the last two decades witness to his attempt to strike a balance between the effort to envision an adequate theological method and the actual discussion of theological issues on the basis of the method he proposes.[102] Besides, from the point of view of substantive theology, Rahner is the central referential point for Tracy.[103]

In *The Achievement of Bernard Lonergan*, Tracy bases his whole description of Lonergan's work in terms of the latter's own change of horizon: from the conceptualist horizon of the schools to the horizon of Aquinas; from the latter to the modern, critical horizon; and from there to the contemporary horizon of historical consciousness.[104] Lonergan's retrieval of Thomas Aquinas went as far as to dissect some central pieces of Aquinas's edifice to find out the very nature, or formal foundations, of that edifice. What Lonergan found at the bottom of his analytical investigation was, in Tracy's view, that Aquinas's speculative theology had an intellectualist and scientific character; that is to say, Lonergan found out that Aquinas's main goal was to analyze and to understand coherently and critically the subject matter of each of the questions he studied, applying to that end the limited power of the intellect. This, in turn, allowed Aquinas to be truly creative in his theological work.[105] Lonergan's discovery of Aquinas's intellectualist and explanatory theo-logy[106] centered his whole work around the act of understanding and allowed him to follow his own route.[107]

Lonergan's second step was to take up the challenges of the empirical scientific revolution and of the Kantian critique of knowledge, moving from the medieval to the modern horizon.[108] In so doing, his previous retrieval of Aquinas was paramount because what Lonergan gained from it was not mainly a set of doctrines on specific issues but rather an interpretation of how Aquinas understood the operation of understanding. That interpretation, in turn, enabled Lonergan to go materially beyond Aquinas precisely by remaining formally attached to him.[109]

Lonergan's main work concerning this second step is *Insight*.[110] Both the scope and the goal of the book are truly ambitious. *Insight* is an attempt to unveil the structure of the process of knowing as such, based on a thorough analysis of the various modes of knowing: common sense, empirical science, mathematics, philosophy, and, ultimately, theology. Thus, Lonergan sought to get at a bedrock that would allow him "to cast into the unity of a single perspective" the viewpoints of Plato, Aristotle, Aquinas, Descartes, Kant, and Maréchal.[111] Lonergan, like Rahner, Coreth, and, in general, all Catholic thinkers who follow, albeit neither uniformly nor uncritically, Maréchal, finds the ultimate foundation of knowledge, its very condition of possibility, in the transcendental nature of knowing disclosed in the self-affirmation of the knower. For Lonergan, as for Rahner and Coreth, God is, finally, that condition of possibility for transcendental thinking.[112]

If *Insight* represents Lonergan's response to the problems raised by critical modernity, his later work, especially *Method in Theology*, marks the third and last step in his career, which is his response to the questions of the contemporary age, namely, historical consciousness and the plurality of contexts, meanings, and interpretations. This response involves a shift "from the medieval achievement of 'reason illuminated by faith,' to the contemporary achievement of 'method illuminated by faith.'"[113] At the basis of this shift to theological method lies, therefore, what Lonergan calls a cultural shift, from the universal and permanent classicist culture to the changing empirical culture.[114] Ultimately, Lonergan's ambition is to devise a method for theology that, formally at least, is not other than *the* method. To that purpose, Lonergan translates the transcendental method into the field of theology. That translation involves categorizing the basic interrelated operations that constitute the invariant structure of knowing, namely, experiencing, understanding, judging, and deciding, through the definition of interrelated theological tasks that correspond to those basic operations. Most of *Method in Theology* consists of giving an explanatory account of those theological tasks. There are eight of these tasks or functional specialties. Tracy divides them into two blocks, namely, mediating theology ("an attempt to encounter the Judaeo-Christian past in its multidimensional, genetic-dialectic development") and mediated theology ("one's own attempt to speak to the present and the impending future from within a basic theological horizon"). To the first block belong research (experiencing), interpretation (understanding), history (judging), dialectic (deciding), whereas the second is integrated, in a converse direction, by foundations (deciding), doctrines (judging), systematics (understanding), and communications (experiencing).[115]

For Lonergan, "the objectification of the normative pattern of our conscious and intentional operations does not admit revision" because it is the very rock, that is to say, the foundation that, given its transcendental character, is the condition of possibility of its own revision. This rock "is the subject in his conscious, unobjectified attentiveness, intelligence, reasonableness, responsibility." Therefore, problems concerning his theological method can only arise from an inadequate categorization of that pattern for theological purposes. In other words, the degree of correctness of the method depends on the varying degree of adequacy of each functional specialty to perform in the field of theology the function that its corresponding foundational-transcendental operation performs in the act of knowing as such.[116]

If Metz characterizes Rahner's theology as a biographical theology, that is, as a theology that unites dogmatics with experience, the same could be said of Lonergan's theology, although bearing in mind the differences between the two authors analyzed above. Indeed, the theological method proposed by Lonergan is not mainly the result of a cold rational analysis (although stringent analysis is an important part of it) but the objectification of Lonergan's own intellectual itinerary. Hence, his methodology is, ultimately, his biography. At the core of that biography lies the endeavor to appropriate in a creative way the theological heritage of Aquinas in order to redefine the theological task, thus overcoming the self-defeating scholastic theology reigning in Catholicism in Lonergan's time. This step marks Lonergan's passage from the undifferentiated consciousness of common sense to the differentiated consciousness of theory. What ultimately emerges from that mediating theology, including exposing Aquinas to the challenges of modernity, is a process of self-appropriation through which Lonergan realizes the transcendental structure of understanding, judging, and deciding.

That signals Lonergan's passage from the world of theory to the realm of self-interiorness. As a result, he formulates and adopts the transcendental precepts (Be attentive, Be intelligent, Be reasonable, and Be responsible), finally accepting the need for an ongoing process of intellectual, moral, and religious conversion. That takes him from interiorness to transcendence. At that point, a new transcendental precept is added to the others: Be loving.

It is precisely on the basis of this whole process of self-appropriation involved in the creative and dialectically critical retrieval of the heritage that he takes up the second task of theology, namely, the formulation of a theology, although from a formal or methodological perspective, that responds to the challenges of historical consciousness and of the plurality of meanings of the new culture. Since reflection on that personal itinerary of conversion-effecting self-appropriation is the basis of the theological method Lonergan proposes, that method, and hence Lonergan's theological contribution, can be justly called, like Rahner's, biographical. In that sense, a parallelism, albeit not identity, exists between Lonergan's itinerary from common sense to transcendence, through theory and interiorness,[117] and Rahner's own process of self-appropriation that, starting from an undifferentiated original experience, advances through the stages of the transcendental-metaphysical and the existential-historical and reaches the mystical-transcendent level.

Lonergan's influence on Tracy's work is foundational. Perhaps the most crucial trait of that influence is that, through Lonergan, Tracy had a firsthand experience of how the Catholic passage from premodernity to critical modernity could be theologically achieved and what that achievement involves. The distance between the pre-retrieval-of-Aquinas Lonergan and the Lonergan of *Method in Theology* is, in terms both of horizon and of theological development, the distance between a Catholicism anchored in a defensive neo-scholasticism as a response to the crises of the Reformation and modernity and a Catholicism able to respond creatively to the challenges of critical modernity. More concretely, through Lonergan, Tracy understood how tradition can be retrieved and revived. He also realized that theology had to be rethought anew if it was going to play a role in a society with competing and conflicting worldviews, in which Christianity in general and Catholic tradition in particular had been, to say the least, called into question.

Tracy inherited from Lonergan three main tools. First, the understanding of theology as a creative effort to express the symbols and doctrines of Christian faith in a reasonable way, whether by means of "faith aided by reason," or of "faith aided by method," or, in a more Tracian way, of a correlation between the Christian message, on the one hand, and common human experience and language, on the other hand. Second, transcendental metaphysics as the ground for religion and theology. Third, transcendental precepts as the ground of the theologian both for critically interpreting the tradition(s) and for formulating a constructive theology appropriate for the new cultural context. With these tools, Tracy turned to the formulation of his own theological project through a critical appropriation of Lonergan.

A Revisionist Theology

In very general terms, Tracy's critique of Lonergan is projective in that it is based on the requirements stemming from Lonergan's own enterprise. In other words, Tracy's basic critique of Lonergan is that the latter does not go as far as the implications and the projection of his own basic positions demand.[118] The central problem, in Tracy's opinion, is that Lonergan does not critically, but only dogmatically, support religious and Christian claims.[119] In other words, the functional specialty "foundations" is just another functional specialty within a theological enterprise that presupposes Christianity instead of being the foundation of religious and Christian claims and, therefore, of theology.[120]

That primary grounding of religious and theological claims he sees lacking in Lonergan is the point at which Tracy initiates his own theological enterprise. His conviction that Lonergan's "foundations" need to be reformulated leads him finally to develop his own fundamental or foundational theology in his work *Blessed Rage for Order*. At the center of Tracy's disagreement with Lonergan lies Tracy's own different existential and intellectual context. In Lonergan's case, the central triggering question had been the crisis of neo-scholasticism and the need for overcoming a conceptualist theology self-entrenched behind its own tautologies. Lonergan stretched his work up to the point of dealing with the contemporary phenomenon of historical consciousness by taking a further step from cognitional theory to methodology. For Tracy, however, the crisis brought about by historical consciousness is the triggering question. He takes Lonergan's methodological turn for granted, and, within it, he demands a critical justification of religious and theological claims. His perception of the crisis of cognitive religious claims is so acute that, in his opinion, Lonergan's foundation of religious claims is not enough because it does not take sufficiently into account the full nature of the crisis. Tracy's view of the context at the beginning of the 1970s points out the crisis of religious cognitive claims ushered in by the process of secularization in Western culture, the radical theological problematization of religious and Christian claims expressed by the theology of "the death of God," the crisis of a too naive Enlightenment unveiled by the "masters of suspicion," and the plurality of claims concerning worldviews in general and religious and Christian views in particular.[121] The obvious question then, *the* question for Tracy, is how to ground "the truth-value of the claims to ultimacy of religious and explicitly theological language."[122]

On the question of which concrete factors influenced Tracy's critique of, and distance from, Lonergan, a comparative analysis with Metz and Gutiérrez can be enlightening. In the case of Metz, this work argues that, apart from his personal traumatic experiences during World War II, his widening horizon as a result of his friendship with Bloch and of his acquaintance with the work of Adorno, Horkheimer, and Benjamin gave him a new view of history and society. It is precisely this new view that made him take a critical step away from Rahner, prompting him to affirm that the transcendental solution was insufficient because it immediately jumped into "the final," thus bypassing the tensions, ambiguities, and contradictions at work in history. Therefore, he moved to the formulation of a political, historically aware, theology. Gutiérrez, in turn, took a reinterpretive distance from the European *nouvelle théologie* as a result of his experience of the social, cultural, religious, and political problems of his people, his acquaintance with Marxism and dependency theory, and his appropriation of the Peruvian thinkers Mariátegui, Vallejo, and Arguedas. That led him to reinterpret both history and the theological sources in a liberation key.

In the case of Tracy, the critical distance from Lonergan is mediated by a widening of his intellectual horizon as a result of his exposure to several influential thinkers and currents. The critical radicalization of the late 1960s manifested itself in the Anglo-American theological realm through the "death-of-God theology," that is, the theological appropriation of the apotheosis of secularization that, supposedly doing away with God and theology, obliged the theologian to come to terms with the tension between the autonomy and the heteronomy of the self vis-à-vis God. Process theology offered Tracy a critique of classical theology and an exemplary model of a modern theological paradigm. Paul Tillich showed Tracy both the need to incorporate a phenomenological analysis of the human situation into the theological task and, more important, the main way to do theology in the era of historical consciousness, namely, the correlation between human situation and Christian message. Moreover, Tracy learned from Tillich how to use Lonergan's notion of self-transcendence to get out of the dilemma of autonomy-heteronomy. Mircea Eliade made Tracy aware of the religious-sacred invariant structure of the human being through his phenomenological-comparative analysis of the systems of symbolic representation-reenactment that appear in a historical exploration of religions. Finally, and crucially, Ricoeur gave Tracy a systematization of the importance and power of symbol as disclosive of reality and of its relation to thought and put Tracy on the hermeneutical path, lending him a tool to retrieve "the Christian fact" critically.

It is on those complex bases that he takes a distance from what he thinks is Lonergan's dogmatic grounding of theology, excessive dependency on classical categories, insufficient consideration of the meaning of symbol, and lack of ability to integrate the phenomenological into the transcendental. On those bases, too, he launches his own phenomenological-hermeneutical-transcendental theological project. Lest it be thought that the critical distance they took severed the links of Metz, Gutiérrez, and Tracy with their basic reference (Rahner, *nouvelle théologie*, and Lonergan, respectively), it must be stressed that the three of them have developed their own works in a tensional ongoing relation to those basic references.

Tracy takes from Lonergan the focus on methodology as necessary to the theological task in the age of historical consciousness but seeks to remedy the insufficiency of the move by placing the emphasis on the grounding of religious, theological, and Christian claims within that task. Lonergan's shift from interiorness to historical consciousness makes methodology a necessary but not sufficient condition for the theological task. Since historical consciousness brings about a radical questioning of religious and theological claims in general, and of Christian claims in particular, such claims must be grounded anew from within the new historical situation, that is to say, bearing in mind, and responding to, the challenges posed by the crisis of authority, the relativization of all claims as purely historical, the reinterpretation of the sources as time-conditioned, and the new awareness of the subject as responsible for conducting history. Therefore, fundamental theology takes center stage.[123] Whereas for Lonergan the theological method centered around how to appropriate the Christian tradition and how to restate it in a manner that suits the contemporary context, Tracy seeks a model of theology capable of taking into account all the problems that historical consciousness poses to theology, making the analysis and elucidation of those problems an intrinsic task of the theological enterprise.[124]

Tracy calls that model for contemporary theology a revisionist model of critical correlation.[125] Tracy shows how theology has tried to respond to the crisis of modernity and of critical modernity through five theological models: the orthodox, which disregarded modern claims and was the favorite model of Catholic theology until the 1950s; the liberal, best represented by Schleiermacher, which embraced modern claims and tried to reformulate both the method and the symbols of Christian faith within the new context; the neo-orthodox, represented by Barth in its radical version but also by Tillich, the Niebuhrs, and Rahner, and interpreted by Tracy as a critical moment "in the larger liberal theological tradition"; the radical, which, as illustrated by the theology of the "death of God," represents the acceptance by theology of autonomous secularity; and the revisionist model, best represented by process theology but also practiced by Gregory Baum, Langdon Gilkey, and others. The last model tries to build upon the experience of the previous four and understands the central task of contemporary Christian theology to be "the dramatic confrontation, the mutual illuminations and corrections, the possible basic reconciliation between the principal values, cognitive claims, and existential faiths of both a reinterpreted postmodern consciousness and a reinterpreted Christianity."[126] According to Tracy, the revisionist model cannot seek easy solutions that disregard the permanent achievements of the four previous models but must steer its own way, bearing in mind the results the mutual corrections of the other four models yield.[127]

Tracy gives an extended explanation for choosing the term "revisionist." He argues that there are both historical and systematic reasons for doing so.[128] In any event, it is clear that such a denomination stems from the fact that both dogmatic religious belief and dogmatic secular belief have been shaken to their very foundations and proven insufficient in the contemporary situation.[129] Therefore, and taking into account that the previous theological models used to respond to such a situation have all run into trouble despite their relative value, he seeks to develop a new, revisionist model that takes into account the need of being critical as regards both faith and the secular mind. Consequently, Tracy argues that "for the revisionist model for theology, the self-referent is a subject committed at once to a contemporary revisionist notion of the beliefs, values, and faith of an authentic secularity and to a revisionist understanding of the beliefs, values, and faith of an authentic Christianity," thus "challenging both the more usual self-understanding of secularity (viz., a nontheistic and anti-Christian secularism) and the more usual self-understanding of Christianity (viz., as an anti-secular, religious supernaturalism)."[130]

Tracy's main goal is firmly to ground religious and theological claims, overcoming every sort of extrincism or dogmatism. Therefore, his model seeks to establish, first of all, an inner relationship between the two principal sources for theology, namely, Christian texts, on the one hand, and common human experience and language, on the other hand.[131] The obvious question concerning Tracy's term "Christian texts" is whether those texts include only the scriptural or also the texts produced throughout Christian history, usually called tradition. This question has historically opposed Protestant and Roman Catholic theologies. Assuming that there exists a general consensus among Christian confessions in accepting the need for both scripture and tradition, Tracy affirms "that the scriptures remain the fundamental although not exclusive expression of that Christian faith."[132]

Concerning the second source, whereas Tillich distinguishes between the sources of theology and the medium through which the theologian appropriates them, namely, experience, Tracy, who disagrees with that distinction, makes common human experience and language one of the sources of theology.[133] Tracy has a broad understanding of experience that includes not only sensuous experience but, in a clearly Lonerganian fashion, a nonsensuous experience of the self whose conscious appropriation leads finally to a transcendental analysis that unveils the conditions of possibility of understanding, acting, and existing. Such immediate or, in Rahnerian terms, original experience is appropriated through the mediation of phenomenological analyses and, ultimately, through a philosophical analysis that, itself, includes a phenomenological moment and a transcendental, final moment.[134]

Process thought plays an important role too in Tracy's actually pointing to experience as a source for theology. In fact, Ogden had already used the term "common human experience."[135] Tracy himself points out the richness and originality of the notion of experience within the Anglo-American tradition in general and within process thought in particular. More specifically, Tracy understands that this notion of experience ultimately enables process thought to appropriate the "turn to the subject" and to take it "to its logical and liberating conclusion."[136] However, Tracy's linking of language to common human experience as a theological source, thus going beyond Ogden, is based on his increasing awareness of the importance of language as vehicle and expression of experience. Hence, the import of hermeneutics for the theological task becomes a must.[137]

In order to establish an inner connection between the two sources, Tracy calls for a critical correlation that presupposes an investigation of both and a determination of the truth-status of the results of that investigation.[138] Tracy borrows the notion of correlation from Tillich but makes it clear that he modifies it by transforming Tillich's simple correlation into a critical one. Tillich, in Tracy's view, picked up the questions from the human-situation pole whereas the answers came always from the Christian pole. Rather than a correlation, says Tracy, Tillich's method "juxtaposes questions from the 'situation' with the answers from the 'message.'" For him, Tillich's final goal can only be achieved if the method "develops critical criteria for correlating the questions and the answers found in both the 'situation' and the 'message.'"[139]

Tracy distinguishes two moments within critical correlation. The first moment is a comparison of the results of the investigations of the two sources of theology in order to see how each result relates to the other and whether an initial positive correlation between the two can be established. However, such a moment is not enough. Before the second moment of correlation takes place, the truth-status of the results of the investigation of the two sources must be clarified using a metaphysical mode of reflection.[140] Once that has been accomplished, then the final moment of critical correlation can take place. That final moment will probe whether the criteria of adequacy that rule the analysis of the first source can be applied to the second source and whether the criteria of appropriateness that rule the analysis of the second source can be applied also to the first source. If such is the case, then it would have been established that there exists a positive correlation between the two terms, and, consequently, religious, theistic, and christological claims will have been sufficiently established.[141]

Hence, first, he brings the phenomenological moment, that is, the phenomenological exploration of the religious dimension of common human experience and language, to bear on the theological task. Tracy chooses phenomenological analysis as the method of investigation of the religious di-

mension of common human experience and language because he considers it
the best suited for that task. Furthermore, Tracy, aware as he is of the evolution undergone by phenomenology, deems hermeneutic phenomenology
(Gadamer, later Heidegger, and Ricoeur) especially well suited for unveiling the religious dimension of experience and language, given "the crucial
question of the linguistic and symbolic character of our experience."[142]

Second, a historical-hermeneutical moment takes place concerning the investigation of Christian texts, in order to establish that the categories used
by the theologian are appropriate to the meanings expressed in the Christian
texts. Therefore, the main question is how those texts can be adequately interpreted. Tracy's claim is that hermeneutical theory is the best method to
achieve this goal, and he adopts Ricoeur's interpretation theory. The core
of that theory is Ricoeur's attempt to integrate dialectically the operations
of *Erklären* and *Verstehen* (in Dilthey's terminology), the reality of the system and the importance of the event, objectivity and subjective engagement,
problem and mystery (in Gabriel Marcel's terms), the mode of knowing
that characterizes natural sciences and that of human sciences, critique and
creative ideation, norm and comprehension. Interpretation is an ongoing
back and forth between those two terms. Thus, Ricoeur seeks critically to
appropriate the Heidegger-based hermeneutics of Gadamer while incorpo-
rating intrinsically to the hermeneutical task the element of critique and
norm reclaimed by Karl-Otto Apel and Jürgen Habermas.[143]

Third, it is the role of philosophical reflection to determine the truth-
status of the results of the other two moments. Thus, fundamental theology
for Tracy "is best understood as philosophical reflection upon both the
meanings disclosed in our common human experience and the meanings
disclosed in the primary texts of the Christian tradition."[144] Tracy is aware
that philosophical argumentation is on shaky grounds in the contemporary
context. However, following other thinkers before him and along the same
argumentative line as Tillich and Ogden, Tracy maintains that metaphysical
reflection is necessary in order to show the truth of religious and theological claims because those claims concern the ultimate ground of the whole
of reality and, consequently, can only be properly assessed by a discipline
whose scope is that whole of reality and the nature of whose argumentation
is finally transcendental—namely, metaphysics.[145]

By so defining the revisionist model, Tracy seeks to make theology public
in a critical-modern context of plurality and critical thought. That context,
clearly, is mainly the U.S. context, whose tradition has strong links with
Anglo-Saxon Europe. In more general terms, that context has usually been
defined as the Western-culture context.[146] At the level of Christian fundamental theology, publicness means that religious, theistic, Christian-theistic,
and christological claims must be adequately grounded. Those claims can
be said to be adequately grounded when they are not dependent on purely

dogmatic statements but can be shown to be internally coherent, existentially meaningful in the current situation, and the condition of possibility for human knowledge and action (in the case of the first two claims) or a relatively adequate and disclosive response to the ultimate needs and longings of human existence (in the case of Christian-theistic and christological claims).[147] The shift from criteria of metaphysical adequacy to probe the truth-status of religious and theistic cognitive claims to criteria of relative experiential adequacy to probe the truth-status of specifically Christian-theistic and christological claims shows that the latter, since they are a further specification of general religious and theistic claims that originated in a particular tradition or symbol-system, cannot be proved to be metaphysically true but only relatively adequate according to experience. Here, fundamental theology approaches systematic theology.[148]

In the second part of *Blessed Rage for Order,* Tracy tries to show how his method of correlation works in practice. First, analyzing those human limit-experiences, like death, that question the meaning of existence and cannot be totally accounted for without reference to a transcendent reality or being, he proceeds from this limit-analysis to show how several philosophical traditions that use different strategies acknowledge the religious dimension of common human experience and language. Faithful to his overall approach, present throughout his whole career, of searching for a broad ground upon which he can build up his own position, Tracy takes here two crucial steps. First, gaining insight from the approach to religion of both the theological-phenomenological tradition (Schleiermacher-Otto-Tillich) and the tradition of human sciences (Weber-Berger-Geertz), Tracy gives up the goal of offering a single definition of religion and tries, instead, to describe "certain signal characteristics peculiar to any language or experience with a properly religious dimension" using the concept "limit."[149] That concept is the central piece of the limit-analysis that unfolds through the phenomenological, historical-hermeneutical, and metaphysical steps of Tracy's substantive application of his revisionist model of fundamental theology to show that, actually, religious, theistic, and christological claims are coherent, meaningful, and true. He uses the concept of "limit" because he thinks that all significant religious language and experience, whether explicit or implicit, at least implies "a limit-experience, a limit-language, or a limit-dimension."[150]

Tracy's second step is to use the contributions of several traditions of thought, namely, process thinking, transcendental method, linguistic analysis, and existential phenomenology, to analyze the religious meaning of common human experience and language.[151] In every case, the strategy is the same: those limit-questions and limit-experiences show that science, morality, and everyday experience cannot be fully explained from within themselves and that, therefore, they are not self-contained. On the contrary, they can make sense only if a broader and transcendent horizon is acknowledged. Furthermore, the implications involved in the limit-nature of those questions and situations seem to be illuminated by the use of religious language. In other words, religious symbols are meaningful in that they seem to represent adequately the content of common experience and have, in that sense, disclosive or re-presentative power.[152]

After having shown the religious dimension of common human experience and language, he analyzes the religious language of Christian texts and tries to establish that there exists a true and positive correlation between that religious language and the religious dimension of common human experience and language. Here, Tracy tries to justify a thesis that is symmetrical to the one concerning the religious dimension of common human experience and language, namely, that explicitly religious language and, specifically, Christian language have a limit-character disclosive of certain limit-experiences. In order to do so, he follows the linguistic analyses of Ian Ramsey and Frederick Ferré that display the limit-character of religious language. A second step is to show that the language of the New Testament has also that character, using the insights of biblical literary criticism and Ricoeur's philosophical interpretation of those insights. The third step, using again linguistic analysis and hermeneutics, is to point out that, in fact, the language used in the New Testament is suggesting a possible mode-of-being-in-the-world, namely, with explicit faith, with complete trust, and with unrestricted love. The final step is to show that such a suggestion does not point to a transworldly mode of existence but makes existential sense in that it seems to re-present adequately and to disclose our most basic human experience.[153] The point, typical of revisionist theology, is to avoid both extrinsic supernaturalism and pure immanentism and to show that the Christian proposal of a mode-of-being-in-the-world is both profoundly human and yet transcendent. It is precisely this tension that Tracy wants to capture with his terms "limit-to" and "limit-of." Tracy's conclusion referring to limit-experiences and limit-languages is that "in terms of criteria of existential meaningfulness, there seem good reasons to affirm the reality of both a religious dimension of our common experience and the existential significance of the originating language of the Christian religious heritage. In terms of the criteria of coherent logical meaning, there also seem solid reasons to affirm that the category 'limit' is a useful if merely initial index of religious meaning."[154]

Having established that there exists a true and positive correlation between religious language and the religious dimension of common human experience and language, Tracy moves on to show the truth of the cognitive claim concerning the affirmation of God as the ground and referent of existence. To achieve that goal, he discusses the question of whether or not metaphysics is the right mode of reflection to justify that claim. Since the religious experience and language are limit-experience and limit-language, the concept that cognitively articulates the ground of that religious experience and language, that is, the concept of God, must be logically a limit-concept. Metaphysics is the "mode of analysis which can investigate the cognitive claims of that kind of limit-concept."[155]

To sustain this claim, Tracy discusses the positions of Ramsey, Ferré, Ogden, and Anders Nygren. An important point related to the discussion is the relationship between the conceptual language of metaphysics and the symbolic language of religion upon which metaphysics reflects. Tracy's position is clear. Religious language has cognitive and noncognitive uses. Primary religious language, although it involves implicit cognitive claims, is, by nature, evocative, tensional, and provocative through the use of symbols, images, metaphors, and the like. A hermeneutical-phenomenological-linguistic mode of analysis is the most appropriate to investigate those noncognitive uses of primary religious language. A primary task of metaphysics is to investigate the cognitive claims of that language. Its secondary task is to explicate conceptually the thematic meanings of primary-symbolic religious language. Tracy seems to imply that the categories of process thought are the most adequate to render conceptually explicit the tensive meaning of primary religious language. For him, of course, such a claim does not imply a sort of Hegelian superseding of religious re-presentation by metaphysical concepts. On the contrary (another typical move of revisionist theology), it offers a third way out of the dilemma of rationalism (Hegel)-fideism (Kierkegaard, Barth). Concerning the question of myth in religious language, Tracy thinks that, if taken literally, myths are misinterpreted, whereas they have a positive function when interpreted for what they are, namely, nonliteral re-presentations of basic beliefs.[156]

Within the different traditions of metaphysical reflection, Tracy rejects the transcendental tradition for being "unwilling to break with the classical theistic concepts of Aquinas."[157] Instead, he claims that the best resource to formulate appropriately the meaning and truth of God is the tradition of process thought, because of its use of a dipolar concept of God that is internally coherent, appropriate to the Christian texts, and adequate to the demands of common experience in the contemporary context. Theologically, process thought is for Tracy thoroughly revisionist in that it is committed to the authentic values of secularity while affirming an understanding of God and religious experience that is truly Christian and truly adequate to modern consciousness. Because process thought is intrinsically characterized by the categories of sociality, temporality, relationality, and becoming, its understanding of God overcomes the aloofness of classical theology's God and presents a God who, although absolute because God's existence depends on no other being, is completely related to all other beings. This dipolar understanding of God is, in Tracy's opinion, appropriate to the image of the loving and related God that emerges from scripture and adequate to the experience of the modern subject. For Tracy, God, as eminently social

and temporal, seems to be the genuine limit-concept that his whole investigation has been seeking. This limit-concept is both internally coherent
and meaningful.[158] Ogden's work helped Tracy to realize the shortcomings
of Lonergan's classical outlook and profoundly influenced his revisionist
project. However, Tracy's positive view of process thought in the matter
of validating Christian-theistic cognitive claims does not mean that process
thought can provide by itself a full "resolution of the contemporary theological situation."[159] Among other problems, process thought seems to be unable
to come up with a symbolic language that can resonate existentially.[160]

The last step is to validate the christological claim, that is to say, to show
in which sense the christological interpretation of theistic religion is meaningful and true.[161] The christological claim, inasmuch as it is a matter-of-fact
claim, cannot be metaphysically validated but must be existentially validated. Therefore, the criteria to achieve that goal are criteria of relative
adequacy to experience.[162] In other words, whereas God can be presented
as a metaphysical necessity due to the absolute-grounding character of the
concept God, such a case cannot be built as regards christological claims
because Christ is not necessary in the terms God is. The goal, therefore,
is to show that christological claims make sense because they disclose real
limit-possibilities of being that respond to the implications of both theistic
claims and grounding human experience. The strategy used by Tracy to show
the relative existential adequacy of christological claims is to analyze both
several meaningful facts of the common human situation and the existential
meanings of the factual-re-presentative limit-character of christological texts
in order to correlate critically the results of the these two analyses.

The relevant facts of common human experience are the need for story,
fiction, and symbol; the existence of "evil"; and the realization that facts
are not only restricted to actualizations of possibilities but also include re-
presentations of possibilities.[163] Clearly, Tracy is preparing the way to make
the story of Jesus the Christ both meaningful and adequate as a story that
discloses a mode-of-being-in-the-world that human beings recognize both
as truthful to their existential-historical experience and as transformative
of their condition. In analyzing these facts, Tracy, following his practice
throughout the book, reviews several traditions and uses them critically to
build his own position. Thus, in the case of the human need for fiction,
Tracy uses linguistics, literary criticism, phenomenology, hermeneutics, and
anthropology. His claim is that even if one admits the need for demythologizing and for hermeneutics of suspicion, as he does, still an adequate
understanding of human existence needs not only conceptual analysis but
also story, symbol, image, myth, and fiction because they perform a necessary function in disclosing new possibilities for existence. Moreover, and
this is a crucial insight in Tracy's whole enterprise, fiction and concept are
internally interrelated because, in the words of Ricoeur quoted by Tracy,

"The symbol gives rise to [critical] thought; yet thought is informed by and returns to the symbol."[164]

In analyzing the fact of the existence of evil, Tracy borrows mainly, but not only, from two sources: from Ricoeur's linguistic-hermeneutical phenomenology and from Reinhold Niebuhr's correlational anthropological theology. Evil, claims Tracy closely following Niebuhr, is not metaphysically necessary but is inevitable. For him, one of the main achievements of neoorthodox theology, and particularly of Niebuhr, is its powerful rendering of an authentically human and religious anthropology that both captures the tragic and guilty reality of evil in existence and, by interpreting it in the religious category of sin in the wider context of God's work of creation and redemption, opens possibilities for its transformation. Tracy writes, thus correcting one of process thought's shortcomings and signaling one of the lines of his own position, that revisionist theology must incorporate that central achievement of neoorthodox theology "into its own twin vision of a common faith in the worthwhileness of existence which sustains us even beyond good and evil and a reflective belief in a credible, a suffering and loving Christian God." In order to do so, revisionist theology "might look anew at the story of Jesus the Christ and attempt to articulate some of its transformative existential possibilities."[165]

In articulating the third fact, and especially in showing that not only facts but also symbolic re-presentations actualize a possibility, Tracy combines again insights coming from different thinkers. One of them is Ogden's notion of re-presentation as possibility that is central to his Christology.[166] A second author who, although not mentioned, is important to Tracy's articulation is Eliade and his understanding of the functions of religious rituals, myths, and symbolic language as disclosive of *the* real and as instruments to retrieve it.[167] The third author that resounds in Tracy's depiction of symbolic re-presentation as actualization of a possibility is Ricoeur, for whom symbolic language, like the poetic, creates "new configurations expressing the meaning of reality," through which "new ways of being in the world [the similarity with Tracy's 'mode-of-being-in-the-world' is striking], of living there, and of projecting our innermost possibilities onto it are also brought to language."[168] For Tracy, the central point is that "the primordial symbols of our culture are not *mere possibilities*. They are facts."[169] Certain historical figures, Tracy mentions the "slain Kennedy brothers and Martin Luther King," become symbols disclosing new possibilities of being regardless of whether or not they actualized those possibilities.[170] Precisely whether or not the christological affirmations fulfill that function is what theology must analyze, especially bearing in mind "the fact of the presence of evil and the fact of the need for symbolic expressions in our lives."[171]

In analyzing the christological texts, Tracy's final aim is to rearticulate the positive existential meanings of Christology, showing that they are faithful to both our common experience and the primary meanings of the scriptural texts. Those existential meanings are present in the New Testament accounts of the words, deeds, and destiny of Jesus. Tracy claims that those words, deeds, and destiny can be sufficiently reconstructed with the aid of historical methods as to provide "the text" that must be hermeneutically interpreted, a text summarized by the Christian limit-symbol of the cross-resurrection of Jesus the Christ. For Tracy, the referent of the sense of this text is "the disclosure of a new, an agapic, a self-sacrificing righteousness willing to risk living at that limit where one seems in the presence of the righteous, loving, gracious God re-presented in Jesus the Christ."[172] This limit-way-of-being can be existentially sensed as a true human possibility and, even more, as the ideal "which represents in and with truth *the* truth of our lives."[173] That, in turn, implies being forced to decide with eschatological urgency whether to embrace that limit-way-of-being.[174]

The conclusion reached by Tracy is that what is re-presented by the proclamation of Jesus Christ as Lord is indeed "the basic faith and the only God whom all humanity experiences."[175] Referring to this "basic faith" in the meaning of existence, Tracy comes to affirm, thus unveiling the unmistakable modern character of his approach, that "an explicit and full recognition of this faith as, in fact, *the* common faith shared by secularist and modern Christian is perhaps the most important insight needed to understand the contemporary theological situation in its full dimensions and its real possibilities."[176] Those initial words of *Blessed Rage for Order* resound at the end of the chapter on Christology that crowns his effort to put his revisionist method to work: "For Christians, christological language suffices because it fulfills certain factual understandings of human and divine reality: the fact that our lives are, in reality, meaningful; that we really do live in the presence of a loving God; that the final word about our lives is gracious and the final power is love."[177]

Tracy's entry into the systematic field from the perspective of his revisionist model of fundamental theology leads him, finally, to try to show how the revisionist model can work in the field of practical theology too.[178] After discussing the liberal and the neoorthodox practical theologies, Tracy focuses on the new praxis-led theology, mainly represented by political and liberation theologies. Their main achievement for Tracy is the retrieval of the societal and political dimension of Christianity. The main problems Tracy sees in them are their lack of concern for criticizing their own theological symbols and interpretations and their paying too little attention to critical social analyses with a strong empirical basis.

Several comments seem important as a conclusion to this discussion of Tracy's proposal of a revisionist fundamental theology. Tracy's agenda at the time was thoroughly influenced by the problems posed to religion by modernity and critical modernity. Therefore, he sought to define a "critical-modern" model of theology capable of responding to those problems.[179] In that sense, Tracy's enterprise is similar to the critical-modern theologies of both Metz and Gutiérrez. The three thinkers develop a critical-modern apologetics that, ultimately, aims at reconciling the utopian, emancipatory, and liberating thrust of modernity with the Christian message. Thus Metz argues that only a reason grounded on the narrative of dangerous, unmasking, provocative memories of Christianity can be rescued from its otherwise destructive madness (as proven by the Holocaust) if left alone to itself. Gutiérrez, in turn, connects the possibility of ultimate liberation to God's love, manifested in Jesus Christ, and thinks that authentic emancipation stems from a praxis based on solidarity with the poorest and most exploited and dispossessed as a requirement of that love of God for them. For Tracy, the symbols of Christianity are the authentic rendering of what is implied by the faith of secularity. The three thinkers, therefore, define their theological positions in relation to the emancipatory enterprise of critical modernity. In that sense, the three of them are creatures of critical modernity. Tracy defines the character of this creature when he writes that "the post-modern intellectual believes that he must remain in fundamental fidelity to the critical exigencies of the liberal period" and that what is needed is, following Habermas, "a retrieval of the radically critical and thereby emancipatory power of human rationality itself."[180]

However, as in the cases of Metz and Gutiérrez, this critical-modern model of theology has become increasingly problematic for Tracy and has been significantly transformed by him without being dropped altogether.[181] As a result, Tracy has focused on reworking the main symbol of Christian faith, namely, the trinitarian God, using strategies and resources structurally neglected by his initial model. In other words, in Lonergan's terms, Tracy has changed and is changing his basic interpretive horizon.

The modern thrust of Tracy's revisionist model of fundamental theology is tensionally related to Lonergan's enterprise. Simplifying perhaps a little too much, *Blessed Rage for Order* marks Tracy's shift from a transcendental model of modern theology, yet classical in its categories and of Catholic-Thomistic descent, to a revisionist model of modern theology in modern categories of Christian-American-process descent. That *Blessed Rage for Order* can be understood as the result of Tracy's encounter with process thought as paradigmatically modern and that, therefore, Tracy's revisionist model is of Christian-American-process descent (inasmuch as process theology is clearly Christian instead of Catholic and unmistakably American in origin and character) can be justified in purely statistical terms. Schubert Ogden is the most quoted author in the book, closely followed by Lonergan. But, if to the citations of Ogden one adds the numerous citations of other process thinkers such as Whitehead, Charles Hartshorne, and John Cobb, then the statistical argument becomes overwhelming.

Beyond these statistics, the analysis of Tracy's thought developed so far clearly shows the central role that the main tenets of process thought, mainly as understood by Ogden, play in his fundamental theology. With Ogden, Tracy's basic aim is to show that the common faith of secular and Christian people alike (the basic faith in the meaning of existence) positively correlates with the Christian message. Moreover, Tracy follows Ogden's (and Tillich's) understanding of theology as correlation of experience and Christianity, as well as Ogden's criteria of adequacy and appropriateness in justifying theological claims. In addition, also with Ogden (although with Lonergan, Tillich, and Schleiermacher too), Tracy maintains that philosophy is the central partner of theology in the latter's effort to show the truth of the theistic claims involved in human experience. Furthermore, and crucially, Tracy adopts the process critique of classical theism and its dipolar-panentheistic understanding of God as the best way (albeit not without problems) to represent in an adequate and appropriate manner that cornerstone-symbol of Christianity. Finally, Tracy also follows Ogden in affirming that Jesus the Christ is the best re-presentation of both the truth and the possibilities of human existence and of the dipolar nature of God.

Although Tracy's shift from Lonergan to process theology is clear, such a shift does not imply a rejection of the Lonerganian model but a relocation of its central tenets, especially the emphasis on method and transcendental reflection, within the revisionist model.[182] In other words, *Blessed Rage for Order* marks the intensification of the critical-modern strand present in Tracy's theology. In that sense, that work, Tracy would claim, is not a rejection of Lonergan but, so to speak, an intensification of Lonergan's logic, bringing it to its completion.

Tracy uses different traditions to control and correct the positions of his two main theological partners, Lonergan and Ogden, and to build his own position. Because plurality of theological models and disciplines is a basic fact for Tracy's revisionist theology, Tracy builds up his case consciously drawing upon different sources and traditions on the basis of the organizing principle or backbone of his revisionist model. Far from adopting a defensive or negative attitude concerning that plurality of views, Tracy believes that such plurality is positive because the different stances help to understand better the complexity of the problems under analysis insofar as they look at them from different angles. Therefore, by discussing them and discriminating among them following the organizing principle of his revisionist model, he uses them to formulate his constructive position. This basic attitude toward plurality is one of the two central assumptions of *Blessed Rage for Order* and of Tracy's whole enterprise.[183]

In interpreting modernity and the situation in general, Tracy uses the insights of the two main critical moments of modernity, namely, "the masters of suspicion" and the Frankfurt School. In interpreting human experience and language he uses a vast array of philosophical positions and human sciences, among which the phenomenological turn (Husserl), the existential-ontological turn (Heidegger), the hermeneutical turn (Gadamer), and the hermeneutical-linguistic turn (Ricoeur) play a crucial role. In justifying the truth of the theistic claim, Tracy uses Ramsey's and Ricoeur's limit-analysis, on the one hand, and transcendental reasoning of several kinds (Lonergan, Toulmin, Ogden, Jasper, Heidegger), on the other hand. In defining his theological position, although the two main partners are Lonergan and Ogden, the more general, overall framework is provided by the Catholic (Lonergan and Rahner) and Protestant (Tillich and Reinhold Niebuhr, mainly) versions of neoorthodox theology and by the different practitioners of revisionist theology, among which process theology takes center stage. In interpreting scriptures and tradition, historical and literary critical methods must be applied before the hermeneutical and central interpretive step takes place. Here again, Ricoeur is crucial. Finally, in establishing the key correlation between the symbol Jesus the Christ and existence, the theory of symbols and their existential meaningfulness and disclosive power (Eliade, Ricoeur) and the existential-eschatological meaning of that central Christian symbol (Bultmann, Ogden) are paramount.

In using this plurality of authors and interpretations Tracy does not, in his own words, "rest content in the merely aesthetic pleasure of a pluralist world."[184] It is clear that his openness and positive view of plurality does not entail an easygoing and relativistic attitude concerning the claims to truth of the different positions. As his revisionist model shows, claims to truth must be justified by means adequate to the aim in each case. It is precisely, according to him, by setting criteria to test the adequacy and truth of theological claims that theology can become public. This is the second assumption of Tracy's enterprise.[185]

Finally, not every tradition or discipline has the same importance in Tracy's position. Constructively, it has just been affirmed that Tracy's fundamental theology is mainly, albeit not only, the result of criticizing and revising Lonergan's project using the resources and positions of process theology in general and Ogden in particular. However, this affirmation must be importantly qualified by adding that, in turn, Tracy uses Eliade's and Ricoeur's interpretation of symbolism and Ricoeur's hermeneutics to criticize and correct the shortcomings of process theology. Precisely this linguistic-hermeneutical element of Tracy's thought will become the central one in his attempt to formulate his own project of systematic theology.

Particular Traditions and Publicness

Systematic theology is the real touchstone of the pursuit of publicness as a central feature of Tracy's theological enterprise. In a society like the United States, where over 90 percent of the population affirm belief in God, to justify the theistic claim on public grounds, although important in relation to the cognitive status of religious claims and to the challenge of secularistic cultural currents, is not the most difficult task. Theism is sociologically public, despite the ambiguities concerning its public-institutional relevance. But, bearing in mind the sweeping religious plurality in U.S. society, the real challenge is to justify the public status of a particular tradition and to show that this tradition can contribute to the public realm. In this sense, the question Tracy asks touches the heart of the problem: "In a culture of pluralism must each religious tradition finally either dissolve into some lowest common denominator or accept a marginal existence as one interesting but purely private option?" He concludes that "neither alternative is acceptable to anyone seriously committed to the truth of any major religious tradition. The need is to form a new and inevitably complex theological strategy that will avoid privatism by articulating the genuine claims of religion to truth."[186]

Tracy's central assertion in this respect is that the publicness of the work of a particular tradition is achieved "through, not despite, its particularity." Against the reigning common wisdom, Tracy affirms that the contribution to the common good demands diving into particularity instead of searching for "some lowest common denominator."[187]

Already in *Blessed Rage for Order*, Tracy concluded that the publicness of systematic theology is not and cannot be the same as fundamental theology's. Religious and theistic claims are metaphysical-argumentatively justified. Christian theistic and christological claims, however, can be justified only relatively, insofar as their experiential adequacy is shown. Therefore, the next step in Tracy's revisionist enterprise was to formulate the method of systematic theology and to show how that method worked when dealing with substantive Christian beliefs. To that effect, Tracy wrote *The Analogical Imagination*.

In line with his previous work, Tracy places theology within culture as a particular form of public discourse and public meaning necessary for that wider culture. Both points are crucial to Tracy's enterprise. First, theology in general is not to be considered a mode of reflection placed at the margin of the wider culture, but, so to speak, theology is in its own right a full member and citizen of that culture. Second, its particular form is not to be confused with privateness. Particularity and publicness are not opposed terms. Indeed, every form of public discourse is necessarily a particular one. As public, theology can contribute resources to the wider culture in which the theological discourse takes place. In this sense, Tracy forcefully argues "that all theology is public discourse."[188] In the background, the phantasms of empiricism, instrumental rationality, and privatization threaten to come onto the scene and to destroy this view of theology, first as a public discourse and, second, as something necessary for society. A justification of these claims is therefore needed.[189]

From the point of view of its function, theology can be said to be public insofar as it conveys a meaningful and true disclosure of something that is most relevant for human life in the current circumstances of society. Beyond its function, theology is intrinsically public because it is always an affirmation of God. This affirmation can only be understood as bearing a claim to universality that, as such, necessarily leads the theologian to give public reasons for it. In other words, the radically theocentric character of theology makes it public. "Theology in all its forms is finally nothing else but the attempt to reflect deliberately and critically upon that God. Theology is *logos* on *theos*. Any authentic speech on the reality of God which is really private or particularist is unworthy of that reality." Since the public character of theology is based on its radical theocentrism, conversely, if theologians "are not involved, at least implicitly, in speech about God, then they are not involved in public theological discourse."[190]

In developing their task and justifying their claims, theologians refer to different publics, that is, acquire different modes of publicness depending on what kind of audience and what sort of environment they relate to. Tracy distinguishes three distinct and related publics: academy, church, and society. These various settings lead, in turn, to different, albeit interrelated, theological enterprises, each one with its own criteria of publicness. Far from being an external figure to these environments, the theologian is usually a member of a concrete church and "has been socialized into a particular society and a particular academic tradition and has been enculturated into one particular culture."[191] As such, theologians have a personal synthesis (more or less tensional) of the structures of the three different environments. This synthesis must be rendered explicit in relation to the theological task, with specific and public reflection upon the different claims to meaning and truth coming from each of the publics.

Each of Tracy's three theological subdisciplines, fundamental, systematic, and practical, uses its own mode of discourse, its own criteria of publicness, and is oriented, mainly but not exclusively, to a particular public. Fundamental theology is mainly related to the academic public and uses philosophical language. Systematic theology is mainly addressed to the church and is hermeneutical in character. Practical theology confronts society, uses both hermeneutics and critical social theory, and adopts commitment and loyalty as criteria of truth. The three are, however, internally related, and the three involve an interpretation both of a religious tradition and of the religious dimension of the contemporary situation.[192] All of them have scriptural and traditional warrants. The three need to engage in an ongoing dialogue to sort out, and make progress in, their different interpretations of both religious tradition and society.

The three subdisciplines must be understood, bearing in mind the pair abstract-concrete. The abstract relates to the level of fundamental theology, which, in an exercise of "public philosophy," transcendentally reflects on the conditions of possibility of human thought and meaningful action. Evidently, as Tracy points out, systematic theology, in dealing with a concrete and particular tradition, relates to a more concrete level and uses hermeneutical interpretation as its main tool. Finally, practical theology moves further down the path of the concrete because it uses critical social theory and praxis in order to "verify" orthopraxically the truthfulness and transformative power of the concrete religious tradition.[193]

Focusing on systematic theology, Tracy attempts to show that this subdiscipline is public in character, but bearing in mind that, in matters of faith and particular traditions, there cannot be proofs but only ways to show their relative adequacy to all those who are intelligent, rational, and responsible. This presupposes an understanding of reason far wider and more nuanced than the Cartesian, clear and distinct, one. The task is to make explicit the meaning and truth of the religious tradition, employing the symbols, texts, and persons encompassed by this tradition. In doing so, systematic theology uses hermeneutics as its method because reflecting on a tradition in order to disclose its claims and its representation of reality is necessarily a prototypical act of interpretation. Hermeneutics, however, is not a mere repetition of the tradition but an ever new manifestation of this tradition in each historical circumstance. Moreover, a tradition must be understood not as something alien to theologians but as their own environment to which they adhere in a personal decision that involves a critical moment. The theologian does not repeat the tradition but recreates it. To do so, two elements are necessary for the hermeneutical appropriation of a given tradition: conversation and method; in other words, a hermeneutics of retrieval through conversation cannot eliminate but, on the contrary, requires a hermeneutics of suspicion in order to control the interpretation and to unmask the misunderstandings and distortions of that particular tradition. In this sense, tradition does not oppose a critical approach but rather includes it.[194]

What makes tradition meaningful and worth exploring and making it manifest is its potentiality as disclosive of new possibilities and horizons for human life. Tracy introduces here the notion of the classics as those expressions of the human spirit that "so disclose a compelling truth about our lives that we cannot deny them some kind of normative status."[195] It is, therefore, a paradigmatic expression of the human spirit that, although not adequately expressible, is however "the real."[196] Although the classic is particular in origin and expression, it is public, potentially universal, in effect.

The notion of "the classic" is the central piece of Tracy's proposal for a public systematic theology. In this respect, at the very beginning of *The Analogical Imagination,* he states that "indeed, the heart of the argument of the entire book may be found in the argument on the phenomenon of the classic.

If that argument stands, the rest of the book can follow. If that theory falls, the rest remains, at best, on shaky ground."[197] Tracy's understanding of the classics comes very close to Rahner's understanding of the inspired author. For Rahner, revelation is a transcendental, unthematic, supernatural experience of God that is original in each person. Inspired authors, for Rahner, are those "in whom the self-interpretation of this supernatural, transcendental experience and its history takes place in word and deed. Hence, something comes to expression in the prophets which fundamentally is present everywhere and in everyone, including ourselves who are not called prophets."[198] Rahner's theological anthropology explains, indeed, why a classic resounds in every Lonerganian "intelligent, reasonable, responsible person," demanding attention and transformation. Reading a classic can have those effects because it makes explicit something that, implicitly, is already present to the self in that transcendental, unthematic, original experience of God.[199] The crucial point as regards the classics is that of disclosure, a point that has much to do with the understanding of truth as manifestation. Truth manifests itself through the classic as paradigmatical embodiment of that truth when the person risks an interpretation of that classic. In such a case, the interpreter can have a "shock of recognition" of the truth embodied in the classic.

In all areas of human culture there exist classics. Systematic theology deals with the classics embedded in a particular religious tradition. Insofar as these are true classics and the theologian engages in the adventure of establishing a creative dialogue with them through the hermeneutical procedure of understanding-explanation-understanding, systematic theology can make a public contribution to the task of disclosing the meaning and possibilities of human life.[200] If such a contribution is the result of a daring and fruitful adventure in confronting the classics, it becomes in turn a classic.[201]

A most important point in Tracy's interpretation of the religious classic concerns the double dimension of classical forms of religious expression: manifestation and proclamation. Both forms belong to the classics. Manifestation stresses the experience of radical participation, whereas proclamation relates to the experience of radical nonparticipation. In other words, both dimensions emphasize either the sense of immanence, of belonging, or that of transcendence, of radical otherness, and they issue either in a mystical or in a prophetic attitude. Both dimensions pervade every religion and require each other, although at times, or under certain circumstances, one or the other can win the day. Within Christianity, for instance, Catholics and Orthodox tend to emphasize manifestation and sacraments, whereas Protestants stress proclamation and word. Within Catholicism, however, one can find the sense of manifestation in Rahner, while Metz would rather represent that of proclamation. Despite these different stresses, Tracy makes it clear that "Christianity lives in and by the paradigmatic power of both manifestation and proclamation." Both are so interrelated that "manifestation is always the enveloping presupposition of the emergence and, at the limit, the eruption of the defamiliarizing word of proclamation."[202]

Turning to the content of Christian systematics, Tracy is decidedly clear in affirming that "the event and person of Jesus Christ" constitute the paradigmatical classic as expressed in the scriptures. However, as regards that event and person, the scriptural texts manifest clearly different perspectives. Far from discarding this diversity, Tracy considers it necessary to take it fully into account, distinguishing among genres and developing a proposal for relative adequacy. According to this proposal, the basic expressions of the witnesses would be represented in the genres of proclamation-confession, narrative, symbol, and reflective thought. In turn, the corrective function upon that complex whole would be the task of the "apocalyptic" and "doctrines" genres.[203]

The apocalyptic genre is a central one in order to avoid forgetting the presence of conflict in history and the necessity of looking for justice out of hope based on God's ultimately transforming force, thus challenging all kinds of complacency and of adequacy between historical reality and the reality being disclosed in the event and person of Jesus Christ. The corrective role of doctrine in relation to the event is to mediate the passage from *fides qua* to *fides quae,* from the extraordinary to the ordinary of life and history. These two genres are corrective of the main plot. This central expression of the event is made up of proclamation as the central shocking genre of the event; of narrative as the disclosure of the main characters and issues; of the central symbols of incarnation, cross, and resurrection as manifestation of participation, conflict, and hope; and, lastly, of the reflective thought of both Paul and John with their dialectical and meditative theological renderings of the event and person of Jesus Christ.[204] Every genre needs the others in order to bring to its fullness all its disclosive meaning, and only this innerly related interplay of genres can ensure the relatively adequate theological expression of the event and person of Jesus Christ. The pluralism in the New Testament is crucial because "the New Testament diversity is impelled by the dynamism of the event itself and its self-expression into the otherness of a wide range of responses to, witnesses to, that event: responses which posit themselves in and by the event by implying their own fulfillment in the next needed form."[205]

In the end, only a Christology capable of paying attention to the whole diversity of expressions in the New Testament obtains a relative adequacy. Tracy argues that "Only the whole of the New Testament expressions will disclose with relative adequacy the whole dialectical meaning of both our situation and the event of Jesus Christ." However, each theologian, each interpreter of the event, must risk a journey of intensification into some particular form or genre as the only way to interpret the event. The strategy, therefore, is not and cannot be an irenic one. At the same time, that interpretation through intensification "needs its self-exposure to the corrective of the others, above all of the original witnesses and, eventually, of the whole tradition." Moreover, each emphasis "needs the other as a self-corrective moment in its own particular journey of intensification, not as a merely external corrective or 'reminder' of other aspects of the whole."[206] However, ultimately, only a faith-response that is both highly personal and communal can ensure that the Christ event is present. This is the final criterion of relative adequacy. This faith-response is linked to the way Christians experience the Christ event, namely, "in the many mediated forms of the Christian church." Tracy is resolute in affirming that "It is the tradition of the church that *is* our central mediation to the actual Jesus." Therefore, this centrality of tradition "does call for a faith in the church," although a church that is always under the disclosive and transformative power of the Christ event and therefore called to be an *ecclesia semper reformanda,* capable of overcoming the ambiguity inherent to both tradition and church.[207] The personal and communal faith-response, in turn, requires "to risk a life on that always-already, not-yet vision of what reality ultimately is. For the Christian truly believes in Jesus Christ by risking the kind of life narrated as Jesus' own."[208]

Tracy's revisionist model requires from systematic theology an interpretation of the situation to which the interpretation of the event and the person of Jesus Christ must dialectically correlate. Evidently, in an age of pluralism, there is no central focus of interpretation, especially after "the masters of suspicion" have shattered the naive confidence of the early Enlightenment and unmasked the conflicts, illusions, and distortions of modern culture. This culture, moreover, has its own reasons to be suspicious even of those masters, bearing in mind the dialectics that has affected their own suspicious readings and interpretations of culture. Indeed, modern, current culture is aware of the fact that every expression of the human spirit bears the marks of the dialectics of ambiguity.[209] In such a situation, the only possible way out of a hopeless, chaotic, and uncontrollable position, in an era threatened to be prey to a purely technical, instrumental reason, is to allow the pervading experience of the uncanny, of the uncontrollable, of that which is "not of our making," to become a central issue in interpreting the situation. At the same time, the different experiences of and routes to the uncanny, the different interpretations of the classics, must engage in a critical conversation in which every partner will risk a journey of intensification into that particular experience or route.[210]

Plurality also is the main feature of the Christian response to the situation. This is so on inner grounds, due to the plurality of the tradition and, more radically, of the New Testament itself. However, there is a basic grammar for Christian systematic theology consisting of the most classic symbols and doctrines acknowledged as such in the tradition.[211] Within this basic grammar, there are different routes to a Christian response to the situation. A common feature of this response is a Christian rendering or interpretation of the disclosive recognition "to an uncanny power not our own."[212] There are three most important and paradigmatic focuses of that response, themselves centered around the Christ event as *the* focus: manifestation, proclamation, and action. This third focus, action, is central for both political and liberation theologies.[213]

The response within each focus can follow different routes. Thus, for instance, Tracy points out that manifestation can occur through the mediation of philosophical reflection (Augustine, Schleiermacher, Whitehead, Rahner), through the ordinary that manifests itself as extraordinary in its own concreteness (Francis of Assisi, Bonaventure, Buber, Marcel, Eastern Christianity, Eliade), or through the paradigmatic (icons, sacraments, mystics). Proclamation of the transcendence and unassailable power of the Word is the main focus of the Reformed tradition. Here again different routes can be found, such as, for instance, the different positions among the neo-orthodox: Barth, Bultmann, and Tillich. Finally, the focus on the inner relation between the transforming power of the Christ event and history and praxis is the main feature of both political and liberation theologies. For these theologies, which seek to validate Christianity in history, "we are primarily neither hearers of the word nor seers of a manifestation. But because we have seen and have heard, we are freed to become doers of the word in history."[214] Also here can one find different routes. Thus, for instance, Metz and Gutiérrez come from a previous appropriation of the journey of manifestation, whereas Moltmann, Sölle, and Cone have previously appropriated the journey of proclamation. For all of them reason is practical, and, therefore, any understanding of the transforming power of the Christ event must be historically acted out and made true through a praxis of liberation. Different routes can also be found in another direction when one compares the European and First World accent of political theologies with the Latin American and Third World accent of liberation theologies. The classic in the case of liberation theologies "is the classic not of a text but of an event: the event of a liberating praxis wherein the actions of whole peoples whose disclosive, ignored, forgotten, despised story is at last being narrated and heard in ways which may yet transform us all."[215]

Within this plurality of approaches, a central insight emerges: any given Christian systematic theology remains always intrinsically inadequate to express the full power of the Christ event itself. The task of systematic theology consists therefore in acknowledging that inadequacy to give full theological expression to that original power beyond any conceptual formulation, while, at the same time, seeking to express it as a conceptual rendering of a particular and truthful journey into the disclosive and transforming power of the Christ event. Theology is "a properly reflective language of critique and participation by means of the articulation of theological *concepts* that are neither mere categories nor simple replacements of the originating tensive religious language." The theological journey can be described as that going from original disclosure through symbol to concept and back again to symbol.[216] In order to achieve a relative adequacy in this theological task, both intensification and critique must play their role. Intensification is a necessary moment if theology is to be meaningful at all. Every theologian must express, so to speak, the shock of recognition of the Christ event, the originating religious experience of that event, from a concrete perspective. Only intensification can guarantee truthfulness and meaningfulness. However, the resulting formulation must be open to the corrections and critique coming from other legitimate theological renderings stemming from different particular perspectives. Only that corrective critique can ensure a relative adequacy of the theological interpretation of the Christ event.[217]

Theology so understood uses two main classic languages in performing its task: analogy and dialectics. Analogy, based on a feeling of participation, articulates the sense of similarity-in-difference, whereas dialectics, centered around the experience of nonparticipation, articulates the sense of radical difference. The analogical language is mainly used by those theologies that focus on manifestation, whereas the dialectical language is the preferred language of those theologies focusing on proclamation and transforming action. If analogy can be interpreted theologically as a "yes" qualified by an ultimately clear "no" that avoids the danger of identity, dialectics is basically a "no" behind which always lurks an inevitable, although dialectical to be sure, stronger "yes" that overcomes pure negativity and hopelessness. Either language resorts to the other in order to be truthful to the Christ event. In this respect, the theological language is always an analogical-dialectical language, albeit with different stresses.[218]

A Christian analogical imagination has as focal point the event and person of Jesus Christ. From this focal point, such an analogical imagination will try to establish ordered relationships for the whole of reality. In the Christ event, God, the world, and the self are revealed. In ordering the relationships among God, world, and self, keeping Christ as focal point, both interpreting the situation and living out the implications of that focal event through transformative praxis play a crucial role.[219] Within this overall model of Christian systematic theology, Tracy argues that grace, dialectically understood as always-already and not-yet, is the central reality disclosed in the originating event. That disclosure is the basis for holding a fundamental trust in the whole. The God manifested in Christ is love. The world appears as a beloved reality. The self, in turn, is "gifted and commanded to become loving."[220]

For Tracy, an analogical imagination is a fundamental requirement in the radically pluralistic condition of current culture. Somewhere else he writes that "the word imagination signifies the priority of possibility as the key to pluralism; the qualifier 'analogical' articulates a way to enhance that possibility."[221] This analogical imagination is the main instrument of relating to the different positions of the others within the wide, open, and self-corrective theological, cultural, and public conversation in which the subject matter is allowed by all partners to take over. Christians have a clue to understanding and dealing with plurality in the wider social realm in the pluralism within the Christian tradition itself. By pursuing a truthful journey of intensification into each particular tradition, while being at the same time prepared to be exposed to the other positions, similarities-in-difference and also discontinuities demanding new efforts will emerge in the context of an ongoing conversation whose final destination cannot be foreseen. A conversation so understood, beyond both "indifferentism" and "repressive tolerance," is the only hope and the only way ahead. "The reality of an analogical imagination becomes a live option in our day. That option lives by its belief that the route to the future concreteness of the whole—a truly global humanity—lies through the concreteness of each particularity." In such a situation, "each of us understands each other through analogies to our own experience or not at all."[222]

Publicness in the Whirlpool of Postmodernity

Tracy's own thinking undergoes a journey of intensification into the experience of the radical plurality and ambiguity that are the main features of the postmodern situation. Although his understanding of plurality was already acute and radical, that understanding took an even more decisive turn in the 1980s. Tracy's referential work for this period was *Plurality and Ambiguity*.[223]

The clarity and self-security of the modern method, applied to his fundamental theology in the first half of the 1970s, had already yielded to the more adventurous position of an ongoing hermeneutical conversation as regards systematic theology at the turn of the decade of the 1980s. Intensifying that journey into radical plurality during the 1980s, Tracy exposes himself and his hermeneutics to radical partners for whom the main referents of modernity have ceased to exist, to become just the memory of the mirage of a naive era. To be sure, Plato, Aristotle, Aquinas, Hegel, William James, Dewey, Lonergan, Rahner, Eliade, and Ricoeur continue to be the main referential partners also in this conversation. Also the "masters of suspicion" continue being important partners in Tracy's conversation. However, authors like Saussure, Wittgenstein, Derrida, Rorty, Foucault, and Lacan, among others, take on the role of challengers, most of them as radical heirs to the original destabilizing moves of these "masters of suspicion," especially Nietzsche and Heidegger. The question is not any longer the critique of the Enlightenment but a radical destabilization of the very basis of the

Enlightenment, namely, the self. In this context, the task is not merely that of publicly justifying a particular tradition in a pluralistic society but, much more radically, of defending the possibility of a public realm in a context that heartily welcomes every tradition and particularity insofar as they acknowledge being just particular manifestations in a sea of sheer plurality and flux.[224]

A good example of the depth of the postmodern crisis is the status of the text. For the postmodern deconstructionist, any text has become so unstable that it can hardly bear any substantive and permanent meaning. This threat to the very possibility of a meaningful text is consequently a threat to any serious hermeneutical interpretation of the classics based on the "surplus of meaning" and "disclosive power" of the ever-interpreted-anew classic texts. The realization of this threat would do away with the very basis of the public, potentially universal, discourse defended by Tracy on the basis of a conversation with the classics. For Tracy, Derrida represents the most radical position among the deconstructivists for whom any text, and language in general, dissolves into just a series of differences, that is to say, a radical plurality that prevents the reader from arriving at the meaning of the text. Hence, "the hope for both conversation and argument may seem in vain."[225]

However, Tracy interprets Derrida not as a grounding position but as a corrective one. The latter's critique of the modern approach to knowledge based on pure self-presence does not altogether entail a denial of the very possibility of knowledge. Tracy moves past language as use, as system, and as differential nonsystem, without denying their importance and the relevance of their insights, to language as discourse. Although discourse is always contingent upon language, society, and history, its meaning can be grasped, however critical the process of interpretation might have to be in order to get at that meaning. In this sense, relatively adequate knowledge remains a possibility. More is not possible, but that knowledge is enough.[226] Tracy argues furthermore that the great practitioners of discourse analysis, such as Foucault, Lacan, and Ricoeur, are so pervaded by the ethical-political dimension that "they can be rightly considered as the contemporary heirs of the classic French moralist tradition from Montaigne through Pascal to Camus."[227] In so concluding, he places his own discourse on a firm track. On the one hand, he fully agrees with the poststructuralist critique of discourse, a critique that unmasks the "more of the same" that any discourse can contain. On the other hand, this critique has not finally issued in the joyful "surf of the signifiers" but has a definite ethical substance. In short, postmodernity helps us to decenter our discourse and to take into account otherness and difference without dissolving into a joyfully unethical "everything goes."

If language explodes in radical plurality, history awakens the awareness of radical ambiguity. Radical interruptions, like the Holocaust, sharpen that awareness and radically question the meaning of history. Every tradition involves deep historical ambiguities that must be taken into account in interpreting its classics. In this respect, the classics must be resisted and unmasked if their greatness is to emerge and to allow for new and more fulfilling ways of living to surface.[228]

Western, domineering history must especially let itself be critiqued by the historical accounts of its repressed "others." Here, Tracy meets Metz, Gutiérrez, and many other critical thinkers for whom Western culture and history remain very ambiguous and must be criticized if the ideals of emancipation, justice, and freedom are to be really universal and meaningful in the future. Tracy critiques the "once seemingly clear historical narrative of progressive Western enlightenment," written from the perspective of a self-assured victor. New histories need to be written, even radical antinarratives powerful enough to unmask the ambiguities, interruptions, and repressed memories of official histories. In order to liberate, the memory of a tradition must involve a subversive dimension. Overall, a proper retrieval of the classics of any culture requires the pursuit of different strategies, capable of eliciting both resistance and hope.[229] Here is where postmodernity can be very helpful with its linguistic turn and its analyses of the relationship between language and knowledge, in an intensification of Nietzsche's analysis.[230] Language has been proven biased and the consciousness of the self severely critiqued if attempting to reign over the radical ambiguity of that historically biased language. Postmodern critiques bring to the fore the subversive repressed memories of suffering. Those memories "subvert our most basic modern belief: the belief that somehow we can think our way through once more."[231]

In an important way, Tracy's confrontation with postmodernity confirms his hermeneutical drive and intensifies it, to be sure making it more nuanced and, in a way, more fragile and more aware of its limits and relativity. Although the acknowledgment of this much more fragile status of conscious rationality poses a problem to his previous enterprise in fundamental theology, it also frees that rationality from its own self-defeating self-centeredness. Now, the voices of the others will be heard together with the otherness within the self. Critical conversation, however fragile and difficult, can, therefore, be a source of resistance and hope.

For Tracy, religion can be relevant in this context, bearing in mind its powerful resources to foster resistance: "Above all, the religions are exercises in resistance" and, in this respect, "reveal various possibilities for human freedom."[232] His strategy to demonstrate this follows the path he established for doing theology, namely, to relate meaningfully, and mutually critically, religion and the situation. Having established that the postmodern decentering of the subject and the acknowledgment of the radical plurality and ambiguity of discourse and history are the unavoidable features of the situation, Tracy moves on to critically and mutually relate religion and that situation. To begin with, he is aware that many postmoderns will resist theology. He suspects that the main reason for this is the negative aspects of the history of the religions, including murder, attack on the liberty of the people, dogmatism, wars, and other signs of domineering power. Religions must acknowledge their own negative history of effects if they are to be credible at all. Religion, due to its transcendent and ultimate nature, can also issue in an ultimate evil. Therefore, on the one hand, any religious discourse and any religious tradition must be critically appropriated, since they also partake both in the radical plurality of a language that conditions any discourse and in the radical ambiguity of the history of effects of any tradition. On the other hand, this critical appropriation, no matter how tentative and never ending, may free religion from its own ideological manipulations and set free its powerful liberating resources.

Religion can powerfully help liberate the postmodern subject from self-centeredness because it relates this subject to a transcendent Ultimate Reality. This recentering-decentering of the self prompted by a Reality-centeredness can, in turn, transform both the self and the way the self relates to nature, history, and others. In this sense, postmodernity and religion can help each other. On the one hand, the postmodern subject is a subject potentially open to the radical otherness of religion, free from the strictures of the autonomous modern self that represented a stumbling block in the relation of that self to religion. Religion, on the other hand, can help the now weak, problematized self to be rescued and to be capable of becoming a responsible, related-to-the-others self.[233]

Tracy acknowledges that religious claims are also plural and that religious interpretations conflict among themselves. Far from affirming that all religions are ultimately one as an easy way out of what he thinks would be an irresponsible plurality, he argues that each religious tradition must stand its own ground and enter a responsible conversation with the other religious traditions following the "analogical imagination" strategy. Tracy argues that if that conversation takes place, in which everyone is prepared to risk their own interpretation, then a responsible consensus is likely to emerge.[234]

Interpreting a religion is not a merely cognitive exercise. All strategies can be helpful to unveil the multifaceted and uncontrollable aspects of a religion: explanation, hermeneutics of critique, hermeneutics of suspicion, and hermeneutics of retrieval. Any purported single way to interpret religion is surely leading to reductionism. Besides these different strategies, praxis must also be a key factor in interpreting religion. "Doing," that is to say, living out the truth of that religion and adopting a mystical-political approach to religion, can be crucial in ensuring a full theological interpretation. In this respect, he converses with the insights of liberation theology. He thinks that liberation theology's insistence on the preferential option for the poor and on the importance of hearing how the poor interpret their faith helps theologians to recenter their task by paying attention to the voices of the poor and the oppressed. At the same time, he is also insistent on the need to avoid a new reductionism that would deny the existence of other voices apart from those of the poor and oppressed.[235]

Religion and its classics, insofar as they bear ultimate, universal claims, are, by definition, open to everybody: academy people, ordinary people, believers, nonbelievers, and, in general, to everyone prepared to risk their interpretations. For those prepared to do so, religion can bear important fruits. It can liberate from self-centeredness; it can empower people to accept the other as other; it can free them from a society too controlled by an instrumental reason that colonizes all realms of life and empties the public realm. In any case, despite all the difficulties and conflicting interpretations, not to give up the effort to keep the conversation alive in order to interpret all the classics of all traditions may be, says Tracy, the best source of resistance and hope.

As a summary, Tracy's attempt in *Plurality and Ambiguity* is to show publicly that the conversation with the religious classics, heeding their claims and risking their interpretation, is an important route to rescue the postmodern self. In this sense, it is important to notice the similarity with Metz's insistence on the necessity of rescuing both the modern domineering subject and the postmodern subject of the *Kulturkarneval* on the basis of the dangerous memories of the radical Christian God.

Naming God in an Age That Cannot Name Itself

One of the problems with postmodernity is precisely the ambiguity of such a naming for a time that, although critical to modernity, seems to have problems in finding its own identity.[236] For Tracy, postmodernity is, fundamentally, a turn to the other. Whereas modernity turned to the subject and was centered around the autonomous, self-conscious self, postmodernity turns to all those others who had been marginalized by the basically Eurocentric modern interpretation of history, of reason, and of the self. Postmodernity entails the irruption of all the repressed others who, with their presence, disrupt the modern conversation, unmask it, and make their voices heard. One cannot fail to see the similarity of this interpretation of postmodernity as the irruption of the other with Gutiérrez's interpretation of the Latin American situation, whose main trait is the irruption of the poor, of the marginalized, making their voices heard.

Tracy, however, distinguishes between the postmodern categories of "the other" and "the different." Whereas for him "the other" has a dialectical-ethical-political character, "the different" lacks that character, referring, mainly in thinkers like Jacques Derrida and Gilles Deleuze, to the dissemination of meanings in language, to the undecidability of all meaning. For these latter authors, dialectical otherness does not allow the different to be such because it forces it into a dialectical opposition.[237] Tracy does not frontally oppose Derrida's "different" but considers that the ethical-political dimension in postmodernity, precisely through and in the repressed others pointed out by Levinas, is the most promising and liberating trait of postmodernity.

His theological strategy in this postmodern age is to try to rethink the meaning of the main referent of reality and of the main object of theology, namely, God, the radical other.[238] This turn to God marks the final turn, so far, in Tracy's theological enterprise.[239] His attempt to name God can be seen both as an interruption of his original revisionist theological program and as a logical development of the basic implications of this program in view of the postmodern cultural shift.[240] Although acknowledging the contribution of modern theology to the understanding of God's constitutive relationality, Tracy realizes the limits and pitfalls of that modern theology, arguing that "*Theos* has returned to unsettle the dominance of the modern *logos*."[241] Tracy criticizes the theology of the modern period, "obsessed with finding the exactly right method, the irrefutable modern rational argument, the proper horizon of intelligibility for comprehending and perhaps controlling God." In response to the logos-excess of modern theology, "postmodern theology is an honest if sometimes desperate attempt to let God as God be heard again: disrupting modern historical consciousness, unmasking the pretensions of modern rationality, demanding that attention be paid to all those others forgotten and marginalized by the modern project." This theological shift can be clearly observed in Tracy's own theology, from the method-centered *Blessed Rage for Order*, responding to the cognitive crisis of modern historical consciousness, to his new theological foci, "the other" and naming God through routes other than those preferred by modernity.[242]

The work on three main aspects underlies and fuels Tracy's turn to the other, indeed to God as radical other: interreligious dialogue, the retrieval of premodern religious classics, and the attempt to overcome the modern divisions between thought and feeling, content and form, and theory and practice. Interreligious dialogue and the retrieval of the premodern religious classics provide Tracy with radically, albeit analogical to be sure, new resources to imagine and rethink that God who resists being controlled by the modern logos. The insistence on the vital role played by feeling, form, and practice in any way of construing—that is to say, imagining, understanding, and interpreting—reality at all widens significantly both the notion of reason and the inner link between thought and life and between theology and spirituality. In turn, all these three elements are interrelated and keep feeding back into each other. Overall, from the point of view of the development of his theological program, Tracy's later work can be seen as a way to put to work his hermeneutical approach to theology in and through a model of conversation as the best path to the development of that hermeneutical approach.[243]

Tracy has interpreted postmodernity as an ambiguous age that has difficulties in naming itself.[244] Tracy argues that "Any postmodern thinker who believes that she or he can now leave this ambiguous modern scene and begin anew in innocence is self-deluding." That is the reason Tracy thinks that postmodernity needs as much suspicion as any other tradition. For him, postmodernity's small concern with ethics is its most ambiguous point, although he also thinks that "Postmodern thought at its best is an ethics of resistance. Resistance, above all, to more of the same."[245]

He sees three competing interpretations of the age at work. The first is represented by those for whom the current age still belongs to the age of modernity. Some among them, like Habermas, are aware of, and opposed to, the failures of modernity but interpret postmodernity simply as another critical moment of an unfinished modernity. For them, the solution lies in pursuing further, and more critically, the ideals of modernity.[246] The second interpretation of the age is represented by those who, convinced of the limits, excesses, and oppressive uniformity of modernity, discard the latter as a completely dead-end project and propose a way ahead that, to a great extent, entails a strong antimodern stand. The third interpretation is represented by those for whom postmodernity is definitely a new cultural turn and not merely another critical moment within modernity.

Tracy's own position can be somehow included in the third interpretation of the age, but with very clear stresses. Overall, he sees postmodernity as an age different from modernity, but to which the only possible way is through modernity and not around it—through modernity, because the ideals of universal and emancipatory reason, of justice, and of solidarity cannot be left behind but must necessarily be incorporated into any present and future project. It is important to notice that this is a view shared by Metz, Gutiérrez, and Tracy. These three thinkers share this view on strictly theological grounds. For the three there is no way out of the constitutive ethical requirements of Christianity. All three think that there is no possible interpretation of Christian salvation without a responsible self. It is precisely postmodernity's ethical ambiguity that makes both Metz and Gutiérrez so suspicious of it. Because Tracy is aware of this ambiguity he stresses that postmodernity must have an ethical soul. Simply to replace a grand modern narrative by an equally grand postmodern antinarrative is not enough. It can be a new way of "more of the same." To insist on "the different" is not enough. That different cannot be just the result of either sheer indetermination or proclaimed undecidability of language. "The different" must become also "the other," a real new center and new perspective, capable of decentering reason from the obsessive self and of recentering it around those others who must be taken into account in their otherness. For Tracy, Levinas is one of the best examples of a thinker capable of giving postmodernity the ethical soul it needs.[247]

Despite its ambiguities, the postmodern age brings new resources, intuitions, and strategies other than those of modernity to the task of both interpreting reality and furthering the emancipatory nuclear vision and drive of modernity. Central to these new resources is the postmodern "turn to the other" as a new way of approaching reality away from the modern "turn to the subject." Among the repressed others, premodern classics and resources must be incorporated into postmodern readings of reality without thereby falling back into premodernity. All in all, Tracy, although aware of the pitfalls, temptations, and ambiguities of postmodernity, sees it as a promising and liberating way in whose center the experience of the other, of the uncontrollable, as challenge and as possibility, has taken center stage.

In accordance with his drive to find a way to name God in this postmodern era, Tracy has turned again to new preferred conversational partners,[248] most of them explicitly religious: the classics and the current thinkers of different religions; the Christian mystics; Christian classics that, like Cusanus and Luther, can render powerful readings of God marginalized by modernity; Plato and Platonist readings of Christianity;[249] and, in general, theologies and thinkers aware of the importance of form (like von Balthasar), the importance of practice in relation to theory (like Pierre Hadot and Lonergan), and the importance of rethinking God in terms other than ontological (like Jean-Luc Marion). The new partners have to do with Tracy's insistence on bringing together feeling and thought, content and form, and theory and practice in an attempt to respond to the pitfalls of a modernity that had severed those inner links, thus breaking the unity needed to inform reason properly. This retrieval of lost unity is what leads Tracy in his journey through premodern classics—helped by Hadot, Iris Murdoch, and other current thinkers—in which, for obvious reasons, modernity was not interested at all. Furthermore, in his dialogue with Marion, Tracy is attracted by ways of naming God that are not dependent on an ontological mental framework. In this sense, Marion's *God without Being*, beyond Aquinas's classical theism, provides Tracy with a new and more creative way to express who God is. In addition to these new referents, certain of his previous partners, like Eliade or William James, continue to be among his preferred conversational partners.[250] Still others, like Foucault and Ricoeur, are important referents for Tracy's interpretation both of the situation and of the kind of hermeneutical strategy required to respond to it.[251]

In his attempt to name God, the radical other, in this age, Tracy's involvement in interreligious dialogue is a way of putting into practice his proposal of hermeneutical conversation as the key strategy in risking an interpretation of the world's religious classics.[252] The conversation with other religions is understood as a way of understanding their religious classics not as projected others but in their otherness and difference. This conversation presupposes both a self-respect for his own Catholic resources and tradition and a self-exposure to the otherness and difference of the other traditions and their classics. Besides, the conversation also entails Tracy's willingness to risk his own understanding of reality and God, accepting the challenges coming from the conversation itself.[253] His work in this domain has been especially important in relation to Buddhism, Judaism, Orthodox Christianity, and archaic religions.

Tracy's dialogue with Buddhism is representative of how the interreligious dialogue has come to be an intrinsic part of his way of doing theology. The understanding of the self is one of the issues in which Tracy sees an "analogical imagination" that can bear fruit in a dialogue with Buddhism. Here Tracy sees a multiple fruitful theological conversation among Buddhism, Christianity, and postmodernity, which, in fact, is an exercise in dialogical-correlational theology. On the one hand, Buddhist understanding of the not-self, although clearly different from the Christian notion of the responsible self, can help in understanding better the kenotic, self-abasing character of the self in relation both to God and to the other, liberating that responsible self from its compulsive drive and its possessive individualism.[254] In this sense, Tracy uncovers those resources in the Christian tradition, namely, the radical apophatic, form-avert mystics, that can help most to disclose the similarities-in-difference between Buddhist and Christian understandings of the self. Within this wider dialogue, Tracy establishes an inner-Christian dialogue among different Christian radical apophatic mystics, in order both to interpret his own Christian tradition and to show, as clearly as possible, the most likely similarities, similarities-in-difference, and differences that can be established between Buddhism and Christianity as a result of this exercise of responsible dialogue.

Besides the dialogue with other religions, Tracy also seeks to establish a dialogue with postmodernity, that is to say, with his own interpretation of the current situation. Postmodernity, with its central critique of the modern self and its insistence on otherness and difference, becomes a natural partner in the Christian-Buddhist conversation about how to understand the self and, in the last analysis, Ultimate Reality. Through this conversation, Tracy seeks to establish a mutually critical correlation between his reading of Christianity and his interpretation of the situation as postmodern. In the process, Tracy retrieves mystical-apophatic categories and traditions of Christianity that allow him to find new theological ways for naming God.

In his search for ways to name God, Tracy's central aim is to render a fully Christian interpretation of, in his opinion, the most important metaphor for naming God: the Johannine "God is love." In trying to interpret this contemplative-meditative metaphor, Tracy seeks to expose it to two different but, ultimately, interrelated strands of both the scriptures and the

Christian tradition. The first strand is the apophatic-negative one. The second is made up of the historical, prophetic, and apocalyptic dimensions of the Christian faith.

Luther's understanding of the hiddenness of God is a radical expression of a God that logos cannot control. This hiddenness is so radical that it is not limited to Luther's characteristic dialectic of the hidden-revealed God, of the God revealed *sub contrariis*. Beyond this dialectic, Luther's portrayal of God's hiddenness tries to capture the actually uncontrollable, unfathomable, divinely free God—a God so other as to be absolutely frightening and fearsome. If Luther's rendering of God is that of a hidden-revealed God, the apophatic mystics experience God as comprehensible-incomprehensible. Tracy argues that these two ways of experiencing and expressing God have come very close to each other in current theology. Both ways disclose a God whose otherness and difference cannot at times even be approached by theology.

One of the things these ways take into account is the experience of suffering and evil in history. For Tracy, a theology that takes lightly this experience cannot be considered theology today.[255] In this sense, theology must open itself to the experience of evil and suffering and must be done from that experience, taking into account the different forms in which that experience has been expressed and, most of all, the praxis of resisting evil and suffering with hope. This is the only way theology can be done, thus overcoming a fundamental problem of modern thought, namely, the separation of thought from feeling, of content from form, and of theory from practice.

Postmodern thought and theology, in this respect, value very much the premodern felt unity of God, self, and cosmos, within which reason was understood in a participatory manner. Postmodern thinkers are also rediscovering the premodern importance of the different forms of expression in order to convey any given content. Finally, postmodernity is also sensitive to the way in which premodern thinkers related practice to theory.

In his move to name God today, Tracy argues that theology must take into account both all the crucial and plural biblical narratives and also the possibilities of the Greek cultural heritage. In this respect, God, understood as love, must be discovered and named, according to Tracy, by the wide range of possibilities that go from the mystical-meditative to the prophetic-apocalyptic. Only that wide range of narratives, of experiences, and of practices can render today an understanding of God as love that not only recovers a deep sense of participation or felt unity but also is capable of taking into account the frightening experiences of tragedy, of interruption, and of radical evil in history.

Chapter 5

The *Exitus*
from Transcendentality to History
and the *Reditus*
from History to the Mystery of God

The central thesis of this work can be summarized as follows: the three models of post-Rahnerian theology follow the double movement of *exitus-reditus* in relation to Rahner's theology. They exit transcendentality and move to history and society in order to place the discussion on God not at the preemptive level of the transcendental analysis of the conditions of possibility of knowing and being but at the level of the conditions of history and the experiences of nonidentity found in that history. Having done that, the three theologies retrieve the hiddenness and the incomprehensibility of God, thus coming back in a kind of recapitulatory way, each through its own theological journey and in its own terms, to the mystery of God in which Rahner himself recapitulated his theological enterprise.[1]

Theology under the Conditions of History

Rahner's crucial turn to the subject consisted in exiting the barren dogmatic approach of the schools to enter the domain of the subject and of historicity understood as an existential dimension of that "subject." This crucial turn allowed Rahner to link dogma with experience; revelation with historicity; and theology with anthropology. By doing so, Rahner established an inner relationship between grace and nature.

The post-Rahnerian theologians that we studied above move further from historicity-as-existential-dimension to the concreteness of history; from the abstract Rahnerian subject to the concrete subjects and nonsubjects in particular societies and cultures; and from the transcendental identity found in the original experience to the concrete experiences of nonidentity found in those particular histories, societies, and cultures. The catastrophes in history, the real presence of evil, and the experiences of discrimination, systemic injustice, and radical ambiguity are the challenges that function as *loci theologici* in the three post-Rahnerian theologies. In this respect, although these three models pursue further the historical and anthropological drive of Rahner's theology, their focus is very different, in that they approach God from those powerful experiences of nonidentity. Therefore, it could be concluded that the very intensification of Rahner's method leads these authors to approach God not from the basic Rahnerian experience of identity but from the disquieting and deeply disturbing experiences of nonidentity found in history.

In that sense, political, liberation, and public theologies are inextricably interwoven with the particularity and concreteness of the social, cultural, and historical contexts in which they were born and in relation to which they formulate the central themes of Christianity and, ultimately, the question of God. In doing so, political, liberation, and public theologies follow different paths in response to the concrete social, cultural, and historical challenges each of them confronts.

Political theology, born in the context of a highly developed, and historically complex, German society, seeks to respond, on the one hand, to the privatization of religion, typical of the developed societies of Europe. On the other hand, political theology wants to formulate Christian theology in a way that accounts for the concrete experiences of nonidentity in the history of those societies in general and of Germany in particular, namely, the Enlightenment, Auschwitz, and the Third World. By responding to those challenges, political theology tries to help both theology itself and the church to overcome the danger of being co-opted by modernity and aims at rescuing the subject from its loss of identity in a society that has colonized reason and separated it from its own history.

Liberation theology was born as a theological response to the experiences of systemic poverty, death, and nonpersonhood, in the context of a society founded on the grounds of colonization, dependence, and underdevelopment, in which the excluded, the nonpersons, have started to make their voices heard. In this respect, liberation theology represents a radically new kind of theological voice, namely, a voice that represents the so-called Third World theologies.[2] Liberation theology seeks to formulate Christian theology from the perspective of the nonpersons. In that sense, this theology wants to respond, on the one hand, to the experience of suffering and death. On the other hand, it aims at interpreting Christianity in a way that is relevant to people's liberation from all kinds of exclusions, dependencies, and exploitations.

Public theology comes from the highly pluralistic, powerful, diverse, and rather individualistic society of the United States in which a public and common realm must be nurtured by the contribution of the different particular traditions—traditions based in a variety of societies, cultures, and histories, some of them historically oppressed and exploited. Public theology seeks to overcome the dangers of privatization at the hands of a colonizing instrumental reason; of tribalization at the hands of a fundamentalism that risks denying altogether the value of reason; and of interpreting traditions in a too sanguine manner, unable to take into account their own systemic distortions, their ambiguous histories of effects, and their triumphalistic and excluding self-centeredness. Positively, public theology aims at making Christian theological claims public and at contributing to a postmodern society with the liberating and critical resources of the Christian tradition.

These three theological projects have a twofold common ground. First, they are firmly anchored in the reinterpretation of the Catholic theological tradition carried out by Karl Rahner, Bernard Lonergan, and the theologians of the French *nouvelle théologie*. Second, the three of them are born into late modernity, value positively the emancipatory drive of the Enlightenment, and seek to formulate Christian theology in a way that establishes a positive dialogue with modernity while, at the same time, criticizing it on different accounts but, ultimately, on strictly theological grounds.

The Three Models in Dialogue: The Theological Method

In assessing the nature and methodological approach of these theologies, it is important to pay attention to some fundamental issues. One of these issues is that these theologies share Rahner's attempt to establish a correlation between human experience and Christian faith. Another issue is the methodological role played by praxis, especially in liberation and political theologies. A third important issue concerns the methodological importance of social sciences and critical social theory for these theologies. Finally, their approach to the biblical texts and their use of them must also be explored.

Correlation and the Role of Praxis

The two basic anchorings of their common ground, namely, reinterpreted, re-created tradition and the late-modern situation, give these theologies a correlational character. In the case of Rahner, that correlational role is made clearly explicit in the anthropological grounding of his theology, that is to say, in the inner link he establishes between theology and anthropology, between revelation and human experience, between grace and nature, and between human history and the history of salvation. Rahner tries to make Christianity reasonable, meaningful, and relevant to the modern subject by intrinsically relating revelation and human experience.

The correlational role of theology, however, is different in each of the three post-Rahnerian models. Political theology emphasizes the apocalyptic strand of the Christian tradition in order to interrupt radically the situation created by a colonizing, evolutionistic-triumphalistic, and oppressive modernity. Metz seeks to relate, to be sure, the Christian message to this situation that does away with the subject and causes massive suffering and sheer annihilation. These experiences of nonidentity are the ground upon which Metz wants to formulate a postidealistic theology, that is to say, a theology that reflects on God not on abstract grounds but on the basis of the concrete realities and experiences of history.

His is also a practical theology, a theology that, like Gutiérrez's, recognizes *Der Primat der Praxis* (the primacy of praxis) as well as its epistemological correlate, namely, that truth must be done. As concerns Christianity's claims, the main problem for Metz is not the cognitive crisis of Christianity vis-à-vis modernity. On the contrary, Metz is convinced that Christianity has a most relevant and liberating message concerning the current situation. The problem lies elsewhere and is twofold: on the one hand, that message has been privatized, and its constitutive social-political-practical dimension has been lost; on the other hand, the subject that must do the truth of that message, namely the Christian church, has been co-opted by modernity and is utterly unable to do the truth and unwilling to pay the price of its orthodoxy in the practice of its life. Consequently, the two central concepts of political theology are praxis and subject.[3]

Theology itself is understood as a practical hermeneutics of Christianity. For Metz, the main hermeneutical problem lies not in the relationship between dogma and history but in that between theory and praxis, between the understanding of faith and social praxis. Faith can be adequately understood only if interpreted through the hermeneutics of praxis, that is to say, through putting that faith into practice, following Christ under the conditions of society and history. Trying to take a distance from a society centered around functional action, achievement, and success, Metz insists that Christian praxis must be understood both as action and passion, as a way of following Christ both in his active pursuit of the Kingdom of God and in his suffering.

Metz's theology, like Gutiérrez's, is grounded in the spirituality of a social Christian praxis. With Ricoeur and Tracy, truth must be understood more as manifestation than as adequacy. In more theological terms, Metz insists that the neo-testamentarian narrative in itself claims attention and demands acceptance.[4] However, in the case of both Gutiérrez and Metz, full and relevant understanding of that truth, of that narrative, will take place only through and in praxis, that is to say, in the doing of that which is narrated. Since the focal content of that narrative is made up of the dangerous *memoria passionis, mortis et resurrectionis Jesu Christi*, the theological hermeneutics is a hermeneutics of danger, of radical questioning, of radical transformation of the domineering social status.[5]

Metz has also somehow altered his understanding of theology. Although eschatology with an apocalyptic sting was always important for his theology, the theological understanding of Auschwitz prompted Metz to understand the eschatological event as a radical interruption of history. The *Theodizeefrage* has become the center of his later theological work and his way to approach the *Gottesrede*. In that respect, his theology has also taken an even more disruptive turn in relation to history and the situation while the question of God has taken center stage.

Gutiérrez's theology is correlational in its own terms. Gutiérrez's theology wants to relate to the situation of the poor, of the nonpersons in Latin America. His theology, therefore, entails an interpretation of the situation from the perspective of what he calls "the underside of history" and an interpretation of the word of God that can relate to that situation. Correlation takes in Gutiérrez a denouncing-prophetic-transformative character, vis-à-vis both the church and society.

One of the main traits of his theology is its crucial grounding in spirituality. This spirituality, made up of the silence of contemplation and the practice of following Christ, is the *actus primus* of the Christian.[6] Only then comes theology as an *actus secundus*. As such, Gutiérrez understands theology as a critical reflection on Christian praxis in the light of the word. The word and liberating praxis disclose each other in a dialectical way. This is the key hermeneutical principle of liberation theology.

Gutiérrez's theology is also firmly grounded in the life of the church. He, of course, might distinguish among the different publics to which Tracy referred in his revisionist project. However, his is a pastoral-practical theology that presupposes not only faith on the side of the theologian but also that the theologian be a member of the church, a follower of Christ within a community committed both to its own permanent conversion and to the transformation of society in the light of the word. Even more radically, theology is not only the work of an individual but, more and more, the ongoing task, as second act, of the communities that have already taken the first step of following Christ in prayer and Christian praxis. The theologian is from this perspective a committed member of a living and committed church and can be better described, in this sense, as an "organic intellectual" rather than as a private intellectual.

Gutiérrez, moreover, is fully aware of the social-cultural matrix of his liberation theology. He insists that his theology stems from the concrete Latin American situation, in which certain conditions obtain: massive poverty, pervasive religiosity, the highly relevant presence of the Catholic Church, and an "irruption of the poor" in the life of the region, demanding their voices be heard. It is from this particularity that he wants to make a public and universal claim both as regards the Catholic Church and in relation to the world society at large.

Tracy's basic aim is to establish a mutually critical correlation between Christianity and the contemporary situation. However, two main developments have taken place since he first formulated his correlational model of revisionist theology. First, the situation has changed in an important way: late, critical modernity has evolved into postmodernity. Second, Tracy's theological emphasis has varied quite substantially: philosophical-transcendental analysis gave way to hermeneutics, and hermeneutics has taken a more disruptive-ethical turn.

To be sure, these two developments are interrelated. It is also clear that none of the three moments of Tracy's theology, the metaphysical, the hermeneutical, and the disruptive-ethical, has eliminated the other two. The two former moments, especially the hermeneutical, continue to play an important role in Tracy's enterprise. Indeed, the concept of truth as manifestation, as disclosure-concealment, rather than as adequacy, suits quite well the task of knowing or discovering who God as radically other is.[7] However, the disruptive-ethical moment within that manifestation, more tailored to express a disruptive *Theos* that cannot be controlled by *logos,* is gaining momentum in Tracy's attempt to name God in "an age that cannot name itself." This, in turn, has given Tracy's theology an increasingly decisive mystical-prophetic formulation.[8]

Order in Tracy, expressed in his definition of the method and in his distinguishing among the three publics, modes of reflection, and criteria of truth and adequacy, has given way to a far more decentered and condensed approach in which the old order somehow dissolves, while its main elements coalesce, in a way, in a single project: naming God. In this decentered-condensed enterprise, particularity has become fragmented, and the disclosive power of the fragments through the different forms makes method, order, balance, and system simply inadequate and highly problematic.[9] Tracy's attempt to name God, therefore, cannot be easily located in either of the three theological disciplines he describes in *The Analogical Imagination.* Nor can it be said that the main public of this theological project is the academy or the church or society. In that respect, it seems rather a work that is aimed at a plurality of publics and that is being built upon different elements that stem from the different communities: the academy, the church, and society at large, including all the different fragments inside each of these communities. In a different order of things, it is also clear that Tracy's theological enterprise includes new elements: form has become as important as content, practice as important as theory; and it is now clear for him that there cannot be theology without spirituality.

As far as the method of correlation is concerned, then, Tracy is still clearly trying to relate God to the postmodern situation, but because of the very traits of that situation, God can now be heard more disruptively and less correlationally. In other words, the main question is not any longer how to formulate God in a way that is adequate to modern, critical reason but how to let God be God in an age that is looking for new and different ways of construing and imagining reality. One of the essential features of post-modernity is the "turn to the other," especially to all the repressed "others" of a culture controlled by modernity and by modern reason. This means also that God is in a way more "allowed" to adopt a "telling" mode vis-à-vis society, culture, and reason. Although hermeneutics, that is to say, interpret-ing what God "tells," continues to be necessary, the crucial task is, first of all, to hear God's voice as radically other. In that respect, Tracy's theology in the postmodern situation has become more Barthian.

According to its own character and aim, each of these theologies has its own *loci theologici*. For all three of them, the word of God, mainly as man-ifested through and in Jesus Christ and read and kept alive in the church and its tradition, is a crucial *locus theologicus*. However, because they want to relate to concrete histories and experiences in which God must be both discovered and reclaimed, each has its own preferred contextual or situa-tional *locus*. For political theology, the historical defeats and catastrophes, such as Auschwitz, and the need to rescue them constitute that *locus*. For liberation theology, that *locus* must be found in the poor, in the nonpersons, and in their liberation struggle, mainly in Latin America, but also elsewhere. Finally, public theology find its *locus* in a situation, especially but not only in the United States, of radical plurality and ambiguity, of radical crisis of modern reason and of the modern self in which the truth and the claims of the "others" must be heard and theologically assumed.

The Role of Social Sciences and Critical Social Theory

Rahner and the other theologians who brought about a radical revision of Catholic theology insisted on the necessity of using social sciences as partners of theology. This partnership has become real in the post-Rahnerian theologies here analyzed, precisely because they seek to relate to a concrete historical situation. From that aim follows a need to interpret that situation.

For both political and liberation theologies, social sciences and critical social theory play a very important role, especially in the works, *Glaube in Geschichte und Gesellschaft* and *Teología de la liberación,* in which both theologies were most systematically formulated. In the case of political the-ology the main partner is the critical social theory of the Frankfurt School with its insistence on negative dialectics. The main partners of liberation the-ology are the theory of dependency and some aspects of Marxism. Finally, critical social theory plays a corrective role within the process of interpreting conversationally both the modern situation and the Christian classics in the case of public theology. That corrective role must guarantee the unmasking of the possible systemic distortions of modernity and of those classics.

In the case of liberation theology, social theory plays an especially important role because one of the main practical aims of that theology is to transform reality, doing away with poverty, discrimination, and a context given over to death. Understanding the Latin American situation is crucial for that purpose. Gutiérrez insists that Christians not only must aid the poor but, more radically, must denounce those social conditions and the structural causes from which poverty stems—and change them. That, in turn, entails the kind of social diagnosis provided by critical social theory.

However, Gutiérrez has been insistent on the theological centrality of his enterprise. In this sense, he claims that the role of social theory in his theology is important and relevant but not foundational. In other words, Gutiérrez uses social sciences in order to get to know the situation to which his theology is addressed. His strictly theological work, however, is not grounded in the social sciences. Theology has its own sources, of which the word of God and the life of the Christian church in following Christ are the central ones.[10]

In general, although Metz, Gutiérrez, and Tracy have developed their theological projects in close dialogue with critical social theory, they have become more and more theocentric and their theologies have become in that respect more explicitly theological.

Interpretation and Use of Biblical Texts

Christian theology had to face very early the problem of interpreting the Bible. The same problem was one of the main reasons that, later on, Christian theology shifted from the *lectio* to the *quaestio,* thus giving rise to scholasticism. In modernity, the critical interpretation of the Jewish-Christian scriptures has been one of the main questions in relation to modern theology. Both literary and historical-critical methods have played a crucial role in understanding biblical texts in a way that could relate to modern critical reason. For some authors, of whom Bultmann is the most important representative, biblical texts had to be demythologized in order to be existentially meaningful. Other authors have tried to recover the historical truth in the gospels, such as in the case of the famous "quest for the historical Jesus," in order to understand the person and the work of Jesus.

The three post-Rahnerian theologies approach the Bible in a similar way. On the one hand, they take critical methods for granted, both in order to correct certain readings of the Bible that, going beyond the biblical boundaries, claim scientific and historical truth and in order to help, not to govern, the interpretation of the texts through historical, cultural, and literary analyses. On the other hand, their main approach to the Bible does not depend on the results those methods may offer. Critical methods have a corrective and auxiliary character but in no way can have a substantive character in reading scriptures theologically because they simply do not approach them from a salvific viewpoint but only from a scientific perspective. The three approach the texts, therefore, in a rather straightforward manner as inspired texts in which the believers have recognized a salvific truth that is paradigmatic for the Christian community.

Metz has stressed more and more the importance of the biblical narrative and of its grounding character as regards theological reason. In keeping with the theological centrality of concrete history and the concrete social-cultural environment, he totally opposes Bultmann's demythologized understanding of the Bible and insists on the importance of the biblical narrative for the theological task. More precisely, he stresses the narrative structure of the theological argument when he writes that "Ultimately, Christianity is . . . not a community of interpretation and argumentation, but a community of memory and narrative in a practical way."[11] This stress, in turn, is related to Metz's insistence on the theological grounding character of the category of memory.

In this respect, Metz reads the biblical narrative as that narrative that embodies the dangerous memories of suffering that make up the history of salvation and that, in the last analysis, are the main avenue to understanding the work and person of Jesus Christ and the mystery of God in relation to a culture centered around control, achievement, and success, and unable to account for the history of massive suffering and oppression and, especially, for the dead.

From this perspective, Metz is critical of historical methods that, on behalf of a questionable "scientific" history, try to reconstruct a historical text, thus doing away with the identity of the text, itself grounded in narrative and tradition.[12] Metz is especially critical of the reconstruction of the historical Jesus, which, in the name of history, risks marginalizing the stories that constitute the innermost character of the gospel, namely, as essentially a narrative of the subversive and dangerous memory of the passion, death, and resurrection of Jesus Christ, heard, remembered, and reenacted by the Christian community.[13]

Metz's aim in approaching the scriptures is not to have a balanced interpretation of them, which he suspects can end up in a neutral reading. On the contrary, his is a clearly located reading—a reading that pays attention to those texts that stress his interpretation of Christianity in terms of interruption, radical otherness of the Kingdom of God, liberating memories of suffering, praxis of following Christ as the only way to make Christianity manifest, and love of the other as other as foundation of universal solidarity. Metz's preferred sources are the dialectical Pauline texts,[14] those proclamatory texts in John that also stress the dialectic of God-world and God's radical otherness and sovereignty,[15] Mark's passion narrative,[16] Matthew's chapter 25 on the last judgment, the apocalyptic texts in the Book of Revelation, and the lamentation literature in the Old Testament, especially in Job, Psalms, and the Prophets.

Of the three theologians, Gutiérrez is the one who uses scriptures most often and systematically in his theological work. In that respect he can be considered the most biblical of the three, with a special sensibility for the Old Testament.[17] Furthermore, he is a clear example of how to read the scriptures theologically, paying attention to their plain ecclesial sense as the one controlling the reading, while at the same time using all the contributions of biblical critical methods to enrich that reading.[18]

Gutiérrez's constant use of the scriptures is one of the main traits of his theological method. In fact, it can be contended that Gutiérrez's theology is an ongoing meditative-reflective reading of the Bible from the perspective of a communitarian-ecclesial Christian praxis of following Jesus, living by the values of the Kingdom of God under the circumstances of poverty, injustice, and death in Latin America.[19] It is not by chance that one of the best examples of his theology is a direct theological reflection on a book of the Bible: the Book of Job. Gutiérrez always tries to make it possible that the texts speak for themselves.[20]

Although Gutiérrez reads the Bible plainly, he reads it from a concrete perspective, namely, the perspective of the poor and of the underside of history. In this sense, his reading is not a pure search for the meaning of the text but rather a dialogue from that concrete perspective with the God who, having been revealed in Jesus Christ, the very key to interpreting the Bible, is the avenger of the poor and the oppressed, the God of life and the lord of history and creation.

Reading the Bible, furthermore, is not only a personal act but also a communitarian one. For Gutiérrez the Bible must be read by the community of the church that wants to follow Jesus with a clear preferential option for the poor in Latin America. He sees this church represented by the grassroots communities that have taken that path and, most often, are made up of the poor themselves. The members of that church of the people, especially of the poor, have developed a fruitful dialogue with the Bible. They experience the word of God as close and familiar, directly speaking to their lives and concerns.[21]

The Bible is considered in the first place as a history-like narrative concerning the life of Israel or the personal itinerary of concrete people but always trying to express an experience of faith as well as the salvific actions of God in history. In that sense, Gutiérrez sees reading the Bible as a dialogue between two concrete experiences of faith and of historical salvation and hope. The current community of faith, from its own concrete historical conditions, establishes a dialogue with the community of faith whose testimony constitutes the biblical narrative; it also establishes a dialogue from its own history of suffering, hope, and salvation with the history of suffering, hope, and salvation narrated in the Bible.[22]

The living dialogue that takes place from the concreteness of social, historical, and cultural determinations is the main element governing the reading of the Bible within the community of the church that, to be sure, has its own authoritative tradition.[23] Critical methods can be helpful to improve the understanding of the biblical texts because they clarify the context, the conditions, the genre, and the style of the text. According to Gutiérrez, they are necessary to avoid either manipulating the text or a decontextualized and purely literal interpretation of that text.[24]

Despite his using almost all the books of the Bible in his theological work, Gutiérrez has some preferred or key authors and subjects. In terms of subjects, suffering, hope, liberation, promise, justice, gratuitousness, preference for the poor, ethical behavior, following Christ, and judgment are among his preferred ones. In terms of books, Exodus, Psalms, Job, and Isaiah are the most often quoted from the Old Testament. The most often quoted gospel is Luke, although Matthew 25 is one of Gutiérrez's key texts. He uses also John's proclamatory and disclosing texts concerning the role of the Son as truth, way, and life, the relation Father-Son, and the commandment of love. Paul and his dialectical theology of the cross are important for Gutiérrez, who also uses theologically the pastoral letters, James's insistence on the importance of linking faith to ethical behavior through works, and 1 John's "God is love" metaphor.[25]

Tracy has increasingly stressed the importance of narrative in rendering a correct interpretation of scriptures and, more specifically, of the gospels.[26] He approaches biblical texts as those classic texts in which the community of believers has recognized an authentic witnessing to God's revelatory event. In this sense, he does not separate the text from the church community that believes "*in* Jesus Christ *with* the apostles."[27]

Tracy insists that, strictly speaking, Christianity cannot be considered a "religion of the book" like Islam. In this respect, Christianity is rather for him "a religion of a revelatory event to which certain texts bear an authoritative witness."[28] The community that has recognized those texts as authoritative has interpreted them in an ongoing tradition.[29] The reading of the Bible, therefore, must be led by the faith in which the believer partakes with the whole community of the Christian apostolic church.

Critical methods, either historical or literary, can help, although not govern, the reading of scriptures. They can help to clarify some of the fundamental theological issues insofar as they throw light on questions concerning literary genres, historical circumstances, and social-cultural contexts. However, the reading of the texts must be done on the basis of the plain ecclesial sense of their narrative.[30]

Tracy considers the most central narratives in the Bible for a Christian to be the passion narratives and, in general, the different narratives concerning the Christ event. Those narratives, he argues, have resulted from the way the different early Christian communities have experienced and interpreted the Christ event as revelatory. Consequently, the gospel, history-like narratives are innerly related to the faith and the life of those communities. In this respect, he criticizes any attempt to make the Christian interpretation of the Christ event dependent upon the results of the "quest for the historical Jesus."[31]

History-like narrative is crucial for Christian theology. For, although the common confession acknowledges the identity and presence to the community of Jesus as Jesus the Christ, only the details of the gospel narratives can fully render this identity and presence in all their richness. Consequently, the full content of the confession is rendered explicit only in and through the narrative. In other words, confession is intrinsically linked to narrative. Finally, that narrative is acknowledged as authoritatively representing the apostolic understanding of the identity and presence of Jesus as Jesus the Christ.[32]

Unsurprisingly, Tracy not only acknowledges a plurality of renderings of Jesus the Christ within the gospel narratives themselves but highly values such a plurality as a legitimate and necessary manifestation of that multifaceted, and always in need of being reinterpreted anew, Jesus Christ. Therefore, the subsequent theological plurality of readings of those various narratives is also both legitimate and necessary.[33]

However, Tracy's own use of scriptures shows his concern for paying due attention to the different narratives and to the other genres that are related to them throughout the New Testament. He refers to Mark as interruptive, apocalyptic, and nonclosed; Luke as realistic, history-like, not responsive enough to contradiction and conflict, but, nevertheless, appealing to charismatic and Pentecostal Christians, and, at the same time, to those Christians sensitive to justice, ethics, and the poor; Matthew as community-oriented and paying special attention to the differences between Judaism and Christianity; John as meditative, appealing both to mystics and to metaphysical theologians; Paul as developer of the dialectical theology of the cross; the pastoral letters as manifesting concern with doctrine, institution, and tradition; the Book of Revelation, full of excess, intensity, and nonclosure, appealing both to apophatic mystics and to those with an apocalyptic sense of history.[34] Generally speaking, Tracy's own theological approach and instinct place him close to John's meditative gospel and letters. His central metaphor for naming God is 1 John 4:16: "God is love." However, he uses the other narratives and neo-testamentarian genres both as a corrective of the high Johannine Christology and because, more fundamentally, he thinks that only the full range of narratives and genres can render an adequate representation of Jesus the Christ, including thereby new ways of reading the Old Testament made possible by the richness of neo-testamentarian readings.[35]

The Three Models in Dialogue:
The Theological Content

Theologically speaking, the development of these three theologies is a journey headed toward a decreasing positive theological content; a journey in which the more they become genuinely theological, the more also they become negative theologies; in short, a journey of intensification down the *via negationis* toward the mystery of a God whose hiddenness must be taken with full seriousness.[36] In this sense, to talk about the theological content of these theologies means to follow their development into this, so to speak, progressive theological self-emptying.

The three theologians have advanced from an early stage in which historical consciousness, the crisis of cognitive claims in modernity, and the ensuing process of secularization were the main challenges, to a mature and later stage in which their theology confronts, in Metz's terms, the painful and difficult experiences of "nonidentity."

Indeed, Metz's formulation of postidealistic theology as a situational theology that takes into account the concrete experiences of "nonidentity" in history helps in understanding the somehow constitutive "negative" approach of this theology on the grounds of God's hiddenness. God is going to be approached not from the heights of God's presence and power in history but from those concrete experiences that somehow represent God's "failure" and are counterintuitive to the idea of God: the experiences of massive suffering and outright annihilation; of the vanquished and forgotten; of the abiding presence of evil and death in history; of the radical ambiguity of any historical achievement.

Paraphrasing Gutiérrez, God is going to be approached and interrogated from "the underside of history," from the history whose existence is denied or, at least, minimized in, and robbed of, its tragic proportions, so that it can be easily deformed, manipulated, and forgotten. This approach is best represented by Gutiérrez's own work on the most classic book of the Bible concerning the tragic destiny of the innocent: the Book of Job.

As regards the theological core of these theologies, each of them favors a given moment or symbol of Christian salvation. Although the Christ event plays a central role in all of them, compared with Rahner's rather protological understanding of salvation, Metz emphasizes eschatology, Gutiérrez stresses the christological moment, and Tracy insists on the balance of those different aspects within the already–not-yet paradigm of salvation whose main form is the Christ event.

The Deep Ambiguity of History

The crucial theological shift of these theologians has been to make historical, concrete experience the main entry to theology, that is, to understanding both God's nature and work.[37] The classical themes of theology—creation, fall, redemption, church, eschatology—are going to be analyzed in relation to that concrete historical experience that, as explained above, is the experience of nonidentity. Each of the three theologians focuses on a different, albeit related, experience of this nonidentity. In the case of Metz, the key experience is the paradoxical history of effects of the Enlightenment, paradigmatically represented in Auschwitz. Whereas the "official" values of freedom, equality, and universal solidarity are preached, an instrumental *halbierte Vernunft* (halved reason) has taken over the project of the Enlightenment, bringing about domination and massive and systemic annihilation, destroying the subject, voiding the public realm, and enthroning hatred and apathy as social attitudes.

For Gutiérrez, the history of Latin America is a history of colonization, domination, oppression, and denial of the identity and personhood of the "Indians" by the European-Christian "saviors." This history of exclusion is an ongoing one, not limited to the sixteenth-century conquest but manifested still today in the unequal international relations, in the poverty that affects the vast majority of people in the world, and in the ideological, cultural, technological, and economical domination the rich-countries minority exerts over the dependent-poor majority.

In the case of Tracy, the main experience is the sheer plurality of unabridgeable perceptions of reality and, most of all, the radical ambiguity of every historical achievement. Even the classics cannot escape this overarching ambiguity. Their history of effects shows their shortcomings, systemic distortions, and denial of the existence of the "others." Modernity has become especially liable in this respect with its claim to a uniformizing universality that completely excluded and, therefore, oppressed and suppressed the "different."

Because of this theological location, creation will not be primarily understood by these three authors as the protological salvific act of God in which grace, that is to say, God's own self-communication, once and for all is "always-already" present. Rather, creation is going to be historicized and thus understood as the stage in which both the presence of evil and suffering and the salvific action of God take place.[38]

There is an important difference between the way these theologies see the presence of sin and evil in history and Rahner's interpretation of this presence. From his existential-personal perspective and in the framework of his transcendental argument, Rahner understands sin as a metaphysically quasi-impossible reality;[39] original sin as a sort of historical, preexistent co-determination of freedom;[40] and the existence of radical evil as a mysterious reality that, in any case, does not compromise the abiding sovereignty of God.[41] From a historical-theological perspective, especially in the case of political and liberation theologies, the presence of evil in history is a major issue and, therefore, becomes theologically crucial.

For these theologies, history cannot be either easily read as a triumphal progression toward freedom and justice or rendered theologically irrelevant through a transcendental analysis for which grace is necessarily "always-already" present. Such optimistic or transcendental views either contradict the facts or do not take them seriously theologically. If suffering, poverty, evil in its different expressions, and death are not to be forgotten and suppressed by a history read with the eyes of the victors or by a theology that runs so high that it does not touch them in its development, then history must be reread from the perspective of suffering, and Christianity must be reinterpreted also from that perspective.[42]

Metz's theology has had from its very inception some crucial elements that have radically relativized history in general and modern, evolutionary readings of history in particular. Eschatology and hope are two of the most important among them.[43] However, an important change, indeed a process of increasing radicalization in his understanding of history and the history of salvation, can be traced from his *Christliche Anthropozentrik* to his "*Gottesrede* after Auschwitz."[44]

Whereas in his *Christliche Anthropozentrik,* world, history, and Christianity were understood in rather evolutionary terms, his political theology increasingly emphasized both the dangers of an optimistic view of history and the centrality of the memory of suffering in history as a category to interpret and judge it and, most of all, to interpret and envisage the future. History is, therefore, for Metz not primarily the stage of action and progress but, on the contrary, the stage of unredeemed suffering (*passio*) become history's main hermeneutical criterion and judge. This *conversio ad passionem* is the central point of view or perspective from which all Metz's theology stems. In a way, this point of view is Metz's, so to speak, version of Gutiérrez's reading of history from its underside. Metz, however, is in a way more radical, since his category of suffering is constitutively embedded in his negative theology of history and salvation. In order to express the hermeneutical importance of this category, Metz refers very often to the "authority of those who suffer," as when he writes: "I only know a really universal category: *memoria passionis.* And I only know one authority, which cannot be revoked by any Enlightenment or emancipation: the authority of those who suffer."[45]

Metz's *passio* perspective has led him to confront the traditional doctrine of original sin as the central explanation of the presence of evil in history. According to his views, Augustine's doctrine of original sin simply does not respect the biblical theology concerning the reality of evil and the way human suffering is always related ultimately to God. Creation and history, therefore, cannot be simply explained in terms of human freedom and action. Rather, they must be understood, on the basis of the biblical narrative that brings to the fore the memory of suffering, as ultimately being in the hands of a God whose acts remain always hidden to human categories.

Basically, then, the role of human action in history is not to advance in the direction of a limitless progress. Any such triumphalistic understanding of history must be interrupted by the memory of suffering. Indeed, history must be understood precisely on the basis of the interruption caused by the memory of suffering, the interruption that results from heeding the "authority of those who suffer." Human action in history, then, must be led by that memory of suffering to the practice of universal solidarity with all those who suffer, ultimately understanding history in the light of the definitive eschatological interruption through which and in which history is constituted and the dead and forgotten of that history are rescued. This memory of suffering is not mainly a category of the past but an eschatological category, a memory that represents the active, salvific presence in history of God's eschatological salvation.

It is on these bases that Metz judges the emancipatory character of the Enlightenment. Insofar as the Enlightenment is unable to account for the victims and suffering of history, far from being emancipatory it becomes an ideology of oppression and domination. Its results are most clearly seen in the catastrophe of the Holocaust but are also noticeable in a theology and a church praxis that go on mostly unquestioned by this historical interruption.[46]

For Gutiérrez, the history of Latin America and the fact that the vast majority of people in the world belong to the mass of the poor witness to the fact that history has been built upon domination, inequality, exclusion, oppression, and, ultimately, death. It is in that context that he poses the question of the meaning of God's love.[47]

History, however, is not the realm of evil but the stage in which, through salvific acts, God's self-manifestation takes place: God saves and acts in history. In this perspective, Gutiérrez understands creation as God's "first salvific act" in history, within a salvific design whose aim is that all become God's children. This implies, in turn, that "history is one," that is to say, that the history of salvation and human history cannot be separated. Creation, therefore, is a salvific act of God "integrated into the history which is being built by human efforts."[48]

At the time of his *Teología de la liberación,* Gutiérrez had a rather anthropocentric understanding of creation. Human beings were not only the center but also the masters of a creation they were called to dominate.[49] Partaking in that "high anthropology" typical of modernity, Gutiérrez had also a high view of the historical role of human beings. They had been created to collaborate with their free agency in continuing the work of creation and, therefore, to dominate the earth and coparticipate in their own salvation through their historical pursuit of liberation and justice. It is precisely this liberating and mediating role of human self-creation in history that can establish an inner link between creation and salvation.[50]

This understanding of history as the stage in which the salvific design of God takes place, intrinsically united to creation through the mediating human agency in pursuit of freedom and justice, is somewhat reworked by Gutiérrez in his later work. Biblically speaking, whereas his *Teología de la liberación* focuses on the Exodus paradigm, his later work shifts the emphasis to the suffering Job. In his *Teología de la liberación* there are only two references to the Book of Job, both related to the focal relevance of human agency in history. In his later theology, however, his work on Job, in relation to the suffering of the innocent, plays a crucial role. The previous anthropocentric understanding of creation and of the relation between human agency and the rest of creation is now questioned on the basis of God's freedom and sovereignty: human beings are neither the center of creation nor its measure. Creation responds only to God's gratuitousness and design. Gutiérrez writes that "God's discourses are a vigorous rejection of a purely anthropocentric understanding of creation. Not everything that exists was made for the immediate utility of human beings, who may not, therefore, judge everything from their own viewpoint. The world of nature expresses God's creative freedom and joy."[51]

A second crucial point follows from this understanding of creation: not only nature but also history is affected by this recentering of creation. Whereas human self-creation in history was the focal point at the previous stage in Gutiérrez's theology, at this second stage human history and destiny, personified in Job, are ultimately made dependent on God's gratuitous purpose, not necessarily coincident with human pursuits. In recognizing this, human behavior is not limited to ethical-prophetic action but essentially turns to the mystical-contemplative acknowledgment of God's sovereign gratuitousness.[52]

Tracy has progressively questioned his initial view of both creation and history. In fact, his original revisionist project was not directly touched by his later acute perception of the ambiguity inherent in human history. The world, human beings, and history were seriously affected by sin, but, using unmasking critique in due measure, the historical project of modernity, best perhaps represented in "the American experiment," was basically doable and good.[53] Correspondingly, the modern subject and modern reason were firm enough to ground and to perform a metaphysical argument based on a sufficiently accurate interpretation of the situation. In other words, there were crises in history but not interruptions; there was ambiguity, but progress was still possible; there was suspicion, but reason was basically sound and reliable.[54]

Theologically speaking, the analogy-led ordered relations concerning

God, the self, and the world started to become more problematic and less objectifiable the more reason became hermeneuticized and the presence of ambiguity in history more manifest. Correlation between concrete history and Christianity was still pursued but not any longer from "positive" historical experiences but rather from the "negative" experiences of suffering and failure.[55]

For the later Tracy, from *Plurality and Ambiguity* on, creation and history cannot be finally interpreted either as the field of human progress or the stage of a linear history of salvation in which God's salvific acts are presented in a manifest and uncontradictable way.[56] On the contrary, modern interpretations of human progress must be highly suspected of domination and exclusion of those who, according to modernity's cultural standards, are not moderns. In other words the hermeneutical key on whose basis "progress" is unmasked and judged is the reality of exclusion and human suffering.

Creation and history, therefore, cannot be theologically construed either on the basis of a modern-like grand narrative that pays no attention to the details of the biblical narrative of suffering or on a purely biblical intratextual basis, thus ignoring the contradictions and real suffering in concrete human history. On the contrary, both the reality of historical suffering and the details of suffering in the biblical narrative must be the basis upon which the history of salvation must be understood.[57]

Salvation in Jesus Christ

As Christian theologians, Metz, Gutiérrez, and Tracy stress the importance of Christology. Metz emphasizes the *memoria passionis, mortis et resurrectionis Jesu Christi* as the focal paradigm of the Christian understanding of history, salvation, and God on an eschatological horizon. For Gutiérrez, Christ is the very center of God's liberating action in history. Finally, Christology is for Tracy the interpretive key of any understanding of Christianity and of the Christian God.

Metz's Christology is, like all his theology, a Christology that seeks to establish an inner link between the Christian message and the historical situation in an eschatological key. Jesus Christ's salvific power is intrinsically united with his *memoria passionis, mortis et resurrectionis*. Who this Jesus Christ is, is known through this *memoria*. At the same time, his salvific power acts in history through the liberating power of that dangerous *memoria*, as anticipation of the future for all those who are hopeless, oppressed, and vanquished.[58]

Jesus, consequently, cannot be understood either as a triumphant victor or as a purely religious redeemer. Metz wants to preserve both the constitutive *passio* character of the Christ event and the political-historical dimension of his redemption. For Metz, the memory of suffering and death cannot be annulled by the memory of resurrection. The memory of suffering and death is also a constitutive part of the memory of resurrection. They belong together. There is no "Easter Sunday–Christology" without "Holy Saturday–Christology."[59] In this respect, the Christ event, as a foundation of hope in history, must be interpreted as a dangerous memory of suffering that proleptically announces a definitive eschatological salvation. This proleptic announcement both prompts a solidary historical response in favor of all the oppressed and forgotten in history[60] and interrupts any easy affirmation of intrahistorical salvation.[61]

Christ appears closely united in Gutiérrez to his idea of integral liberation. Within liberation theology's understanding of God's salvation in history, Christ is *el liberador* (the liberator).[62] In this sense, although Gutiérrez's theology is also aware of the importance of the eschatological dimension, it has a markedly christocentric and intrahistorical character. More to the point, the intrahistorical dimension of salvation on the basis of Christ's integral liberation is crucial for this theology that seeks to expose both the inner link between Christian salvation and political-ethical transformation of society and the historical role of Christians in bringing about this transformation.[63] Christology, in this sense, is primarily understood in its salvific-redemptive character.[64]

Gutiérrez stresses some traits of Jesus Christ. One of them is his historical, concrete existence. Christ is not an ideal, ahistorical figure but a concrete person who lived and acted in a determined time in history. Another trait of this historical Jesus is his aligning himself with the poor and marginalized people.[65]

But, in his later work, the idea of Christ's action as liberator in history is going to be increasingly complemented by a view of the suffering Christ as radically solidary with the poor of history. In this sense, using Metz's terms, the Christ of *actio* is going to be more and more seen as the Christ of *passio* in the suffering faces of the poor.[66] In this new scenario, the ethical-historical dimension of salvation in Christ is going to be interpreted under the light of God's sovereignty and gratuitousness.[67]

At the time of *Blessed Rage for Order,* Tracy's discussion of Christology was directly related to his enterprise of establishing a critical correlation between the situation and Christianity. In that work, Tracy's understanding of Christianity is clearly christocentric. Christological language is discussed in terms of limit-language, from a basically existential perspective.[68] The systematic-hermeneutical approach of *The Analogical Imagination* focuses on interpreting the Christ gift/grace/event in a balanced way that takes into account both the three main christological statements—incarnation, cross, and resurrection—and the full possibilities of the always-already yet not-yet salvation paradigm.

In his final work on God, Tracy makes it clear once again that the crucial question Who is God? can only be answered through and in Jesus the Christ.

However, there are several new emphases that show Tracy's own theological development. First, the former Christian christocentrism is replaced by theocentric christomorphism. In other words, the Christian God, the very center of Christianity, can only be rendered through the Christ form. Second, on intratextual grounds, Christ is not only manifested in the different forms of the narratives and genres of the New Testament. The full spectrum of forms in the Bible must be also taken into account for that purpose. Third, Tracy's understanding of God through and in Christ turns to the concrete "others" of history in order to read the Christ event, taking into account the history of suffering and oppression of these suppressed others.[69]

A Church That Bears Hope by Following Christ

The church plays different roles in Metz, Gutiérrez, and Tracy. For the three of them, the church is primarily the community that, following Christ in history, announces his truth and bears his hope under the conditions of history.

Radical discipleship entails a danger in practical, sociopolitical terms when guided by the dangerous memory of suffering. The church must embrace this discipleship and its ensuing costs in order to be the witness to God's liberating message and action. Discipleship is therefore one of Metz's key issues, directly related to the practical nature of the Christian faith. Believing and understanding the full content and implications of faith go hand in hand with the practice of discipleship in historical and political terms. There are two crucial traits in the *Nachfolge*. First, its radicalness. Those who follow Christ must be prophets whose life refers constantly in practical terms to the dangerous and subversive memory of Christ. Because the problem of Christianity is its having been co-opted by the model of the *bürgerliche Gesellschaft,* the church must play a clearly prophetic role that must serve both to make Christianity understandable and credible in practical terms and to rescue the subject in a society in which an instrumental reason reigns overall and has converted the subjects into passive practitioners of the ways and aims imposed by this reason. The second trait of the *Nachfolge* is that the disciples must be prepared to pay the price of their praxis. Such a praxis is dangerous and risky because it is based on a dangerous and subversive memory.

For Metz the question of the church is essential because the crisis of Christianity is directly related to the inability of the church actually to announce the Christian message in a relevant way. The problem is that the church approaches its task in a rather theoretical, idealistic way and also understands Christianity in the same way. In other words, because the church does not do the truth it announces, its message completely lacks both meaning and credibility. The truth of Christianity can only be relevant when the community of believers pays the price of its orthodoxy through the dangerous orthopraxis of living out in history and society the implications of the *memoria passionis, mortis et resurrectionis Jesu Christi*.[70] Radical discipleship is crucial to this purpose. One of the main obstacles for the church to embrace this kind of discipleship is the way it is conceived and organized.

Metz thinks that, although the church is in principle "the people of God," it has been in fact traditionally conceived and organized as an institution in which the hierarchy both run and control it, supervising, so to speak, the life of the rather passive faithful. This traditional *Betreuungskirche* (controlling church) has been replaced in the developed, democratic societies by a *Bürgerkirche* (citizen-church: a church according to the needs of the modern citizen) understood as an efficient institution that provides the religious services required by the society that it serves. Neither of these two models can be properly understood as a church, as the community that follows Jesus in history and society.[71]

The church of the community of disciples must be a *Basiskirche* (grassroots church), a church of the people who are called to follow Jesus as a community. This is not a hierarchical, top-down church but rather a bottom-up church as far as initiative within the church is concerned. For Metz this prophetic, grassroots church of disciples is the condition for announcing relevantly the Christian message in developed societies. Actually, Metz sees a living example of this model of church in the grassroots communities of Latin America. They are a prophetic source of hope for the churches in the developed countries and in the rest of the world, especially in the postmodern situation, which requires the recognition of the other as other, both within the church and in society.[72]

In the case of Gutiérrez, the experience of the church that follows Jesus Christ in the Latin American situation of suffering and injustice is both the matrix of his theology and its main practitioner. In this sense, Gutiérrez's theology can be properly named both a church theology and a theology of the church and for the church. Accordingly, his theology is pastorally driven.[73]

In theological terms, Gutiérrez, following the main guidelines of the theology of the church in Vatican II, understands the church both as a sacrament of history and as a universal sacrament of salvation.[74] In this respect, the church is understood not as a self-centered reality but as a reality that lives to be a sign, a sacrament of the Lord and of the Lord's salvific grace, for the world. The church is, then, on the one hand, grounded in God and, on the other hand, living for the world and in a close relation of mutuality with it.[75]

One of the central names of this missionary, sacramental church is "people of God." Although the church is also a human institution, its constitutive character is spiritual; this is to say, the church is the community gathered and inhabited as a people by the Spirit to live in common its faith in the Lord.

Therefore, the church must make visible, in its very organizational structure and in the way it is run, the message that it bears and its spiritual nature.[76] The church is the people of God in history. Once again, this historical, concrete dimension is crucial in Gutiérrez. The historical dimension is essential to the church's nature. Bearing its eschatological hope is the historical task of the church and the main reason for its existence. The church was founded by Jesus Christ in order to give witness in history to God's salvific design as announced by and manifested in him.

Gutiérrez links the historical task and mission of the church in Latin American to the social situation of that region. The mission of the church in Latin America does not consist in the purely religious announcement of an ahistorical message of salvation. Rather, the church, understood as the Christian community and people of God,[77] must read politically "the signs of the time" and announce its message of Christian liberation in relation to the struggle for justice and liberation going on in Latin America. This task, moreover, must be performed not in a distant and detached manner but in the church's active self-alignment with the poor and their liberation struggle. Finally, the poor themselves cannot be seen as mere recipients of the aid of the church but both as subjects of their own liberation and as evangelizers in and of the church.[78]

The church must be guided by the spirit of discipleship. In being a disciple of Christ in history and society, the church does the truth, thus understanding the meaning both of Christ's message and of the Kingdom of God he proclaimed and making that message relevant and meaningful for society at large. Performing this orthopractical task in Latin America under difficult and dangerous conditions, the church pays the price for its orthodoxia with the fertile blood of the martyrs.

In the case of Tracy, his environment is paramount in the way he understands the church. He understands it in two different ways. One is the theological-systematic understanding of the church. The second is directly related to his experience of the Catholic Church in the pluralistic and religiously disestablished context of U.S. society. In this latter sense, the church is concretely understood both as the institution and as the community bearer of the particular identity of the Catholic tradition and shared meanings in that pluralistic society.[79]

For Tracy, then, talking about the church means elaborating on that particular Catholic identity that stems from the specific experience of the Catholic people and the Catholic Church within "the American experiment." One of the main traits of this experiment is its Protestant soul. The Catholic minority, therefore, was not especially welcomed into the experiment, being suspected, among other things, of being "papist" and non-American. The "strange" character of the Catholic Church in the United States was magnified by the fact that, although present in the country from the very beginning of the process of colonization, it gained in importance and social weight as a result of the successive waves of Catholic immigrants from Europe. Thus, it was seen as a church of poor immigrants. Only in the twentieth century have Catholics become a "public" church, playing an increasingly important role in the life of the experiment. Their public voice, seen more naturally and accepted as both Catholic and American, has become a relevant element in the life of the nation, especially in matters concerning social justice and peace.

Due to this particular experience, Tracy's theology has sought both to reflect on the character, ethos, and identity of this particular Catholic tradition and to make it publicly available and meaningful in U.S. society at large.[80] As far as the first of these aims is concerned, Tracy has emphasized the social-communitarian character of Catholicism vis-à-vis Protestant individualism and what he has named the Catholic analogical character in relation to the more dialectical character of Protestantism.[81] As concerns the second aim, he has advanced his proposal of an "analogical imagination."

This experience is somehow embedded in Tracy's sociological and theological approach to the church. Corresponding to his U.S. experience, Tracy considers the church as a "community of moral and religious discourse." Alternatively, he understands that the churches may be considered "voluntary associations exercising a mediating function between the individuals and society as a whole." In any case, both aspects, the more particular and communitarian, on the one hand, and the social-public, on the other hand, must be interrelated in Tracy's opinion.[82] Both sociological aspects, the particular-communitarian and the public one, are, in turn, related to the specifically theological identity of the church.

In referring theologically to the church, Tracy adopts a Christian ecumenical perspective.[83] The church, from this theological point of view, can be best described as an "engifted participatory reality in the event of Jesus Christ" or, following Rahner and, especially, Schillebeeckx, as the "sacrament of Christ and eschatological sacrament of the world." The church, in this respect, cannot be identified with the Kingdom of God. On the contrary, the church remains always under the judgment of the eschatological reality of this kingdom.[84] The church so understood has an intrinsically universal, hence public, character that cannot be eliminated without compromising its very identity.

Within this framework, Tracy stresses the mediating role of the church in relation to the Christ event. This mediation is envisaged by him in two different forms. First, as a tradition understood as an ongoing memory of the Christ event in direct relation with, and dependent on, its reception and interpretation by the apostolic witnesses as expressed in their neo-testamentarian writings.[85] Second, this mediation is viewed as a tradition lived out in the world, that is, through and in the praxis of the *imitatio Christi* in the concrete conditions of history and society. This aspect has been increasingly highlighted by Tracy over the years, both because of his exposure to what he names "practical" theologies, especially political and liberation theologies, and because of his recent emphasis on the necessary link between theory and practice in order to overcome the pitfalls of the modern tradition's notion of reason. Here, the correspondence with Metz's notion of the actualization and validation of orthodoxia through orthopraxis can be clearly observed.[86]

Eschatology as Constitutive of History

If Rahner's core theological understanding of salvation is rather protological, Gutiérrez's christological, and Tracy's christomorphical, Metz's key theological category is eschatology. Indeed, eschatology pervades Metz's theology to such an extent that every other category or theological statement must be understood from a radically, indeed interruptive, eschatological stand.

One of the most important theological paradigms in the late twentieth century has been the classic "already–not-yet" paradigm. Rahner, Gutiérrez, and Tracy formulate their theology within this paradigm. This paradigm tries to make explicit the necessary balance and radical tension between the historical presence and actuality of salvation and its final, eschatological nature; between the incarnated, dead, and resurrected Jesus Christ and the Christ to come at the end of time; between ethical commitment in history and radical inadequacy of every historical achievement. As such, this paradigm is a sign of the importance of eschatology in recent theology.

Metz, however, wants so much to stress the radical nature of eschatology that he is suspicious of this "already–not-yet" formula. The problem for him is twofold. On the one hand, he fears that the strength of the "already" may silence the experience of nonidentity, the memory of suffering, that belongs to the experience of Jesus himself and to the core of the biblical religion. On the other hand, he fears that the radical eschatological dimension, indeed interruption, of Christianity may be simply seen, in practical terms, as the final or definitive step of a salvation that "already" is at hand and grows in history. From this point of view, he insists on the apocalyptic character of Christianity and on the need for stressing the expectancy of the final coming of the Lord. He writes that "the primary question is not the seemingly 'specifically Christian' question of how much salvation we 'already' have and how much 'not yet' (in which time-horizon is here understood the difference between 'already' and 'not yet,' present and future?), but the question of how much time do we have at all (yet)? This is *the* eschatological time-question that is adequate to the non-evolutionary essence of time."[87]

Metz insists constantly that eschatology must be understood as the end of history, as the total and final interruption of history—so total and final that such an interruption is best understood in the biblical category of apocalypse. Because this interruption marks the definitive end of history, it is at the same time the point from which both history and historical action are, in a way, constituted. Without either memory or interruptive end, time and history become just mere repetition of an empty sameness, lacking, in the last resort, both identity and true existence.[88]

Creation, redemption, resurrection, history of salvation, and every Christian statement can therefore be rightly understood only on the basis of both their anamnestic and their eschatological character. Otherwise, they become just myths.[89] The eschatological dimension of Christianity constitutes the very foundation of hope. This hope includes, on the one hand, the historical signs of salvation manifested through and in the resurrection of Christ. However, it preserves, on the other hand, the experiences of nonidentity, the unresolved questions concerning the *passio et mortis Jesu Christi* and, in general, the suffering and evil in history. In the last analysis, Christian hope only can exist as imminent expectancy of the final coming of the Lord.[90]

This radical apocalyptic eschatology has its consequences for the importance of both human action and human responsibility in history. It would seem that the more the interruptive character of eschatology is accentuated, the more fragile and problematized human action in history becomes. In this regard, Gutiérrez and Metz are somehow different. Both stress historical responsibility and transformative action concerning the pursuit of justice, peace, and freedom. However, their different social contexts and concerns prompt them to put different accents on that common transformational thrust.

Metz wants the church to do the truth by following Christ in sociopolitical terms, but he wants to make sure that the *Homo emancipator* mentality does not take over the interpretation of the role of the Christian church in society—a role that, among other things, must also denounce that *Homo emancipator* mentality as one of the causes of domination and oppression in society.[91] Because every historical achievement is under the eschatological judgment and must be interrupted by the memory of suffering, liberating action is also understood rather in the terms of Adorno's negative dialectics. Liberating praxis must go definitely on, but its practical content will always be somehow provisional and ambiguous.[92]

Metz's corrective stress on the *passio* component of Christian praxis to differentiate this praxis from the action-driven domineering social practice, common in developed societies, is very different from the concerns of Gutiérrez, guided by the need to accompany the poor in their pursuit of liberation and justice. Stressing the *passio* element may be adequate in those societies to which Metz refers, but it could be misinterpreted and lead to resignation and passive acceptance of suffering and injustice in a society like the Peruvian one. In fact, historically the Catholic Church in Peru has been accused of having preached resignation or, at least, supported it implicitly.[93] Hence the initial suspicion of liberation theology about popular religiosity.[94]

This does not imply at all that Gutiérrez has disregarded that *passio* element. He knows very well both its Christian meaning and its being a fact in the case of so many Christians that have suffered persecution, torture, and even death for their commitment to the poor and to the pursuit of justice. The question here discussed, therefore, concerns the different emphasis of the two theologians within their common theological framework.

Tracy has increasingly come to appreciate the interruptive character of all those narratives that have been repressed by the reigning standards of modern reason and rationality. In this respect, he agrees with Metz's critique of a domineering reason whose discourse is always a discourse of success, achievement, and victory that disregards those voices and realities that would interrupt it. Indeed, claims Tracy, history cannot any longer be interpreted as an evolutionary and empty succession of "more of the same." The repressed others—Native Americans, African Americans, women, archaic religions, forgotten classics, peoples' narratives of suffering—must be allowed to enter this history and to interrupt it.

Moreover, Tracy has also moved toward a more interruptive understanding of suffering and evil. At the time of *Blessed Rage for Order* and *The Analogical Imagination*, using the already–not-yet paradigm, he interpreted Metz's apocalyptic emphasis as an intensification of the eschatological dimension of Christianity, that is to say, of the "not-yet" element of the paradigm, mainly vis-à-vis the Rahnerian stress on the "always-already."[95] In his more recent work, the interruptive character of the memory of suffering and the centrality of theodicy have surfaced with a new strength. For him, "to develop a *logos* on *theos*—a theology—today is to start by facing evil and suffering."[96] To be sure, Tracy's main approach continues to be an integrative, rounded approach. One thing, however, is changing. Integration is being built not exactly on the same analogical bases of *The Analogical Imagination* but by taking into account the full tension of the different elements that make up the Christian message. It is in this sense that Tracy's theology, although always analogical, has become more interruptive and, consequently, more eschatological.

Encountering the Mystery of God in History

Like Rahner, Metz, Gutiérrez, and Tracy have evolved in a strictly theological way, that is to say, have come to consider the question of God the fundamental, indeed only, question of their theologies after having developed their own models through different stages. Nevertheless, it would be a mistake to think that they have become more "theo-logical" either by retreating from their own historical-concrete approach and turning back to transcendental, idealistic, or intratextual approaches or because their theologies have come to a dead-end and needed to be abandoned and drastically reformulated. On the contrary, their move has come about as the result of a journey of intensification on the basis of their original historical approach.

There is a crucial aspect that is common to the three. The question of God comes to the fore of these theologies as a necessity of recognizing who this God, encountered in history, is. In this sense, it is a practical, not a theoretical, concern. If Tracy wants to name God in an age that cannot name itself; if Gutiérrez, with Job, seeks a way to speak of God in the midst of innocent suffering; and if Metz wants rather to root his *Gottesrede* in a prayer that expresses the *leiden an Gott*, it is not because they have suddenly converted to speculative theology but because they need to find their own way of talking about the God they have encountered in the concrete history in which they have developed their theological enterprises.

This journey into the mystery of God starts with a historical diagnosis. The three theologies make three moves. First, they approach history from the repressed memory and actuality of its failures, catastrophes, and inner ambiguities, namely, from the memory of suffering in Metz, from the "underside of history" in Gutiérrez, and from the radical ambiguities of history and traditions in Tracy. Second, they denounce and discard the modern, Western reading of history as evolutionary progress, this is to say, as an ideology that, although modeled after a concrete instrumental reason, presents itself as the measure of reason, right, and civilization and imposes its views, interests, and history on the others.[97] Third, they call for a reinterpretation of history and of reality on the basis of its "underside," its vanquished and dead, and all its repressed "others."

Theology, as *Gottesrede*, as *un hablar de Dios*, as *theos* on *logos*, is directly challenged by this need to reinterpret history, reason, and reality. This challenge is twofold. First, theology must ask itself whether its own way of talking about God—and therefore about every other reality—has not accepted the main presuppositions of Western modernity concerning reason, history, and reality at large. Modernity's model of reason is in principle an argumentative-autonomous reason. In practice, modern reason has often become an instrumental reason. History and reality, in turn, are interpreted as triumphant-evolutionary. By accepting this interpretation of reason, history, and reality, theology forgets not only the repressed and suppressed "reasons" and "others" but also the constitutive eschatological-critical dimension of Christianity and, most of all, the radical otherness of God. Second, theology must ask itself whether it has not retreated to an idealistic, speculative realm, instead of talking about God from and in the midst of the conflicts and contradictions of the history in which God is profoundly implicated and saves. Metz expresses this powerfully when he writes: "In my view Christianity is not like a postmodern *Glasperlenspiel* [game of marbles], but the most daring staging of world history, because God is involved in it."[98]

Metz, Gutiérrez, and Tracy express these challenges each in his own way, but the three of them adopt both a critical and, up to a point, a postmodern approach to history, reason, reality, and theology, changing approaches and perspectives, widening the limits of reason, opening the doors to the repressed others, bringing new voices to the theological task, and challenging the "official" ways of imagining and representing reality. The three of them are postmodern in their criticism of a Eurocentric and too narrow modernity and, most of all, in their affirmation of the "other." However, they do not have the same opinion of postmodernity. Whereas Tracy values it as a "turn to the other" despite its ambiguities and ethical deficit, Gutiérrez and especially Metz are very critical of it due to what they see as postmodernity's lack of a firm stand concerning the values of justice, emancipation, solidarity, and universality.

Metz wants to change the terms in which theology is conceived. According to him, theology has abandoned its own constitutive logos, namely, the memory of suffering that belongs to the core of the biblical narrative, and has become mainly speculative-argumentative, theoretical, and rather triumphalistic. Along with the memory of suffering, theology has also forgotten the concrete, historical dimension of Christianity, represented both by this memory of suffering and by eschatology as expression of the interruptive end of history. Therefore, theology, the *Gottesrede,* has become idealistic, *situationsfreie Theologie* (situation-free theology), and he wants to formulate a postidealistic theology, directly related to a concrete situation.

Second, Metz also wants to change the terms in which both classical and transcendental theologies have imagined God. The God of these theoretical theologies is a strong God, a God who remains unchallenged and untouched by the tragedies and contradictions of history, a God who, in the end, is invincible. In a God so rendered, the experiences of nonidentity have no relevance and go unnoticed by theology. In Metz's "negative" approach, both the memory of suffering and the temporal-eschatological determination of Christianity must return to the logos of "theo-logy" if this God-talk is to respond to the challenges of those nonidentity experiences.[99]

Third, Metz changes the question concerning God. Faced with the experiences of nonidentity, the question Who is God? must be reformulated as Where is God? in order to make relevant the memory and the actuality of suffering in relation to God. In this respect, the theoretical-speculative question about God must become practical in the face of the massive suffering in the world. The negative nature of Metz's theology pervades the way it addresses the question of God, namely, not on the basis of God's presence but, so to speak, by "missing" God in the midst of suffering and asking about God's whereabouts. For Metz, "This missing God plays between crying and hoping," like Christ on the cross.[100]

Fourth, the approach to the God question and the language of theology must also be different for Metz. Turning from a theoretical to a practical question also conditions the language of theology. God-talk is primarily a "talking to God" before being a "talking about God." Therefore, theology must be anchored in prayer, in a form of speech that is free enough to express the *leiden an Gott,* that is to say, free enough to question God, to complain to God, to show anger and frustration for the inexplicable existence of evil and suffering. In this sense, theology is a reflective language of prayer, a reflection on God that starts with prayer and keeps using that language throughout, because, ultimately, there are no answers to the questions, to the complaints, to the suffering. Referring to the *Gottesrede* as prayer, Metz writes that this kind of prayer "is the homeland of negative theology, it is the prohibition of representing God put into practice, it is a frank refusal to be consoled either by ideas or myths, it is *Gottespassion,* very often nothing else than a soundless sigh of the creature."[101]

Finally, Metz, in a very postmodern-like way, insists that, ultimately, God cannot be properly described with "strong" categories. The categories of the God-language must be "weak"; they must mirror the "vulnerability" of God concerning the presence and "power" of evil and suffering. These "weak" categories are the biblical categories of the beatitudes, of the sermon on the mount; the categories of "poverty," "mourning," and "hunger and thirst for justice"; those categories that express the reality of suffering, longing, and the inability to be consoled and to triumph, while at the same time expressing eschatological hope. Those categories are also the expression and the foundation of "negative theology" because they are a way of expressing Israel's prohibition against representing God in a "positive" way, that is to say, in a triumphant, strong, and clear way. Even the Johannine "God is love" must be "weakly" understood. God's love is not invincible; it bears the marks of the "wound" caused by suffering and sheer destruction.[102] A God who is discovered and remembered in a memory of passion is always a "poor," "endangered," "weak," "vulnerable" God. The God of Israel is "poor" because such a God does not console, does not take away the contradictions, suffering, and anxiety always present in history. Israel remains always "an eschatological 'land of screams,' a land of memory and expectation," and, therefore, absolutely incapable of imagining God in either mythical or idealistic terms, incapable "of being consoled by ideas or myths that are removed from history."[103]

All in all, Metz's *Gottesrede* seeks to express all the tensions involved in the *Gottespassion* concerning the God of biblical monotheism. The believer, together with Israel and with Jesus of Nazareth, the crucified and resurrected Christ, is, on the one hand, passionately attracted to the God of the promise, the only and true hope of life and liberation. On the other hand, the believer, also with Israel and with Jesus Christ, suffers profoundly because of this passion for God and lives this passionate relationship with God as a *passio,* as an inexplicable suffering, *leiden an Gott,* full of questions without definitive answer. God is not a human-made myth whose function is to console either with answers or with power and strength.[104] God is both irritatingly eschatological and "weak," a God with open flanks, vulnerable and suffering. Biblical monotheism is "by no means a system but an event, an eschatological event. As such, it is not a monotheism of political power, but a pathic monotheism with painfully open eschatological flanks." Therefore, the *Gottesrede* is a constitutionally negative language to and about God, only possible ultimately in and through prayer.[105]

Gutiérrez's *hablar de Dios* (talk *about* God) is also essentially an *hablar con Dios* (talk *to* God). It is not possible to talk about God without being befriended by God, without going through all the experiences of a true and deep close relationship with the God of the Bible, including not only obedience, confidence, praise, and love but, as in Job, and indeed in Vallejo, also rebellion, betrayal, grievance, and estrangement. Gutiérrez's main aim is to speak of God as a loving God in the midst of innocent suffering. In doing so, his *hablar de Dios*, his theology, is an *hablar con Dios,* that is to say, a prayer. This is clear in the case of Job, who, time and again, demands to talk directly to God. Gutiérrez refers to his theological method as "a talk enriched by silence."[106] In this respect, he comes very close to Metz's definition of theology as a "reflective prayer-talk" and also to Tracy's insistence that modernity's conceptual way of speaking of God must be replaced by a God-talk based on prayer and contemplation as well as on discipleship and praxis. For the three of them, true prayer is always accompanied by the praxis of discipleship in history.

As with Metz, Gutiérrez's locus for encountering God is history—a history from which a dialogue must be established with the history in which the Bible narrates the experience of God. This history, now read through the eyes of the poor and the oppressed, reveals the face of God in the face of the poor, as in the works of Arguedas, and in the experiences of estrangement, absurdity, and lack of hope encountered in that history, as in Vallejo's case. The latter's poetry is for Gutiérrez a powerful example of how to talk about God by talking and bitterly complaining to God from the historical limit-experience of hopelessness and frustration, thus keeping alive an affirmation of life and of hope. In fact, Vallejo and Arguedas are powerful voices that express the way history is read in Peru from the perspective of the oppressed and the poor and that try to relate that history to the experience of the presence-absence of God. In this sense, they are the voice of the particular and concrete Peruvian story-history from which the dialogue with the story-history of the Bible must be established in order to do theology. Moreover, their literary-mythical-poetical language provides Gutiérrez with a powerful instrument to overcome the strictures of a purely discursive language, opening the theological language to the intuitive and meaning-excessive language it needs to suggest and somehow express the inexpressible.

For Gutiérrez, as for Metz, God is discovered in the experiences of non-identity that take place in history. However, Metz's memory of suffering as that memory in which God is discovered, the memory of the biblical narrative, the war experiences, Auschwitz, becomes in Gutiérrez more actual suffering and actual experience in the life of the poor in Latin America, more of an ongoing, current interruption of a sanguine and victorious rendering of history than of memory; Metz's memory of the dead in history becomes current awareness of the presently dead-alive in Gutiérrez.[107]

Theology, for Gutiérrez, can be carried out only if the theological task and language are rooted in the mystery of God, that is to say, in the paradoxical experience of seeking a God who seems not only to neglect the creature and to remain hidden but also to persecute this creature. It is in the midst of this painful experience that Gutiérrez seeks, with Job, with Arguedas, and with Vallejo, to talk to and about God. In this respect, he also changes the way theology is understood. Theology cannot be carried out as an argumentative discourse based on principles. This kind of academic-speculative God-talk is doomed to failure. Only on the grounds of a living, passionate, struggling, and committed experience can theology become a proper language to and about God.[108] Faced with the suffering of the masses of the poor, the reigning social inequalities and injustice not only in Peru and Latin America but in the worldwide system of social relations, and the death of innocent people, as in Ayacucho, Gutiérrez insists on affirming that the Christian God is the God of life and the God of love of the letter of John. The question about God, then, is also for Gutiérrez a practical question related to the historical experience of suffering and evil.

God, to begin with, is not a consoling God of the poor but the foundation of their hope, resistance, and struggle. The question is crucial in a continent that is both Christian and poor and in which religion has been accused of playing an alienating role. Gutiérrez, following Arguedas, insists that the God in whose name resignation and passive acceptance of oppression and injustice are preached is a *calandria consoladora* (consoling lark). This God is nothing other than an idol, an instrument of oppression, and a way of using religion to justify and maintain the status quo. This *calandria consoladora* must be opposed by the *calandria de fuego* (lark of fire), the liberating force of the God of "the fraternity of the wretched."[109] The consoling idol must be unmasked and replaced by the liberating God.

Therefore, along with Arguedas, Gutiérrez affirms that any God-talk must take into account a very practical question: Which God is the talk about? A central character in one of Arguedas's novels responds to the question of whether he believed in God with another question: "Which God shall it be?" or with the similar question: "How many Jesus Christs are there?"[110] To talk about God in general is not enough. In fact, it can be a way to justify oppression and injustice. In Latin America, from the time of the conquest on, the Christian God has been an instrument and an excuse to make money through injustice, exploitation, and death. Gold in the times of the conquest and money in modern Latin America are the idols to which human beings have been and are being sacrificed, using God and Christian religion as an excuse and a legitimation.[111]

The biblical God is the God that paradoxically appears in all those who have been rejected in society: the "Indians," the poor, the despised, the fool, the malformed, the unadapted, the socially incorrect. This God is revealed in Huamán's *pobres de Jesucristo;* in *los opresos indios, los Cristos azotados de las Indias,* of Las Casas; in all the most peculiar characters of Arguedas: the despised *pongo* of *Los ríos profundos,* the poor and malformed *kurku* of *Todas las sangres,* the *loco Moncada,* the *hermano negro Miguel,* and the *profeta Esteban* in *El Zorro de arriba y el Zorro de abajo.* This God is a different God: the "underside" God, the "fool" God, the "irrational" God, the "malformed" God. This "weak" God is the God of hope, resistance, and liberation.[112]

Vallejo is also a crucial, in a way unsurpassed, partner in Gutiérrez's journey into the mystery of God, into his negative theology.[113] Although Gutiérrez has not written any work on this Peruvian poet, Vallejo is always present whenever Gutiérrez's God-talk reaches its mysterious and painful depth. In Vallejo, God is perceived on the frontier between affirmation and negation—more precisely, in an affirmation despite and because of a negation. A prophet of hope beyond all hope and in the midst of despair, Vallejo is the "negative" poet of religion and God. Vallejo is the paradoxically civil-"atheist" version of Job, but also the Peruvian Job, human, real, historical, and tragically hopeful. His poems, truly complaining, sometimes provoking, prayers to God, maintain a striking parallelism to the language of Job.[114] He, like Job, is a most clear example of the different, tensional dimensions involved in the Metzian term *Gottespassion.*[115]

Gutiérrez finds not only powerful intuitions in Vallejo but also the language of poetry as one of the best languages to express the inexpressible, to point to reality beyond reality, to achieve disclosure through mystery, to cling to hope beyond hope. Indeed, in Vallejo, Gutiérrez finds the "negative" believer, the poet of negative theology, the suffering and compassionate human being[116] who accusingly talks to God and affirms God's profound care through and in God's inexplicable absence, God's true love through and in God's scandalous "hatred," God's power and closeness through and in God's alienating distance-powerlessness in history, God as source of hope through and in God's unacceptable play with creation. Vallejo's passion for God is most profoundly expressed in and through his complaint to God, *el hombre sí te sufre* (man really endures you).[117]

Gutiérrez's dialogical commentary on Job is his most elaborate work on God in the midst of historical innocent suffering. Gutiérrez's aim with this work on Job is not to put to rest the profoundly negative theological poetry of Vallejo with his unanswered, bleeding questions. Rather, Gutiérrez has sought to take up these permanently open questions, to make them the center of his theology, of his *hablar de Dios,* and, with Job, to talk to God and about God on the basis of these questions. For Gutiérrez, both Vallejo and Job are not mere instances of a special, personal experience, but, rather, true representatives of Latin American suffering with a universally meaningful message.[118]

The center of this meditation-conversation is both the suffering of the innocent and innocent suffering. In relation to the historical situation in Latin America, the central question for Gutiérrez is: How to talk of the God of love and justice in the midst of poverty, oppression, and the suffering of the innocent? As in Metz's case, in even more concrete terms from the point of view of those who suffer, the question is: Where are you, my God?[119]

However, Gutiérrez's reading of Job is not centered around the mystery of evil and suffering in history. Gutiérrez's Job is the Job who, despite every counterevidence, aims at believing in God as God in whom he can trust in a totally gratuitous way. Ultimately, therefore, the subject matter of the Book of Job is not, according to Gutiérrez, the theodicy question but the question of the nature of the God/creature relation as a totally gratuitous relation. This is, finally, the thesis of Gutiérrez. The conversation with God, through Job and with Job, is the way by which Gutiérrez discovers the absolutely gratuitous love of God in the midst of the suffering of the innocent in Latin America.

Gratuitousness in Gutiérrez means the absolute lack of motive and reason. In this sense, gratuitousness is a negative concept, a way of referring to the radical "emptiness" of God's love. Gratuitousness, therefore, is the name of God's mystery in Gutiérrez—that which has no reason or motive and, therefore, cannot be explained. The similarity with Rahner is important. For Rahner, God's self-communication, gratuitous and inexplicable, was *the* mystery of Christianity. All other mysteries were derived from this primal mystery. However, Gutiérrez's route to the mysterious-gratuitous God is totally other than Rahner's. Rahner's main route is transcendental-metaphysical; Gutiérrez's is historical-biblical.[120]

One of Gutiérrez's theological contributions is his twofold way to speak about God: the mystical-prophetic God-language. The way to discover the gratuitous love of God is, ultimately, the way of mystical language. This way, however, is preceded by the discovery of the poor and oppressed; by the commitment to justice and to the cause of the poor; by the prophetic language that demands that justice be done in history. Job's discovery of the suffering of the poor and his commitment to justice give him an entry to the gratuitousness of God.[121]

On the one hand, the mystical language without the prophetic one lacks a crucial element, namely, God's preferential love for the poor and God's commandment to do justice to the poor and to love them preferentially—not because the poor are morally good but just because God is good. It is precisely and only through this preferential love that the paradoxical God, hidden from the learned and the powerful and revealed to the uneducated and the poor, can be known. On the other hand, the prophetic language, although necessary, is insufficient to talk about God. The prophetic language must be finally understood within the encompassing mystical language through which God appears as absolutely gratuitous.[122]

Job's final dialogue with God, his listening to God, is his route to contemplation. Job begins to understand that God cannot be comprehended in human categories. God's plans, ways, designs, and justice are not the same as those of the creatures and completely exceed any reason; they are reason-free; they can only be understood within the "emptiness" of God's absolute gratuitousness. God is beyond categories and beyond any logic other than sheer gratuitousness. There is where Job meets, discovers, and enters a new relation of gratuitousness with God.[123]

Like Gutiérrez and Metz, Tracy also has increasingly focused his theology on the question of God. Indeed, a permanent trait of Tracy's work has been his effort to find an adequate language about God that could be meaningful in the late-modern society to which he has tried to relate his theology. His current work on naming God can be interpreted as part of this ongoing project, this time related to the postmodern situation. In this respect, his current centeredness on God is somehow both a response to the needs of the postmodern condition and a result of the liberating effects of that condition.[124] God is rediscovered as the radical other that cannot be controlled by the logos of modernity. In a sense, this God is both the radical affirmation of every otherness and the only possibility of liberating and rescuing all the forgotten and suppressed others in history and in society.

Tracy's journey into the mystery of God is a tensional one between the manifested, eternal God and the hidden, historical God; between the analogically comprehensible, immanent God and the totally other, incomprehensible, transcendent God. All-encompassing love and all-threatening tragedy, as well as sheer, radiant identity and radical, obscuring ambiguity, interact constantly in this journey to a God felt at hand yet always beyond reach, shockingly recognized as present yet tragically absent, true and only truth yet lost in the ambiguity of the human experience. This tensional, dialectical character between hiddenness and manifestation, between relatedness and total otherness, is the centerpiece of Tracy's *logos* on *theos*.

In his search for publicness, for sharing publicly the Christian God, for making God available and known to all, Tracy has, somehow, known all the way through both that Rahner, in the final analysis, was right in his insistence on God's "always-everywhere" presence and, nevertheless, that

Rahner's statement had to be confronted with the historical and biblical experience of God's radical hiddenness. Tracy is essentially a meditative-contemplative thinker, forged in the mold of analogy and manifestation, true to his Catholic identity. He has, however, always known that he had to find a way to convey his God-experience, his faith, his particular Catholic identity, to people with different views, with other faiths, and, most of all, with other grounding experiences.[125] His theology, understood as *logos* on *theos*, as a journey to God, is the result of undertaking this search for publicness in changing circumstances, mainly the change from his initially late-modern project to his later response to the postmodern situation.

Tracy's starting point on his theological route is a double social-historical experience: on the one hand, his heightened awareness of his sharp, constitutive Catholic identity and tradition—an awareness very much due to the particular experience of Catholicism in the United States; on the other hand, his equally sharp consciousness that his particular tradition was just one among other possible traditions both as regards Christianity and in relation to the constitutively pluralistic U.S. society, with all the conflicting and different claims and perspectives that compete yet intermingle within "the American experiment." The question for Tracy in this context was to find a way to make his position a shareable one. At the time of *Blessed Rage for Order* he sought to speak of the Christian God using both a phenomenological and a transcendental-metaphysical route. His God-language came very close to that of process theology, focused on God's radical relationality.

An important point in Tracy's development was his increasing awareness of the radical ambiguity of every tradition. Hermeneutics opened for him new possibilities and demands in his search for a meaningful-shareable God-talk. The previous sharp awareness of plurality was now joined by a heightened awareness of the radical ambiguity inherent in every tradition. In fact, Tracy starts to see "the American experiment" with new eyes, increasingly aware of its inner contradictions, ambiguities, and victims. His God-talk starts to take a "negative" turn. The correlation between Christianity and the situation is increasingly sought through the experiences of failure, oppression, and suffering. The Christian God, now approached from the perspective of concrete histories, is discovered as a source for resistance and hope.

The postmodern condition is read by Tracy also as an ambiguous condition. On the one hand, he reads it as a response to the strictures and failures of modernity; as a cry of liberation from an oppressive modernity masking itself as *the* universal and only way to emancipation and freedom; as a rebellion against a self-centered subject; as an unmasking of a too narrow and self-proud reason; as a doing away with all kinds of grand narratives, replacing them just by fragments. In this respect, postmodernity marks the assault of the repressed others on the fortress of modernity. This is why Tracy insists that the central trait of postmodernity is the "turn to the other."

On the other hand, postmodernity risks losing every reference and drift-ing into a mere playful enjoyment of sheer difference, dissemination, and "otherness." In such a situation, the just-liberated other risks being prey to the Darwinian law of the strongest that stems from the impossibility of sus-taining and defending any substantive affirmation. Postmodernity is open to so many different claims and interpretations and is so unable to adjudicate among them that Tracy refers to postmodernity as an "age that cannot name itself." Postmodernity needs an ethical core—an ethical stand that, to be sure, cannot be a simple remake of the ethics of modernity. However, post-modernity must take up the emancipatory and universal drive of modernity through the recognition and defense of the others, especially the marginal-ized, the poor, the repressed and oppressed others. In a way, Tracy is trying to say that this "age that cannot name itself" must be fully transformed into "the age of 'the other.' "

This is the situation in which and from which Tracy tries to "name God." By the term "naming God" Tracy means a God-language that can free the whole range of possibilities of the "otherness" of God; a language not con-trolled by the strictures of modern reason; a language that, despite its limits, "lets God be God." Tracy is trying to speak about the God who is inter-rupting all modern kinds of God-talk by appearing under those forms that were unimaginable within the limits of modern reason: the forms of the radically apophatic mystics, the hidden and scandalous forms of massive suffering and annihilation, the "empty" forms of the negative thinkers, the forms beyond being, the forms of excess of the Johannine "God is love." The God of the grand narrative, the "positive" God, is suddenly being shattered and replaced by the weak, "negative" God who is disclosed just through "fragments."[126]

What Tracy ultimately is looking for is nothing other than a totally re-lated yet totally other God—a God who, being *the* paradigmatically other, becomes the referent for "the age of 'the other,' " the possibility of affirma-tion of every "other" and every "otherness."[127] This God, hidden-revealed, comprehensible-incomprehensible, can only be discovered through all the possibilities of a God-language that is truly and fully mystical-prophetic, contemplative and ethical, manifestative and disruptive, capable of hint-ing at all those dialectical, even conflicting, fragments of the mysterious, uncontrollable other-God.

Whereas Metz wants to rescue and to find a firm foundation for the dead and forgotten of history and Gutiérrez seeks to liberate and to find hope for the poor and all those who suffer innocently, Tracy is looking for ways to affirm and give hope to every "other," especially to the repressed "others." In this sense, the three of them, each one by his own route, come to discover and to affirm God as a mystery, as nonidentical, as gratuitous, as uncontrollable "other."

Notes

Chapter 1: Karl Rahner and the Turning Point in Catholic Theology

1. For a general understanding of the ground of Rahner's thought, see Karl Rahner, *I Remember* (New York: Crossroad, 1985), 20–49; Herbert Vorgrimler, *Karl Rahner verstehen: Eine Einführung in sein Leben und Denken* (Freiburg im Breisgau: Herder, 1985), 64–83, English translation, *Understanding Karl Rahner: An Introduction to His Life and Thought* (New York: Crossroad, 1986); Karl-Heinz Weger, *Karl Rahner: Eine Einführung in sein theologisches Denken* (Freiburg im Breisgau: Herder, 1978), 13–39, English translation, *Karl Rahner: An Introduction to His Theology* (New York: Seabury, 1980); Anne Carr, *The Theological Method of Karl Rahner* (Missoula: University of Montana Scholars Press, 1977), 7–60.

2. Martin Heidegger, *Being and Time* (New York: Harper and Row, 1962), 21–64.

3. Rahner, *I Remember*, 46.

4. Karl Rahner, *Geist in Welt*, reworked by Johannes Baptist Metz (Munich: Kösel, 1957), English translation, *Spirit in the World* (New York: Herder and Herder, 1968).

5. See Thomas Aquinas, *Summa Theologiae* I, Q.12 (hereafter *ST*) (Madrid: Editorial Católica, 1955); Karl Rahner, "An Investigation of the Incomprehensibility of God in St. Thomas Aquinas," in *Theological Investigations* (hereafter *TI*) (New York: Seabury, 1979), 16:244–54; idem, "On Recognizing the Importance of Thomas Aquinas," in *TI* (New York: Crossroad, 1983), 13:3–12.

6. See Karl Rahner, "Einführender Essay," in Johannes Baptist Metz, *Christliche Anthropozentrik: Über die Denkform des Thomas von Aquin* (Munich: Kösel, 1962), 9–20.

7. I am deeply indebted to Bernard McGinn for my reading of Aquinas, especially for his clear insights on the metaphysics of knowledge, on ontology, and on the overall Neoplatonic structure (*exitus-reditus*) of the *Summa Theologiae*. In relation to Rahner, my work with Anne Carr has helped me to understand the importance of Rahner's method and overall approach in moving Catholic theology forward by retrieving tradition to make it understandable to modern Christians.

8. This happened, therefore, before he studied with Albert the Great. See James A. Weisheipl, O.P., *Friar Thomas D'Aquino: His Life, Thought, and Works* (Washington, D.C.: Catholic University of America Press, 1983), 18.

9. For instance, Aquinas follows Aristotle only to a certain point beyond which he resorts to the sources of Christian revelation, as is the case in his interpretation of "sacred doctrine" as a science and in his understanding of the soul. Metz has analyzed in depth the relation between Aquinas's way of thinking (*Denkform*) and that

of Aristotle. See Metz, *Christliche Anthropozentrik*, 43–59, 97–115, an important early work by Metz that will be examined in the next chapter.

10. Aquinas, *ST* I, Q.1; Karl Rahner, *Hörer des Wortes: Zur Grundlegung einer Religionsphilosophie*, revised by Johannes Baptist Metz (Munich: Kösel, 1963), 205–21, English translation, *Hearers of the Word* (New York: Herder and Herder, 1969), 167–80.

11. *TI*, 16:9.

12. To explore the commonality between Rahner and others on the return to ontology, on the dialogue with Kant, on the influence of Heidegger and Maréchal, and on the transcendental reading of Aquinas, see the articles by Otto Muck, Gustav Siewerth, Johannes B. Lotz, and Emerich Coreth, in Johannes Baptist Metz et al., eds., *Gott in Welt: Festgabe für Karl Rahner*, vol. 1 (Freiburg im Breisgau: Herder, 1964). Rahner pointed several times to his shared views in these matters with other thinkers. See, for instance, *I Remember*, 41–46.

13. See Weger, *Karl Rahner*, 24–38; Francis P. Fiorenza, introduction to Rahner, *Spirit in the World*, xl–xliii; Carr, *Theological Method*, 44–54. The latter is a very comprehensive and perceptive analysis of the relationship between Rahner and Maréchal.

14. Johannes Baptist Metz, "Widmung und Würdigung," in Metz et al., *Gott in Welt*, 1:8–11; Carr, *Theological Method*, 44; Weger, *Karl Rahner*, 28.

15. For thorough discussions of the different authors Rahner deals with in *Geist in Welt*, and of the influence of each of the authors on Rahner's position, see Carr, *Theological Method*, 10–54; Fiorenza, introduction, xix–xlv; Weger, *Karl Rahner*, 28–37.

16. Rahner, *Spirit in the World*, liii, where he talks of "a thoroughgoing determination of knowing by being." One of the main problems in interpreting Kant is the necessity of taking into account the whole development of his project in relation to the critique of knowledge. His steps from "pure reason" to "practical reason" and from the latter to "judgmental reason," coming finally to deal with "religion within the limits of pure reason," are, to this day, one of the most thorough and systematic philosophical accounts ever given not only of human knowledge but, implicitly, of human nature. Seen from this perspective, Kant's whole project is not only a critique of knowledge, which it explicitly is, but also, though implicitly, an ontology. In this respect, although one cannot talk of "a thoroughgoing determination of knowing by being" in relation to Kant, one does find in the progressive unfolding of his project a being that always underlies the knowing and that, so to speak, grows more and more important with each step taken by Kant.

17. Johannes Baptist Metz, foreword to Rahner, *Spirit in the World*, xiii–xviii.

18. Rahner, *I Remember*, 45–46; David Farrell Krell, "General Introduction: 'The Question of Being,'" in Martin Heidegger, *Basic Writings: From "Being and Time" (1927) to "The Task of Thinking" (1964)*, ed. David Farrell Krell (New York: Harper Collins, 1977), 15–16.

19. Heidegger explains his whole ontological project in his introduction to *Being and Time*, 21–64. Unfortunately, Heidegger never completed the project, so he never sorted out *the* question of being. Moreover, since there was a *Kehre* in his thought, there is an inconclusive debate on the question of whether or not he changed his mind

with respect to his early central tenets. Rahner himself did not have a final opinion in this respect (see Rahner, *I Remember*, 44–45). For Heidegger's understanding of the *Destruktion* of the history of ontology, see his *Being and Time*, 41–49, and the translator's note to that term in Heidegger, *Basic Writings*, 64.

20. There is a noteworthy similarity between Heidegger's understanding of *Dasein* as the being distinguished from other beings "by the fact that, in its very Being, that Being is an *issue* for it" (Heidegger, *Being and Time*, 32) and Rahner's understanding of human existence when he says that "man exists as the question about being" (Rahner, *Spirit in the World*, 58).

21. Heidegger, *Being and Time*, 36–40, 78–90.

22. Rahner's notions of "existentiell" and "existential" are related to his categorial/transcendental analysis of human existence, that is to say, to his distinction between the actual existence of, for example, concrete human knowledge (categorial knowledge) and the conditions of possibility of such a knowledge (transcendental knowledge). For an understanding of these terms in Heidegger and Rahner, see the editor's note in Heidegger, *Basic Writings*, 55, and the translator's note in Karl Rahner, *Foundations of Christian Faith: An Introduction to the Idea of Christianity* (New York: Crossroad, 1987), 16.

23. The question will be examined later in detail. For an understanding of the supernatural existential, see Rahner, *Foundations*, 126–33.

24. See Heidegger, *Basic Writings*, 105–12; Rahner, *Foundations*, 17–23.

25. See *TI*, 16:245–54; Rahner, *Foundations*, 33–35; Heidegger, *Basic Writings*, 102–8.

26. Aquinas, *ST* I, Q.84, AA.6–7.

27. Rahner, *Spirit in the World*, 61–65, 406–8. The question of historicity comes to the fore in a much clearer form in *Hearers of the Word*, 130–63, and plays an even more crucial role in Rahner's later theology.

28. Weger, *Karl Rahner*, 24.

29. For a short and perceptive analysis of Rahner's approach and of the foundations of his thought, see Metz, "Widmung und Würdigung," and idem, foreword to Rahner, *Spirit in the World*. For a thorough analysis of Rahner's method, see Carr, *Theological Method*, esp. chap. 3.

30. Carr says that "Discussion of Rahner's thought should begin at his own starting point: human experience as a whole" (Anne E. Carr, "Starting with the Human," in Leo J. O'Donovan, ed., *A World of Grace: An Introduction to the Themes and Foundations of Karl Rahner's Theology* [New York: Crossroad, 1989], 17). Carr points also to the development of Rahner's theology in relation to experience in *Theological Method*, 56.

31. See Johann Baptist Metz, *Glaube in Geschichte und Gesellschaft: Studien zu einer praktischen Fundamentaltheologie* (hereafter *GGG*) (Mainz: Matthias-Grünewald, 1977), 195–203 (my trans.).

32. The terms "transcendental" and "transcendent" may be confusing and need further clarification. The term "transcendental" refers to the condition of possibility of concrete human existence. In this sense, Rahner says that human knowledge and freedom and love are only possible because human beings are open to "being as such." This openness is the transcendental structure that makes actual knowledge,

freedom, and love possible. The term "transcendent," in turn, refers to that horizon and ground of being, God for Rahner, in whom human beings discover both the fountain and the ultimate end of their existence.

33. For this understanding of Rahner, I am totally indebted to Ottmar John and to his comments in his seminar " 'Ästhetisierung der Politik'—Die Bedeutung von Benjamins Erfahrungsbegriff für die Theologie," in the winter semester 1990/91 at the University of Münster.

34. It has already been said in this work that Rahner's starting point was always a religious one. This must be stressed again lest an inaccurate picture of Rahner's work emerges. In that respect, it would be wrong to think that prayer was not present at the first stage of Rahner's project. As a matter of fact, his first publication ("Warum uns das Beten nottut," *Leuchtturm* 18 [1924/1925]) refers directly to prayer, and practically at the time he wrote *Spirit in the World,* the most philosophical of his works, he wrote his first prayerbook, *Worte ins Schweigen* (Innsbruck: Felician Rauch, 1938).

35. Carr says that "Rahner's metaphysics of knowledge is deepened as theological anthropology into a metaphysics of mystery" (Carr, *Theological Method,* 167). Rahner wrote extensively on grace. A good understanding of this concept can be found in *Foundations,* 116–33. A systematic account of grace is given in Rahner's contribution to the article "Grace," in *Sacramentum Mundi.*

36. Rahner, introduction to *Spirit in the World,* xxxii.

37. Rahner, *Spirit in the World,* 68–71; idem, *Foundations,* 14–17.

38. Rahner, *Foundations,* 17.

39. Ibid., 20–21.

40. Rahner discusses the meaning of transcendental reflection in "Reflections on Methodology in Theology," in *TI* (New York: Seabury, 1974), 11:87–93. On the crucial Rahnerian difference between "transcendental" and "categorial," a difference that he never fully discusses, see L. Bruno Puntel, "Zu den Begriffen 'transzendental' und 'kategorial' bei Karl Rahner," in Herbert Vorgrimler, ed., *Wagnis Theologie: Erfahrungen mit der Theologie Karl Rahners* (Freiburg im Breisgau: Herder, 1979), 189–98. Puntel points to the heart of what constitutes the real counterpart of the transcendental reflection when he writes: "What a person 'really' does and understands is always more than what this person explicitly defines and articulates" (190 [my trans.]). Puntel describes this relationship in these words: "Categoriality is the thematized, interpreted, conceptually theorized transcendentality. It intrinsically refers back to transcendentality, which, according to Rahner, never can be totally and finally grasped, and is aimed at (self-)explanation, at (self-)interpretation, and, in this sense, at categoriality" (190 [my trans.]). For Rahner's description of this relationship, see *Spirit in the World,* 405.

41. Rahner, *Spirit in the World,* 391; idem, *Foundations,* 21.

42. "Transcendental experience, of course, is not merely an experience of pure knowledge, but also of the will and of freedom" (Rahner, *Foundations,* 20).

43. Ibid., 35.

44. Ibid., 33.

45. Ibid., 21.

46. Ibid., 26–43, is Rahner's actualized synthesis of *Hearers of the Word.*

47. Rahner, *Foundations*, 35–37.

48. For an understanding of these concepts, see Rahner, "Grace," in *Sacramentum Mundi*, and the section "A Gratuitously Self-Giving God: The Supernatural Existential" below.

49. Rahner, *Foundations*, 39.

50. These three are also "existential" structures of humanness. See ibid., 40–41.

51. Although Rahner defended this necessary linkage between ultimate decision about oneself before God and concrete decisions in history, he also warned that no easy and mechanistic connection between the two can be established. Whether, despite the apparent direction of all categorial decisions of the individual, the latter's ultimate decision is in fact pointing in a different direction belongs to the realm of the unfathomable relation between God and the individual. Rahner explores this issue masterfully in "Experience of the Spirit and Existential Commitment," in *TI*, 16:24–34.

52. See ibid., 16:41, 138–75, for a thorough discussion of the unity between salvation history and history as such.

53. In order to explore the ethical implications of Rahner's theology, see Karl Rahner, *Im Gespräch*, ed. Paul Imhof and Hubert Biallowons, vol. 2, 1978–82 (Munich: Kösel, 1983), 41–47, where Rahner explains the two dimensions of following Christ: the mystical and the ethical-political; ibid., 278–83, on the issue of salvation and emancipation; ibid., 307–10, for some opinions on the role of the church in relation to the pacifist movement; idem, *The Christian Commitment* (New York: Sheed and Ward, 1963), esp. 3–74, 145–48. The latter is crucial to understanding the ethical implications of Rahner's theology before he turned more explicitly to the question of the political dimension of Christianity in his later writings. Several authors have commented on the questions of freedom and ethics in Rahner. See, among others, Carr, "Discussion"; James F. Bresnahan, "An Ethics of Faith," in Donovan, *World of Grace*, 169–84; Jörg Splett, "Über die Einheit von Nächsten-und Gottesliebelaienhaft (Idiota de unitate...)," in Vorgrimler, *Wagnis*, 299–310; Gregor Zasche, "Der Preis der Nachfolge-theologisch gesehen," in Vorgrimler, *Wagnis*, 387–92.

54. "The original objectivity of the experience of self necessarily takes place in the subjectivity of its encounters with other persons in dialogue, in trustful and loving encounter. Man experiences himself by experiencing the other *person* and not the other *thing*" (*TI* [New York: Crossroad, 1983], 13:127).

55. Ibid., 128.

56. Ibid., 126; Karl Rahner, *TI* (Baltimore: Helicon, 1969), 6:231–49; idem, *Im Gespräch*, 2:41–47. Rahner refers here explicitly to Metz. In fact, the confrontation with Metz's theology led Rahner to develop those implicit elements of his own theology that relate to the political and historical action of the believer and of the church. For a collection of texts where Rahner deals with these aspects of his theology see Karl Rahner, *Politische Dimensionen des Christentums: Ausgewählte Texte zu Fragen der Zeit*, ed. Herbert Vorgrimler (Munich: Kösel, 1986). For a synthetic and critical appraisal of the relation between Metz and Rahner, see Vorgrimler, *Karl Rahner verstehen*, 152–57. For a thorough discussion of the same subject, see Titus F. Guenther, "Rahner and Metz: Transcendental Theology as Political Theology" (Ph.D. diss., University of St. Michael's College, 1988).

57. Rahner, *Foundations*, 322. Rahner's writings on the church are numerous through his whole career and cover many different aspects. Every volume of his *Theological Investigations* contains several essays about the church. Rahner wrote extensively on the question of the church in the light of Vatican II. A key point within this question concerns the relationship between church and world. To explore some of the issues Rahner dealt with in relation to the church, see *Foundations*, 322–401, clearly Rahner's best work on the nature and mission of the church; Karl Rahner, *Strukturwandel der Kirche als Chance und Aufgabe* (Freiburg im Breisgau: Herder, 1989), for an understanding of Rahner's program of transformation of the church; Karl Rahner, *TI*, vol. 14 (New York: Seabury, 1976); *TI*, vol. 20 (New York: Crossroad, 1981); *TI*, vol. 22 (New York: Crossroad, 1991), three volumes totally devoted to the church, especially interesting for understanding Rahner's vision of the future of the church and the church's relation to society; *TI*, 10 (New York: Herder and Herder, 1973), 293–389, where Rahner develops his view of the relationship between church and world; Vorgrimler, *Wagnis*, 341–568, for analyses concerning Rahner's theology in relation to the church by various authors and from different perspectives.

58. Rahner, *Foundations*, 412. The text is within the section "Remarks on Christian Life" that develops a theology of the sacraments.

59. Metz refers to Rahner's theology as "mystical biography in the form of dogmatics" (Metz, *Glaube*, 203 [my trans.]). Vorgrimler also places the mystical-biographical drive of Rahner's theology at the very center of that theology. In referring to it he describes it as "a life-story with God" and as "confirmation and interpretation of the experience of God" (*Karl Rahner verstehen*, 12 [my trans.]). See ibid., 11–30, for an analysis of the centrality of the mystical dimension in Rahner's theology. Carr points to the mystagogical character of Rahner's theology as something that gains momentum in Rahner's later writings (see *Theological Method*, 208).

60. Rahner, *Foundations*, 21.

61. In Karl Rahner, *Sehnsucht nach dem Geheimnisvollen Gott: Profil, Bilde, Texte*, ed. Herbert Vorgrimler (Freiburg im Breisgau: Herder, 1990), 13 (my trans.).

62. The following are key texts concerning the theological elaboration on the experience of the transcendent: Karl Rahner, "Experience of the Self and Experience of God," in *TI*, 13:122–32; idem, "Experience of the Spirit and Existential Commitment," in *TI*, 16:24–34; idem, "Experience of Transcendence from the Standpoint of Christian Dogmatics" and "Experience of the Holy Spirit," in *TI*, 18:173–210; idem, "Man in the Presence of Absolute Mystery," in *Foundations*, 44–89.

63. Karl Rahner, *TI* (New York: Crossroad, 1983), 18:196–97.

64. Ibid., 193.

65. Ibid., 202–7; Rahner, *Im Gespräch*, 1:277–81.

66. Rahner, *Foundations*, 22.

67. Ibid., 116. Rahner uses the German word *Selbsmitteilung*, which has been translated into English as "self-communication." Although the translation is accurate, there is the risk of understanding the expression in purely epistemological or gnoseological terms, as if what it is passed on were information or knowledge. In order to avoid this, the German word *Selbsmitteilung* could be translated as "self-

sharing-with," so that God's self-communication to human beings is understood as God's own being gratuitously shared by God with human beings.

68. Ibid., 117–18.

69. "Grace, the really supernatural grace, which God is, is the innermost center of human existence" (Weger, *Karl Rahner,* 80 [my trans.]).

70. Rahner, *Foundations,* 126–33; idem, *TI* (Baltimore: Helicon, 1961), 1:297–382, esp. 311–13; idem, *TI* (Baltimore: Helicon, 1966), 4:165–88, esp. 182–85.

71. Just before Rahner came to formulate the concept of the supernatural existential, Henri de Lubac had tried to reach the same conclusion, especially in his work *Surnaturel: Études historiques* (Paris: Aubier-Montaigne, 1946), but without getting at the breakthrough brought about by Rahner. Henri de Lubac addressed again the issue and formulated more precisely his position (also countering what he calls some misunderstandings on the part of Rahner in relation to his [de Lubac's] own position) in his *Le mystère du surnaturel* (Paris: Aubier-Montaigne, 1965). Finally, he came back to the subject in his book *Petite catéchèse sur nature et grâce* (Paris: Librairie Arthème Fayard, 1980). The author describes nature and the supernatural as correlative, giving more weight than Rahner to the distinction between the two. Although he does not attack the theological soundness of Rahner's supernatural existential, he does not see much use in it.

72. Rahner, *Foundations,* 123–24.

73. For Rahner's view on nature as a "remainder concept," see *TI,* 1:300–315.

74. See in that sense Rahner, *Foundations,* 138–75.

75. Karl Rahner, *The Christian Commitment* (New York: Sheed and Ward, 1963), 38–61.

76. See Rahner, *Foundations,* 181. For a masterful application of the transcendental method to Christology, see ibid., 206–12.

77. Ibid., 65–66. Carr captures very well the importance of Rahner's theology of mystery and how it marks "a movement toward simplicity and integration in Rahner's thought" (Carr, *Theological Method,* 163–67 and 268–69). Vorgrimler points to the same in "Grundzüge der Theologie Karl Rahners," in Rahner, *Sehnsucht,* 39–40.

78. Rahner, *Foundations,* 21–22.

79. *TI,* 16:244–54. This text shows how masterfully Rahner is capable of reinterpreting tradition and, in this case, Aquinas's theology in this crucial matter. Aquinas treats the question of the incomprehensibility of God in *ST* I, Q.12, AA.5, 7, and 8. On the one hand, Rahner picks up the central affirmation of the incomprehensibility of God and then, overcoming some of the dangers of the Thomistic analysis implicit in Aquinas's stress on the insurmountable distance between God and the creature, digs in the ontological foundations of Aquinas's own thought to finally show how, if sense is to be made of Aquinas's position, one must respect the two terms of such a position, namely, direct vision and manifestation of the incomprehensibility. This is only possible if that incomprehensibility is understood as belonging to the very being of the human person.

80. *TI,* 16:253–54.

81. Rahner, *Im Gespräch,* 1:310.

82. Rahner, *Foundations,* 137.

83. Ibid., 13.

84. Rahner, *Im Gespräch*, 1:248 (my trans.). For a systematic and full account of Rahner's theology of the Trinity, see Karl Rahner, "Der dreifaltige Gott als tran-szendenter Urgrund der Heilsgeschichte," in *Mysterium Salutis*, 2:317–401. A short summary can be found in *Foundations*, 133–37.

85. Rahner, *Spirit in the World*, chapter 4.

86. Rahner, *Foundations*, 46. See the whole section (44–51) on the word "God," as well as on God as "holy mystery" (65–68).

87. Ibid., 14–17.

88. Here too Rahner is close to Aquinas. The latter discusses the appropriateness of metaphors in sacred doctrine and concludes that to use them is both necessary and helpful. One of the reasons is that "what He [God] is not is clearer to us than what He is. Therefore similitudes drawn from things farthest away from God form within us a truer estimate that God is above whatsoever we may say or think of Him" (*ST* I, Q.1, A.9).

89. Vorgrimler, in Rahner, *Sehnsucht*, 13 (my trans.).

90. Carr, *Theological Method*, chaps. 3 and 4.

91. Ultimately, the subject matter transcendental theology investigates "are the *a priori* conditions in the believing subject which enable him to recognize the fundamental truths of his faith" (*TI*, 13:46).

92. See Rahner, *Im Gespräch*, 1:31–32, where Rahner attributes this way of rethinking dogmas to the influence of Heidegger's critical and creative mode of thinking. See also ibid., 1:33–42 for Rahner's ideas on the relation to the con-temporary context, on the relationship between theology and kerygma, and on the transcendental method.

93. Ibid., 1:40 (my trans.).

94. Ibid., 2:222–23.

95. Rahner, *Foundations*, 176–322. Carr has analyzed in depth the importance of Rahner's Christology and how it paradigmatically shows both how the method works and its impact on the theological conclusions (see *Theological Method*, 126–36).

96. "Transcendental Christology allows one to search for, and in his search to understand, what he has already found in Jesus of Nazareth" (see Rahner, *Foun-dations*, 212). On the relation between transcendental and categorial revelation, see ibid., 153–61.

97. Rahner, *Foundations*, xi–xii.

98. Among these, *Sacramentum Mundi, Mysterium Salutis* (probably the most important Catholic systematic theology written since Vatican II with the participation of theologians from different countries, unfortunately not translated into English), and J. Höfer and Karl Rahner, eds., *Lexikon für Theologie und Kirche* (Freiburg im Breisgau: Herder, 1957–) deserve to be mentioned. The fact that a systematic theology can only be written by a team of theologians that specialize in the disciplines and issues they write on does not solve completely the problem of the inevitable fragmentation in theology and of the ensuing pluralism. Teamwork is useful but has also clear limits (see Rahner, *Foundations*, 7–8)).

99. Rahner, *Foundations*, xii–xiii, 6–7; *TI*, 13:39, 80–102.

100. Rahner, *Im Gespräch*, 2:150–51 (my trans.).

101. A good example is Rahner's "Allgemeine Grundlegung der Protologie und theologischen Anthropologie," in *Mysterium Salutis,* 2:406–20, where his opening, short contribution to the section "Der Anfang der Heilsgeschichte" puts into perspective the subsequent contributions.

102. Rahner, *Foundations, 7.* Rahner writes in this text about that diversity and the problems that it poses for the unity of theology. It is clear that Rahner could not master the methods required to sort out some of the questions he had to face, implicitly or explicitly, in his systematic writings. He therefore had to borrow conclusions from other theologians with expertise in those matters. That is something he could do, although always tentatively, in certain disciplines like exegesis and history, but such a procedure had its clear limits, as Rahner himself acknowledges in the same text without offering a final solution to the problems derived from it for any systematic enterprise, even if developed by a team.

103. A clear example is Rahner's "Der dreifaltige Gott als transzendenter Urgrund der Heilsgeschichte," in *Mysterium Salutis,* 2:317–405, which is the section on *de Deo Trino* within the larger treatise on *de Deo,* in which other theologians also collaborate. The articles by Rahner in the dictionary *Sacramentum Mundi* are also a good example of the impact of his method on his systematic theology. Finally, much of his *Theological Investigations* also exemplify it, as for instance his essay "Theos in the New Testament," *TI,* 1:79–148.

104. See David Tracy, *The Analogical Imagination: Christian Theology and the Culture of Pluralism* (New York: Crossroad, 1981), 162 and 185n.31.

105. Rahner, *Hearers of the Word,* 175–76.

106. Rahner, *Foundations, 7.*

107. Ibid., 7–8; idem, *TI,* 13:61–66 and 75–102.

108. Rahner, *Foundations,* 8.

109. Ibid., 5–8.

110. See Rahner, *Im Gespräch,* 2:115–16, on the rejection of Metz as professor in Munich, and 137–46, on the case of Küng; ibid., 1:256–58, also on the same case of Küng; *TI,* 14:3–134, where Rahner analyses various questions related to the teaching office in the church.

111. William V. Dych, "Theology in a New Key," in O'Donovan, *World of Grace,* 1–16.

112. To avoid misunderstanding of these terms, see how Rahner himself described them in *Im Gespräch,* 2:222.

113. Ibid., 2:272–73 (my trans.).

114. Vorgrimler insists that God as absolute mystery is the center of what a person and a theologian can know and say about God. See *Karl Rahner verstehen,* 158–62, and Vorgrimler's essay in Rahner, *Sehnsucht,* 39–50, where he describes Rahner's personal and theological convergence toward the mystery of God as "nicht Reduktion, sondern Konzentration."

Chapter 2: Johann Baptist Metz

1. These three theologians have expressed their views on political theology throughout their entire work. However, the three following works are representative

of their understanding of political theology: Dorothee Sölle, *Politische Theologie* (Stuttgart: Kreuz, 1982); Jürgen Moltmann, *Politische Theologie-Politische Ethik* (Munich: Kaiser, 1984); and Johannes Baptist Metz, *Glaube in Geschichte und Gesellschaft: Studien zu einer praktischen Fundamentaltheologie* (hereafter *GGG*) (Mainz: Matthias-Grünewald, 1977). Moltmann's work is especially interesting from the North American perspective since it includes a discussion of "civil religion" and of the "American dream" from the point of view of political theology.

2. See Gustavo Gutiérrez, *Teología de la liberación: Perspectivas* (hereafter *TL*) (Lima: Centro de Estudios y Publicaciones, 1971), English translation, *A Theology of Liberation* (Maryknoll, N.Y.: Orbis Books, 1973). Without attempting the task of giving a full bibliography on liberation theology, it may be helpful here to point out some general works that can be useful in understanding its overall program. Methodologically, other than Gutiérrez's already cited book, two works are helpful: Juan Luis Segundo, *The Liberation of Theology* (Maryknoll, N.Y.: Orbis Books, 1976), and Clodovis Boff, *Theology and Praxis: Epistemological Foundations* (Maryknoll, N.Y.: Orbis Books, 1987). An invaluable collection of documents related to Latin American liberation theology in English can be found in Alfred T. Hennelly, ed., *Liberation Theology: A Documentary History* (Maryknoll, N.Y.: Orbis Books, 1990). For a multinational approach to liberation theology with contributors from all over the world, see Marc H. Ellis and Otto Maduro, eds., *The Future of Liberation Theology: Essays in Honor of Gustavo Gutiérrez* (Maryknoll, N.Y.: Orbis Books, 1989). For an overview of liberation theology and its critics, see Arthur F. McGovern, *Liberation Theology and Its Critics: Toward an Assessment* (Maryknoll, N.Y.: Orbis Books, 1989).

3. See, for instance, the enlightening theological-historical study concerning the Evangelische Kirche in Germany by Wolfgang Huber, *Kirche und Öffentlichkeit* (Munich: Kaiser, 1991).

4. Within the Catholic sphere, John Courtney Murray can be considered a classic and a pioneer. For an overview of his work, see Robert W. McElroy, *The Search for an American Public Theology: The Contribution of John Courtney Murray* (Mahwah, N.J.: Paulist, 1989). For a view of the concern public theology awakens in theologians belonging to different denominations, see Robin W. Lovin, ed., *Religion and American Public Life: Interpretations and Explorations* (Mahwah, N.J.: Paulist, 1986).

5. Mark Schoof renders an interesting account of the development of Catholic theology in its confrontation with modernity. Schoof, although from an exclusively European perspective, correctly points to the different threads and movements that finally converged in Vatican II. To be sure, he gives Rahner credit for his decisive contribution, but he is able to show how and to what extent other theologians and schools also labored over several decades to prompt a turning point in Catholic theology. See Mark Schoof, *A Survey of Catholic Theology: 1800–1970* (Glenn Rock, N.J.: Paulist Newman, 1970). For another view on the evolution of Christian theology and a more critical appraisal of Rahner's theology within that evolution, see Hendrikus Berkhof, *Two Hundred Years of Theology: Report of a Personal Journey* (Grand Rapids, Mich.: Eerdmans, 1989).

6. See Johann Baptist Metz, *Unterbrechungen: Theologisch-politische Perspektiven und Profile* (Gütersloh: Gütersloher Verlagshaus Gerd Mohn, 1981), 16.

7. See the Pastoral Constitution on the Church in the Modern World (*Gaudium et Spes*), in Walter M. Abbot, ed., *The Documents of Vatican II* (Piscataway, N.J.: New Century, 1966), 199–308. To be sure, this pastoral constitution is intrinsically related to the Dogmatic Constitution on the Church (*Lumen Gentium*), in ibid., 14–101, and cannot be understood otherwise.

8. See Charles Davis, *Theology and Political Society* (Cambridge: Cambridge University Press, 1980), 1–27.

9. See *GGG*, 3–11, for an understanding of apologetics in a positive way.

10. See Dorothee Sölle, Johann Baptist Metz, and Karl-Josef Kuschel, *Welches Christentum hat Zukunft?* (Stuttgart: Kreuz, 1990), 21.

11. See Ekkehard Schuster and Reinhold Boschert-Kimming, *Trotzdem Hoffen: Mit Johann Baptist Metz und Elie Wiesel im Gespräch* (Mainz: Matthias-Grünewald, 1993), 9.

12. For a short, but well-documented, account of German history, see Ulf Dirlmeier et al., *Kleine deutsche Geschichte* (Stuttgart: Philip Reclam, 1995). Dirlmeier's introduction to the book is very enlightening regarding the complexity and identity of German history.

13. In this respect, see the critical analysis in historical perspective of the German nation in Thomas Ebermann and Rainer Trampert, *Die Offenbarung der Propheten: Über die Sanierung des Kapitalismus, die Verwandlung linker Theorie in Esoterik, Bockgesänge und Zivilgesellschaft* (Hamburg: Konkret Literatur, 1995), esp. 168–210.

14. See the Economist, *Pocket World in Figures* (London: Hutchinson Business Books, 1991).

15. See Mario von Baratta, ed., *Der Fischer Weltalmanach 1997* (Frankfurt am Main: Fischer Taschenbuch, 1996), 125, 145.

16. See, inter alia, Ebermann and Trampert, *Die Offenbarung der Propheten*, 16, where they speak of West Germany as *die Okkupanten*.

17. See Robert M. Seltzer, *Jewish People, Jewish Thought: The Jewish Experience in History* (New York: Macmillan, 198)], 355ff.

18. On the question of the relation of Europe to Islam, see Bernard Lewis, "Die Islamische Sicht auf und die moslemische Erfahrung mit Europa," in Otto Kallscheuer, ed., *Das Europa der Religionen: Ein Kontinent zwischen Säkularisierung und Fundamentalismus* (Frankfurt am Main: S. Fischer, 1996), 67–95. In general, this volume contains interesting essays concerning some central aspects of the religious identity(ies) of Europe. On the question of the role of the Ottoman Empire between Eastern Christianity (Russia) and Western Christianity (Hapsburgs, papacy, France), see Dan Diner, "Zwierlei Osten: Europa zwischen Westen, Byzanz und Islam," 97–113.

19. See Collin Randlesome et al., *Business Culture in Europe* (Oxford: Heinemann, 1990), 1–57.

20. Metz speaks of a *kollektives Trauma* when he refers to the Hitler-Diktatur, as well as of a *Kulturkatastrophe in der Nazizeit* (see *Unterbrechungen*, 76 and 81). The research concerning the Hitler era has not stopped. New literature keeps coming up, trying to enlighten the understanding of the darkest episode of humankind

in modern times, in an ongoing soul-searching endeavor. As Julius H. Schoeps says, "Also in the future will we anxiously ask ourselves: What really made so many Germans become mass murderers?" (see Julius H. Schoeps, ed., *Ein Volk von Mördern?* *Die Dokumentation zur Goldhagen-Kontroverse um die Rolle der Deutschen im Holocaust* [Hamburg: Hoffmann und Campe, 1996], 10 [my trans.]). Some, like Elie Wiesel, belong "to the small minority for which this tragedy, which compares to nothing in its range and gravity, will always remain unexplained. An unexplainable" (ibid., 47 [my trans.]).

21. See Christian Meier, "Verurteilen und Verstehen: An einem Wendepunkt deutscher Geschichtserinnerun," in Ernst Nolte et al., *Historikerstreit* (Munich: Piper, 1987), esp. 51–58; Wilhelm von Sternburg, *Warum wir? Die Deutschen und der Holocaust* (Berlin: Aufbau Taschenbuch, 1996), 21–52; also the essays in Schoeps, *Ein Volk.*

22. See Wilhelm von Sternburg, *Warum wir? Die Deutschen und der Holocaust* (Berlin: Aufbau Taschenbuch, 1996).

23. See Daniel Jonah Goldhagen, *Hitler's Willing Executioners: Ordinary Germans and the Holocaust* (New York: Alfred Knopf, 1996).

24. See in this respect the different essays in Schoeps, *Ein Volk,* especially the essays by Omer Bartov, "Ganz normale Monster"; Josef Joffe, " 'Die Killer waren normale Deutsche, also waren die normalen Deutschen Killer' "; Hans-Ulrich Wehler, "Wie ein Stachel im Fleisch"; and Ulrich Herbert, "Die richtige Frage."

25. See Ernst Nolte, "Vergangenheit, die nicht vergehen will," in Nolte et al., *Historikerstreit,* 39–47.

26. See Meier, "Verurteilen und Verstehen," 55–61; Jürgen Habermas, "Eine Art Schadensabwicklung: Die apologetischen Tedenzen in der deutschen Zeitgeschichtsschreibung," in Nolte et al., *Historikerstreit,* 62–76.

27. See Hans Mommsen, "Suche nach der 'verlorenen Geschichte'? Bemerkungen zum historischen Selbstverständnis der Bundesrepublik" and "Neues Geschichtsbewußtsein und Relativierung des Nationalsozialismus," in Nolte et al., *Historikerstreit,* 156–88; Martin Broszat, "Wo sich die Geister scheiden: Die Beschwörung der Geschichte taugt nicht als nationaler Religionsersatz," in ibid., 189–95. A short and enlightening discussion of the different explanations of the Holocaust can be found in Bartov, "Ganz normale Monster," 64–65.

28. See the World Bank, *World Development Report 1991: The Challenge of Development* (New York: Oxford University Press, 1991).

29. See the Economist, *The World in 1992* (London: Economist Publications, 1991), 30–31; *The Economist* 7750 (21 March 1992): 56–59; *New York Times,* March 18, 1992; the Economist, *Pocket Europe,* 2d ed. (London: Economist Publications, 1994), 79; Bodo Harenberg, ed., *Harenberg Lexikon der Gegenwart: Aktuell '97* (Dortmund: Harenberg Lexikon, 1996); *The Economist* 7985 (3 October 1996): 138; Robert Hettlage and Karl Lenz, *Deutschland nach der Wende: Eine Bilanz* (Munich: C. H. Beck'sche Verlagsbchhandlung, 1995), 222–51.

30. This embarrassment of Germany when called to assume its international responsibilities in time of conflict seemed to disappear when Germany, contrary to the will of most of its partners in the European Community and of the United States, forced the other members of the community to recognize Croatia and Slovenia by

the end of 1991. If the former embarrassment was criticized by the international community, the same happened when Germany showed its new assertiveness and its will to assume its international role. Especially the U.S. government seemed to be upset by the new German attitude. The last steps in the direction of becoming a world power seem to be Germany's demand to be a member of the UN Security Council (see *Frankfurter Allgemeine Zeitung*, September 25, 1996, 3) and the progressive participation of its army in international peace missions like the one in Kosovo in 1999.

31. See Fritz Stern, *Dreams and Delusions: National Socialism in the Drama of the German Past* (New York: Vintage Books, 1989). The author, a German-born professor at Columbia, argues that the idealism of the German soul has usually entailed a lack of realism, an inability to confront past history, and a tendency to take refuge in unattainable dreams. The result has been disaster and devastating delusion, as in the case of Hitler (see 3–21).

32. "The angst of being German raises to the point of a neurosis that leads many born-Germans to emigration and fiercely to oppose all Germans as latent fascists" (Ulrich Wickert, "Weshalb noch Angst vor Deutschland," in Ulrich Wickert, ed., *Angst vor Deutschland: Die neue Rolle der Bundesrepublik in Europa und der Welt* [Hamburg: Hoffmann und Campe, 1994], 22 [my trans.]).

33. Even before the beginning of the Second Reich, in 1835, Heinrich Heine warned the French, "Beware! I mean to be friendly with you and, therefore, I tell you the bitter truth. You have more to fear from the liberated Germany than from the entire Alliance" (as quoted in Ebermann and Trampert, *Die Offenbarung der Propheten*, 181 [my trans.]).

34. See Carola Stern and Heinrich A. Winkler, *Wendepunkte deutscher Geschichte: 1848–1990* (Frankfurt am Main: Fischer Taschenbuch, 1994); in Wickert, *Angst vor Deutschland*, see the following: Friedrich Schorlemmer, "…Und den Kindern werden die Zähne stumpf," 35–47; Günter Grass, "Wider den Einheitsstaat," 67–78; Patrick Süskind, "Deutschland, eine Midlife-crisis," 117–28; Heleno Saña, "Deutschlands neuer Patriotismus: Der Wille zur Macht," 159–69; Arthur Miller, "Die 'unsicheren' Deutschen," 185–94. Lea Rosh's words are, in this respect, a tragic testimony when she writes:

In the swimming-pool, also in the future they will say that the Jews themselves are to blame.
These Germans are hopeless.
They just do not know it.
But I know it.
I am afraid of them.
Always

See Lea Rosh, "…bis Vergessen einkehrt…," in Wickert, *Angst vor Deutschland*, 139 (my trans.).

35. *Deutsche Frage* can be translated as "German question," meaning the question about the identity and political and geographical boundaries of Germany.

36. Jürgen Kocka, for instance, refers to the process of reunification as *"Bundesrepublikanisierung der gescheiterten DDR"* (see Jürgen Kocka, *Vereinigungskrise: Zur Geschichte der Gegenwart* [Göttingen: Vandenhoeck & Ruprecht, 1995], 135).

37. "Revolution from outside and from above. This lets East Germans become objects of the change, instead of being active protagonists of that change" (ibid., 148). For a discussion of the *Deutsche Frage*, see Immanuel Geiss, *Die Deutsche Frage: 1806–1990* (Mannheim: B. I. Taschenbuch, 1992). For a more historical discussion of the main turning points in modern Germany, see Stern and Winkler, *Wendepunkte deutscher Geschichte*. For critical appraisals of the recent process of reunification, see the essays in Wolfgang Dümcke and Fritz Vilmar, eds., *Kolonialisierung der DDR: Kritische Analysen und Alternativen des Einigungsprozesses* (Münster: Thomas Dominikowski Agenda, 1995); also the essays by Grass, Süskind, and Saña in Wickert, *Angst vor Deutschland*. For a different point of view, see Hans-Dietrich Genscher, "Wir wollen ein europäisches Deutschland, nicht ein deutsches Europa," in Wickert, *Angst vor Deutschland*, 323–30. For still another view, see Steffen Heitmann, "Revolution und Wende: Über den schwierigen Aufbau des vereinten Deutschlands," in Heimo Schwilk and Ulrich Schacht, eds., *Die Selbstbewusste Nation: "Anschwellender Bocksgesang" und weitere Beiträge zu einer deutschen Debatte* (Frankfurt am Main: Ullstein, 1996), 447–56; *Frankfurter Allgemeine Zeitung*, September 25, 1996, 8. For an overall assessment of the process of reunification, see the different essays in Hettlage and Lenz, *Deutschland nach der Wende*, as well as Kocka's work. In relation to the European Union, see *ZEIT Punkte* 4 (1996): esp. 74–76; Joscha Schmierer, *Mein Name sei Europa: Einigung ohne Mythos und Utopie* (Frankfurt am Main: Fischer, 1996), 156–207; Kocka, *Vereinigungskrise*, 151–69; *The Economist* 7983 (20 September 1996): 27–28 and 7984 (27 September 1996): 21–24; "Europe, L'utopie blesée," *Le Monde Diplomatique*, Manière de voir 22, esp. 6–19.

38. On the issue of the Frankfurt School, see Rolf Wiggershaus, *Die Frankfurter Schule: Geschichte, theoretische Entwicklung, politische Bedeutung* (Munich: Deutsche Taschenbuch, 1987). On the Bauhaus, see Bauhaus-Archiv, Museum f. Gestaltung, ed., *Bauhaus-Archiv. Museum: Sammlungs-Katallog (Auswahl): Arkitechtur, Design, Malerei, Graphik, Kunstpädagogik* (Berlin: Mann Gebr., 1984). On expressionist art, see Reinhold Heller, ed., *Vom Expressionismus zum Widerstand: Kunst in Deutschland 1909–1936* (Munich: Prestel, 1991). On the question of the Nazi persecution of artists in Germany, see Stephanie Barron et al., *"Degenerate Art": The Fate of the Avant-Garde in Nazi Germany* (Los Angeles: Los Angeles County Museum of Art, 1991). A critical appraisal of the work of the Bauhaus in America can be found in Charles Jencks, *Modern Movements in Architecture* (New York: Penguin Books, 1986).

39. See, for instance, F. D. E. Schleiermacher, *Hermeneutik und Kritik*, ed. Manfred Frank (Frankfurt: Suhrkamp, 1977).

40. The Evangelical Church is more a federation of different and autonomous churches than a church. It actually reunites thirteen Lutheran, two Reformed, and twelve United (the Unionskirche was a result of the administrative union of Lutherans and Reformed that took place in Prussia in 1817) *Landeskirchen* under the umbrella of the Evangelische Kirche in Deutschland (EKD). See Franz-Xaver Kaufmann, *Religion und Modernität: Sozialwissenschaftliche Perspektiven* (Tübingen: J. C. B. Mohr, 1989), 133–35. In terms of numbers, Catholics became the biggest minority in former West Germany, representing 47 percent of the total population by 1990. In

former East Germany, Evangelicals are the biggest religious minority, with Catholics amounting only to 6 percent of the population. Overall, Catholics make up about 34 percent and Evangelicals around 35 percent. See Mark S. Hoffman, ed., *The World Almanac and Book of Facts* (New York: Pharos, 1989 and 1992); Felician A. Foy, O.F.M., ed., *1992 Catholic Almanac* (Huntington, Ind.: Our Sunday Visitor Publishing Division, 1991); Bodo Harenberg, ed., *Harenberg Lexikon der Gegenwart: Aktuell '97* (Dortmund: Harenberg Lexikon, 1996), 211–12.

41. The 1919 constitution of the Weimar Republic explicitly mentions the right of those churches that are corporations of public law to the church-tax system. The status of the churches remains currently unchanged, and the practice of the church-tax has continued to this day without being interrupted even by Hitler (during communist rule, state-collected church-taxation was abolished in East Germany, although the churches continued to collect the *Kirchensteuer* themselves). See Ernst Gottfried Mahrenholz, *Die Kirchen in der Gesellschaft der Bundesrepublik* (Hannover: Fackelträger, 1972), 12–27, 30–31, 36–41, 175–81. Mahrenholz argues that the constitutional norm "There is no established church" clearly formulated in the Paulskirchenverfassung of 1848, and later in the Weimar constitution of 1919 and in the constitution of the Federal Republic in 1949, must be understood in practice as "There are two established churches"; see John McManners, ed., *The Oxford Illustrated History of Christianity* (New York: Oxford University Press, 1990), 367–69.

42. See Johann Baptist Metz, *Jenseits bürgerlicher Religion: Reden über die Zukunft des Christentums* (Munich: Kaiser, Matthias-Grünewald, 1980), English translation, *The Emergent Church: The Future of Christianity in a Postbourgeois World* (New York: Crossroad, 1987), where, critically reviewing the identity and presence of the Catholic Church in former West Germany, Metz criticizes the quasi-compensatory role money plays in the relation between religion and the members of the church and speaks of the "question about the quasi-ideological status of the church-tax" (17 [my trans.]). Although the church-tax is periodically debated, in general, most citizens seem to think that the church efficiently provides social services with part of the money coming from that tax, such as kindergartens, schools, and hospitals. An example of this is the opinion of a member of the German parliament from the SPD who was for the continuation of the current church-tax system because he thought, following Bismarck's opinion, that the church-tax is the most social tax. See *Frankfurter Allgemeine Sonntagszeitung*, March 1, 1992, 5.

43. Despite the ongoing ecumenical collaboration and dialogue, each church, Evangelical and Catholic, holds its own separate chairs and faculties. There is only one instance in Germany of mixed theological faculty, Der Theologische Institut an der Universität Bielefeld. This is a clear example of how deep the separation between the two took root at the time of the Reformation and how the subsequent political agreements established a situation of mutual nonaggression based on a clear separation of the two churches.

44. See Erwin Gatz, "Caritas und soziale Dienste," in Anton Rauscher ed., *Der soziale und politische Katolizismus: Entwicklungslinien in Deutschland 1803–1963* (Munich: Günter Olzog, 1982), 2:312–51.

45. See Mahrenholz, *Die Kirchen,* 58–60. Although recognizing the important

occasions on which both churches opposed the Hitler regime, the author critically affirms that this opposition was not against the inhuman Third Reich per se but only against the attacks of the regime against the churches. Only individual churchpeople opposed the abuses of Hitler regarding the Jews and the concentration camps; see Heinz Hürten, *Kurze Geschichte des deutschen Katholizismus: 1800–1960* (Mainz: Matthias-Grünewald, 1986), 209–42. For Hürten, the position of organized Catholicism was clearly contrary to Hitler and favorable to the mainly Catholic Zentrumspartei or Volkspartei (in Bavaria) during the 1933 elections that gave Hitler the victory. However, this resistance softened very quickly in the few weeks after Hitler's victory, and, shortly thereafter, the new political order outlawed all important Catholic organizations. The conclusion for Hürten is that "the Third Reich meant the end of German Catholicism" (241 [my trans.]). For Gotto, Hockerts, and Repgen, the German bishops adopted a clear line of action, according to which the most important goal was to resist the Nazi regime by means of protecting the identity and public rights of the Catholic Church from the massive ideological and practical attacks of that regime against all forms of dissent. These authors conclude that the German episcopate never understood their mission to be an active resistance against the regime and its practice (see Klaus Gotto, Hans Günter Hockerts, Konrad Repgen, "Nationalsozialistische Herausforderung und kirliche Antwort: Eine Bilanz," in Klaus Gotto and Konrad Repgen, eds., *Die Katholiken und das Dritte Reich* [Mainz: Matthias-Grünewald, 1990], 173–90).

In *Jenseits bürgerlicher Religion*, 43–47, Metz supports the same thesis as Mahrenholz. In Dorothee Sölle and Johann Baptist Metz, in conversation with Karl-Josef Kuschel, *Welches Christentums hat Zukunft?* (Stuttgart: Kreuz, 1990), 28–29, Metz refers to the situation of the Catholic community in his village in these words: "We prayed for *Führer, Volk*, and *Vaterland*, led by a Parish priest who was not at all a Nazi" (my trans.).

For an analysis of the position of the Evangelische Church in relation to National Socialism and the Holocaust, see Georg Denzler and Volker Fabricius, *Christen und Nationalsozialisten* (Frankfurt am Main: Fischer Taschenbuch, 1993). For a summary of the most important documents of the Catholic and Evangelical Churches during the Nazi regime, see ibid., 249–363. For an interesting quantitative analysis of several religious factors during the same period, see Gotto and Repgen, *Die Katholiken*, 199–206.

46. See in this respect Georg Denzler, *Widerstand oder Anpassung: Katolische Kirche und Drittes Reich* (Munich: R. Piper, 1984), 35–41.

47. See Dietrich Albert, "Der Heilige Stuhl und das Dritte Reich," in Gotto and Repgen, *Die Katholiken*, 28. Albert seems to agree both with Pius XII's interpretation of the situation in Germany and with his papal justification of the role of the concordat and of the Catholic Church during the Nazi era. For an account of Pius XII's position, see Denzler, *Widerstand oder Anpassung*, 41, 44, 58, 67–69.

48. Endlösung can be translated as "final solution," meaning the decision made by the Nazi regime to exterminate the Jews in the concentration camps.

49. For the text of this unpublished encyclical and some of the reasons why it was never published, see Georges Passelecq and Bernard Suchecky, *The Hidden Encyclical of Pius XI* (New York: Harcourt Brace, 1997).

50. See Denzler, *Widerstand oder Anpassung*, 63–73; Denzler and Fabricius, *Christen und Nationalsozialisten*, 148–78.

51. See Gemeinsame Synode der Bistümer in der Bundesrepublik Deutschland, *Unsere Hoffnung: Ein Bekenntnis zum Glauben in dieser Zeit*, in Synodenbeschlüsse no. 18 (Bonn: Sekretär der Gemeinsamen Synode der Bistümer in der Bundesrepublik Deutschland, Dr. Josef Homeyer, 1976), 22.

52. See Mahrenholz, *Die Kirchen*, 12–15; Johannes Wallmann, *Kirchengeschichte Deutschlands seit der Reformation* (Tübingen: J. C. B. Mohr, 1993), 95–97, 175–78.

53. Mahrenholz, *Die Kirchen*, 18–20; Hürten, *Kurze Geschichte*, 33–61.

54. Hürten, *Kurze Geschichte*, 122.

55. Ibid., 122–35, 146–50, 245–46.

56. See Metz, *Unterbrechungen*, 51 and 54 (my trans.).

57. Johannes Baptist Metz, *Advent Gottes* (Munich: Ars Mundi, 1959).

58. See Johann Baptist Metz, "Theologie als Theodizee?" in Willi Oelmüller, ed., *Theodizee-Gott vor Gericht?* (Munich: Wilhelm Fink, 1990), 114–15.

59. Emerich Coreth, 1919–, is one of the best representatives of the generation of German Jesuit thinkers that followed the path of transcendental Thomism inaugurated by Maréchal. His best-known work is *Metaphysik: Eine methodisch-systematische Grundlegung* (Innsbruck: Tyrolia, 1961), English translation, *Metaphysics* (New York: Herder and Herder, 1968).

60. See summary in *Scholastik* 38 (1953).

61. Johannes Baptist Metz, *Christliche Anthropozentrik: Über die Denkform des Thomas von Aquin* (Munich: Kösel, 1962).

62. See his preface in Rahner, *Spirit in the World*, xlviii.

63. See his preface to Rahner, *Hearers of the Word*, ix.

64. For a detailed analysis of the changes introduced by Metz in Rahner's works, see Roger Dick Johns, *Man in the World: The Theology of Johannes Baptist Metz* (Missoula: University of Montana Scholars Press, 1976), 72–78. For a discussion of the relationship between the two at the initial steps of Metz's theology, see Guenther, "Rahner and Metz," 36–43.

65. Metz, *Christliche Anthropozentrik*, 47.

66. Ibid., chap. 2.

67. Hence, subjectivity belongs "theologically speaking, in formal predefinition, to the very event of revelation" (ibid., 98 [my trans.]).

68. Ibid., 107.

69. Ibid., 124–34.

70. Ibid., 127 (my trans.).

71. See "Vorwort zur 5. Auflage," in Metz, *Glaube in Geschichte und Gesellschaft: Studien zu einer praktischen Fundamentaltheologie*, 5th ed. (Mainz: Matthias-Grünewald, 1992), 9.

72. *GGG* (1977), 12 and n. 18.

73. Johann Baptist Metz, *Zur Theologie der Welt* (hereafter *ZTW*) (Mainz: Matthias-Grünewald, 1968), 57–58, English translation, *Theology of the World* (New York: Herder and Herder, 1969).

74. *Concilium* 16 (1966).

75. See preface to *Concilium* 6 (June 1965).

76. See Johannes Baptist Metz, "Unbelief as a Theological Problem," *Concilium* 6 (June 1965), in which he states that unbelief is becoming "a central question of theology itself" (59).

77. Ibid., 62.

78. Ibid., 62–77.

79. See, for instance, Johann Baptist Metz, "The Controversy about the Future of Man: An Answer to Roger Garaudy" *Journal of Ecumenical Studies* 4, no. 2 (1967).

80. Ibid., 231.

81. See Johann Baptist Metz, "Konkupiszenz," in Heinrich Fries, ed., *Handbuch theologischer Grundbegriffe*, vol. 1 (Munich: Kösel, 1962).

82. *GGG*, 143–45.

83. This first essay is called "Weltverständnis im Glauben: Christliche Orientierung in der Weltlichkeit der Welt heute." Metz opens the essay with a footnote in which he states that he is attempting to interpret in a positive way, on the basis of theological reasons, the increasing worldliness of the world.

84. *ZTW*, 14, 21.

85. Ibid., 18.

86. Ibid., 25 (my trans.).

87. Ibid., 37, 40–41.

88. Ibid., 15–16, 26–28.

89. See Francis P. Fiorenza and Johann Baptist Metz, "Der Mensch als Einheit von Leib und Seele," in *Mysterium Salutis;* and Metz, "Konkupiszenz."

90. *ZTW*, 44–45.

91. See Johannes Baptist Metz, "Theologische und metaphysische Ordnung," *Zeitschrift für katholische Theologie* 83 (1961), English version, "The Theological World and the Metaphysical World," *Philosophy Today* 10, no. 4 (1966).

92. Ibid. (English version), 256–57.

93. Ibid., 258.

94. Ibid., 263n.24.

95. A concise and illuminating analysis of Metz's development in this early phase can be found in Francis P. Fiorenza, "The Thought of J. B. Metz: Origin, Positions, Development," *Philosophy Today* 10 (1966). Fiorenza points to the importance of the concern with history as the factor that "led Metz to break with transcendental-existential philosophy" (249). However, as stated above, the importance of history in Metz's work cannot be thought to be a late development. As Fiorenza himself points out, Metz's understanding of freedom, for instance, is far more existential-historically oriented than Rahner's already at the time of *Christliche Anthropozentrik*. See also Johannes Baptist Metz, "Freiheit als philosophisch-theologisches Grenzproblem," in Johannes Baptist Metz et al., eds., *Gott in Welt: Festgabe für Karl Rahner,* vol. 1 (Freiburg: Herder, 1964).

96. See Metz, *Unterbrechungen*, 58–69.

97. Ernst Bloch, *Atheismus in Christentum: Zur religion des Exodus und des Reichs* (Reinbek bei Hamburg: Rowohlt Taschenbuch, 1970), English translation, *Atheism in Christianity: The Religion of the Exodus and the Kingdom* (New York: Herder and Herder, 1972).

98. Ibid., 15–16 (my trans.).

99. See Johann Baptist Metz, "Facing the Jews: Christian Theology after Auschwitz," *Concilium* 175 (October 1984): 32.

100. Bloch, *Atheismus in Christentum,* 17; Johann Baptist Metz, "Ende der Zeit?" in *Frankfurter Allgemeine Zeitung,* July 13, 1991 (my trans.).

101. *GGG,* 149 (my trans.).

102. The essay was published first in 1964 and later included in *ZTW,* 51–71.

103. *ZTW,* 56–64, 71.

104. Published first in 1966 and included in *ZTW,* 75–89.

105. Bloch, *Atheismus in Christentum,* 45–47.

106. My trans. Metz develops this concept explicitly in his article "Gott vor uns: Statt eines theologischen Arguments," in Siegfred Unseld, ed., *Ernst Bloch zu Ehren: Beiträge zu seinem Werk* (Frankfurt: Suhrkamp, 1965).

107. That truth must be "done," one of the central tenets of both political and liberation theologies, does not entail the denial of the importance of orthodoxy. In fact, the primacy of orthopraxis over orthodoxy is based in the old adage *primum vivere deinde philosophare,* expressed in the Thomistic distinction between first act and second act. To be a Christian, a follower of Christ, is the first act of faith. To understand logically and in a proper way what is being practiced is the second act. The first, although prior to the second, requires the second for its proper articulation, whereas the second is void of any meaning if the first is lacking. This intrinsic complementarity is stressed by both political and liberation theologies.

108. *ZTW,* 83–88 (my trans.).

109. For this position toward Marxism, see Metz, "Gott vor uns." For some examples of Metz's confrontation with Marxism, see Metz, "Controversy"; Milan Machoveč, Johannes Baptist Metz, and Karl Rahner, *Can a Christian Be a Marxist? A Dialog among a Marxist Philosopher and Two Christian Theologians* (Chicago: Argus, 1969). In the 1960s, the Paulus-Gesellschaft organized several discussions on the issue of Marxism and Christianity attended by Metz. See Paulus-Gesellschaft, *Christentum und Marxismus heute: Begegnung von Christen und Marxisten,* vol. 1 (Munich: Dokumente der Paulus-Gesellschaft XIII, 1966). For a detailed analysis of the relationship between Metz's theology and Marxism, see the important analysis of Metz's theology by Nedjeljko Ancic, *Die "Politische Theologie" von Johann Baptist Metz als Antwort auf die Herausforderung des Marxismus* (Frankfurt: Peter D. Lang, 1981). Later, in the 1980s, Metz gave a summarized account of the relationship between Christian theology and Marxism, in Johann Baptist Metz, "Thesen zum theologischen Ort der Befreiungstheologie," in Metz, ed., *Die Theologie der Befreiung: Hoffnung oder Gefahr für die Kirche?* (Düsseldorf: Patmos, 1986), 149–53. According to this account, there is no interest-free truth. Truth is always linked with distinct interests. (Here the relation not only to Marx but more concretely to Habermas's *Erkenntniss und Interesse* [Frankfurt am Main: Suhrkamp, 1968] is clearly noticeable.) In the case of Christian theology, and more precisely of political and liberation theologies, the interest in universal justice is the premise of the truth claim. This interest is the practical ground of the knowledge of truth to which the *Primat der Praxis* in the theological enterprise refers (ibid., 150–51). Marxism has developed a second point that is also a central question for biblical Christianity: the question of

the historicity of the world and of humankind, in which both profane and salvation history are intimately intertwined, and in which also Christians, on the basis of their hope in the God of justice, give witness to that hope through their own liberating praxis. In that sense, both political and liberation theologies take very seriously the Marxian interest in a historical liberating praxis and, in turn, account for two central elements in becoming a subject that Marxism does not account for: the forgotten and the dead, on the one hand, and historical guilt, beyond any Manichaean class division, on the other hand (ibid., 151–53). Still later, in the 1990s, after the political break of communism in Europe, Metz thinks that Marxism continues to be important for theology. Whereas the *jüdische Geist* has discovered what history is, Marx, not unrelatedly also a Jew, has actualized in a social-critical way this discovery within European history and, thereby, has also actualized in a more pointed way the *Theodizeefrage* (see Schuster and Boschert-Kimming, *Trotzdem Hoffen*, 18).

110. The essays are "Kirche und Welt im Lichte einer 'politischen Theologie'" and "Christliche Verantwortung für die Zukunftsplannung in einer weltlichen Welt," *ZTW*, 99–115 and 132–46.

111. *ZTW*, 102 (my trans.).

112. Ibid., 103.

113. See in this respect *GGG*, 16, where he refers to the "primacy of practical reason" as the "central problem of the Enlightenment" (my trans.).

114. *ZTW*, 105.

115. See ibid., 133 and 133n.4.

116. Ibid., 134–35.

117. Ibid., 106–7.

118. Ibid., 107–16 and 122–27.

119. See *GGG*, 45n.2 and 47 n.3.

120. By the end of the 1960s, Metz felt obliged to justify why he had chosen the term "political theology" to designate his theology, bearing in mind that this term had already been used by Carl Schmitt with a very different meaning and purpose. (For a very enlightening analysis of the convergences and differences between the two, see Michael J. Rainer, "Carl Schmitt und Johann Baptist Metz in Fremder Nähe? Bemerkungen zu zwei Leitkonzepten politischer Theologie im 20. Jahrhundert," in Jürgen Manemann, ed., *Demokratiefähigkeit* [Münster: LIT, 1995]; for a succinct and revealing history of the term "political theology," see Francis Schüssler Fiorenza, " 'Political Theology': An Historical Analysis," *Theology Digest* 25, no. 4, [1977].) Metz acknowledged that he chose the term "political theology" not because he thought the term was totally appropriate but because of the lack of an appropriate and better alternative to it (see Johann Baptist Metz, " 'Politische Theologie' in der Diskussion," in Helmut Peukert, ed., *Diskussion zur "politischen Theologie"* [Mainz-Munich: Matthias-Grünewald, Kaiser, 1969], 268–69nn. 6 and 29).

121. Metz, " 'Politische Theologie' in der Diskussion," 268–73. In defining the relation between theology and praxis, Metz thinks that political theology is so intimately close to a transformative, political ethics that he affirms that "political theology is the specific Christian hermeneutics of a political ethics as transformative ethics" (ibid., 282 [my trans.]). The hermeneutical task, and here Metz refers to Habermas's *Erkenntniss und Interesse,* is constitutively related to a praxis

of transformation both of the conditions and of the horizon of understanding (ibid., 283).

122. See Ottmar John, "Fortschrittskritik und Erinnerung: Walter Benjamin, ein Zeuge der Gefahr," in Edmund Arens, Ottmar John, and Peter Rottländer, *Erinnerung, Befreiung, Solidarität: Benjamin, Marcuse, Habermas und die politische Theologie* (Düsseldorf: Patmos, 1991), 13–80.

123. Ibid., 15–31 (my trans.).

124. Ibid., 31–76; Walter Benjamin, "Über den Begriff der Geschichte," in *Gesammelte Schriften* (Frankfurt am Main: Suhrkamp, 1974), 1.2:700–701.

125. For an interesting analysis of some aspects of the dialogue between political theology and the Frankfurt School, see also the essays by Edmund Arens on Habermas and Peter Rottländer on Marcuse in *Erinnerung, Befreiung, Solidarität.* For an enlightening work on how Habermas and Adorno relate to theology, see José Antonio Zamora, " 'Transcendencia desde dentro,' 'Idea de reconciliación': Habermas y Adorno frente a la teología," *Taula* 23–24 (1995): 25–66.

126. Examples of it are the following works: Johann Baptist Metz, Jürgen Moltmann, and Willi Oelmüller, *Kirche in Prozess der Aufklärung* (Munich, Mainz: Kaiser, Matthias-Grünewald, 1970); Jörn Rüsen, Eberhard Lämmert, and Peter Glotz, eds., *Die Zukunft der Aufklärung* (Frankfurt: Suhrkamp, 1988).

127. Hans Blumemberg, *Die Legitimät der Neuzeit* (Frankfurt: n.p., 1966); Hermann Lübbe, *Religion nach der Aufklärung* (Graz: Styria, 1986).

128. In relation to GGG, the English title, *Faith in History and Society,* can be misleading on the question of the relationship between Christianity and history and society, due to the ambiguity of the preposition *in.* The thesis is not that Christians have faith in history and society in the sense of believing in those realities but that Christianity is a faith with a constitutive sociohistorical element and that, therefore, it must be lived out in history and in society. The German title is precise in this sense: not *Glaube an Geschichte und Gesellschaft* but *Glaube in Geschichte und Gesellschaft.*

129. See especially GGG, 44–76.

130. Ibid., 22 (my trans.).

131. See also ibid., 195–203, where Metz explains how Rahner's theology can be an example of the inner relationship between fundamental theology and dogmatics.

132. Ibid., 61 (my trans.).

133. Metz, *Jenseits bürgerlicher Religion,* 9 (my trans.).

134. GGG, 14–15 (my trans.).

135. In reference to that inability, he affirms that "Catholics enclose themselves in a firm, and not least political, *corpus catholicum*" (GGG, 16) (my trans.).

136. Ibid., 23–25

137. Ibid., 25–29.

138. H. Richard Niebuhr, *The Kingdom of God in America* (Middletown, Connecticut: Wesleyan University Press, 1988), 193.

139. "Von der produktiven Ungleigzeitigkeit der Religion: Eine Antwort an Jürgen Habermas," in Metz, *Unterbrechungen,* 11–19.

140. GGG, 29–43.

141. Ibid., 49–50.

142. Ibid., 47–48. Metz had already hinted at the importance of memory and narrative in his last essay of *ZTW* (146) and had formulated his *memoria-These* in " 'Politische Theologie' in der Diskussion," 284–96. Later, he kept working on this question, to make it a central piece of political theology.

143. Walter Benjamin, "Der Erzähler," in *Illuminationen* (Frankfurt: Suhrkamp, 1961); T. W. Adorno, *Minima Moralia: Reflexionen aus dem beschädigten Leben* (Frankfurt: Suhrkamp).

144. *GGG*, 182–90 (my trans.).

145. Ibid., 47–51.

146. Johann Baptist Metz, *Zeit der Orden? Zur Mystik und Politik der Nachfolge* (Freiburg im Breisgau: Herder, 1977), English translation, *Followers of Christ: The Religious Life and the Church* (New York: Paulist, 1978).

147. *GGG*, 68–74.

148. See Metz, *Jenseits bürgerlicher Religion*, 8.

149. The issue runs throughout Metz's works. Some instances in which Metz deals explicitly with it are *Jenseits bürgerlicher Religion*, a collection of essays that expand Metz's thought in connection with the need for a Christianity and a church that, far from becoming a merely compensatory ideology and service-center, must retrieve their own power and their distinct, shocking identity in a world dominated by the liberal mind and ideology; Franz-Xaver Kaufmann and Johann Baptist Metz, *Zukunftsfähigkeit: Suchbewegungen im Christentum* (Freiburg im Breisgau: Herder, 1987), 93–165; "Welches Christentum hat Zukunft?" in *GGG*, 120–35, an essay in which Metz explores the meaning of the notion of the church as a church of the people, a church that takes seriously its own memory and the meaning of its dogmas and that converts itself to the church of the new people of God.

150. For an early formulation of the liberating power of the memory of suffering, see Metz's *Befreiendes Gedächtnis Jesu Christi*.

151. *GGG*, 54–55.

152. Jürgen Moltmann, *The Crucified God: The Cross of Christ as the Foundation and Criticism of Christian Theology* (London: SCM, 1974).

153. *GGG*, 54 (my trans.).

154. Johann Baptist Metz, "The Future in the Memory of Suffering," *Concilium* 76 (1972). See also Johann Baptist Metz and Jürgen Moltmann, *Meditations on the Passion: Two Meditations on Mark 8:31–38* (New York: Paulist, 1974), in which Metz writes that there cannot be talk of salvation except by and through the messianic history of suffering, rejection, and decline, despite the fact that our modern, only-always-progress-oriented society cannot endure the foolishness and scandal of the messianic truths and announcements.

155. See Johann Baptist Metz, "Erlösung und Emanzipation," in *GGG*, 104–19, previously published in *Stimmen der Zeit* 3 (1973).

156. Ibid., 107 (my trans.).

157. Ibid., 113.

158. Benjamin, "Über den Begriff der Geschichte," in *Gesammelte Schriften* 1.2: 697 (my trans.).

159. *GGG*, 97–100.

160. Ibid., 161–211.

161. Ibid., 150.

162. Ibid., 155 (my trans.).

163. "Ermutigung zum Gebet," in Johann B. Metz and Karl Rahner, *"Ermutigung zum Gebet"* (Freiburg: Herder, 1977), 34.

164. Metz gives a very illuminating and concise account of the evolution of his theology after *GGG* in his preface to the fifth edition of that work ("Vorwort zur 5. Auflage"). He characterizes his theology as postidealistic. By this Metz means its corrective nature with respect to a *situationsfreie Theologie* and its ability to cope with three experiences of nonidentity that belong to the current situation of both society and theology: the Enlightenment, Auschwitz, and the Third World. In doing so, he is pursuing further his understanding of political theology as a theology that, unlike idealistic theology, is constitutively oriented to take into account history and its tragedies, its irreparable failures, and its inconsolable suffering, seeking to turn that experience of nonidentity into the hermeneutical key of the *Gottesrede*. An insightful analysis of Metz's latest positions can be found in Reyes Mate, *Mística y política* (Estella: EVD, 1990).

165. See the World Bank, *World Development Report 1990: Poverty* (Oxford: Oxford University Press, 1990), iii.

166. An introduction to this vast issue can be found in David Harvey, *The Condition of Postmodernity: An Enquiry into the Origins of Cultural Change* (Oxford: Basil Blackwell, 1980).

167. Johann Baptist Metz, "Mit den Augen der Opfer," a conversation with Peter Hertel in *Mit dem Gesicht zur Welt* (Würzburg: Echter, 1996), 18 (my trans.).

168. It is an open question whether postmodernity is a real cultural innovation or just a reactive outburst to the rationalism (and the imperialism) of modernity, whether it is a real alternative or just a dead-end road. Although postmodernity forces the recognition of some of the pitfalls of modernity and brings a much-needed fresh air to counter the stiffness and arrogance of modernity, it is too wide and undifferentiated (and eclectic) to constitute a clear alternative, not to mention the difficulty its strongest philosophical positions have in sustaining themselves against the radical questioning of the very presuppositions of thought. For a discussion of this issue, see Wolfgang Welsch, *Unsere postmoderne Moderne* (Weinheim: VCH Verlagsgesellschaft, 1993); idem, ed., *Wege aus der Moderne: Schlüsseltexte der Postmoderne-Diskussion* (Weinheim: VCH Verlagsgesellschaft, 1994), a collection of essays that reflect different views on the nature of postmodernity.

169. For a Metzian synthetic diagnosis of this society, see *Jenseits bürgerlicher Religion*, 51–54, 95–99.

170. See Johann Baptist Metz, "Gotteskrise: Versuch zur 'geistigen Situation der Zeit,' " in Johann Baptist Metz et al., *Diagnosen zur Zeit* (Düsseldorf: Patmos, 1994), 81–82.

171. Ibid., 82–83.

172. See, for instance, Steve Brouwer, Paul Gifford, and Susan D. Rose, eds., *Exporting the American Gospel: Global Christian Fundamentalism* (New York: Routledge, 1996); Martin Riesebrodt, "Zur Politisierung von Religion: Überlegungen am Beispiel fundamentalistischer Bewegungen," in Kallscheuer, *Das Europa der Religionen*, 247–75.

173. See Johann Baptist Metz, "Religion, ja—Gott, nein," in Johann Baptist Metz and Tiemo Reiner Peters, *Gottespassion: Zur Ordensexistenz heute* (Freiburg im Breisgau: Herder, 1991) (my trans.).

174. See Johann Baptist Metz, "Gotteszeugenschaft in einer Welt der religionsfreundlichen Gottlosigkeit," *Ordensnachrichten* 2 (1992).

175. See Johann Baptist Metz, "Theologie gegen Mythologie: Kleine Apologie des biblischen Monotheismus," *Herder Korrespondenz* (April 1988); idem, "Zur Rettung der Vernunft: Der Geist Europas und der Geist des Christentums," *Süddeutsche Zeitung* 27/28 (October 1990). Especially in the first of these two articles, Metz makes an interpretation of the God of the Bible, the God of radical monotheism, a monotheism that theology betrays sometimes, trying to find mystifying and, ultimately, mythological grounds for its explanation.

176. See Johann Baptist Metz, "Wider die zweite Unmündigkeit: Zum Verhältnis von Aufklärung und Christentum," in Rüsen, Lämmert, and Glotz, *Die Zukunft der Aufklärung*, 82.

177. See Metz and Peters, *Gottespassion*, 40n.20, where Metz gives a summary of his "anamnestic anthropology."

178. *Der Spiegel* 23 (1976): 209.

179. Metz, "Theology gegen Mythologie," 191–93.

180. Johann Baptist Metz, "An der Schwelle zum dritten Jahrtausend oder Wohin ist Gott?" a contribution to the Concilium International Theological Congress, Louvain, September 9–13, 1990.

181. Metz, "Theologie gegen Mythologie," 187–89.

182. Ibid., 189–90.

183. He is referring to an article by Francis Fukuyama published in 1989, later expanded in Francis Fukuyama, *The End of History and the Last Man* (New York: Free Press, 1992).

184. See Johann Baptist Metz, "Ende der Zeit?" *Universitas* 6 (1992): 592–97.

185. Johann Baptist Metz, "Das Christentum und der europäische Geist," in Peter Koslowski, ed., *Europa imaginieren: Der europäische Binnenmarkt als kulturelle und wirtschaftliche Aufgabe* (Berlin: Springer, 1992).

186. See Johann Baptist Metz, "Unity and Diversity: Problems and Prospects for Inculturation," *Concilium* 204 (1989): 80.

187. See Metz, "Zur Rettung der Vernunft"; idem, "Gott und Aufklärung"; idem, "Das Christentum und die Fremden: Perspektiven einer multikulturellen Religion," in Friedrich Balke et al., eds., *Schwierige Fremdheit: Über Integration und Ausgrenzung in Einwanderungsländern* (Frankfurt: Fischer Taschenbuch, 1993), 225–26, where he speaks of a technical, domineering Europe and a Europe of the political Enlightenment; and idem, "Mit den Augen der Opfer," 23.

188. See Metz, "Zur Rettung der Vernunft."

189. Ibid., 80–84. This is an important point to be compared in chapters 4 and 5 with David Tracy's strategy of intensification of tradition as the only appropriate way to establish a fruitful dialogue among the different traditions.

190. See Johann Baptist Metz, "Kirche nach Auschwitz," in Marcel Marcus, Ekkehard W. Stegemann, and Erich Zenger, eds., *Israel und Kirche Heute: Beiträge zum christlich-jüdischen Dialog* (Freiburg im Breisgau: Herder, 1991), 119–20. See

also in this respect José Antonio Zamora, *Krise, Kritik, Erinnerung: Ein politisch-theologischer Versuch über das Denken Adornos im Horizon der Krise der Moderne* (Münster: LIT, 1995), 367–92, where the author analyzes how the original, biblical, apocalyptic character increasingly faded in the encounter of Christianity with Gnosticism and the Hellenistic Neoplatonism through Irenaeus, Origen, and Eusebius, and how this has influenced an idealistic interpretation of history and salvation in modern theology from Harnack on.

191. See Metz, "Das Christentum und die Fremden," 217.

192. See *GGG*, 4.

193. See Johann Baptist Metz, "Lateinamerika mit den Augen eines Theologen," *GI Prisma* 2 (1989): 46; idem, "So viele Anlitze, so viele Fragen: Lateinamerika mit den Augen eines europäischen Theologen," in Johann Baptist Metz and Hans-Eckehard Bahr, *Augen für die Anderen: Lateinamerika—eine theologische Erfahrung* (Munich: Kindler, 1991), 13–15.

194. Metz, "So viele Anlitze," 54–55; idem, "Vorwort zur 5. Auflage," 9–10; idem, "Die Dritte Welt und Europa: Theologisch-politische Dimensionen eines unerledigten Themas," *Stimmen der Zeit* 211 (1993): 3.

195. Metz, "Die Dritte Welt und Europa," 9, 19.

196. Johann Baptist Metz, "Ein Dialog der Theologen," in Johann Baptist Metz and Peter Rotländer, eds., *Lateinamerika und Europa: Dialog der Theologen* (Munich: Kaiser, Matthias-Grünewald, 1988), 19–20.

197. See Metz, "Unity and Diversity," 84.

198. Schuster and Boschert-Kimming, *Trotzdem Hoffen*, 30–32.

199. See Metz, "Vorwort zur 5. Auflage," 14, where, in referring to the other, he speaks of "the disclosure of 'God's mark' in the experience of the other's alteriry" (my trans.).

200. See, among others, Johann Baptist Metz, "Solidarische Freiheit," *Concilium* 2 (1992); idem, "Das Christentum und die Fremden," 225–28; idem, "Zur Rettung der Vernunft."

201. See Metz, "So viele Anlitze," 11–62.

202. Ibid., 52–53.

203. See Metz, *Zeit der Orden?* 45–47; idem, *Gottespassion*, 36–38, works written in 1977 and 1990, respectively, in which Metz goes back and reinterprets his early work *Armut im Geiste* (Munich: Ars Sacra, 1962).

204. See Metz, *Die Theologie der Befreiung*, 155 (my trans.).

205. Metz, *Zeit der Orden?*, 45–48; idem, *Jenseits bürgerlicher Religion*, 118–24; idem, "Das Konzil—'der Anfang eines Anfangs'?" *Orientierung* 22 (1990): 248–50; idem, *Die Theologie der Befreiung*, 155–56.

206. Metz, "So viele Anlitzen," 48–50; idem, "Die Dritte Welt und Europa: Theologisch-politische Dimensionen eines unerledigten Themas," *Stimmen der Zeit* 211 (1993): 6–9; idem, "Ein Dialog der Theologen . . . ," 20–22; idem, "Das Konzil," 246–48; idem, "Unity and Diversity," 79–84; idem, *Die Theologie der Befreiung*, 154; idem, "Im Aufbruch zu einer kulturell polyzentrischen Weltkirche," in Franz-Xaver Kaufmann and Johan Baptist Metz, *Zukunftsfähigkeit: Suchbewegungen im Christentum* (Freiburg im Breisgau: Herder, 1987).

207. Metz, "So viele Anlitze," 50–54.

208. See, inter alia, Metz, "Mit den Augen der Opfer," 19–21.

209. See mainly Metz, *Die Theologie der Befreiung*, 149–57; idem, "So viele An-litze," 41–61. For an interesting view from the perspective of liberation theology in relation to the issues discussed above, see the essays by Gustavo Gutiérrez, "Theorie und Erfahrung im Konzept der Theologie der Befreiung," Leonardo Boff, "Europäische Freiheitstraditionen und lateinamerikanisches Befreiungskonzept," and Juan Carlos Scannone, "Die Rolle des Volkskatholizismus in Lateinamerika," in Metz and Rotländer, *Lateinamerika und Europa*.

210. See Metz, "Vorwort zur 5. Auflage."

211. Ibid. (my trans.).

212. See Johann Baptist Metz, "Facing the Jews: Christian Theology after Auschwitz," *Concilium* 175 (1984): 29.

213. Ibid.

214. The phrase is ambiguous because the Spanish word *sueño* may have two different meanings. It can mean either slumber or dream. Therefore, the English translation could be "Reason produces monsters if asleep" or "Reason produces monsters if it dreams."

215. See Metz, "Vorwort zur 5. Auflage," 16n.20. For a detailed analysis of the discussion about theodicy in modernity, see Hans-Gerd Janßen, *Gott— Freiheit—Leid: das Theodizeeproblem in der Philosophie der Neuzeit* (Darmstadt: Wissenschaftliche Buchgesellschaft, 1989).

216. Theodor W. Adorno, *Negative Dialektik* (Frankfurt: Suhrkamp, 1975), 354–55.

217. Johann Baptist Metz, "Theodizee-empfindliche Gottesrede," in Metz, ed., *Landschaft aus Schreien: Zur Dramatik der Theodizeefrage* (Mainz: Matthias-Grünewald, 1995), 82–83.

218. See Johann Baptist Metz, "Theologie als Theodizee?" in Willi Oelmüller, ed., *Theodizee—Gott vor Gericht?* (Munich: Wilhelm Fink, 1990).

219. Metz does not want to deny the importance of the Greek spirit for Christianity. As always, he wants to correct what he thinks is the imbalance of that Greek spirit in the formulation of Christian faith; however, Metz does not specify what he understands as a balanced contribution of Greek thought to Christianity ("Theologie als Theodizee?" 111–13).

220. Ibid., 114–16.

221. Ibid., 114. The translation of *leiden an Gott* into English is not easy. The idea is that suffering in the Bible is always both related and directed to God by those who suffer as the one ultimately responsible for it. Clearly in Job, in the Prophets, in the Psalms, and, most radically, in the passion narrative of Mark (see esp. Mark 15:33–38), those paradigmatic believers suffer the deathly consequences of unconditionally believing in God, feel that such a destructive suffering is directly related to God, and get no answers to the questions that in their anguish they address to God. In the last resort, says Metz, all of them *leiden an Gott*.

Metz's first entry into this *leiden an Gott* took place through his analysis of the meaning of Christian prayer, at a relative early stage in his formulation of the main themes of political theology. See in this respect his work *Ermutigung zum Gebet*, published in 1977, in which he already refers to Job, the Prophets, the Psalms, and the gospel of Mark.

222. For a summary of Metz's understanding of Christianity, see Johann Baptist Metz, "Communicating a Dangerous Memory," in Fred Lawrence, ed., *Communicating a Dangerous Memory: Soundings in Political Theology* (Atlanta: Scholars Press, 1987), 37–53. See also Tiemo Rainer Peters in *Börsenblatt für den deutschen Buchhandeln* (March 7, 1989).

223. Metz's overall theological approach is, in a way, close to Barth's. In a sense, Metz, like Barth, is a dialectical theologian for whom there is no possible answer to the question of God other than in a dialectical way in which both affirmation and negation come together. This *unversöhnlicher Widespruch*, in Barth's words, comes very close to the Metzian *Unversöhnheit*, before which one only can surrender into God while *leiden an Gott*. However, in arriving at that dialectical conclusion, common to both, Barth and Metz use different ways. Whereas Barth's question is how to talk about God respecting God's absolute otherness, Metz's political theology approaches the question of God from the experience of suffering and failure in history. In that respect, he comes close to Bonhoeffer's (and Gutiérrez's) "view from below" (or underside) as the vantage point to discover what God and Christianity are. For a condensed view on Barth's notion of dialectical theology, see Karl Barth, "Das Wort Gottes als Aufgabe der Theologie," in Karl-Josef Kuschel, ed., *Lust an der Erkenntnis: Die Theologie des 20. Jahrhunderts* (Munich: Piper, 1986), 103–7. For Bonhoeffer's approach, see Dietrich Bonhoeffer, *Letters and Papers from Prison* (New York: Macmillan, 1971), 17, 360–63.

224. Johann Baptist Metz, "Die Rede von Gott angesichts der Leidensgeschichte der Welt," in *Stimmen der Zeit* 117 (1992): 317–20; idem, *Theologie als Theodizee?* 116–18; Schuster and Boschert-Kimming, *Trotzdem Hoffen*, 52–54.

225. See Metz, *Ermutigung zum Gebet*, 21–22 (my trans.). A most enlightening work on Metz's theology and, especially, on its spiritual dimension is James Matthew Ashley, *Interruptions: Mysticism, Politics, and Theology in the Work of Johann Baptist Metz* (Notre Dame, Ind.: University of Notre Dame Press, 1998). Ashley superbly examines Metz's *leiden an Gott* spirituality and translates it as "suffering onto God" (127–29, 153–63, 218n.31).

226. See, for instance, Metz, *Ermutigung zum Gebet*.

227. Metz, *Landschaft aus Schreien*, 84 (my trans.).

228. See especially Schuster and Boschert-Kimming, *Trotzdem Hoffen*, 44–55.

Chapter 3: Gustavo Gutiérrez

1. See the World Bank, *World Development Report: 1991* (New York: Oxford University Press, 1991) 204; idem, *World Development Report: 1999/2000* (New York: Oxford University Press, 2000), 230–31, 251; Instituto Nacional de Estadística e Informática, Dirección Nacional de Censos y Encuestas, *Compendio Estadístico 1989–90* (Lima: Instituto Nacional de Estadística e Informática, 1990); the Economist, *Pocket World in Figures 1995* (London: The Economist Books/Hamish Hamilton, 1994), 26.

2. For a description of the measures adopted by the government of Fujimori and a detailed analysis of their impact on the population up to 1990, see Instituto

Cuánto, *Ajuste y economía familiar: 1985–1990* (Lima: Instituto Cuánto, 1991). For the financial deficit, see Bodo Harenberg, ed., *Harenberg Lexikon der Gegenwart: Aktuell '97* (Dortmund: Harenberg Lexikon, 1996), 464.

3. See Instituto Cuánto, *Ajuste y economía familiar,* 30.

4. In relation to the increasing importance of the *informales,* see Hernando de Soto et al., *El otro sendero: La revolución informal* (Lima: Instituto Libertad y Democracia, 1986). The thesis is that the rise of the *informales* (mainly those who have nothing and have started to be active in business outside the legal and official framework that was a hindrance to them) in Peru amounts to a social revolution against the rigidity, inefficiency, and corruption of the legal and official system. According to de Soto, the way ahead is to favor this pacific social revolution and to debureaucratize the state, scrapping its mercantilist traditional nature. Peru, and other nations too, can be saved not by the state but by the activity of the citizens.

5. One example of the underlying reflections can be found in Carlos Milla Batres, ed., *En qué momento se jodió el Perú* (Lima: Editorial Milla Batres, 1990), a collection of essays by several intellectuals and political thinkers.

6. See World Bank, *World Development Report: 1999/2000,* 290.

7. See *The Economist* 7756 (April 25, 1992): 48; United Nations Development Program, *Human Development Report 1999* (Oxford: Oxford University Press, 1999), 3.

8. For a description of urban poverty in Peru and for support of the figures concerning poverty in this note, see Instituto Cuánto, *Ajuste y economía familiar.* For figures concerning macroeconomic magnitudes, see Instituto Nacional de Estadística e Informática, *Dirección Nacional.* For a short depiction of living conditions of a poor family in an urban shantytown see the World Bank, *World Development Report 1990: Poverty* (Oxford: Oxford University Press, 1990), 24–25. For a revealing study about the political attitudes and practices of shantytown dwellers, see Susan C. Stokes, "Politics and Latin America's Urban Poor: Reflections from a Lima Shantytown," *Latin American Research Review* 26, no. 2 (1991): 75–101. The author depicts the complexity of those attitudes and practices and warns about the danger of interpreting them in a too simplistic manner.

In relation to Sendero, see Carlos Iván Degregori, *Ayacucho 1969–1979: El surgimiento de Sendero Luminoso: Del movimiento por la gratuidad de la enseñanza al inicio de la lucha armada* (Lima: Instituto de Estudios Peruanos, 1990); idem, *Qué difícil es ser Dios: Ideología y violencia política en Sendero Luminoso* (Lima: El Zorro de Abajo, Ediciones, 1989); idem, "*Sendero Luminoso": I, Los hondos y mortales desencuentros; II, Lucha armada y utopía autoritaria,* 7th ed. (Lima: Instituto de Estudios Peruanos, 1989); Gustavo Gorriti Ellenbogen, *Sendero: Historia de la guerra milenaria en el Perú I* (Lima: Editorial Apoyo, 1990). In relation to the impact of Sendero on rural communities in general, and on the teachers living in those communities in particular, see Juan Ansión et al., *La escuela en tiempos de guerra: Una mirada a la educación desde la crisis y la violencia* (Lima: CEAPAZ, TAREA, Instituto Peruano de Educación en Derechos Humanos y Paz, 1992). I owe many interesting insights in relation to Sendero to Charles Kenney, a former member of the Instituto Bartolomé de Las Casas of Lima, and to Manuel Piqueras, who teaches sociology at the Universidad Católica de Lima and has published numerous studies on violence and peace.

One of the many debates in Peru concerns the economic situation and the path to follow in order to overturn it. As in other parts of the world, basically two different stands exist, both related to the controversy surrounding the orthodox policies promoted worldwide by the international financial organisms. One, adopted by the Fujimori government, follows substantially the policies of adjustment, privatization, and liberalization recommended by the International Monetary Fund and the World Bank, whereas the second one criticizes it because of its high social costs and its being a copy of outside models that may not work adequately in Peru. A presentation of the position on which the policy of adjustment of Fujimori is based can be found in *World Development Report 1991,* 1–11. The difference between the position of the World Bank and that of Fujimori is that the latter has done practically nothing to establish a cushion, as the World Bank advocates, for the poor, who are terribly hit by the economic measures of stabilization. For a different view of what development means and of how to promote it in Peru, see Javier Iguíñiz Echeverría, "Hacia una alternativa de desarrollo," *Páginas* (Lima) 113 (February 1992): 6–30. On the economic relevance of the *informales* and on the need for promoting small entrepreneurship as a path to development, see Fernando Villarán, "El fenómeno Fujimori o la crisis de las ideas convencionales," *QueHacer* (Lima) 64 (June 1990): 30–35. I am deeply indebted to both Javier Iguíñiz and Fernando Villarán for their contribution to my understanding of the Peruvian economy through the discussions I held with them.

9. Most authors attribute the origin of that discrimination to the conquest and to the subsequent colonization. However, as Iguíñiz points out, discrimination in Peru has also roots in preconquest times (see Iguíñiz, "Hacia una alternativa," 21).

10. See, for instance, Gutiérrez's own view in *En busca de los pobres de Jesucristo* (hereafter *BPJ*) (Lima: Instituto Bartolomé de Las Casas, Centro de Estudios y Publicaciones, 1992), 577, English translation, *Las Casas: In Search of the Poor of Jesus Christ* (Maryknoll, N.Y.: Orbis Books, 1993). For an idea of the cultural and political situation before and during the Inca Empire, see, besides the bibliography referred to by Gutiérrez, Carlos Daniel Valcárcel, *Historia del Perú autóctono* (Lima: Editores Importadores S.A., 1982), 1–35. The author has a very positive view, although perhaps a little bit idealized, of the achievements of the Incas, especially in relation to the integrative character of their Andean political vision, their educational system, and their advanced and deeply socialist economy. Valcárcel critiques the inability of the Europeans to capture the uniqueness of the Inca economy as a paradigm of universal importance. For a seventeenth-century history of the Incas, see Bernabé Cobo, *History of the Inca Empire,* trans. and ed. Ronald Hamilton (Austin: University of Texas Press, 1979).

11. See Huamán Poma, *Nueva crónica y buen gobierno,* ed. Carlos Araníbar (Lima: Ediciones Rikchay Perú, Instituto de Apoyo Agrario, 1990). For an introduction to the work and to Huamán Poma, see the foreword by Carlos Araníbar to the work just cited. For an analysis of the theological importance of Huamán, see Alberto Maguiña Larco, "Guamán Poma y la evangelización," *Páginas* (Lima) 107 (February 1991): 43–52; Gustavo Gutiérrez, *Dios o el oro en las Indias: Siglo XVI*

(Lima: Instituto Bartolomé de Las Casas–Rimac, Centro de Estudios y Publicaciones, 1989), 12–14; idem, *BPJ*, 24–28, 92–93, 271–72, 616–28, where Gutiérrez analyzes the parallelism between the perspective and theological approach of both Bartolomé de Las Casas and Huamán (Guamán in Gutiérrez) Poma de Ayala.

An account of the Spanish conquest is given by Guillermo Prescott, "Historia de la conquista del Perú," in Valcárcel, *Historia*, 270–356. For a detailed account, see José Antonio del Busto Duthurburu, *Historia general del Perú: Descubrimiento y conquista* (Lima: Librería Studium, 1978). A summarized and systematic description of the Spanish colonization of Peru and of the main means and institutions used for that purpose can be found in Julio Cotler, *Clases, estado y nación en el Perú* (Lima: Instituto de Estudios Peruanos, 1978), 21–70.

12. See *BPJ*.

13. See Gutiérrez, *Dios o el oro*, 10n.2; *BPJ*, 637–41.

14. See José Carlos Mariátegui, *Seven Interpretive Essays on Peruvian Reality* (Austin: University of Texas Press, 1971), 7, 24.

15. See Washington Delgado, "¿Cuándo se jodió el Perú?" in Milla, *En qué momento*, 55, where the author argues that a few years after 1828, the year in which the natives were granted all their citizen rights, they lost half of their land.

16. See Huamán Poma, *Nueva crónica*, 78–79.

17. Mariátegui, *Seven Interpretive Essays*, 22–25.

18. See Cotler, *Clases*, 245, 295.

19. For an analysis of the nature of elections in Peru, see Jorge Basadre, *Elecciones y centralismo en el Perú: Apuntes para un esquema histórico* (Lima: Centro de Investigación de la Universidad del Pacífico, 1980).

20. See Curt Cadorette, *From the Heart of the People: The Theology of Gustavo Gutiérrez* (Oak Park, Ill.: Meyer-Stone Books, 1988), xii.

21. See Rodolfo Cerrón-Palomino, *El quechua: Una mirada de conjunto* (Lima: Centro de Investigación de Lingüística Aplicada, Universidad Mayor de San Marcos, 1980), 4, 41–44, 51–54. According to Cerrón-Palomino, Quechua is not perceived by native people as a positive asset, but as a hindrance. They want to learn Spanish to have access to the benefits of the Spanish-dominated urban life. In consequence, Cerrón-Palomino thinks that the survival of the native language is not simply a question of teaching it, but that it has profound political, economic, and social implications. A very interesting work about bilingual education, its policy, problems, strategy, and future, is Nancy H. Hornberger, *Haku Yachaywasiman: La educación bilingüe y el futuro del Quechua en Puno* (Lima-Puno: Programa de Educación Bilingüe de Puno, 1989).

22. See Cotler, *Clases*, 39.

23. José María Arguedas, *Los ríos profundos* (Lima: Editorial Horizonte, 1988), 12–26. In Gutiérrez's breathtaking analysis of Arguedas's work, he masterfully shows the theological implications of this passage (see Gustavo Gutiérrez, *Entre las calandrias: Un ensayo sobre José María Arguedas* [hereafter *EC*] [Lima: Instituto Bartolomé de Las Casas–Rimac, Centro de Estudios y Publicaciones, 1990], 75–78).

24. See Jean-Pierre Tardieu, *Noirs et Indiens au Pérou (XVIe-XVIIe siècles): Histoire d'une politique ségrégationniste* (Paris: Éditions L'Harmattan, 1990), 60.

25. Gutiérrez, *Dios o el oro*, 142–44.

26. Tardieu, *Noirs et Indiens*, 47–87, 125–26.

27. See Cotler, *Clases*, 106.

28. A good collection of essays on these matters can be found in Wilfredo Kapsoli et al., *Primer seminario sobre poblaciones emigrantes* (Lima: Consejo Nacional de Ciencia y Tecnología, 1987). An interesting article on the question is Mary Fukumoto, "Asian Influences in the Americas: The Chinese and Japanese in South America," *The New World: A Smithsonian Quincentenary Publication Dedicated to the Americas* 3 (spring/summer 1992): 6–7. See also José Carlos Mariátegui, *Peruanicemos el Perú* (Lima: Empresa Editora Amauta, 1970), 130.

29. Mariátegui, *Peruanicemos el Perú*, 65. Cotler, in *Clases*, follows the same interpretation. This Mariateguist thesis is widely shared by many thinkers in Peru, as the essays in Milla, *En qué momento*, show.

30. The paradigmatic expression of such a project is the novel by José María Arguedas, *Todas las sangres* (Lima: Editorial Horizonte, 1987). The book has become a classic in Peru, and, although the types presented in it are, too be sure, "ideal types" that respond to Arguedas's own views, it is a referential point for all thinkers interested in formulating an integrative national project.

31. See Milla, *En qué momento*, 11.

32. On the crucial importance of the native peasants in the socialism of Mariátegui, see Alberto Flores Galindo, "José Carlos Mariátegui: Sociedad campesina y socialism indoamericano," in Carlos Franco, ed., *El Perú de Velasco*, 3 vols. (Lima: Centro de Estudios para el Desarrollo y la Participación, 1983), 1:125–34. On the ideas of Haya and Mariátegui, see Carlos Franco, "Haya y Mariátegui: Los discursos fundadores," in Franco, *El Perú de Velasco*, 1:135–65; Cotler, *Clases*, 201–26. On the different nature and success of their political activities, see ibid., 232–36. On the influence of the APRA and of its founder on Peru, see ibid., 227–383. On how Mariátegui saw the reasons for his rupture with Haya, see José Carlos Mariátegui, *Invitación a la vida heroica: Antología* (Lima: Instituto de Apoyo Agrario, 1989), 335–38, 364–67.

33. See Cotler, *Clases*, 290, and Instituto Nacional, *Dirección Nacional*, 1:157.

34. From the point of view of the political participation of the masses, see Héctor Béjar, "Los movimientos sociales y los partidos políticos desde 1930 hasta 1968: Su significado en términos de participación popular," in Franco, *El Perú de Velasco*, 183–91. On the boom of the masses in the last two decades, see José Matos Mar, *Desborde popular y crisis del Estado: El nuevo rostro del Perú en la década de 1980* (Lima: José Matos Mar, 1988).

35. See Cotler, *Clases*, 353–83; Francisco Guerra García, "El régimen oligárquico: Procesos políticos," in Franco, *El Perú de Velasco*, 236–38; Arturo Valdés Palacio, *Una revolución itinerante* (Lima: Instituto de Propiedad Exclusiva de sus Trabajadores, 1989), 6; Carlos Franco, "Los significados de la experiencia velasquista: Forma política y contenido social," in Franco, *El Perú de Velasco*, 2:318–23.

36. An example of a mixed, but mostly critical, review is Delgado, "¿Cuándo se jodió el Perú?" 63–64.

37. Degregori, "*Sendero Luminoso*," 29.

38. See Cotler, *Clases*, 382–83.

39. See Franco, *El Perú de Velasco*, 2:415–16, 3:915.

40. See ibid., 3:929.

41. See Jeffrey Klaiber, S.J., *La iglesia en el Perú: Su historia social desde la independencia* (Lima: Fondo Editorial de la Pontificia Universidad Católica del Perú, 1988), 386–97, 401–7. Cotler's opinion is rather similar (*Clases*, 326). For a global assessment of the Velasco regime, see the different articles included in Franco, *El Perú de Velasco*. An inside account of the main expropriations of American companies and of the conflicts involved thereby can be found in Valdés Palacio, *Una revolución itinerante*. The author was both a member of the COAP, the influential committee advising president Velasco, and the secretary at cabinet meetings.

42. On the group ONIS, see Luis Pásara, *Radicalización y conflicto en la Iglesia peruana* (Lima: Ediciones El Virrey, 1986), 45–50, 68–77; Klaiber, *La iglesia*, 381–83, 390.

43. See Hubert Jedin, ed., *History of the Church Reformation and Counter-Reformation* (New York: Seabury, 1980), 5:575–78.

44. See *BPJ*, 423–27.

45. For an idea of the complexity of the issue, see Isacio Pérez Fernández, O.P., *Bartolomé de las Casas en el Perú: El espíritu lascasiano en la primera evangelización del imperio incaico (1531–1573)* (Cusco: Centro de Estudios Rurales Andinos "Bartolomé de las Casas," 1988).

46. See Cotler, *Clases*, 33–40.

47. See Gutiérrez, *Dios o el oro*, 11; *BPJ*, 13, 236–53, 288–99, 545–56.

48. See Gutiérrez, *Dios o el oro*, 27–30; *BPJ*, 35–71.

49. See Thomas Eggensperger and Ulrich Engel, *Bartolomé de las Casas: Dominikaner—Bischof—Verteidiger der Indios* (Mainz: Matthias-Grünewald, 1991), 37–70.

50. The book has recently been translated into English: Bartolomé de las Casas, *The Only Way*, ed. Helen Rand Parish (Mahwah, N.J.: Paulist, 1992), with a well-documented introduction by the editor. For an analysis and assessment of the work of Las Casas and of his battle to improve the situation of the natives, and also for the struggle between pope and king, other than Parish's introduction just cited, see Pérez Fernández, *Bartolomé de las Casas*; Eggensperger and Engel, *Bartolomé de las Casas*; Gutiérrez, *Dios o el oro; BPJ*; Jedin, *History of the Church*, 6:232–40.

51. See Pérez Fernández, *Bartolomé de las Casas*, 398.

52. Ibid., 438n.140, 583–650.

53. See Jedin, *History of the Church*, 6:234–37.

54. Ibid., 6:236.

55. Cotler, *Clases*, 54; Jedin, *History of the Church*, 6:244.

56. See Catalina Romero, *Iglesia en el Perú: Compromiso y renovación (1958–1984)* (Lima: Instituto Bartolomé de Las Casas–Rimac, 1987), 35–42.

57. See Cotler, *Clases*, 308; Romero, *Iglesia*, 37–38; Pásara, *Radicalización*, 13–14; Klaiber, *La iglesia*, 34; Gustavo Gutiérrez, *Líneas pastorales de la iglesia en América Latina* (Lima: Centro de Estudios y Publicaciones, 1970), 18.

58. See Cotler, *Clases*, 308–15; Romero, *Iglesia*, 12; Pásara, *Radicalización*, 37; Klaiber, *La iglesia*, 43–45.

59. See the collection of documents produced by all the conferences: Episcopado

Latinoamericano, *Conferencias Generales: Río de Janeiro, Medellín, Puebla, Santo Domingo* (Santiago de Chile: San Pablo, 1993), 44–45, 76–79.

60. Klaiber, *La iglesia,* 43–47. Romero analyzes the period more from the perspective of the social-critique role played by the church, and also in more dynamic terms, as an advance toward a clearer definition of the church vis-à-vis the unjust situation in which the majority of the population lived (Romero, *Iglesia,* 10–20).

61. See *TL,* 157 (my trans.).

62. See Cotler, *Clases,* 323–24.

63. On the theory of dependency, see Arthur F. McGovern, *Liberation Theology and Its Critics: Toward an Assessment* (Maryknoll, N.Y.: Orbis Books, 1989), 125–29, where the author analyzes this theory and provides the basic bibliography on it.

64. See Romero, *Iglesia,* 43–50. For this author the importance of Medellín lies on its view of evangelization, which encompasses all aspects concerning human liberation, thus being the beginning of a new era of Christianity and of the Catholic Church in Latin America.

65. See Episcopado Latinoamericano, *Conferencias Generales,* 83–223.

66. Ibid., 109 (my trans.).

67. See Gustavo Gutiérrez, "The Church and the Poor: A Latin American Perspective," in Giuseppe Alberigo, Jean-Pierre Jossua, and Joseph A. Komonchak, eds., *The Reception of Vatican II* (Washington, D.C.: Catholic University of America Press, 1987), 171–93. For an analysis of Medellín in relation to Vatican II from different theological disciplines, see José Dammert et al., *Irrupción y caminar de la iglesia de los pobres: Presencia de Medellín* (Lima: Instituto Bartolomé de Las Casas, Centro de Estudios y Publicaciones, 1989).

68. See Gustavo Gutiérrez, "Significado y alcance de Medellín," in Dammert et al., *Irrupción,* 26.

69. Ibid., 30.

70. See Gustavo Gutiérrez, "Two Theological Perspectives: Liberation Theology and Progressivist Theology," in Sergio Torres and Virginia Fabella, eds., *The Emergent Gospel: Theology from the Underside of History: Papers from the Ecumenical Dialogue of Third World Theologians, Dar es Salaam, August 5–12, 1976* (Maryknoll, N.Y.: Orbis Books, 1978), 246.

71. In this sense, see Jean-Ives Calvez, "Medellín and Puebla in the Perspective of the World Church," in Edward L. Clearly, ed., *Born of the Poor: The Latin American Church since Medellín* (Notre Dame, Ind.: University of Notre Dame Press, 1990), 183–96.

72. See Gustavo Gutiérrez, *Teología de la liberación: Perspectivas,* 7th ed. (Lima: Centro de Estudios y Publicaciones, 1990), 64n.1. The text of the address, delivered by Gustavo in a meeting held at Chimbote, can be found in Hennelly, *Liberation Theology,* 62–76.

73. Gustavo Gutiérrez, *The Power of the Poor in History* (hereafter *PPH*) (Maryknoll, N.Y.: Orbis Books, 1983), 212–14.

74. See Episcopado Latinoamericano, *Conferencias Generales,* 381; Hennelly, *Liberation Theology,* 253–58.

75. This is Romero's central thesis (see Romero, *Iglesia,* 60–63). An invaluable collection of documents showing the changes taking place in the Latin American

church is the series Signos, with five volumes published until now: *Signos de reno-*
vación: Recopilación de documentos post-conciliares de la iglesia en América Latina
(Lima: Comisión Episcopal de Acción Social, 1969); *Signos de liberación: Testi-*
monios de la iglesia en América Latina 1969–1973 (Lima: Centro de Estudios y
Publicaciones, 1973); *Signos de lucha y esperanza: Testimonios de la iglesia en*
América Latina 1973–1978 (Lima: Centro de Estudios y Publicaciones, 1978); *Sig-*
nos de vida y fidelidad: Testimonios de la iglesia en América Latina 1978–1982
(Lima: Centro de Estudios y Publicaciones, 1983); *Signos de nueva evangelización:*
Testimonios de la iglesia en América Latina 1983–1987 (Lima: Centro de Estudios
y Publicaciones, 1988); *Signos de identidad solidaria: Testimonios de la iglesia en*
América Latina 1988–1992 (Lima: Centro de Estudios y Publicaciones, 1993).

76. Pásara sees in this period the peak of what he calls the radicalization of the
Peruvian church, when the work with grassroots organizations gained momentum
(see Pásara, *Radicalización*, 77–79). For Klaiber, however, the new period marks
a shift from the social-political church of the 1968–75 period to a social-pastoral
church. At the base of this shift lies, in Klaiber's opinion, a certain disenchantment
with the possibilities of changing reality rapidly by political means. The political
euphoria felt in the church after Medellín, and during the Velasco regime, faded
away, giving way to a greater emphasis on the pastoral nature of the mission of the
church (see Klaiber, *La iglesia*, 412–13).

77. Episcopado Latinoamericano, *Conferencias Generales*, 250.

78. See Romero, *Iglesia*, 57–58; the text finally approved can be found in
Conferencia Episcopal Peruana, *Documentos de la Conferencia Episcopal Peruana*
1979–1989 (Lima: Ediciones VE, 1989), 253–73. The thesis of Pásara is that the radicality and rigidity of those militant Catholics committed to the cause of the poor and
to the promotion of a grassroots church have increasingly encountered the reactive
radicality and rigidity of those Catholics who totally disagree with those liberation-
oriented views. For Pásara, both groups seem unable to live together within the
Peruvian church, which finds it difficult to redefine itself in democratic and pluralistic terms (see Pásara, *Radicalización*, 10). Romero points to the division and the
tensions within the Peruvian church and has a somehow similar interpretation of
them: the cause of those tensions lies in the active role the church adopted regarding
its option for the poor (see Romero, *Iglesia*, 57–60). However, whereas Romero's
views are clearly supportive of that active role of the church on the side of the
poor, Pásara adopts a rather critical stance before it, due to the, in his interpretation, excessive radicality of the most dynamic groups that represent that option for
the poor.

79. See in that respect Gustavo Gutiérrez, "Hacia el quinto centenario," in Juan
Ansión et al., *Quinto centenario y nueva evangelización* (Lima: Centro de Estudios y Publicaciones, 1992), 11–24; Jon Sobrino, "The Winds in Santo Domingo
and the Evangelization of Culture," in Alfred T. Hennelly, S.J., ed., *Santo Domingo*
and Beyond: Documents and Commentaries from the Historic Meeting of the Latin
American Bishops Conference (Maryknoll, N.Y.: Orbis Books, 1993), 168, where
Sobrino states that Medellín is still "the unsurpassed symbol of the new evangelization." For an analysis of the importance and of the meaning of the term "new
evangelization" in John Paul II, see Cecilia Tovar, "Juan Pablo II y la nueva evan-

gelización," in Ansión et al., *Quinto centenario,* 93–124. Very perceptively, Tovar notices that the term is closely linked with the pope's awareness of a new histori- cal beginning centered around the notion of celebration and remembrance brought about by the new millennium (two millennia since the gospel was first announced, one millennium since the evangelization of the Slavs, a half-millennium since the evangelization of Latin America).

80. See the essays by Edward L. Clearly, O.P., "The Journey to Santo Domingo," and Alfred T. Hennelly, S.J., "A Report from the Conference," in Hennelly, *Santo Domingo and Beyond;* Gustavo Gutiérrez, "Una agenda: La IV Conferencia de Santo Domingo," and Francisco Chamberlain, S.J., "La realidad, Santo Domingo y Juan Pablo II," in *Paginas* 119 (1993). As these essays show, Rome not only set up the agenda of the conference; it also controlled its presidency and rejected the working document that, although it had already been severely chopped and polished, still represented the enormous preparatory work for the conference undertaken by every national church in the region.

81. See the essays referred to in the previous two notes.

82. See Robert McAfee Brown, *Gustavo Gutiérrez: An Introduction to Liber- ation Theology* (Maryknoll, N.Y.: Orbis Books, 1990), 22–25. The author gives interesting biographical information about Gutiérrez and provides a good introduc- tion to his work in the broader context of the processes taking place in Latin America and in the Catholic Church. For an understanding of the movement known as *la nou- velle théologie,* see Schoof, *Survey of Catholic Theology,* 93–121, 194–210. Schoof is able to relate the movement to other efforts going on mainly in the German-speaking world, thus providing an enlightening comparison of the two traditions.

83. Something to bear in mind, because it is paradigmatic for Gutiérrez, is that Catholic intellectuals, such as Péguy, Claudel, Bernanos, Mauriac, Mounier, and, most of all, Maritain, accomplished a double task: to assert their Catholic identity in the intellectual milieu and to reflect on the conditions of that assertion. Maritain formulated one of the most articulate responses to the problem of the supersed- ing of religion and philosophy by science posed by Comte (see Jacques Maritain, *Distinguer pour unir; ou, Les degrés du savoir* [Paris: Desclée de Brouwer, 1932]). He also devised an active role for Christians in politics and society in his probably most influential work, *Humanism intégral: Problèmes temporels et spirituels d'une nouvelle chrétienté* (Paris: Aubier-Montaigne, 1936).

84. A well-known polemic arose in the mid-1970s between Míguez Bonino and Moltmann. Míguez Bonino critiqued Moltmann and other European theologians for retreating to a neutral critical function in theology. Moltmann responded by saying that Míguez Bonino's theology was based ultimately on the same theological principles that the theologians he was critiquing and that liberation theologians in general did in fact not contribute much to the theological enterprise from a strictly Latin American perspective (see Hennelly, *Liberation Theology,* 195–204).

85. On recognizing the decisive influence of French theology and thought on Gutiérrez, as well as of other European thinkers, Frei Betto writes that "there is no denying the European roots springing from Maritain's integral humanism, Mounier's committed personalism, Teilhard de Chardin's progressive evolutionism, de Lubac's social dogmatics, Congar's theology of the laity, Lebret's theology of development,

Comblin's theology of revolution, or Metz's political theology" (see Frei Betto, "Gustavo Gutiérrez: A Friendly Profile," in Marc H. Ellis and Otto Maduro, eds., *The Future of Liberation Theology: Essays in Honor of Gustavo Gutiérrez* [Maryknoll, N.Y.: Orbis Books, 1989], 32). As a matter of fact, references to these and other authors run throughout Gutiérrez's foundational work, *Teología de la liberación,* which he published first in 1971. On the constitutive Peruvian identity of Gutiérrez's theology, see Curt Cadorette, "Peru and the Mystery of Liberation: The Nexus and Logic of Gustavo Gutiérrez's Theology," in Ellis and Maduro, *Future,* 49–58, and also Cadorette, *From the Heart of the People,* esp. 30–82. Two interesting works that witness to a sincere European desire to understand and to benefit from liberation theology are Johann Baptist Metz and Peter Rotländer, eds., *Lateinamerika und Europa: Dialog der Theologen* (Munich: Kaiser, Matthias-Grünewald, 1988) and Johann Baptist Metz, ed., *Die Theologie der Befreiung: Hoffnung oder Gefahr für die Kirche?* (Düsseldorf: Patmos, 1986). In the latter, the articles by Schnackenburg, Kasper, and Metz show how a critical collaboration can foster a mutual understanding between the Latin American and the European perspectives.

   Another interesting collection of essays that gauge the contribution of liberation theology to the theological enterprise is Gregory Baum et al., *Vida y reflexión: Aportes de la teología de la liberación al pensamiento teológico actual* (Lima: Centro de Estudios y Publicaciones, 1983). Metz's contribution to this work, prior in time to that discussed in the previous paragraph, establishes a parallelism between the role played by the religious orders in the twelfth century in renewing the church and the role played by grassroots communities and liberation theology in renewing the church and theology today. Metz calls it a second Reformation. Also interesting is Chenu's article, because it shows how the praxis-based method of liberation theology coheres with Vatican II and with the elimination of the dualism nature-supernature or world history–history of salvation. Moreover, liberation theology is for Chenu a legitimate development of that nondualistic notion of nature-supernature that, in turn, contributes to flesh it out theologically. In that sense, Chenu helps to understand the link between *la nouvelle théologie* and Gutiérrez's theology.

   86. The work was published in 1968. It consists of a series of talks delivered first in 1964 and then reworked and presented before a group of leaders of Catholic students in 1967. Gutiérrez incorporated this work into his book *Teología de la liberación,* chaps. 4 and 5, although introducing some important modifications.

   87. *TL,* 72–88, 210–32; Gustavo Gutiérrez, *Beber en su propio pozo: En el itinerario espiritual de un pueblo* (hereafter *BPP*) (Lima: Centro de Estudios y Publicaciones, 1983), 62–63; idem, *Dios o el oro,* 188–91.

   88. *ST* I, Q.1.

   89. Gutiéerrez, *Líneas pastorales,* 9–10. That sciences, philosophy, and theology are interrelated (each of them, however, being placed on a different level) is the main thesis of Maritain in his work *Distinguer pour unir; ou, Les degrés du savoir.* The first part of the title witnesses to the Thomist outlook of Maritain's thought, an outlook that has permeated also Rahner's and Gutiérrez's thought.

   90. Gutiérrez, *Líneas pastorales,* 11–12. The Thomistic distinction between first and second acts is already encountered here. Although Gutiérrez's own theology is understood as critical reflection, he acknowledges that the other two historical

functions of theology, the spiritual and the scientific, are also permanent traits of Christian theology.

91. Gutiérrez, *Líneas pastorales*, 6. He presents theology in his foundational work as "critical reflection on historical praxis in the light of the Word" (see *TL*, 85 [my trans.]). This definition of theology encompasses the classical task of theology as *fides quaerens intellectum*, which Gutiérrez calls *inteligencia de la fe* (*TL*, 67).

92. *TL*, 433.

93. See Gustavo Gutiérrez, *La verdad los hará libres: Confrontaciones* (hereafter *LV*) (Lima: Instituto Bartolomé de Las Casas–Rimac, Centro de Estudios y Publicaciones, 1986), 146.

94. Gutiérrez, *Líneas pastorales*, 8.

95. See *Lumen Gentium* 48.

96. *TL*, 143–48.

97. Gutiérrez, *Líneas pastorales*, 13 (my trans.).

98. That perspective was already present in the article by Juan Luis Segundo, "The Future of Christianity in Latin America," in Hennelly, *Liberation Theology,* 29–37, written in 1962. For Segundo, "Latin America is a *Western* world on the move" (29). The church faces the fast dechristianization of social Christendom. The only valid way ahead is to set up a program of evangelization aimed at the promotion of Christians with a mature and personal faith capable of dealing with the new parameters of the modern world.

99. See Brown, *Gustavo Gutiérrez,* 25.

100. Gutiérrez, *Líneas pastorales*, 14–21.

101. Ibid., 26–27. This danger stems from the creation of Christian political parties and unions, of which one of the most operative in Latin America has been the Chilean Christian Democratic Party led by Eduardo Frei.

102. See *TL*, 129.

103. Gutiérrez, *Líneas pastorales*, 22–23.

104. An enlightening comparison between the way Maritain and Gutiérrez see salvation and its social presence can be found in J. Dean Brackley, "Salvation and the Social Good in the Thought of Jacques Maritain and Gustavo Gutiérrez" (Ph.D. diss., University of Chicago, 1980). For Brackley, Maritain stresses the difference (not to separate but to unite) between nature and grace and therefore between the order of salvation and the social order, whereas Gutiérrez emphasizes that salvation takes place in and through the social good. Brackley also claims that Maritain has a rather individualistic approach, whereas Gutiérrez, if anything, has a social bias (see ibid., 121–22). Interestingly for the purpose of this work, Brackley points to Rahner's understanding of the relation between nature and the supernatural as that which allowed Gutiérrez to go beyond Maritain's position (ibid., 221–51).

105. In *TL*, Gutiérrez will call this model "the distinction of planes" (see *TL*, 132–36).

106. Gutiérrez, *Líneas pastorales*, 27–29.

107. See Cecilia Tovar, "UNEC: Cincuenta años de camino," *Páginas* (Lima) 111 (October 1991): 92–94.

108. Gutiérrez, *Líneas pastorales*, 29–31.

109. Ibid., 70. Here, Gutiérrez moves theologically toward a definition of the role

of the church, that of being prophetic, that is central to liberation theology and that will be actually taken up both by Medellín and by Puebla.

110. Gutiérrez points out that the notion was already present in Blondel (ibid., 72).

111. Ibid., 71–74.

112. Ibid., 77–78.

113. Ibid., 80–84.

114. See *PPH*, 16–22, among others.

115. Gutiérrez, *Líneas pastorales*, 85–88.

116. English translation, "Toward a Theology of Liberation," in Hennelly, *Liberation Theology*, 62–76.

117. See Brown, *Gustavo Gutiérrez*, 28–29.

118. This pattern—introduction, three points, conclusion—is characteristic of Gutiérrez's presentations (see Brown, *Gustavo Gutiérrez*, 48).

119. See Hennelly, *Liberation Theology*, 62–65. Gutiérrez has always been insistent on the necessity of reflection. Action, the positive response to God's call led by charity, can become pure activism if abandoned to itself. Because he is convinced of the need for reflection, Gutiérrez founded the Instituto Bartolomé de Las Casas as a center of documentation and reflection. This institute focuses on research and reflection concerning the social sciences and theology. The aim is to provide theology with an analysis of Peruvian society that enables the formulation of a liberating interpretation of faith that takes into account the reality of that society in its different dimensions, as well as its possibilities and constraints. It is not by chance that the institute bears the name of Las Casas. Driven by his pastoral endeavor and by his never-ending attempt to improve in practice the situation of the Indians, Las Casas never disregarded reflection. On the contrary, action and reflection run side by side, are indeed intrinsically interrelated, in Bishop Las Casas. For Gutiérrez, Las Casas was not only a bishop and a social activist but also a ground-breaking theologian with a privileged insight into reality.

120. The expression was widely used by Vatican II. Already Pope John XXIII had referred to the "distinctive characteristic" of our age that had to be analyzed by the church in order to understand the situation and to discover the work of the spirit in history. Vatican II popularized the expression "discerning the signs of the times" with a similar meaning (see Joseph Gremillion, ed., *The Church and Culture since Vatican II: The Experience of North and Latin America* [Notre Dame, Ind.: University of Notre Dame Press, 1985], 12, 209).

121. Hennelly, *Liberation Theology*, 65. Here, Gutiérrez is applying to the Latin American situation what Chenu and Danielou had already demanded in the European context, namely, the use of social sciences (including Marxism) as partners of theology. Rahner also stressed the need for that partnership. What is new in Gutiérrez in relation to his European forerunners is that he not only claims the necessity of the partnership but puts it into practice.

122. Ibid., 67–68.

123. Pope Paul VI, encyclical letter, *Populorum Progressio*, in Gremillion, *Church and Culture*, 387–415.

124. The influence of these two documents on both Gutiérrez and Medellín is pervasive. Of the eighty-eight notes included in four key documents of Medellín (Justice,

Peace, Family and Demography, and Poverty of the Church), forty-two refer either to *Populorum Progressio* (sixteen) or to *Gaudium et Spes* (twenty-six). The rest break down as follows: other addresses by Paul VI (twenty), other Vatican II documents (eleven), references to the scriptures (fourteen), Latin American bishops (one).

125. Hennelly, *Liberation Theology*, 69.

126. Gutiérrez will speak later of integral salvation (see *TL*, 271). The notion of integral salvation fully coheres with an integrative view of the relation between nature and grace embraced by Gutiérrez, a view based on Rahner. If the natural is "always and already" constitutively touched by the supernatural, then everything that is natural pertains at the same time to the realm of salvation. Everything must be rescued and brought into communion with God.

127. Hennelly, *Liberation Theology*, 70. Gutiérrez grounds this affirmation in *Populorum Progressio*. At this stage, Gutiérrez still uses the concept of development, following the interpretation that Paul VI gives the notion of "integral development" in *Populorum Progressio*, to the point of affirming that "in this perspective, we understand development as liberation" (*TL*, 69).

128. *TL*, 71–72.

129. Ibid., 74. This is the same thesis Metz maintained in order to justify the legitimate worldliness of the world.

130. "The encounter with God takes place in the encounter with our neighbor" (ibid., 74).

131. Ibid., 75. Gutiérrez claims that it is characteristic of Christianity to keep that dialectic between radicalization and relativization of human action in history.

132. The framework Medellín-Puebla has been used by many analysts of liberation theology such as Brown, Klaiber, Lois (see the interesting work Julio Lois, *Teología de la liberación: Opción por los pobres* [Madrid: IEPALA, Fundamentos, 1986], esp. chap. 1), Oliveros, and Gutiérrez himself.

133. See Brown, *Gustavo Gutiérrez*, 34.

134. See Hennelly, *Liberation Theology*, 48–57.

135. See Gustavo Gutiérrez, "Liberation Movements and Theology," *Concilium* 93 (1974): 135–46.

136. See in that respect Brown, *Gustavo Gutiérrez*, 11–14, which analyzes the mutual influence between Medellín and Gutiérrez and which calls Medellín "the breakthrough."

137. Sodepax stands for Commission on Society, Development, and Peace, a body jointly created by the Pontifical Commission on Justice and Peace and by the World Council of Churches. The commission organized a conference in Switzerland in 1969 to discuss the theology of development. Gutiérrez came up with a sharp critique of the notion of development, proposing instead the term "liberation" as more fitting to the reality and aspirations of Latin America.

138. Gutiérrez has always followed a progressive path in writing his books. Typically, he starts to develop them at conferences and then continues to rework and to contrast his germinal ideas with different audiences. After some years, during which the material is polished and expanded, it finally is published in book form. Only two works have been directly written as books, namely, *Hablar de Dios desde el sufrimiento del inocente: Una reflexión sobre el libro de Job* (hereafter *HD*) (Lima:

Centro de Estudios y Publicaciones, 1986), English translation, *On Job: God-Talk and the Suffering of the Innocent* (Maryknoll, N.Y.: Orbis Books, 1987) and *EC,* even though the latter underwent some expanding since its first version. As Brown points out (see Brown, *Gustavo Gutiérrez,* 34–35), Gutiérrez's *TL* grew out of his previous works, step by step, in the second half of the 1960s, until finally it became the epoch-making formulation of liberation theology at the beginning of the 1970s. Gutiérrez himself acknowledges this in *TL,* 64. An enlightening analysis of the genesis and evolution of liberation theology in general and of Gutiérrez in particular from the mid-1960s to the late 1970s is Roberto Oliveros Maqueo, *Liberación y teología: Génesis y crecimiento de una reflexión, 1966–1976* (Lima: Centro de Estudios y Publicaciones, 1977). Also interesting for understanding how liberation theology came about, from a more detached approach than Maqueo's, is Christian Smith, *The Emergence of Liberation Theology: Radical Religion and Social Movement Theory* (Chicago: University of Chicago Press, 1991).

139. See Gustavo Gutiérrez, "Significado y alcance de Medellín," in José Dammert et al., *Irrupción,* 55, where he writes that "This 'turn' to concrete people marks the life of the Latin American church in these years" (my trans.).

140. This is one of Gutiérrez's central points in *TL* (62). See also *PPH,* 21, 201–2; Gustavo Gutiérrez, "Statement by Gustavo Gutiérrez," in Sergio Torres and John Eagleson, eds., *Theology in the Americas* (Maryknoll, N.Y.: Orbis Books, 1976), 310–11; idem, "Freedom and Salvation: A Political Problem," in Gustavo Gutiérrez and Richard Shaull, *Liberation and Change* (Atlanta: John Knox, 1977), 92–93. A concise and insightful analysis of Gutiérrez's shift in perspective can be found in Rebecca S. Chopp, *The Praxis of Suffering: An Interpretation of Liberation and Political Theologies* (Maryknoll, N.Y.: Orbis, 1986), 46–63. See also Robert McAfee Brown, "Preface: After Ten Years," in *PPH,* xii.

141. See Gutiérrez, "Two Theological Perspectives," 248–49.

142. A sample of this latter work are Salustiano Alvarez et al., *San Agustín y la liberación: Reflexiones desde Latinoamérica* (Iquitos, Lima: Centro de Estudios Teológicos de la Amazonia, Centro de Estudios y Publicaciones, 1986); Pablo Thai-Hop, *Tomás de Aquino: Teólogo militante* (Lima: Ediciones IPEP, 1988).

143. Chapters 6, 7, and 8 of *TL* are the decisive part of the book for understanding the new perspective adopted by Gutiérrez.

144. See Hennelly, *Liberation Theology,* 64–65.

145. See Gustavo Gutiérrez, *Teología de la liberación: Perspectivas* (Salamanca: Ediciones Sígueme, 1972), 118–26, 352–62. It is widely known that Gutiérrez's use of class-struggle analysis was heavily opposed from some quarters. He tried to dispel all misunderstandings by rewriting the whole section dealing with that category for the fifteenth anniversary edition of *TL.* Problems also arose in relation to the theory of dependency, presently discarded as a correct tool to explain the problems of the poor countries. Gutiérrez also confronted such problems in the new edition of his book. These shifts will be analyzed later in this chapter.

146. Gutiérrez provides extensive bibliography concerning the theory of dependency in *TL,* 158–70, as well as a good discussion on the subject. A complementary discussion of the main points of this theory and a comparison of it with the theory of imperialism can be found in the collection of essays, René Villarreal, ed.,

Economía internacional: II, Teorías del imperialismo, la dependencia y su evidencia histórica (Mexico City: Fondo de Cultura Económica, 1979). Particularly interesting are the essays by Fernando H. Cardoso, Theotonio Dos Santos, Aldo Ferrer, Osvaldo Sunkel, and Gunder Frank. These essays are interesting because they show the opinion of some of the founders of the theory of dependency (although it would be more accurate to speak of theories of dependency in the plural rather than in the singular) at different points in time throughout the 1970s. A very enlightening discussion of the different theories concerning development in Latin America is Cristóbal Kay, *Latin American Theories of Development and Underdevelopment* (London: Routledge, 1989). For a discussion of the theory of dependency in relation to liberation theology, see McGovern, *Liberation Theology*, 125–29, 164–76. This author distinguishes between the theory of dependency as such and the fact of dependency. He discusses the theory and its critics, acknowledging the insufficiency of its analysis, while showing that the fact of the Latin American dependency in relation to the rich countries, especially the United States, is undeniable. See also Arthur F. McGovern, "Dependency Theory, Marxist Analysis, and Liberation Theology," in Ellis and Maduro, *Future*, 272–86; Peter G. Moll, "Liberating Liberation Theology: Towards Independence from Dependency Theory," *Journal of Theology for Southern Africa* 78 (March 1992): 25–40.

147. See *TL,* 96–98.

148. For Theotonio Dos Santos, the Cuban Revolution greatly influenced the Latin American intellectual activity during the 1960s (see Theotonio Dos Santos, "La cuestión de la teoría de la dependencia," in Villarreal, *Economía internacional,* 488).

149. Cardoso claims that the ECLA developed an original economic theory of development that started with Raúl Prebisch in the late 1940s and that evolved with the times and the changes in the economic scene. One evolved product of that original contribution was, according to Cardoso, the theory of dependency. See Fernando H. Cardoso, "La originalidad de la copia: La CEPAL y la idea de desarrollo," in Villarreal, *Economía internacional,* 175–215.

150. See Brown, *Gustavo Gutiérrez,* 25–26.

151. See *TL,* 158–70, esp. 166.

152. See *TL,* 157, 170. Gutiérrez affirms that "dependency and liberation are correlative terms" and that "to characterize Latin America as a dominated and oppressed continent, naturally leads to speak of liberation."

153. *PPH,* 45–46.

154. See Gustavo Gutiérrez, "Two Theological Perspectives: Liberation Theology and Progressivist Theology," in Torres and Fabella, *Emergent Gospel,* 240.

155. *TL,* 98–108. Gutiérrez repeats here an idea he had already developed in his "Hacia una teología de la liberación." However, Gutiérrez modifies his previous understanding of modernity by introducing this time the new awareness concerning economic and unconscious determinants of human behavior unveiled by Marx, Freud, and those who, like Marcuse, use both of them in their analyses.

156. See in that respect *TL,* 90.

157. Ibid., 174–79.

158. His most famous work, a true classic of the 1970s, is Paulo Freire, *Pedagogy of the Oppressed* (New York: Herder and Herder, 1970), which by 1990 had been

reprinted thirty-two times in English. A short article, very representative of his work, is Paulo Freire, "Conscientizing as a Way of Liberating," in Hennelly, *Liberation Theology*, 5–13.

159. *TL*, 181–210. It is important to notice that in bringing about this change in the church, certain minorities, notably among the clergy and among lay Christian militants, play an outstanding role; see *PPH*, 31, where Gutiérrez talks about "the most vital sectors of the people of God in Latin America" in referring to that transforming minority.

160. *TL*, 208–10.

161. See "Medellín Documents," in Gremillion, *Church and Culture*, 449–50, 455–58.

162. Compare for instance the 1972 edition of *TL*, 352–62, with Medellín's statements in Gremillion, *Church and Culture*, 450–51, where the call is for transcending antagonisms and moving toward unity.

163. See Gremillion, *Church and Culture*, 448–52.

164. Ibid., 452–54.

165. Ibid., 471–76.

166. *TL*, 353–64.

167. David A. Krueger, "The Economic Ethics of John A. Ryan and Gustavo Gutiérrez" (Ph.D. diss., University of Chicago, 1988), 157–215, is a help in understanding this issue, although some of the obscure points Krueger identifies in his work have been clarified in Gutiérrez's later work, probably not accessible to Krueger at the time of his writing.

168. See *TL*, 96–115.

169. See Krueger, "Economic Ethics," 167–84, for a discussion of the relationship between political, liberation, and scientific rationality.

170. For a perceptive analysis of how Gutiérrez uses both social sciences and Marxism, see Curt Cadorette, *From the Heart of the People*, 83–114.

171. *TL*, 1972 ed., 353–54, especially n. 49.

172. See *PPH*, 45.

173. See *LV*, 83–84.

174. *TL*, 174.

175. See Alberto Flores Galindo, "Presentación," in Mariátegui, *Invitación*, 20.

176. See Jorge Basadre, introduction to Mariátegui, *Seven Interpretive Essays*, xxv.

177. See Oliveros, *Liberación y teología*, 274–79, for an analysis of the notion and the role of utopia in Gutiérrez. See also Krueger, "Economic Ethics," 184–88.

178. Gutiérrez partakes the Enlightenment's basic orientation toward the future over against the prestige of the past characteristic of premodern thought (see *TL*, 319). Modern humankind is decidedly future-oriented, a trait also stressed by Metz in his *ZTW*. Liberation lies in the future, but for this future to happen those who want and hope for it must make a commitment to transform current society (*TL*, 320). Commitment, in turn, is based on active hope as understood by Bloch in his *Das Prinzip Hoffnung*, that is, as a force that subverts the existing order and that is the key of human existence (*TL*, 323–25). For an analysis of Gutiérrez's appropriation of Bloch, see Curt Cadorette, *From the Heart of the People*, 98–103.

179. *TL,* 353–59. In *BPJ,* Gutiérrez discusses the likely connection of Thomas More's *Utopia* with Las Casas's utopian project (*esquema comunitario*) for building up and organizing adequately an indigenous community. According to some authors, More might have read a first draft of Las Casas's project and used it as a basis for his famous work (see *BPJ,* 112–17).

180. See *TL,* 95–96, 107–8, 176–77; *PPH,* 29.

181. See in that respect Gustavo Gutiérrez, "Marxismo y Cristianismo," in CE-DIAL, *Cristianos latinoamericanos y socialismo* (Bogotá: Ediciones Paulinas, 1972), 15–34. The influence of Mariátegui is clearly recognizable in this view of Marxism. For Gutiérrez's relation to Althusser, see Cadorette, *From the Heart of the People,* 89–93.

182. See Antonio Gramsci, "La filosofia di Benedetto Croce," in *Quaderni del Carcere,* Edizione critica dell'Istituto Gramsci (Torino: Giulio Einaudi editore, 1977), 2:1207–1362. For a good anthology in English of his writings in prison, see Antonio Gramsci, *Selections from the Prison Notebooks,* ed. and trans. Quintin Hoare and Geoffrey Nowell Smith (New York: International Publishers, 1971). In this book, Hoare and Smith provide a very enlightening historical introduction to the work of Gramsci.

183. *TL,* 107, 363.

184. Ibid., 363.

185. Ibid., 355–58.

186. *TL,* 146–53, 239–46. Gutiérrez had already formulated these basic positions in his *Líneas pastorales de la iglesia en América Latina* and in "Hacia una teología de la liberación." See in that respect the section "First Steps of Gutiérrez's Theology," above.

187. See *TL,* 5–12. The question of method will be discussed in chapter 5.

188. See Luis Alberto Gómez de Souza, "La fuerza histórica de la reflexión de Gustavo Gutiérrez," in by Cardinal P. E. Arns et al., *Teología de la liberación: Perspectivas y desafíos: Ensayos en torno a la obra de Gustavo Gutiérrez* (Lima: Instituto Bartolomé de las Casas, Centro de Estudios y Publicaciones, 1989), 83.

189. Brown, *Gustavo Gutiérrez,* 27; Cadorette, *From the Heart of the People,* 76.

190. Mariátegui, *Seven Interpretive Essays,* xxxiii.

191. Ibid., 124–25.

192. Ibid., 139, 145.

193. Mariátegui, *Peruanicemos el Perú,* 64.

194. Mariátegui, *Invitación,* 13–14; idem, *Seven Interpretive Essays,* 152.

195. The theory of dependency was deemed immature by Gutiérrez himself at the time he wrote *TL,* and he considered it insufficient in 1978 (see *PPH,* 78). Over the last decade, that theory has been increasingly under attack from scientific quarters. The other tool used by Gutiérrez as the key device in interpreting social organization and the forces that move history, namely, Marxist class struggle, has been the object of many criticisms that judge it sociologically insufficient, anthropologically reductionist, and outdated even in the economic realm, the discussion of which exceeds the limits of this work.

196. *TL,* 363.

197. See Juan Luis Segundo, "Two Theologies of Liberation," in Hennelly, *Liberation Theology,* 353–66.

198. Ibid., 362–66.

199. *TL,* 171–72, 181–83.

200. See above the sections "Understanding the Latin American Situation" and "The Role of the Church."

201. *TL,* 235.

202. Ibid., 141–46.

203. Ibid., 210–20.

204. The notion of popular religion is by no means easy to define or to establish, due precisely to the different and complex layers and threads that make it up. A brief survey of the analysis of that notion by liberation theologians can be found in McGovern, *Liberation Theology,* 89–91. A most interesting work on the subject is Michael R. Candelaria, "Popular Religion and Liberation: An Examination of the Discussion in Latin American Liberation Theology" (Ph.D. diss., Harvard University, 1987), which acknowledges the difficulties involved in formulating the nature of popular religion.

205. Gustavo Gutiérrez, *La fuerza histórica de los pobres* (Lima: Centro de Estudios y Publicaciones, 1979), English translation, PPH.

206. *BPP,* 12; *TL,* 15.

207. See *BPP,* 180.

208. *PPH,* 76.

209. Ibid., 103.

210. See Gustavo Gutiérrez, "En nuestras manos," in Catalina Romero and Ismael Muñoz, eds., *Liberación y desarrollo en América Latina: Perspectivas* (Lima: Instituto Bartolomé de Las Casas, Centro de Estudios y Publicaciones, 1993), 145. In relation to Gutiérrez's change of emphasis, Lois speaks of a shift of the hermeneutical matrix, that is, a shift from the significative minorities to the popular majorities as main agents of the liberation struggle (see Lois, *Teología,* 41).

211. *PPH,* 105. See the discussion of this point in Lois, *Teología,* 236–37.

212. See Gustavo Gutiérrez, "Statement by Gustavo Gutiérrez," in Torres and Eagleson, *Theology in the Americas,* 310–11; idem, "Two Theological Perspectives," 241, 253n.23, where he says that "the women of these groups are doubly exploited, alienated, and oppressed"; *PPH,* 37, 190, where he speaks of "the exploited classes, oppressed cultures, and ethnic groups that suffer discrimination"; idem, "Liberation Movements and Theology," *Concilium* 93 (1974): 139; idem, "Liberation, Theology and Proclamation," *Concilium* 96 (1974): 57–58.

213. *TL,* 16–20.

214. See *PPH,* 73n.30, where Gutiérrez asserts that "the native peoples and cultures of Latin America are not yet adequately represented in our efforts of theological reflection."

215. *PPH,* 97–98, 123, 193; idem, "Liberation, Theology and Proclamation," 69.

216. *PPH,* 97–98, 123–24, 193, where he explicitly says that "one of the values of the people of Latin America is popular religion." For a more detailed analysis on Gutiérrez's treatment of popular religion, see Cadorette, *From the Heart of the People,* 31–39. An issue that Gutiérrez has not explored very far concerns the re-

lationship between evangelization and culture in Latin America. For a view that, far from being opposed to Gutiérrez's insistence on the need for social critique and liberating praxis, is an enrichment and, somehow, a balance to it, see Juan Carlos Scannone, "Evangelization of Culture, Liberation, and 'Popular' Culture: The New Theological-Pastoral Synthesis in Latin America," in Gremillion, *Church and Culture,* 74–89.

217. In the 1980s Gutiérrez also devoted a substantial amount of work to the task of clarifying his positions, especially after those positions came under the close scrutiny of the Congregation for the Doctrine of the Faith at the Vatican. See, in that respect, Brown, *Gustavo Gutiérrez,* 136–55.

218. This is especially true in relation to the question of God.

219. In order to dispel misunderstandings, it must be pointed out that, in his main work, *Teología de la liberación,* he uses the Bible massively: forty-five books of the Bible are cited, and the total number of biblical references amounts to 405. In relation to spirituality and God, Gutiérrez uses biblical poetry (Job, Psalms), religious mystical poetry (Teresa de Avila, Juan de la Cruz), and secular mystical poetry, especially César Vallejo.

220. *TL,* 311–18.

221. Ibid., 312.

222. *BPP,* 11.

223. However, the work that goes the deepest into exploring the adventure of the encounter with God is *HD,* Gutiérrez's book on Job. The reason is that Gutiérrez finds in Job all the ingredients that make that adventure a tragedy. In that sense, Job's struggle bears the clearest resemblance with the situation of the poor in Latin America, because, as Job, they also believe in God despite their innocent suffering.

224. Title of one of the books by Mariátegui discussed above.

225. *BPP,* 45. Gutiérrez claims that the birth of new spiritualities in the history of Christianity responds to profound historical changes occurring at the time those spiritualities come to life. For him the cases of the spirituality of the mendicant orders and Ignatian spirituality are two clear examples that confirm his hypothesis. In general, Gutiérrez thinks that a new spirituality emerges when a reordering of the foundational axes of Christian life occurs as a result of a central intuition that responds to the times (ibid., 135).

226. Ibid., 16. The expression, according to Gutiérrez, has its origin in Bernard of Clairvaux, for whom, in matters of spirituality, people must "drink from their own wells."

227. Ibid., 37–44, 62.

228. Ibid., 139.

229. Ibid., 134.

230. Ibid., 58, 112–36.

231. Ibid., 59. That encounter that is due to the Lord's initiative is, according to Gutiérrez, the primordial basis of faith. It echoes Rahner's God's self-communication (see *TL,* 256–57).

232. *BPP,* 85–111.

233. Ibid., 35–54.

234. See, among others, Gutiérrez, "Una agenda," 14, where he laments that the

Conference of Santo Domingo did not mention the existence of those martyrs and their importance for the Latin American church.

235. *HD*, 11.

236. Ibid., 12–18.

237. Caring for and liberation of the poor are features of God stressed in *TL* (see *TL*, 86–105).

238. This is the second trait explored by Gutiérrez in his work on Job. The two traits respond to the classical immanent and transcendent dimensions of God.

239. See Gustavo Gutiérrez, *El Dios de la vida* (hereafter *DV*) (Lima: Instituto Bartolomé de Las Casas, Centro de Estudios y Publicaciones, 1989), 26, English translation, *The God of Life* (Maryknoll, N.Y.: Orbis Books, 1991).

240. See Karl Rahner, *The Trinity* (New York: Seabury, 1974), 15–24.

241. *HD*, 19.

242. *PPH*, 169–221; Gutiérrez, "Two Theological Perspectives," 227–55.

243. See Hennelly, *Liberation Theology*, 358. Here, Segundo understands ideology in the Marxian way, as something that distorts reality, and not as the necessary mediation for faith and theology that is his other understanding of ideology. For that second understanding, see Juan Luis Segundo, *The Liberation of Theology* (Maryknoll, N.Y.: Orbis Books, 1976).

244. *DV*, 109–17.

245. Ibid., 117–21. Gutiérrez quotes Léon Bloy's dictum "money is the blood of the poor."

246. See *BPJ*, 608–15.

247. Ibid., 588–96.

248. See, for instance, *PPH*, 169–221.

249. Cadorette, *From the Heart of the People*, 76.

250. Quoted in *EC*, 24 (my trans.).

251. See Washington Delgado, prologue to *EC*, xv.

252. *EC*, 11.

253. Ibid., 17.

254. See José María Arguedas, "No soy un aculturado...," in José María Arguedas, *El zorro de arriba y el zorro de abajo* (Lima: Editorial Horizonte, 1988), 13–14.

255. See Luis Alberto Ratto, interview, "La vivificante obra de José María Arguedas," in *Páginas* (Lima) 100 (1989): 67–70.

256. See José María Arguedas, *Relatos completos* (Lima: Editorial Horizonte, 1987), 53–72, 105–20.

257. *EC*, 66–85, 94.

258. For a detailed bibliography on Arguedas's work, see the vast array of writings to which Gutiérrez refers in his study of Arguedas. For an analysis of the relationship between Arguedas's and Gutiérrez's works, see Cadorette, *From the Heart of the People*, 67–75. On the question of the project of a new Peru and the contributions of Arguedas, Mariátegui, and Gutiérrez to it, see Guillermo Nugent, "La construction de la vida en el Perú como identidad histórica moderna," in *Páginas* (Lima) 100 (1989): 125–57. The article includes an interesting discussion on the understanding of rationality.

259. Job is Gutiérrez's most cherished hero, and the author of the discourses of Job in the book is his most admired author. He has repeated many times that, once in heaven, one of his main aims will be to meet that author, to satisfy his curiosity concerning many questions he is keeping until that moment, and to share with that author in the bliss of seeing answered those questions that the book cannot solve but that will become clear in heaven.

260. *HD,* 71–89.

261. Ibid., 65.

262. Ibid., 151–52.

263. Ibid., 194.

264. Ibid., 192–202.

265. In that sense, Gutiérrez argues that "the combination of these two dimensions, prayer and commitment, strictly constitutes what we call practice. Theology of Liberation comes from it" (*TL,* 36 [my trans.]). A most interesting discussion of this mystical-prophetic dimension of Christian practice, according to liberation theology, can be found in *LV,* 11–17, 79–82.

266. *TL,* 113–15.

267. In other words, Job's story is the story of the suffering of the innocent. Such a suffering is a permanent trait of human history and experience for which God, according to the Book of Job, cannot be blamed and for which, ultimately, there is no convincing explanation.

268. It could be argued that the two main parameters of Gutiérrez's theology, mainly after his work on Job, are those he sees as the fountain of the theological creativeness of Bartolomé de Las Casas, namely, a sense of the mystery of God and of God's love for the least (*BPJ,* 274).

269. The point is made especially clear in Gustavo Gutiérrez, "Liberación y desarrollo: Un desafío a la teología," in Romero and Muñoz, *Liberación y desarrollo,* where Gutiérrez analyzes some of the most important developments of liberation theology and points out new challenges.

270. The economic policy of adjustment put in place in the 1990s all over the world is affecting every country and economy in the world, but it has been especially painful for the poorest countries. Moreover, it is said that there are no alternatives to the market-governed-economy model. That is why some refer to the current situation as a situation under the sway of a *pensée unique* (see Ignacio Ramonet, "La pensée unique," *Le Monde diplomatique,* January 1995, 1, where the author affirms that "since the fall of the Berlin Wall, the downfall of communist regimes, and the demoralizing of socialism, the arrogance, the pride, and the insolence of this new gospel have reached such a level that one can, without exaggeration, call this ideological furor modern dogmatism" [my trans.]).

271. See Brown, *Gustavo Gutiérrez,* 131–56; Hennelly, *Liberation Theology,* 348–50, 367–74, 393–414, 461–513.

272. Gutiérrez refers to this, arguing that "in that *kairos,* Christians in the region are experiencing a tense and intense moment of *solidarity,* of reflection, and of *martyrdom*" (*TL,* 14 [my trans.]).

273. See *LV.*

274. Gustavo Gutiérrez, "Mirar lejos," in *TL,* 7th ed., 9–60. The section he mod-

ified was the most controversial of his original work, dealing with the relationship between Christian love and class struggle. (Compare "Fraternidad cristiana y lucha de clases," in 1972 ed., *TL,* 352–62, and "Fe y conflicto social," in 7th ed., *TL,* 396–408. The replacement of the term "class struggle" by that of "social conflict" signals the direction of the changes introduced by Gutiérrez in his most paradigmatic work.)

275. *TL,* 7th ed., 12 and 14 (my trans.).

276. Ibid., 27 (my trans.). Gutiérrez has further developed this theme of God's preference for the poor and the destitute in his work on Las Casas. In this respect, as Pedro Trigo very perceptively says, "this book about Las Casas's thought also is a book about Gustavo Gutiérrez's thought" (see Pedro Trigo, "Las Casas y Gustavo Gutiérrez: A propósito de 'En busca de los pobres de Jesucristo,' " *Páginas* [Lima] 129 [October 1994]: 70 [my trans.]).

277. That social sciences play an auxiliary role in theology does not at all mean that they are dispensable. Although their role is not the central one in the theological enterprise, they do have an important role in that enterprise, especially in the case of liberation theology (something similar can be argued as regards the other two theologies analyzed in this work, namely, political theology and public theology). Indeed, they are indispensable in order to analyze the causes of the dire situation of the poor. Gutiérrez insists once and again that describing this situation is not enough. Its causes must be discovered so that they can be eradicated and liberation brought about. See, in this sense, his "Liberación y desarrollo," 29.

278. *LV,* 83–94. Both questions are important in order to clarify the nature of liberation theology, especially in responding to those who see it as (or accuse it of) merely being a theological camouflage for theses that stem from debatable social theories.

279. See especially Gutiérrez, "Liberación y desarrollo," 22–25.

280. *LV,* 95–112; *TL,* 396–408.

281. *TL,* 16–24. Gutiérrez stresses particularly the issues concerning women, races, cultures, as well as the role of popular religion. See also McGovern, *Liberation Theology,* 83–104.

Chapter 4: David Tracy

1. This does not imply that there are not other ways in which Vatican II Catholic theology has evolved in the United States. Some of them will be mentioned later in the chapter.

2. Although de Tocqueville's classic, *Democracy in America* (New York: Harper and Row, 1966), may be an exception, not even he could get rid of some pre-established European views in assessing the U.S. situation (see Martin E. Marty, *Religion and Republic: The American Circumstance* [Boston: Beacon, 1987], 53–57). Needless to say, the author of the present work, also a foreigner, considers himself bound by the same kind of limitations.

3. George Washington, already in his First Inaugural Address in 1789, referred to the new course steered by the United States according to its Constitution as "the experiment entrusted to the hands of the American people" (see George Washington, "First Inaugural Address," in Daniel J. Boorstin, ed., *An American Primer* [New York: Meridian Classic, 1985], 193). In his "Farewell Address," he continued to

express his conviction that the political system of the Union was "well worth a fair and full experiment" (see George Washington, "Farewell Address," in Boorstin, *American Primer*, 217).

4. Dutch colonizers also came to the East Coast, settling along the Hudson Valley. See Samuel Eliot Morison, *The Oxford History of the American People*, vol. 1, *Prehistory to 1789* (New York: Penguin Books, 1972), 95–96.

5. For a description of the different colonizers in the territories of the current United States and Canada, see ibid., 1:68–155.

6. See, for instance, Daniel J. Boorstin, *The Americans: The Colonial Experience* (New York: Random House, 1958), 1–143. For Boorstin, three ideals were projected by different groups of Englanders onto the American land: the religious, the philanthropic, and the socioeconomic. The first partially succeeded, the second failed, and the third was highly successful. The thesis of the author is that America deeply transformed the ideals and ideas of the European colonizers, forging a truly American culture.

7. See Richard D. Heffner, *A Documentary History of the United States*, 4th ed. (New York: NAL Penguin, 1985), 9. Heffner follows Crèvecoeur, who in 1782, six years after the Declaration of Independence and five before the convention that devised the Constitution, wrote that "the American is a new man, who acts upon new principles; he must therefore entertain new ideas, and form new opinions" (ibid., 9).

8. See Samuel Eliot Morison, ed., "The Mayflower Compact," in Boorstin, *American Primer*, 19–25.

9. See Boorstin, *The Americans: The Colonial Experience*, 116; and Heffner, *Documentary History*, 9–10.

10. The biblical language pervades most of the political discourses delivered at crucial moments by the presidents of the nation and by other politicians up to our time. The invocation to God and to divine providence are already part of the Declaration of Independence. In his First Inaugural Address, Washington clearly saw the hand of God leading the United States of America toward the fulfillment of its mission and thought that the future of liberty and of the republican form of government depended on the result of the American experiment (see George Washington, "First Inaugural Address," in Boorstin, *American Primer*, 192–93). Jefferson described the young nation "advancing rapidly to destinies beyond the reach of mortal eye," as a "successful experiment" and as "the world's best hope" (Thomas Jefferson, "First Inaugural Address," in Heffner, *Documentary History*, 74). For him, the United States was called to serve as an example to other nations so that the "Empire of Liberty" could extend to the whole world (see Robert Tucker and David C. Hendrickson, *The Empire of Liberty: The Statecraft of Thomas Jefferson* [Oxford: Oxford University Press, 1990]). Alexander Hamilton was also convinced of the worldwide mission of the new nation (see Alexander Hamilton, James Madison, and John Jay, *The Federalist Papers*, ed. Garry Wills [New York: Bantam Books, 1982], 54–55).

11. This was the aspect that powerfully caught the attention of Tocqueville because it strongly contrasted with the experience of the French Revolution. He notices that one of the strongest beliefs of the Enlightenment philosophers was that religion had to retreat and ultimately disappear "as enlightenment and freedom spread." He sees, however, that "the facts do not fit this theory at all" because "in America the

most free and enlightened people in the world zealously perform all the external duties of religion" (Tocqueville, *Democracy in America*, 295).

12. See David Tracy, "Particular Classics, Public Religion, and the American Tradition," in Robin W. Lovin, ed., *Religion and American Public Life: Interpretations and Explorations* (Mahwah, N.J.: Paulist, 1986).

13. None of these traditions, though, are themselves univocal. For instance, Lovin's perceptive analysis of the republican tradition shows how the utopian ideals of the Enlightenment, as well as its great appreciation of reason, are but one side of the philosophical and political views that determined the shape of the nascent nation. The other side was formed by the empiricist and individualist ideas developed in eighteenth-century Britain. These ideas substantially curtailed reason's ability to deal with final ends and grounding principles and centered on how individuals could pursue their personal interests and desires without falling into a Hobbesian warfare. Thus, Lovin claims, a covenantal culture that pursued substantive ends was replaced, or at least modified, by a society based on a procedurally social contract (see Robin W. Lovin, "Social Contract or a Public Covenant?" in Lovin, *Religion*). Robert N. Bellah's interpretation of the formation of American society in his work *Habits of the Heart* identifies three threads: the biblical, the republican, and the philosophy of individualism (see Robert N. Bellah et al., *Habits of the Heart: Individualism and Commitment in American Life* [New York: Perennial Library, 1986], 27–35). Lovin's analysis, by placing the individualistic strand within the republican thread, shows the ambiguities and tensions inherent in the nation.

14. See National Conference of Catholic Bishops, *Economic Justice for All: Pastoral Letter on Catholic Social Teaching and the U.S. Economy* (Washington, D.C.: United States Catholic Conference, 1986), 4. The bishops also mention other instances of "conflict and suffering," such as the struggle for female suffrage, the workers' movement, and the more recent civil rights movement. For Bellah, see Robert N. Bellah, *The Broken Covenant: American Civil Religion in Time of Trial*, 2d ed. (Chicago: University of Chicago Press, 1992), 37.

15. See Heffner, *Documentary History*, 15. Unfortunately, Jefferson himself was far from being consistent with the truths he proclaimed as self-evident (see Edwin S. Gaustad, "On Jeffersonian Liberty," in Jerald C. Brauer, ed., *The Lively Experiment Continued* [Macon, Ga.: Mercer University Press, 1987], esp. 95–101, where Gaustad shows that, in dealing with Native Americans and African Americans, Jefferson contradicted his own principles).

16. This dark side has, to be sure, a bright flip-side that preaches and practices equality, openness to the stranger, emancipation, empowerment of the dispossessed, and peace grounded in justice for all. The point made here is that this bright side did not operate in the case of the Native Americans except in a very few occasions.

17. Alfonso Ortiz, himself a Native American, contends that the name "Indians" is an unwarranted overall generalization and a European invention and abstraction that does not take into account the sheer diversity of the Native American population. This population must be viewed, according to Ortiz, as made of many "native American peoples" (see Alfonso Ortiz, "Indian/White Relations: A View from the Other Side of the 'Frontier,'" in Frederick E. Hoxie, *Indians in American History* [Arlington Heights, Ill.: Harlan Davidson, 1988], 10).

James Brown shows that "the population in North America in 1492 was probably 3–5 million" and that "more than 170 North American languages are known, excluding those within the area of Mexican civilization" (see James A. Brown, "America before Columbus," in Hoxie, *Indians*, 21, 42). That gives an idea of the cultural diversity and complexity of the human reality that was designated with the term "Indians."

18. Hoxie affirms that Native Americans were less than 1 percent of the total population in 1887 (see Frederick E. Hoxie, "The Curious Story of Reformers and the American Indians," in Hoxie, *Indians*, 206). Bearing in mind that the population in 1887 was around 60 million (see Mark S. Hoffman, ed., *The World Almanac and Book of Facts* [New York: Pharos, 1989 and 1992], 74), it follows that there were about 600,000 Native Americans. The last census of 1990 shows that the American Indian population is 1.9 million, a mere 0.75 percent of the total U.S. population (ibid., 77).

19. See William T. Hagan, "How the West Was Lost," in Hoxie, *Indians*, 198–201.

20. See Frederick E. Hoxie, "The Curious Story of the Reformers and the American Indians," in Hoxie, *Indians*, 220; Charles F. Wilkinson, "Indian Tribes and the American Constitution," in Hoxie, *Indians*, 119–25; Eric Black, *Our Constitution: The Myth That Binds Us* (Boulder, Co.: Westview, 1988), 114–16. For the different policies followed by the U.S. government concerning the native peoples, see Angie Debo, *A History of the Indians of the United States* (Norman: University of Oklahoma Press, 1970), esp. 299–422.

21. The settlers were not interested at all either in respecting the natives or in assimilating them. Their elimination or displacement was the only choice they accepted both in theory and in practice. On such a move depended their own progress. From that point of view they completely adhered to the view of the natives as "lawless savages," an alibi that enabled them to advance their interests at the expense of the natives, even killing them proudly (see R. David Edmunds, "National Expansion from the Indian Perspective," in Hoxie, *Indians*, 160–61).

22. See ibid., 159–60; Tucker and Hendrickson, *Empire of Liberty*, 304–6n.102.

23. See Kenneth M. Morrison, "Native Americans and the American Revolution: Historic Stories and Shifting Frontier Conflict," in Hoxie, *Indians*, 95–106.

24. See Black, *Our Constitution*, 115; Walter L. Williams, "American Imperialism and the Indians," in Hoxie, *Indians*, 231–45.

25. See Hoxie, "Curious Story," 205–21.

26. See Ortiz, "Indian/White Relations," 1–16.

27. It would be completely wrong to think of slavery as a uniquely American practice. Slavery existed in Egypt and other parts of Africa and was practiced also in Europe and Asia; in short, slavery was "a universal phenomenon that has been practiced in almost all countries" (see Lerone Bennett Jr., *Before the Mayflower: A History of Black America*, 5th rev. ed. [New York: Penguin, 1984], 10–27). Concerning the slave trade in Africa in modern times, it seems that the Muslims practiced it several decades before the Europeans entered it in 1444.

28. Ibid., 29.

29. Ibid., 27–45; Morison, *Oxford History of the American People*, 1:128, 136;

Boorstin, *The Americans: The National Experience* (New York: Random House, 1965), 181–82.

30. See Black, *Our Constitution,* 48, where he argues that, in relation to the Declaration of Independence, the Constitution was "essentially a conservative counter-revolution."

31. See Tucker and Hendrickson, *Empire of Liberty,* 8, on the question of Jefferson's ambiguity regarding slavery; also Bennett, *Before the Mayflower,* 76.

32. See Boorstin, *The Americans: The Colonial Experience,* 182.

33. Heffner, *Documentary History,* 110–13; Bennett, *Before the Mayflower,* 76–77; Samuel Eliot Morison, *The Oxford History of the American People,* vol. 2, *1789 through Reconstruction* (New York: Penguin Books, 1972), 252–64.

34. See Boorstin, *The Americans: The Colonial Experience,* 183–90.

35. Bennett, *Before the Mayflower,* 51.

36. Ibid., 77–85.

37. See ibid., 87–95 for a short description of those conditions; Boorstin, *The Americans: The Colonial Experience,* 190–92; Henry Louis Gates Jr., ed., *The Classic Slave Narratives* (New York: Penguin, 1987), a collection of testimonial narratives written by slaves after they were freed.

38. Bennett, *Before the Mayflower,* 96, 99.

39. Ibid., 99–111; Boorstin, *The Americans: The Colonial Experience,* 190–99, for whom the role of what he calls "the invisible churches" was the crucial one in forming the black community and its soul.

40. Black, *Our Constitution,* 44–45.

41. Ibid., 121; Bennett, *Before the Mayflower,* 214–54.

42. Daniel J. Boorstin, *The Americans: The Democratic Experience* (New York: Random House, 1973), 301.

43. Black, *Our Constitution,* 120.

44. Ibid., 120–22; Samuel Eliot Morison, *The Oxford History of the American People, 1869–1963* (New York: Penguin Books, 1972), 3:106–11; Bennett, *Before the Mayflower,* 255–96.

45. See Nicholas Lemann, *The Promised Land: The Great Black Migration and How It Changed America* (New York: Random House, 1992), where the author describes and analyzes the different elements, achievements, and frustrations of this migration, together with the social policies and political struggles that accompanied it.

46. For an idea of the thought and life of these two leaders, see Martin Luther King Jr., *Why We Can't Wait* (New York: Penguin, 1964); Stephen B. Oates, *Let the Trumpet Sound: The Life of Martin Luther King, Jr.* (New York: Penguin, 1985); Malcolm X and Alex Haley, *The Autobiography of Malcolm X* (New York: Ballantine Books, 1973).

47. See for instance James H. Cone, *Black Theology and Black Power* (San Francisco: Harper, 1969), and his later work, James H. Cone, *Martin & Malcolm & America: A Dream or a Nightmare?* (Maryknoll, N.Y.: Orbis Books, 1992).

48. This must be qualified by saying that, in fact, liberal capitalism has never been put into practice in its pure form, and, in not a few occasions, so-called liberal capitalistic economies, such as that of the United States, have prospered in clear

contradiction to the theoretical principles of liberal capitalism. Rather than freedom and equal opportunity, monopolistic practices and inequality of power that hindered free competition have been permanent forces in a market that, as the economic theory says, is always imperfect.

49. See Heffner, *Documentary History,* 49–59; Black, *Our Constitution,* 27–30.

50. See Heffner, *Documentary History,* 91–129; Black, *Our Constitution,* 47–52, where the author argues that progressive democracy was represented by the Declaration of Independence, whereas the Constitution was a reaction of the ruling class against it; Boorstin, *The Americans: The National Experience,* 400–430; Tucker and Hendrickson, *Empire of Liberty,* 33–47.

51. See the World Bank, *World Development Report: Development and the Environment* (New York: Oxford University Press, 1992), 223, 277; idem, *World Development Report 1999/2000* (New York: Oxford University Press, 1999), 230–31; A. G. Kenwood and A. L. Lougheed, *The Growth of the International Economy 1820–1990: An Introductory Text,* 3d ed. (London: Routledge, 1992), 17; Herbert Stein and Murray Foss, *An Illustrated Guide to the American Economy: A Hundred Key Issues* (Washington, D.C.: AEI, 1992), 6–7; Kathleen Burk, "The International Environment," in Andrew Graham and Anthony Seldom, *Government and Economies in the Postwar World* (London: Routledge, 1990), 9–29.

52. Black, *Our Constitution,* 113–36.

53. See Tucker and Hendrickson, *Empire of Liberty,* 157–171; Morison, *Oxford History of the American People,* 2:311–29.

54. See Heffner, *Documentary History,* 208–19.

55. See Stein and Foss, *Illustrated Guide,* 109, 118–27; Lemann, *Promised Land,* 281–91, where the author offers an interesting discussion of the "underclass," comparing the different authors on that question; J. Larry Brown and H. P. Pizer, *Living Hungry in America* (New York: New American Library, 1987), for an analysis of the people suffering from hunger and of the causes of such a situation.

56. See *New York Times,* September 5, 1999.

57. For an enlightening and succinct analysis of the matter in relation to Washington, Franklin, Hamilton, Madison, Adams, and Jefferson, see A. James Reichley, *Religion in American Public Life* (Washington, D.C.: Brookings Institution, 1985), 85–114. The overall conclusion is that all of them, albeit in different degrees, held deistic or rationalistic views on religion and that all of them thought that the American experiment needed the support of the transcendent truths of religion. In Adams' words, "A patriot must be a religious man" (ibid., 104).

58. See Gaustad, "On Jeffersonian Liberty," 37–215; idem, *Dissent in American Religion* (Chicago: University of Chicago Press, 1973), where the author points out that "schism was, quite early, an American way of life" (10); Marty, *Religion and Republic,* 11–50, 197–325; idem, *Protestantism in the United States: Righteous Empire,* 2d ed. (New York: Scribner's, 1986); idem, *A Nation of Behavers* (Chicago: University of Chicago Press, 1976), where Marty classifies the religious variety according to different patterns of behavior, rather than on doctrinal or sociopolitical bases; idem, *Pilgrims in Their Own Land: 500 Years of Religion in America* (New York: Penguin, 1984), a description of how the fact of the different waves of immigration and a kind of restlessness in the American soul are the principles of variety and change

that characterize "American religion"; Sidney E. Mead, *The Lively Experiment: The Shaping of Christianity in America* (New York: Harper and Row, 1963), in which Mead analyzes the rise and changes experienced by Protestant denominationalism.

59. See, among others, Marty, *Pilgrims in Their Own Land,* ix.

60. See Robert Wuthnow, *The Restructuring of American Religion* (Princeton, N.J.: Princeton University Press, 1988), 17, 164–65, 303–4; Hoffman, *World Almanac and Book of Facts,* 724–25; Edwin S. Gaustad, "America's Institutions of Faith," in William G. McLoughlin and Robert N. Bellah, eds., *Religion in America* (Boston: Houghton Mifflin, 1968), 123.

61. Bellah has been one of the most outspoken prophets in this area, and he has kept pressing the issue over the years (see Bellah, *Broken Covenant;* idem et al., *Habits of the Heart;* idem, *The Good Society* [New York: Alfred A. Knopf, 1991]). For a different view, see Richard John Neuhaus, *The Naked Public Square: Religion and Democracy in America* (Grand Rapids, Mich.: Eerdmans, 1984); Peter L. Berger, *A Far Glory: The Quest for Faith in an Age of Credulity* (New York: Free Press, 1992), 51–62.

62. Marty, *Religion and Republic,* 77–94, esp. 82. Reinhold Niebuhr is one of the most powerful prophetic figures of American life from a religious perspective; nevertheless, he was always convinced of the importance of constructive action. His insights concerning the overpowering tendency of the United States in the international field, its self-righteousness, its juvenile use of its strength, its naivete, and its self-defeating liberal presuppositions led him both to challenge the character of the nation and to offer a theological depiction of both person and society. That depiction, in which God is the transcendent center and savior of a creature that must acknowledge its not necessary but inevitable sinful condition, was for Niebuhr the only coherent account of human nature (see Reinhold Niebuhr, *The Nature and Destiny of Man,* vol. 1, *Human Nature* [New York: Charles Scribner's Sons, 1941]; idem, *The Nature and Destiny of Man,* vol. 2, *Human Destiny* [New York: Charles Scribner's Sons, 1943]; idem, *The Irony of American History* [New York: Charles Scribner's Sons, 1952]).

63. The classic here is John Dewey, *A Common Faith* (New Haven: Yale University Press, 1934).

64. Mead, *Lively Experiment,* 135. Within the denominational strand of American Christianity, there are also further distinctions. See H. Richard Niebuhr, *The Kingdom of God in America* (Middletown, Conn.: Wesleyan University Press, 1988).

65. Historically, mainly Protestantism, until the current century; from then on, Protestantism, Catholicism, Judaism, and Lutheranism; lately, Islam, Buddhism, and other religions are also present in U.S. society.

66. Marty is, for good reasons, not a great admirer of "civil religion" and prefers to see the soul of the nation as informed by the participants that, from religious and secular quarters, come to the national public realm (Marty, *Religion and Republic,* 53–76).

67. See the discussion in John Dewey, *The Public and Its Problems* (New York: Henry Holt, 1927), esp. 12.

68. Robert W. McElroy, *Search for an American Public Theology: The Contribution of John Courtney Murray* (Mahwah, N.J.: Paulist, 1989), 4.

69. See Marty, *Religion and Republic,* 95, 97–122.

70. McElroy, *Search,* 185n.12.

71. See Marty, *Nation of Behavers,* 80–105, where he points out the crusading nature of fundamentalist positions that fit the confrontational model "Christ against culture" in the relationship with society; Neuhaus, *Naked Public Square,* 36, where Neuhaus concludes that the New Right *"wants to enter the political arena making public claims on the basis of private truths"* and that such a move must be resisted because "public decisions must be made by arguments that are public in character"; Wuthnow, *Restructuring,* 178–80, which offers a differentiation between evangelicals and fundamentalists on the basis of how the former, unlike the latter, "had in mind the creation of a philosophically defensible biblical theology."

72. Neuhaus could be a representative of this second position. A different variety of this second position is that of Stanley Hauerwas (see *A Community of Character: Toward a Constructive Christian Social Ethic* [Notre Dame, Ind.: University of Notre Dame Press, 1981]).

73. For an interpretation of Reinhold Niebuhr as public theologian, see Marty, *Religion and Republic,* 97–122; Richard Harries, ed., *Reinhold Niebuhr and the Issues of Our Time* (Grand Rapids, Mich.: Eerdmans, 1986); Dennis P. MacCann, *Christian Realism and Liberation Theology: Practical Theologies in Creative Conflict* (Maryknoll, N.Y.: Orbis Books, 1981), 6–130; Robin Lovin, *Reinhold Niebuhr and Christian Realism* (Cambridge: Cambridge University Press, 1995).

74. See David O'Brien, *Public Catholicism* (New York: Macmillan, 1989), 4.

75. "For most of their history in the United States, Catholics had walked a tightrope between America's dominant culture, which they perceived to be in one way or another hostile to their faith, and Roman leadership, which was in many ways implicitly anti-American" (O'Brien, *Public Catholicism,* 220).

76. See H. R. Niebuhr, *Kingdom of God,* where, quoting André Siegfried, the author affirms that "Protestantism is America's 'only national religion and to ignore that fact is to view the country from a false angle' "; Marty, *Pilgrims in Their Own Land,* 227, who points out that Americans "thought of themselves as Protestants" and that, "pleased with their nation, they wanted it to be somehow homogeneous"; idem, *Nation of Behavers,* 70–71; Mead, *Lively Experiment,* 134–35; Will Herberg, "Religion and Culture in Present-Day America," in Thomas T. McAvoy, ed., *Roman Catholicism and the American Way of Life* (Notre Dame, Ind.: University of Notre Dame Press, 1960), 7, where he states that until the twentieth century, "Normally to be born American meant to be a Protestant," and formulates his thesis, very popular in the 1950s and 1960s, that in this century the United States has been transformed "from a *Protestant* country into a *three-religion* country," by which he means Protestantism, Judaism, and Roman Catholicism; Winthrop S. Hudson, "Protestantism in Post-Protestant America," in McAvoy, *Roman Catholicism,* 20.

77. See Gaustad, *Religious History,* 237–38; James Hennesey, *American Catholics: A History of the Roman Catholic Community in the United States* (New York: Oxford University Press, 1981), 246–47, 252–53.

78. Quoted in Jay P. Dolan, *The American Catholic Experience: A History from the Colonial Times to the Present* (Notre Dame, Ind.: University of Notre Dame Press, 1992), 421. As Dolan puts it, "Kennedy was telling the voters that he would

take orders from the people, not the Pope" (ibid., 421). Yet his Catholicism cost him many votes, and he won by the slimmest of margins (see John Tracy Ellis, *American Catholicism*, 2d rev. ed. [Chicago: University of Chicago Press, 1969], 187–88).

79. See Ellis, *American Catholicism*, 84–87; Hennesey, *American Catholics*, 56–58, 117–19, 182–83, 246–47. Within the Catholic Church, the understanding of authority originated tensions already in the colonial period. The main tensions then concerned the role of the laity in the government of parishes. The controversy known as Trusteeism took root and embroiled bishops and laity over an extended period of time (Dolan, *American Catholic Experience*, 165–92).

80. See Heinz Robert Schlette, "Religious Freedom," in *Sacramentum Mundi,* vol. 5.

81. For the text of the encyclicals, see Claudia Carlen, ed., *The Papal Encyclicals (1740–1981)*, 5 vols. (Ann Arbor, Mich.: Pierian, 1990). According to Dolan, the consequences of Pius X's encyclical *Pascendi Dominici Gregis* for the Catholic Church in the United States were intellectually devastating, signaling the end of the effort to come to grips with modernity, and securing the triumph of conservatism (Dolan, *American Catholic Experience*, 318–19). The resulting situation put Catholics in the United States "in a strange stance; they were both 100 percent American, loyal patriots to the core, and 100 percent Roman, loyal Catholics to the core. It was a unique blend of religion and nationalism which most other Americans failed to understand" (ibid., 320). Equally, the definition of the infallibility of the pope by Vatican I in 1870 did not contribute to the improvement of the image of the Catholic Church in the United States. The proposal at the council to proclaim papal infallibility was initially resisted by a majority of the American bishops present in Rome, although finally half of them voted for the definition (Hennesey, *American Catholics*, 168–71).

82. Yet the thought of both Leo XIII and Pius XI was still in tension with the American experiment. Their worldviews were not born of that original mixture of covenantal Protestantism and Enlightenment rationalism. Freedom for them in no case could apply to whether or not "true religion," that is, Catholicism, was embraced, since there was only one truth, Christ's, and it totally had been entrusted to the Catholic Church (see Pius XI, *Mit Brennender Sorge*, in Carlen, *Papal Encyclicals*, 3:525–35, esp. nos. 18–22; idem, *Ubi Arcano Dei Consilio*, in Carlen, *Papal Encyclicals*, 3:225–39, esp. nos. 41–46). Neither could they accept the principle of separation of church and state, although they were prepared to accept that religious freedom in the United States at least allowed the Catholic Church to go about its business without hindrance. However, that church "would bring forth more abundant fruits if, in addition to liberty, she enjoyed the favor of the laws and the patronage of the public authority" (see Leo XIII, *Longinqua*, in Carlen, *Papal Encyclicals*, 2:363–70, esp. no. 6; Hennesey, *American Catholics*, 200, where he quotes Bishop Ireland as saying of the encyclical that "the unfortunate allusion to Church & State cannot be explained to Americans"). Not until Vatican II would the Catholic Church proclaim the principle of religious freedom, under the impulse of U.S. bishops and theologians, especially Murray, thus removing an important stumbling block concerning the public image of Catholics in the United States.

83. On Ryan, and in general on social Catholicism, see O'Brien, *Public Catholi-*

cism, 167–82; Aaron I. Abell, "The Catholic Factor in the Social Justice Movement," in McAvoy, *Roman Catholicism,* 70–83; Dolan, *American Catholic Experience,* 334–46, 401–7; Hennesey, *American Catholics,* 234–56; Joseph P. Chinnici, O.F.M., *Living Stones: The History and Structure of Catholic Spiritual Life in the United States* (New York: Macmillan, 1989), 137–45, for an analysis of Ryan's thought in relation to his vision of the Christian life; John A. Coleman, *An American Strategic Theology* (New York: Paulist, 1982), 85–97, for an examination of the work of Ryan as public theology.

84. See National Conference of Catholic Bishops, *Justice in the Marketplace: Collected Statements of the Vatican and the U.S. Catholic Bishops on Economic Policy, 1891–1984* (Washington, D.C.: United States Catholic Conference, 1985), 367–83.

85. Dolan, *American Catholic Experience,* 342–46.

86. In Marty's opinion, Catholicism in the country has shifted from "public Catholicism" to "pluralism" in the two decades that followed Vatican II (Marty, *Invitation,* 180–210). Catholics seem to think and to act now with a much greater deal of freedom and distance from their hierarchy than they did before Vatican II, "taking from their church what they want and discarding what they do not" (George Gallup Jr. and Jim Castelli, *The American Catholic People: Their Beliefs, Practices, and Values* [Garden City, N.Y.: Doubleday, 1987], 178; Andrew M. Greeley, *The Catholic Myth: The Behavior and Beliefs of American Catholics* [New York: Macmillan, 1990], 91).

87. O'Brien, *Public Catholicism,* 244–49.

88. Chinnici, *Living Stones,* 209–13.

89. Obviously, this typology is a simplification of how the different theologians understand their work and must be taken as a description of "ideal types" that can never be found in their purity in reality.

90. A detailed analysis of this period will be developed below. Tracy describes Lonergan's evolution and new project in David Tracy, *The Achievement of Bernard Lonergan* (hereafter *ABL*) (New York: Herder and Herder, 1970).

91. The same applies to the Catholic heroes of Vatican II, Rahner, Congar, Chenu, and de Lubac, and, in general, to all those who at crucial cultural junctures have had to retrieve their tradition to make it relevant in a deeply transformed context.

92. See, for example, for a comparison of the two hermeneutical approaches, Bernard Lonergan, *Method in Theology* (hereafter *MT*) (Minneapolis: Seabury, 1973), 127, and David Tracy, *Blessed Rage for Order: The New Pluralism in Theology* (hereafter *BRO*) (New York: Seabury, 1975), 73–79.

93. David Tracy "God, Dialogue, and Solidarity: A Theologian's Refrain," in James M. Wall and David Heim, eds., *How My Mind Has Changed* (Grand Rapids, Mich.: Eerdmans, 1991), 89.

94. Ibid., 92.

95. David Tracy, "Literary Theory and Return of the Forms for Naming and Thinking God in Theology," *Journal of Religion* 74, no. 3 (July 1994).

96. "Thomist" in the sense that Aquinas's work can be understood as "modern" insofar as it is an attempt to formulate critically and scientifically a theological in-

terpretation of reality in a systematic way. To that end, Aquinas uses a method of argumentation, based on strict logical criteria, that seeks to justify and adjudicate philosophical and theological claims bearing in mind and discussing all other counterclaims. Unfortunately, although the Aquinas of the treatises and the *Summa(ae)* has been thoroughly analyzed, the meditative Aquinas, the mystical Aquinas, as recent research is helping to understand, has been to a great extent disregarded (see in this regard Jean-Pierre Torrell, O.P., *Saint Thomas d'Aquin, maître spirituel: Initiation 2* [Paris: Éditions du Cerf, 1996], a very insightful analysis of Aquinas's spiritual dimension and work, in which the author argues that "following the tradition of Saint John the evangelist and of the Church Fathers, the orientation of Thomas Aquinas's theology is clearly contemplative and as profoundly spiritual as doctrinal" (vi [my trans.]) and gives important clues for understanding the whole enterprise of Aquinas in a spiritual key [see esp. 265–98 and 495–513]).

97. A very succinct and similar interpretation of Tracy's theological development can be found in William D. Dean, *History Making History: The New Historicism in American Religious Thought* (Albany: State University of New York Press, 1988), 67–68.

98. The aim of this section is to analyze Lonergan's thought insofar as it has influenced Tracy's work. Besides Lonergan's works, one of the main means of reaching that goal will be Tracy's study of Lonergan's work up to 1965, namely, *ABL*. For an insightful and summarized analysis of Lonergan's overall intellectual development, see *ABL*, 224–31.

99. See Tracy, *ABL*, 1–12, for an enlightening analysis of Lonergan's ground-questions and of his commonalities with Rahner.

100. Ibid., xiv.

101. See Michael O'Callaghan, "Rahner and Lonergan on Foundational Theology," in Matthew L. Lamb, ed., *Creativity and Method: Essays in Honor of Bernard Lonergan, S.J.* (Milwaukee: Marquette University Press, 1981), 123.

102. David Tracy, "God, Dialogue, and Solidarity," 91, where Tracy quotes Rahner's statement, "But we cannot spend all our time sharpening the knife; at some point we must cut," and then affirms that "the only way to cut accurately is to try to analyze questions of method simultaneously with substantive theological topics." Referring to his books *Blessed Rage for Order* and *The Analogical Imagination,* he writes that "about half of each book is on method, the other on testing the method with substantive theological issues (God, revelation, Christ)."

103. Tracy's overall theological outlook is deeply linked with Rahner's theological paradigm shift and with the central position of that paradigm, namely, the intrinsicality of grace (uncreated grace) as constitutive of the person, that is, in Rahner's terms, the notion of the supernatural existential (see above, the first section of chapter 2, for a discussion of Rahner's influence on Tracy, Gutiérrez, and Metz).

104. For an explanation of how Tracy understands the terms "horizon" and "horizon-analysis," see *ABL*, 7–21.

105. That is, Aquinas fully developed the principle that fueled theological thought after Augustine, *fides quaerens intellectum,* bringing the consequences of that principle to the point of building an encompassing philosophic-theological "theory-edifice." See, in this respect, David Tracy, *Lonergan's Interpretation of St. Thomas*

Aquinas: The Intellectualist Nature of Speculative Theology (hereafter *LITA*) (Rome: Pontificia Universitas Gregoriana, Facultas Theologica, 1969), esp. 37–41. Aquinas's stringent intellectual endeavor in pursuit of a chain of arguments that would lead him to the final clarification of the question under examination was the basis of his scientific theological method. Lonergan was more interested in that method than in the actual content of Aquinas's work.

106. *LITA,* 45. Tracy opposes intellectualist to conceptualist, and explanatory to descriptive. By conceptualist, Tracy understands a theology that is only interested in concepts or definitions, that is to say, a manual-based theology with ready answers to every question, but uninterested in understanding. Contrariwise, an intellectualist theology is concerned mainly not with answers but with the very operation of understanding (ibid., 37–38). The explanatory element is also crucial in understanding Aquinas's project in regard to the earlier Christian theology. Aquinas's contribution is to elaborate a theory that explains not only the contents of doctrine but also the coherence of that doctrine on a rational basis. In other words, Aquinas means the passage from an Augustinian symbolical, pretheoretical, or at least not fully theoretical theology, to a scientific and theoretical theological discourse. In Tracy's words, "Aquinas succeeded in bringing *theory* to bear on religious truth" (*ABL,* 48).

107. *LITA,* 43–44, where Tracy affirms that Lonergan's work on Aquinas gave him the key to all his "later achievements"; he refers to Lonergan's "secure intellectualism which allows him to further differentiate, develop, thematize and order a theory of meaning for contemporary philosophical and theological needs."

108. *ABL,* 82.

109. Tracy sees Lonergan's whole program as a realization of Leo XIII's adage *vetera novis augere et perficere* and writes that this adage "is an important hermeneutic principle for recognizing the continuity between Lonergan's earlier work (on the *vetera* of the Catholic theological tradition, more specifically on St. Thomas Aquinas) and his later work (on the *nova* of the modern and contemporary periods, i.e., from the critical work of *Insight* on)" (*LITA,* 33–34n.84). Tracy also describes Lonergan's work on Aquinas as "the effort of the young Lonergan to reoriginate the Catholic theological tradition by a return to and a recovery of its authentic intellectualist origins in Aquinas" (*ABL,* 22).

110. Bernard J. F. Lonergan, *Insight: A Study of Human Understanding,* revised student's edition (London: Longmans, 1958).

111. Ibid., xxii.

112. Ibid., 636–39, for an analysis of how transcendence is already implicit in the very existence of ever-questioning transcendental thinking. In Tracy's view, Lonergan's "critical method does not eliminate the notion of 'God' but heuristically formulates it as the unrestricted act of understanding and proceeds to work out its general attributes" (*ABL,* 174).

113. *ABL,* 204, where Tracy reproduces Lonergan's own formulation of the shift.

114. *MT,* xi.

115. *ABL,* 240, 242.

116. *MT,* 19–20.

117. Tracy writes of Lonergan's intellectual development in terms of the four exigencies, namely, systematic, critical, methodical, and transcendent, "expressing the

movement from level to level of self-transcendence" ("Lonergan's Foundational The-
ology: An Interpretation and a Critique" [hereafter LFT], in Philip McShane, ed.,
Foundations of Theology: Papers from the International Lonergan Congress 1970
[Dublin: Gill and Macmillan, 1971], 199).

118. Ibid., 220.

119. Ogden affirms in a similar way that Lonergan "arrives at his metaphysical
conclusions, not by following his method, but by uncritically employing a traditional
category, which is to say, by in effect appealing to authorities and treating as self-
evident what is by no means so to everyone" (Schubert Ogden, "Lonergan and
the Subjectivist Principle," in Philip McShane, ed., *Language, Truth, and Meaning:
Papers from the International Lonergan Congress 1970* [Dublin: Gill and Macmillan,
1972], 233).

120. See David Tracy, "Method as Foundation for Theology," *Journal of Religion*
50 (July 1970): 318, for just the bare formulation of the problem; idem, *LFT*, 214–
22, for Tracy's developed explicitation of the critique.

121. *BRO*, 3–21.

122. *LFT*, 214. For a discussion and assessment of Tracy's critique of Lonergan,
see Gerald M. Boodoo, "Development and Consolidation: The Use of Theological
Method in the Works of David Tracy" (Ph.D. diss., Katholieke Universiteit Leuven,
1991), 50–87.

123. This, however, does not imply that Tracy restricts the theological task to
the foundational step. On the contrary, at the time of *Blessed Rage for Order*, he
envisioned the theological enterprise as encompassing four disciplines: fundamental, systematic, historical, and practical within the same revisionist model (see *BRO*,
237–40). Later, by the time of *The Analogical Imagination*, though, he spoke only
of three, namely, fundamental, systematic, and practical, making historical theology
a moment within each of those three, no longer disciplines but subdisciplines (see
David Tracy, *The Analogical Imagination: Christian Theology and the Culture of
Pluralism* [hereafter *AI*] [New York: Crossroad, 1981], 54–58). In both instances,
Tracy sees these disciplines, later subdisciplines, as mutually related and interde-
pendent, thus adapting to his own revisionist model Lonergan's methodological
contribution of functional specialties.

124. In other words, in Lonergan's terms, Tracy's horizon is different from Lonergan's. Lonergan made an attempt in his *Method in Theology* to take into account
some of Tracy's critiques. That is clear in his notions of meaning and symbol, in
his paying more attention to the phenomenology of religion (see Tracy's recognition
of this in *BRO*, 53–54), in his awareness of the importance of hermeneutics, and
in his affirmation that the task of theology is to bridge the gap between doctrines
and experience. However, these moves only cover part of the ground Tracy seeks to
cover with his own enterprise.

125. On Tracy's understanding of model, see *BRO*, 34n.1, where he claims to
use Lonergan's notion of model, that is, model as an interlocking set of terms and
relations concerning the subject matter of a discipline.

126. Ibid., 32.

127. Ibid., 41n.65.

128. Ibid., 32.

129. See Tracy's opening analysis of the crisis of both in ibid., 4–14, where he refers to "the disenchantment with mystification" and "the disenchantment with disenchantment."

130. Ibid., 33.

131. Ibid., 43.

132. Ibid., 44.

133. Ibid., 43–45; Paul Tillich, *Systematic Theology,* vol. 1, *Reason and Revelation, Being and God* (Chicago: University of Chicago Press, 1951), 34–40.

134. *BRO,* 64–68.

135. See Schubert Ogden, "A Christian Natural Theology?" in Delwin Brown et al., eds., *Process Philosophy and Christian Thought* (Indianapolis: Bobbs-Merrill, 1971), 114, an article first published in 1965.

136. *BRO,* 173.

137. Ibid., 47–48.

138. Ibid., 45–46, 79.

139. Ibid., 46. Elsewhere, though, Tracy points out that, although Tillich's formulation of the method rather juxtaposes than correlates situation and message, the way Tillich used that method was, in many cases, a true two-way correlation (see David Tracy, "Tillich and Contemporary Theology," in James Luther Adams et al., eds., *The Thought of Paul Tillich* [San Francisco: Harper and Row, 1985], 266).

140. *BRO,* 54–55.

141. Ibid., 79–81. An important shift in understanding the method of correlation took place later, at the time of *The Analogical Imagination.* In this work, Tracy, following Schillebeeckx, introduces the term "mutually" before "critical correlation." From the beginning of the 1980s on, therefore, Tracy speaks always of a "mutually critical correlation" between Christianity and the situation. This move aimed at indicating "the fuller range of possible correlations between some interpretation of the situation and some interpretation of the tradition" (see *AI,* 88n. 44; idem, "God, Dialogue, and Solidarity," 89).

142. *BRO,* 47–48.

143. Ibid., 72–79. Tracy follows the theory of interpretation as Ricoeur presented it in a colloquium of the faculty at the Divinity School of the University of Chicago in 1971 (*BRO,* 60n.37). The work was reworked and published later (see Paul Ricoeur, *Interpretation Theory: Discourse and the Surplus of Meaning* [Fort Worth, Tex.: Christian University Press, 1976]). For Ricoeur's understanding of the hermeneutical tradition and his position in relation to that tradition, see Paul Ricoeur, *Hermeneutics and the Human Sciences,* ed. and trans. John B. Thompson (Cambridge: Cambridge University Press, 1981), 43–62. For his relation to social critical theory, see ibid., 63–100. For his position in relation to Gadamer and Habermas, see Ricoeur, "Ethics and Culture: Habermas and Gadamer in Dialogue," *Philosophy Today* 17, no. 2/4 (1973). For an enlightening analysis of the evolution of Ricoeur's thought and of his confrontation with Gadamer's hermeneutics and with social critical theory, see Javier Bengoa, *De Heidegger a Habermas: Hermenéutica y fundamentación última en la filosofía contemporánea* (Barcelona: Editorial Herder, 1992), 83–124, 125–87.

144. *BRO,* 43.

145. Ibid., 55, and, most of all, 153–56, where he embraces Ogden's position;

Boodoo, "Development and Consolidation," 109–12, for an analysis of Tracy's understanding of the philosophical task.

146. On the cultural limits (and limitations) of Tracy's model of theology, see Boodoo, "Development and Consolidation," 86n.271, where, referring to its clear cultural anchoring, Boodoo writes that "though the foundational theology set out there claims a common human experiential base, its use of and contextualization within the Anglo-American Christian tradition, questions its claims to a broader experiential base." It is precisely Tracy's increasing realization of his cultural and religious roots and determinations that has led him to broaden significantly his horizon and, consequently, the scope of his project in his later work. At the same time, it must be immediately added that such horizon broadening has not prompted Tracy to claim that he has achieved a universal standpoint that, beyond his own tradition, adequately represents all others, thus trying a new strategy to impose his views on others. On the contrary, his expanding horizon has led him to move not beyond his tradition but precisely to the inner core of that tradition, while at the same time entering an increasingly deep, and therefore difficult and problematic, dialogue with other traditions. Evidence for these views will unfold throughout the rest of the chapter.

147. Tracy defines the publicness of theology as the application to the theological enterprise of "publicly available criteria for meaning, meaningfulness, and truth" (*BRO*, 34). For a more developed discussion of public criteria and modes of argumentation not only for fundamental theology but also for systematic and practical theologies, see Tracy, "Modes of Theological Argument," *Theology Today* 33 (1976–77): 387–95.

148. *BRO*, 80–81.

149. Ibid., 92–93.

150. Ibid., 93. For Tracy's important qualifications of his understanding and use of the concept of "limit," see ibid., 111n.11, where Tracy acknowledges the influence of mainly Ian Ramsey and Ricoeur on his interpretation of the limit-character of religious language. For an analysis of the differences between Ricoeur and Tracy on this question and for a critical assessment of Tracy's use of limit-analysis, see Boodoo, "Development and Consolidation," 129–62.

151. *BRO*, 94.

152. Ibid., 94–109. In his analysis, Tracy discusses the positions of Lonergan, Toulmin, Ogden, Jaspers, Maslow, Heidegger, and Tillich, showing his way of advancing his own constructive discussion through an open and critical dialogue with the representatives of the main positions concerning the matter under scrutiny.

153. Ibid., 119–34.

154. Ibid., 132–36.

155. Ibid., 148.

156. Ibid., 160–63.

157. Ibid., 172, where he also claims that "classical Christian theism is neither internally coherent nor adequate as a full account of our common experience and of the scriptural understanding of the Christian God."

158. Ibid., 175–83. On process theology's understanding of God and on its critique of classical theism, see Schubert Ogden, *The Reality of God and Other Essays*

(London: SCM, 1967); idem, "Toward a New Theism," in Brown et al., *Process Philosophy,* 173–87, which is a reworked version of an article originally written in 1966.

159. *BRO,* 187–88.

160. Ibid., 187–91. In a more recent discussion (1989) of Ogden based on the role argument, conversation, and myth play in Plato's work, Tracy goes much further than he does in the position just discussed—so much as to wonder whether it would not be possible for Ogden "to affirm, through his own dialectical inquiry, the truth of Plato's defense of the truth-status of both myth and art" (David Tracy, "Argument, Dialogue, and the Soul in Plato," in Philip E. Devenish and George L. Goodwin, eds., *Witness and Existence: Essays in Honor of Schubert M. Ogden* [Chicago: University of Chicago Press, 1989], 102).

161. *BRO,* 191.

162. Ibid., 225n.12.

163. Ibid., 205.

164. Ibid., 209. There is an interesting parallelism between this insight of Ricoeur and Rahner's insight that there is an ongoing, tensional dynamic between an original experience that intrinsically looks for conceptualization and the need for that conceptualization to go back to the original experience because it never can reflect and mediate it adequately (Karl Rahner, *Foundations of Christian Faith: An Introduction to the Idea of Christianity* [New York: Crossroad, 1987], 15–17). For Ricoeur's critical assessment of Rahner's hermeneutics, see Paul Ricoeur, " 'Response' to Karl Rahner's Lecture: On the Incomprehensibility of God," in David Tracy, ed., *Celebrating the Medieval Heritage: A Colloquy on the Thought of Aquinas and Bonaventure,* special supplement of *Journal of Religion* 58 (1978): 128.

165. *BRO,* 214.

166. See, for instance, Schubert Ogden, *Christ without Myth: A Study Based on the Theology of Rudolph Bultmann* (London: Collins, 1962), 170–92.

167. See, for instance, Mircea Eliade, *Myth and Reality* (New York: Harper and Row, 1963); idem, *The Sacred and the Profane: The Nature of Religion* (New York: Harper, 1961); idem, *Images and Symbols* (New York: Sheed and Ward, 1969).

168. Ricoeur, *Interpretation Theory,* 60.

169. *BRO,* 215.

170. Ibid., 216.

171. Ibid., 218.

172. Ibid., 221.

173. Ibid.

174. Ibid., 223. The parallelism with Bultmann is clear here. Tracy's entry into Christology forces him to enter also the complex world of controversies around that field. In general terms, Tracy's position follows rather closely Ogden's Christology and, therefore, is a critical revision and appropriation of Bultmann's existential Christology. However, besides other authors discussed by Tracy, his Christology uses extensively the hermeneutical principles formulated by Ricoeur. With Ricoeur, Tracy rejects any author-addressees-centered interpretation and advocates an objective or text-as-ideal-meaning-centered interpretation.

175. Ibid. Tracy borrows from Ogden the term "basic faith," something that all

humanity experiences (see Ogden, *Reality of God,* 34, 37, 43; idem, "Toward a New Theism," in Brown et al., *Process Philosophy,* 182; idem, *On Theology* [San Francisco: Harper and Row, 1986], 69–72, 106–7).

176. *BRO,* 8.

177. Ibid., 223.

178. For Tracy, "historical theology seeks to reconstruct the past meaning for the present; fundamental and systematic theologies deal with the significance of Christian faith for the present; practical theology, finally, projects the future possibilities of it. Thus, the first issues in *historia,* the second in *theoria,* and the third in *praxis"* (ibid., 240). Tracy follows Ogden here rather closely. For instance, the relationship of theology with past, present, and future can be found also in Ogden, *On Theology,* 8–15.

179. Tracy, for instance, programmatically embraces the "morality of scientific knowledge" and "the faith of secularity," which is *"the* common faith shared by secularist and modern Christians" (*BRO,* 7–8). Furthermore, the strong "modern" character of his theology is clear when he affirms that "the Christian theologian holds that a proper understanding of the explicitly Christian faith can render intellectually coherent and symbolically powerful that common secular faith which we share" (ibid., 9). Tracy's final claim is that "Christian faith is at heart none other than the most adequate articulation of the basic faith of secularity itself" (ibid., 10). However, Tracy's view on that faith of secularity is far from being naive and overoptimistic. On the contrary, he firmly believes that the "disenchanters" have, in turn, been "disenchanted." The time of the first Enlightenment is definitively over, especially after the unmasking operations of its naive presuppositions, perversions, and destructive potential performed, first, by Marx, Freud, and Nietzsche and, second, by the Frankfurt School. Modernity is by itself ambiguous. Therefore, it is either critical or destructive. It is precisely at this critical secular faith and at its practitioners that the revisionist project is aimed (ibid., 10–14).

180. Ibid., 12–13.

181. This is clear in Metz's dramatic change from *Christliche Anthropozentrik* to his latest work and in Gutiérrez's increasing attention to popular culture and religiosity and mounting disappointment with social sciences and other typically critical-modern interpretive tools. In Tracy, the focus on the modern concern with argument and concept has been replaced by a focus on how to name and think God in a postmodern time.

182. First of all, on both scores of trying to define a model for theology and of formulating a method for fundamental theology, Tracy can be said to be foundationally Lonerganian. Besides, Tracy relies on Lonergan at different stages, as, for example, showing the religious and theistic implications of scientific inquiry (*BRO,* 96–100). Even more basically, Lonergan works as a referential partner for Tracy in the sense that he shows at every important point how his position stands in relation to Lonergan's.

183. Ibid., 3.

184. Ibid., 249.

185. Ibid., 3.

186. *AI,* xi. Tracy is fully aware of the difficulties involved in his project when

he writes that "At first sight it seems counterintuitive to suggest that systematic theologies are public. For systematic theologies, after all, are theological expressions of a particular tradition's construal of reality from the vantage point of that religious particularity" (David Tracy, "Defending the Public Character of Theology," in James M. Wall, ed., *Theologians in Transition* [New York: Crossroad, 1981], 116).

187. Tracy, "Defending," 117. In another text, he writes that "every classic religious tradition can be honored as bearing public resources not despite but through their very particularity." This is so because classic particularities "remain public insofar as they function as disclosive of truths about our common situation" (David Tracy, "The Foundations of Practical Theology," in Don S. Browning, ed., *Practical Theology* [San Francisco: Harper and Row, 1983], 70–71).

188. *AI*, 3.

189. Ibid., 7–15, for a discussion of some of the trends in society.

190. Ibid., 51, 52.

191. Ibid., 25.

192. See the enlightening essay by Matthew Lamb, "David Tracy," in Dean G. Peerman and Martin Marty, eds., *A Handbook of Christian Theologians,* enlarged ed. (Nashville: Abingdon, 1985), 677–90. In Lamb's view, Tracy seems to be "attempting to establish mutually critical correlations between the subdisciplines of fundamental, systematic, and practical theologies" (682). Lamb notices that Tracy has changed the way of designating the specialties of fundamental, systematic, and practical theology. Whereas he called them disciplines in *BRO*, he calls them subdisciplines in *AI*. This, for Lamb, is another indication of Tracy's intensification of the inner mutually critical correlations among the three specialties (689). The essay is especially interesting because, among other things, it compares Tracy's and Lonergan's developments.

193. For a succinct account of how the movement from abstraction to concreteness proceeds through the three disciplines, see Tracy, "Foundations of Practical Theology," 80.

194. See the discussion over these issues in *AI*, 99–107.

195. Ibid., 108.

196. *AI*, 130. In this case, Tracy follows Eliade's notion of the sacred and the primordial or essential. Because the paradigmatic is a representation of the sacred, "the paradigmatic is the real" for Eliade (see esp. Eliade, *Sacred and the Profane,* 11–13).

197. *AI*, xii.

198. Rahner, *Foundations,* 158.

199. See *AI*, 162, where Tracy discusses Rahner's position and the intimate relationship between fundamental and systematic theologies in Rahner.

200. For Tracy, to take the full risk of interpreting the religious classics is "to risk entering the most dangerous conversation of all. For there the most serious questions on the meaning of existence as participating in, yet distanced, sometimes even estranged from, the reality of the whole are posed" (*AI*, 155). Evidently, there is not and there cannot ever be only one interpretation of a classic. Interpreting the classics entails always entering a conflict of interpretations.

201. This is the case with certain Christian theologians like Augustine, Aquinas,

Luther, and, more recently, with those theologians who, like Schleiermacher, Barth, Tillich, the Niebuhrs, Rahner, and Lonergan, can be seen as potential classics (ibid., 132–33).

202. Ibid., 214–15.

203. Ibid., 264.

204. Ibid., 265–87.

205. Ibid., 308.

206. Ibid., 312, 313, 314.

207. *AI*, 320, 322, 323–24. In this sense, Tracy considers it important to pay attention to the Christologies of both liberation and political theologies with their "Christian critique of ideologies grounded in the mystical-political reality of the praxis of authentic Christian faith" (ibid., 327). Consequently, hermeneutics and Christian ideology-critique belong together in the task of interpreting the classic event and person of Jesus Christ as mediated by the tradition (ibid., 328). The "communal character of the tradition" must be matched by the "collegial character of theology" if criteria of relative adequacy are to be developed "for resolving the inevitable conflicts to trust in the Spirit released by that Christ event in the church to discern and to guide the church in its fidelity to Jesus Christ" (ibid., 328–29).

208. Ibid., 332. This is Tracy's way of saying what both political and liberation theologies say, namely, that truth must be "done." One important point stressed by Tracy is the dialectical character of the Christ event. On the one hand, that event is revealing and disclosive. On the other hand, God appears as the hidden and even, sometimes, absent. This dialectics of the hidden-revealed God, already present at this stage in Tracy's theology, will become one of the central points in Tracy's later developments.

209. Tracy refers here to what is possibly the most famous dictum in this respect, namely, Benjamin's insistence that every product of civilization is at the same time a product of barbarism (ibid., 351).

210. Ibid., 363.

211. Tracy argues that "every theology worthy of the history of the classic self-understanding of Christianity" recognizes these doctrines and symbols "as the paradigmatic candidates for Christian response and recognition—God, Christ, grace; creation-redemption-eschatology; church-world; nature-grace, grace-sin; revelation; faith, hope, love; word-sacrament; cross-resurrection-incarnation. *All* these symbols, like Everest, are simply there" (ibid., 373).

212. Once again, truth as manifestation that elicits a shock of recognition is central in Tracy's understanding of how the Christian response operates. In this sense, he argues that "by its own disclosive force, that power transforms each theologian's interpretations of both situation and tradition." The core of this experience can be expressed by affirming, as H. R. Niebuhr did, that Christ is the transformer of culture (ibid., 374). Disclosure and transformation become, therefore, key, and mutually complementary, criteria for truth in systematic and practical theologies (ibid., 407).

213. Ibid., 376.

214. Ibid., 390.

215. Ibid., 398.

216. Ibid., 407–8.

217. Ibid., 422.

218. Tracy sees clear examples of this mixed language in Barth, Bultmann, Tillich, Moltmann, Metz, and Gutiérrez. He sees a paradigmatic expression of this bipolarity in Tillich's understanding of Christian theology as based on "Protestant principle and Catholic substance" (ibid., 419).

219. Ibid., 421–30. Tracy offers a succinct account of the journeys of systematic theologians, arguing that those journeys occur when the theologians are "concentrated in some theological paradigmatic focal meaning employed to interpret the originating religious event, expanding that focal meaning into relationships with all reality—God, self, world—exposing all those understandings to the fuller range of the symbol system and the entire range of live options and questions in the situation" (ibid., 454).

220. Ibid., 446.

221. David Tracy, "Christianity in the Wider Context: Demands and Transformations," in William Schweiker and Per M. Anderson, eds., *Worldviews and Warrants: Plurality and Authority in Theology* (Lanham, Md.: University Press of America, 1987), 8. On the question of plurality and pluralism, see ibid., 2–8, where Tracy argues that plurality is a fact, whereas pluralism is a positive assessment of this fact. In any case, pluralism can be neither eclecticism nor indifferentism nor "repressive tolerance." Pluralism is a strategy to acknowledge and to appropriate the other as a representation of a potentially productive new possibility of being-in-the-world.

222. *AI*, 449 and 451.

223. David Tracy, *Plurality and Ambiguity: Hermeneutics, Religion, Hope* (hereafter *PA*) (San Francisco: Harper and Row, 1987).

224. Tracy had already argued in *AI* that one of the dangers of the radically plural society was accepting unproblematically a kind of happy plurality that radically did away with the public realm. He referred to it as a "relaxed pluralism of privacies" (*AI*, 451). Metz's diagnosis of the present time in postindustrial societies also stresses the postmodern cultural tendency to accept happily everything without accepting thereby any personal engagement with anything. As regards religion, for instance, he describes this cultural situation as a situation of a "religion-friendly-godlessness," dominated by the *postmoderne Kulturkarneval.*

225. Ibid., 59. For Tracy, Derrida's analysis leaves us just with the "abyss of indeterminacy." The core of Derrida's position is, so to speak, the radicalization and intensification of Saussure's insights. In an enlightening analysis, Tracy surveys the main shifts within the global linguistic turn. In his view, an intensification can be observed from Wittgenstein's plurality of language use through Heidegger's plurality in every discourse of language to Derrida's plurality within language. He concludes that "Whether or not language becomes discourse in Derrida himself is a genuine puzzle" (ibid., 60).

226. Tracy moves in a sort of Hegelian way through the different stages of the critique of the text back to the final retrieval of its relevance. As he puts it, we must "turn from an interpretation of language-as-object back to an interpretation of language-as-use. We must turn from the deconstruction of words to a chastened interpretation of texts. Indeed, at its best, deconstructive criticism is also discourse" (ibid., 62).

227. Ibid., 64.

228. Ibid., 66–70. There is also the risk of retiring into a subtle mode of complacency, namely, "universal and ineffectual guilt." Therefore, tradition must be both assumed and confronted. To illustrate that, Tracy argues that "To risk conversation with our classic texts should be more like meeting such characters as Amos and Isaiah, Ruth and Jeremiah, Oedipus and Antigone, even Medea and Herakles, than it is like conceiving the classics simply as further examples of ideology" (ibid., 69).

229. Ibid., 70, 72–76. Given the complexity of any tradition, its critical retrieval can only be achieved by using different strategies. Especially important are the strategies of resistance, attention, and hope. Resistance to one own's tradition is also hope in that tradition. The use of religion may be a relevant strategy to resist distortions. The Christian symbols of evil, sin, and, most crucially, grace can be extremely helpful in coming to terms with the ambiguities of a history that, nevertheless, is not without hope. In turn, religions must be themselves critiqued and liberated from their own distortions and ambiguities.

230. Tracy thinks that "the leitmotiv of all the pluralistic strategies of deconstruction" may be found in Nietzsche's denials of the existence of truth, which for him is a mere illusion (ibid., 76).

231. Ibid., 77.

232. Ibid., 84.

233. Tracy sees in Kierkegaard's understanding of sin, grace, and the decentered Christian self a good example of how theological insights can speak "with all the force of the most radical French postmodernists" ("God, Dialogue, and Solidarity," 93).

234. *AI*, 98. The point is a very difficult one, and Tracy only approaches it from the point of view of the necessity of establishing a serious ongoing conversation among the interpreters of the religions.

235. Ibid., 141n.56.

236. See, for instance, David Tracy, "On Naming the Present," *Concilium* 1 (1990): 80.

237. See David Tracy, *Dialogue with the Other: The Inter-religious Dialogue* (hereafter *DWO*) (Grand Rapids, Mich.: Eerdmans, 1991), 71.

238. See David Tracy, "The Return of God in Contemporary Theology," unpublished manuscript, 1994.

239. For Tracy, theology's main drive is to say and mean "God." In a postmodern time, this means to render God's name "in and through the honest confusions, terrors and hopes of this age, our age—the age that cannot name itself" ("God, Dialogue, and Solidarity," 99).

240. Tracy acknowledges that he "may never be ready to attempt that third volume of the projected theology," referring to the third part, on practical theology, of his revisionist program. He admits he is not prepared yet, not only because he has not sorted out all the basic issues involved thereby but "also, indeed primarily, because I have changed the focus of my theological thought" (ibid., 91). More concretely, this focal shift has to do with a certain relativization of his modern hopes at the time he wrote *Blessed Rage for Order*. The new postmodern cultural setting entails a severe critique of basic elements of that modern hope. That makes Tracy shift his theology

toward the new foci: "the other" and naming God. However, he does so precisely because he wants to preserve the basic hope of modernity in a postmodern age, the hope that true enlightenment, true emancipation, true reason, true justice, and true solidarity are a possibility in history.

241. See David Tracy, "Return of God."

242. Eliade's persistent influence on Tracy's thought can hardly be overstressed. Tracy's theological insight of the disruptive emergence of that ultimate repressed other, God, in the present age, bears striking similarities to the untamable presence of the sacred, emerging always anew both to disrupt the profane and to liberate human beings from the oppressive constraints of the profane reality (see, in this respect, Tracy's own interpretation of Eliade in relation to the emergence of the archaic others in postmodernity, in *DWO*, 48–67).

243. See, for instance, *DWO*, xi, where he describes the essays included in this book as explorations that "may help other theologians and philosophers to test the model of dialogue for hermeneutics and the mystical-prophetic model for theology."

244. See Tracy, "On Naming the Present," 66, where he states that "We live in an age that cannot name itself." This age, defined by default as postmodern, is also an ambiguous one.

245. See David Tracy, "Theology and the Many Faces of Post-Modernity," *Theology Today* 51, no. 1 (April 1994).

246. Tracy agrees with Habermas on two important issues: the originally emancipatory character of modernity and the need to overcome instrumental reason, rescuing the life-world and the public realm on the basis of a communicative reason. Tracy, however, argues that Habermas's social-evolutionary understanding of history and, above all, his inability to acknowledge the public character of the liberating resources of art and religion prevent him from overcoming the strictures of modern reason and from rescuing the emancipatory character of reason and modernity in a postmodern age (see, in this respect, Tracy, "On Naming the Present," 72).

247. Ibid., 79.

248. What is meant here by the term "preferred conversational partners" are those conversational partners who are especially provoking and creative as regards Tracy's new concerns.

249. Over the last years, Tracy has been insisting on the retrieval of classical Greek thought. One of the strands of that thought needing to be retrieved is Plato's thought, as well as Platonism and Christian Neoplatonism. Plato's intellectual journey is especially enlightening for Tracy. Having adopted an initially radical Socratic demythologizing stand in his dialogues, Plato's understanding of reason undergoes a subtle transformation to take an unexpected turn in his *Timaeus*. In this dialogue, Plato comes to acknowledge that the mythological, symbolic language is the only possibility to get a glimpse of a unbounded reality that, being unbounded, cannot be represented by a merely discursive-dialectical reason. See in this respect David Tracy, "Argument, Dialogue, and the Soul in Plato," where Tracy argues that Plato expressed in the *Timaeus* "the truth of any great myth or any great work of art that manifests the truth of the intrinsic kinship of soul and cosmos" (101).

Tracy's interest in Plato, however, does not end with Plato's rediscovery of the importance of myth. Tracy is also most interested in the genre of Plato's work, namely, the dialogue. For Tracy, the crucial information is that "There is no other text for Plato's philosophy. It is all in the dialogues" (see David Tracy, "Iris Murdoch and the Many Faces of Platonism," in William Schweiker and Maria Antonacio, eds., *Iris Murdoch and the Search for Human Goodness* [Chicago: University of Chicago Press, 1996]). The point for Tracy is that, unlike the treatise, the dialogue is a genre that shows that true knowledge requires a personal transformation, an intellectual journey of the soul to the Truth, the Good, the Beautiful. The inner unity between form and content makes itself manifest in the dialogue genre. In the same line, dialogues involve a link between argument and character that unveils the inner link between reason and the transformation of the soul. Theory is an empty notion without the spiritual exercise through which one can appropriate it.

250. See, in this respect, *DWO*, 27–67, for Tracy's assessment of the insights of both James and Eliade as being most fruitful in the postmodern age.

251. Ricoeur, as has already been argued, is crucial to Tracy's hermeneutical approach. What Tracy values especially in Ricoeur is his ability to understand the hermeneutical constitution of reason, while, at the same time, through his advocation of explanation, critique, and suspicion, avoiding the pitfalls of a hermeneutics of mere retrieval. As regards Foucault, it might be argued that he is for Tracy the most insightful thinker in deconstructing and exposing the illusions and distortions of modernity. Tracy argues furthermore that, in his unmasking of those illusions and distortions, Foucault must be considered a postmodern heir to the great ethical tradition of the Enlightenment.

252. See *DWO*, xi, where Tracy argues that "it will not be possible to attempt a Christian systematic theology except in serious conversation with the other great ways."

253. See, in this respect, ibid., 73, where Tracy defines the conditions for developing a fruitful "analogical imagination" in the interreligious dialogue. Dialogue itself can only occur when "the subject-matter and not the subject's consciousness is allowed to take over" (ibid., 95).

254. Tracy refers explicitly here to "the gospel dialectic of 'to gain the self, one must lose the self'" (ibid., 78).

255. See David Tracy, "Evil, Suffering, and Hope: The Search for New Forms of Contemporary Theodicy" (unpublished manuscript, 1995), where he argues that "To develop a *logos* on *theos*—a theology—today is to start by facing evil and suffering." This is almost identical to Metz's understanding of what theology is today in his reflections on the *Theodizee Frage*.

Chapter 5: The Exitus from Transcendentality to History and the Reditus from History to the Mystery of God

1. What is meant here is that each one of the three authors discovers the mystery of God in his own particular way. As Tracy points out, whereas for Rahner that mystery is expressed in and through the incomprehensibility of God, in the case of Metz God appears mainly as hidden. Again, according to Tracy, God's incomprehensibility comes to the fore in Gutiérrez, although certain traits of God's hiddenness are also present in his work. Finally, Tracy himself prefers to refer to the hidden-

incomprehensible God (see David Tracy, "The Tenderness and Violence of God: The Return of The Hidden God in Contemporary Theology," in *Lumière et Vie* [1996]).

2. This naming is somehow misleading, given the wide differences among the various Third World theologies. However, it stresses an important point, namely, that these theologies are formulated in those regions of the world in which poverty, exclusion, and injustice reign. This is a new phenomenon, bearing in mind that, until the late 1960s, the so-called First World, and especially Europe, was the only social and cultural context in which Christian theology was being formulated.

3. Johann Baptist Metz, *Glaube in Geschichte und Gesellschaft: Studien zu einer praktischen Fundamentaltheologie* (hereafter *GGG*) (Mainz: Matthias-Grünewald, 1977), 147.

4. See ibid., 48.

5. See, esp., ibid., 78–82.

6. In this respect, Gutiérrez masterfully and wisely affirms that "Theology is a talk constantly enriched by silence" (Gustavo Gutiérrez, *La verdad los hará libres: Confrontaciones* [hereafter *LV*] [Lima: Instituto Bartolomé de Las Casas–Rimac, Centro de Estudios y Publicaciones, 1986], 13 [my trans.]). Without silence, prayer, and contemplation, there cannot be any theology.

7. In this sense, the disruptive turn is an inner moment within the overall hermeneutical enterprise of Tracy. Therefore, this new stress in his theology cannot be isolated from hermeneutics. The point is rather that new, more disquieting and uncontrollable voices, aspects of reality, and faces of God are entering the conversation with more "telling" strength. They demand not so much to be understood and interpreted but to be heard and heeded.

In relation to the metaphysical moment of Tracy's theology, it is clear that, although always playing an implicit, behind the scenes, role, its centrality was related to Tracy's formulation of fundamental theology at the time of *Blessed Rage for Order*. Its role now is far more muted and, somehow, more precarious (David Tracy "God, Dialogue, and Solidarity: A Theologian's Refrain," in James M. Wall and David Heim, eds., *How My Mind Has Changed* [Grand Rapids, Mich.: Eerdmans, 1991], 92–93). However, it is always there, because, following Rahner's insight, there is no human thought that is not intrinsically and, at least inchoately, metaphysical.

8. A radically "other" God that cannot be controlled by reason must be meditated upon, discovered rather than understood. In this sense, Tracy refers to the wide range of possibilities along the "mystical-meditative" spectrum. Moreover, this uncontrollable God must be allowed to disrupt and even interrupt all historical discourses and ways. Therefore, Tracy thinks this God must also be expressed in the full range of possibilities within the "prophetic-apocalyptic" spectrum.

It is interesting to notice how importantly Tracy sees his work and experience with the Catholic theological review *Concilium* for his awareness of the necessary polycentrism of theology and for his shift toward this mystical-prophetic theology (see *On Naming the Present: God, Hermeneutics, and Church* [hereafter *ONP*] [Maryknoll, N.Y.: Orbis Books, 1994], xi–xii). It is hardly surprising that Rahner was one of the main cofounders of *Concilium* and that Tracy had served many years on its board of directors, together with both Gutiérrez and Metz (among others).

Two further aspects deserve special analysis in this respect. First, *Concilium* has been very instrumental in giving Tracy a different perspective from that of his academic environment at the University of Chicago. This new perspective has been Catholic in the two senses of the word: (*a*) mainly related to Catholic theology although with a theologically intrinsic ecumenical dimension; (*b* related to a church with a catholic, universal, pluriregional outlook and presence. A second aspect of *Concilium*'s influence on Tracy concerns the pastoral dimension of the periodical. As Tracy himself acknowledges in the text quoted above, *Concilium* was always, from its very inception, something more than a theological review. Born in the aftermath of Vatican II, it was a pastoral project on three different accounts. First, as a theological enterprise, the main aim was not only to improve theological research but also to promote a pastorally guided theology, that is to say, a theology that could present in a reasonable, meaningful, and relevant way the Christian message, bearing in mind the different challenges pointed out by Vatican II and the new tasks of the Catholic Church in the world following the guidelines of the council. Second, *Concilium* was also pastoral because it wanted to contribute to the task of the permanent conversion and reform of the Catholic Church, so that this church could really be the community that could bear witness to the Lord and to the Kingdom of God. Finally, *Concilium* was also a pastoral project because it wanted theologically to join the struggle for bringing about in the world the values of that kingdom, namely, the values of justice, peace, and love.

9. At least at this stage of Tracy's work on naming God, in which the work itself is obviously fragmented and inconclusive. However, the inadequacy and difficulty of method, order, balance, and system is not simply a question of work-stage. Rather, it stems from the very basis of Tracy's decentered, disruptive theological approach in his later work.

10. See *LV,* 90–95.

11. *GGG,* 193 (my trans.).

12. See ibid., 190–92.

13. Ibid., 192–94.

14. Metz quotes Paul's dialectical texts very often. In fact, Paul is Metz's most quoted biblical author although he does not like what he sees as Paul's too individualistic understanding of redemption and salvation (see, for instance, Johann Baptist Metz, *Jenseits bürgerlicher Religion: Reden über die Zukunft des Christentums* [Munich: Kaiser, Matthias-Grünewald, 1980], English translation, *The Emergent Church: The Future of Christianity in a Postbourgeois World* [New York: Crossroad, 1987], 81).

15. John's gospel is the gospel Metz explicitly quotes most often.

16. Paradoxically, Mark's gospel is the gospel Metz most seldom explicitly quotes, although its latent presence, especially as regards the passion narrative and the apocalyptic-interruptive dimension, is pervasive throughout his work.

17. Consider, for instance, his use of scriptures in *Teología de la liberación: Perspectivas* (hereafter *TL*) (Lima: Centro de Estudios y Publicaciones, 1971), English translation, *A Theology of Liberation* (Maryknoll, N.Y.: Orbis Books, 1973). This book contains 230 quotations from 26 books of the Old Testament and 175 quotations from 19 books of the New Testament.

18. Apart from the massive use of the scriptures in his theological works, a clear

example of how Gutiérrez approaches and reads the Bible is his work, *Compartir la palabra: A lo largo del Año Litúrgico* (Lima: Instituto Bartolomé de Las Casas, Centro de Estudios y Publicaciones, 1995), a sermon-genre commentary on the Sunday and holy day readings of the three liturgical years.

19. This way of putting Gutiérrez's theological method is related to his own definition of theology as "a critical reflection on Christian praxis in the light of the Word."

20. See in this respect p. 26 of the preface to his work, *El Dios de la vida* (hereafter *DV*) (Lima: Instituto Bartolomé de Las Casas, Centro de Estudios y Publicaciones, 1989), 26, English translation, *The God of Life* (Maryknoll, N.Y.: Orbis Books, 1991).

21. *DV*, 21–23.

22. Ibid., 22–23.

23. Concreteness of experience and of interests coming from this experience is central to Gutiérrez's understanding of establishing a dialogue with the biblical texts. Faith, experience, hope, and history are the leading elements in the dialogue. However, there is another important component ruling the dialogue, namely, the authoritative reading of the tradition of the church. In this respect, Gutiérrez writes that revelation must be understood as "la Escritura que vive en la Tradición" (scripture alive in tradition) (see *LV*, 122). Therefore, reading the Bible that lives in the church is always for Gutiérrez an act of the church.

24. See *DV*, 23–24.

25. Also for Gutiérrez this is the all-encompassing way of naming God that must be proclaimed and understood in the midst of injustice and of the suffering of the innocent (see ibid., 29).

26. In order to understand his evolution after *The Analogical Imagination*, see David Tracy, "On Reading the Scriptures Theologically," in Bruce D. Marshall, ed., *Theology and Dialogue: Essays in Conversation with George Lindbeck* (Notre Dame, Ind.: University of Notre Dame Press, 1990), where he acknowledges the importance of Frei's work on narrative for his own development.

27. See *ONP*, 121, where he insists on the importance of that common Christian confession as regards the foundational status of the Bible in relation to the apostolic faith.

28. See *ONP*, 121. Tracy insists on both the distinction and the connection between event as revelatory and text as authoritative, in order to avoid both the pitfall of fundamentalism and the danger of losing the authoritative control of faith by the text. However, Tracy makes it clear that Christianity is not a religion centered around a book but around the revelatory-salvific Christ event.

29. Tracy expresses it by saying that Catholics "understand God foundationally in and through Scripture-in-tradition." He argues that such an approach is different from both the older Roman Catholic "Scripture and tradition" and the Reformation's "Scripture alone" (see David Tracy, "Approaching the Christian Understanding of God," in Francis Schüssler Fiorenza and John Galvin, eds., *Systematic Theology: Roman Catholic Perspectives* [Minneapolis: Augsburg Fortress, 1991], 135).

30. See *ONP*, 123–25; "On Reading the Scriptures," 61n.24.

31. For a discussion of Tracy's position as regards the "quest for the historical

Jesus," and, more generally, concerning the use of critical methods, see *The Analogical Imagination: Christian Theology and the Culture of Pluralism* (hereafter *AI*) (New York: Crossroad, 1981), 233–41. Tracy's position is clear: "The relevant Jesus for theology is the actual Jesus in the event of Jesus Christ—the Jesus remembered by the tradition and community as re-presentative of God's own presence among us and as mediated to individuals and community in all the classic words, sacraments, and actions expressing the Christ event in the present community, in conformity with the original apostolic witness" (239).

32. See Tracy, "On Reading the Scriptures," 39–40.

33. This does not mean that Tracy enjoys sheer plurality concerning the biblical rendering of Jesus the Christ. This plurality of biblical readings is legitimate because it concurs with the common confession and the common narrative (ibid., 46, where he summarizes his position, stating that "the common Christian confession and, more fully, the 'plain sense' of the passion narrative should define but should not confine the possible range of Christian construals of the common narrative and confession").

34. Ibid., 44–46.

35. See, for instance, Tracy's "Evil, Suffering, and Hope: The Search for New Forms of Contemporary Theodicy" (unpublished manuscript, 1995) and "On Reading the Scriptures," 51–57, where he discusses the need for the full range of possibilities offered by the tensional mystical-prophetic readings of the scriptures with the passion narratives at their center.

36. Tracy's distinction between the incomprehensible and the hidden God can be helpful here to understand what is meant by "negative" theology. Although Tracy has also become increasingly aware of the hiddenness of God, that hiddenness is Metz's and Gutiérrez's entry into the mystery of God. In this respect, their negative theology goes beyond Pseudo-Dionysius's *via remotionis,* which refers mainly to the incomprehensibility of God, later analyzed and assumed by Aquinas as *via negationis.* Metz and Gutiérrez take another "negative" route, namely, God's hiddenness, that, as in Luther, also comes to assert the impossibility of knowing what God is (see Tracy, "Tenderness and Violence of God").

37. Referring to how history is understood in these theologies, Tracy writes: "For history here as the locus of God's actions will mean neither what will now read as the homogeneous and empty evolutionary time of liberal and modern theologies of historical consciousness, nor the historicity of the solitary individual of existentialist and transcendental theologies. Rather history will now be seen as the focus of God's self-disclosure in the survival, struggle, and conflict of oppressed and forgotten people, living and dead: in otherness, difference, marginality" (ibid.).

38. Metz insists that his theology has a corrective character. In that sense, he does not claim that Rahner is ultimately wrong in his theological assertion of the definitive character of God's gracious self-communication. The problem is rather Rahner's insensitivity to the interruptions in history. More concretely, Metz cannot understand how Rahner's theology would have been equally formulated had the two world wars and the horror of the Holocaust not happened. Therefore, his insistence on making theology responsive to the horrors of history, abandoning its too strong protological approach.

39. See Karl Rahner, *Foundations of Christian Faith: An Introduction to the*

Idea of Christianity (New York: Crossroad, 1987), 102, where Rahner, following his transcendental reasoning, states that every "no" to God "always derives the life which it has from a 'yes' because the 'no' always becomes intelligible only in the light of the 'yes,' and not vice versa." However, concerning the actual possibility of this contradictory "no" happening radically, he concludes that "We shall have to allow this possibility to exist as the 'mystery of evil.' "

40. Ibid., 108–12.

41. In ibid., 91–93, Rahner takes a rather sociological-phenomenological approach and comes to the conclusion that "a person today" does not experience the radicalness of evil and does not have an acute sense of guilt. However, he admits the existence of radical evil, although this evil does not pose any threat to God's abiding sovereignty (ibid., 105–6). In other words, always reasoning transcendentally, nothing can represent, in Metz's terms, a radical challenge, an experience of "nonidentity," vis-à-vis God's abiding presence. At the same time, however, Rahner cannot be discounted as a naive optimist. He knows very well, like Benjamin, that every historical act is a radically ambiguous act (ibid., 109).

42. Metz is the most sensitive theologian in this respect. In relation to Rahner, the main problem is not that the latter has a liberal, sanguine understanding of both history and theology. True, Rahner does not escape an evolutionary-progressive view of history within which he tries to reinterpret the Jesus Christ event (see the section "Christology within an Evolutionary View of the World," in *Foundations*, 178–203). However, in no way does he accept the rosy interpretation of history that ignores and suppresses the existence of suffering, ambiguity, and evil. The problem, as already pointed out several times in the preceding pages, is rather that his transcendental analysis voids the theological import of the scandal of suffering and evil because, as Metz says, the transcendental solution is "always-already" present, untouched, and therefore necessarily unchallenged, by the realities of history.

43. In order to understand this as the *Grundimpuls* (fundamental impulse) of Metz's theological enterprise, it is interesting to notice Metz's own account of his tragic and life-lasting war experience in his early youth. He was only sixteen when he, together with his classmates and other young people, was drafted into Hitler's army toward the end of World War II. One evening, he was dispatched with a message to the battalion headquarters. At his return to his company next morning he found all its members dead. He remembers running away with a soundless shriek having taken hold of him. That day, all his childhood dreams and representations of reality were wounded for good, leaving him with a profoundly disquieting angst that has never abandoned him thereafter. Metz writes that he did not decide to go to the analyst to come to terms with this trauma but to live with it in the light of his own faith; to pray to God and to talk about God on the basis of this experience. In this sense, he interprets this experience as a grounding experience concerning his own view of history, of religion, of God, and, therefore, as an experience that has marked his entire theology (see his contribution to Ekkehard Schuster and Reinhold Boschert-Kimming, *Trotzdem Hoffen: Mit Johann Baptist Metz und Elie Wiesel im Gespräch* [Mainz: Matthias-Grünewald, 1993], 49–50, where referring to the lasting importance of that experience, he writes that "up to this day I do not remember but a soundless scream, in which probably all my childhood dreams and what one calls

'child-trust' were destroyed" and that "I have not gone later to the psychologist with this experience, but rather to church; not in order to find a solution for these experiences and memories, but to believe in God and to talk to God with them").

44. He speaks from "God-talk in the *conversio ad passionem*" (see Johann Baptist Metz, "Wie ich mich geändert habe," in Jürgen Moltmann, ed., *Wie ich mich geändert habe* [Gütersloh: Chr. Kaiser/Gütersloher Verlagshaus, 1997], 42).

45. Schuster and Boschert-Kimming, *Trotzdem Hoffen*, 29–30.

46. In this respect, Metz especially criticizes Pannenberg's *universalgeschichtliche Hermeneutik* (universal-historical hermeneutics) and also Moltmann's interpreting the current situation of Christianity on the basis of the modern history of freedom revolution (see *GGG*, 52 and 139).

47. This interpretation of history and its theological relevance is a permanent trait of Gutiérrez's theology that runs throughout his entire work. However, the work in which he has analyzed this issue most deeply historically, philosophically, and theologically is *En busca de los pobres de Jesucristo* (hereafter *BP*) (Lima: Instituto Bartolomé de Las Casas, Centro de Estudios y Publicaciones, 1992), English translation, *Las Casas: In Search of the Poor of Jesus Christ* (Maryknoll, N.Y.: Orbis Books, 1993). It is misleading to see this work as mainly historical, although it is doubtless part of Gutiérrez's attempt to reread history from the "underside of history." Apart from its undeniable historical rigor, this book on Las Casas condenses all the different strands of Gutiérrez's theology under the historical mantle. The work can be seen as a representation of the vast drama of history, with the different historical actors and sufferers, philosophers and learned, prophets and mercenaries, taking their place on the stage to play out what seems to be the unavoidable outcome of an unavoidable conflict in which the weak are finally dispossessed of their rights, oppressed, and displaced to the margins of a society that condemns them to the category of "nonpersons." On this vast stage, Gutiérrez presents the different strategies of power; the ambiguous role of the official church; the role of the prophets, martyrs, and saints in the church, true bearers of an always threatened but living hope; and, finally, how God's paradoxical almightiness and love are manifested in the radical powerlessness of the suffering poor.

It would be totally wrong to interpret the book as a pessimistic and resigned way of looking at human history from a religious point of view that would finally accept injustice and death as unavoidable while just trying to console and preach resignation to the victims. To begin with, one of the things that Gutiérrez appreciates most in Las Casas is his social analysis, that is to say, his going beyond the recognition of the situation of oppression, poverty, and death to the analysis of the causes of such a situation. Second, Gutiérrez highly values Las Casas's civil struggle for the rights of the "Indians." In this sense, Las Casas's efforts are not limited to the sphere of the church but are mostly aimed at the civil realm in which the decisions are made that bring death to the natives. Finally, Gutiérrez also likes Las Casas's behavior in relation to the church. On the one hand, the church must be solidly aligned with "the poor of Jesus Christ." On the other hand, the church must assume the political consequences of such an option and do everything it can to do away with the final causes of oppression and death.

Read in this way, the work presents itself as paradigmatic. Gutiérrez insists from the very beginning of the book that he does not want to make of Las Casas a forerunner of liberation theology. However, his constant shifting between Las Casas's time, situation, and challenges and the current situation and challenges of Latin America and of the Latin American church, thus establishing a parallelism between the two, reinforces the paradigmatic character of the book.

48. See *TL*, 86–87.

49. Ibid., 90.

50. Ibid., 90, 101.

51. See Gustavo Gutiérrez, *Hablar de Dios desde el sufrimiento del inocente: Una reflexión sobre el libro de Job* (hereafter *HD*) (Lima: Centro de Estudios y Publicaciones, 1986), 64, English translation, *On Job: God-Talk and the Suffering of the Innocent* (Maryknoll, N.Y.: Orbis Books, 1987). Gutiérrez also elaborates on this idea, with more explicitly ecological considerations, in his book *El Dios de la vida* (see *DV*, 165–66, where he insists on the need for paying more attention to the ecological concerns from the perspective of the poor).

52. Whereas *HD*'s second part is entirely devoted to the ethical-prophetic dimension, the third and final part of this work focuses on the centrality of the mystical-contemplative dimension, "beyond justice," concerning the way human beings must relate to God (see esp. *HD*, 192–202, and also *DV*, 294–308).

53. This does not imply that Tracy is not interested in "the American experiment" any longer. The point is rather that he reads this experiment in a different, more dialectical way and that he brings new disquieting and interruptive resources to the task of interpreting and renewing it.

54. This, of course, refers basically to Tracy's thought at the time of *Blessed Rage for Order: The New Pluralism in Theology* (hereafter *BRO*) (New York: Seabury, 1975), 73–79.

55. Explaining his change of perspective, Tracy wrote already in 1981 that "the profound negativities of human existence—personal, societal, and historical—seem so pervasive in this age that any route to fundamental trust must be far more circuitous, tentative, and even potholed than I had once hoped." Accordingly, "that trust has now become subtly transformed by being arrived at only through a route highlighting the negative at every moment of the theological journey." In relation to his theological emphasis on analogy, he wrote: "The classic language of analogy (the language of somehow ordered relationships) remains my real theological home. Yet now the analogies emerge more tentatively through (not in spite of) the various languages of radical negative dialectics" (see "Defending the Public Character of Theology," in James M. Wall, ed., *Theologians in Transition* [New York: Crossroad, 1981], 121–22).

56. On Tracy's critique of this linear and rather problem-free understanding of history of salvation, see *ONP*, 52–53, where he writes that "Even earlier biblical theologies of 'the God who acts in history' (von Rad, Wright) are no longer adequate to disclose the disturbing and interruptive hiddenness of the God who does act in history."

57. Ibid., 49–53.

58. See *GGG*, 79.

59. See, in this respect, Metz's later insistence on *Karsamstagschristologie* in

"Gotteskrise: Versuch zur 'geistigen Situation der Zeit,'" in Johann Baptist Metz et al., *Diagnosen zur Zeit* (Düsseldorf: Patmos, 1994) 80, where he writes that "the Easter Sunday–Christology has pervaded too much of our prayer with a vanquisher-language and has taken away prayer's capacity to be sensitive to catastrophe. We need a sort of Holy Saturday–language, a Holy Saturday–Christology, a Christology of weak categories, a Christology whose Logos can still be frightened and change under this fear." Once again, Metz insists on the necessity of correcting a Christology that is too much formulated on the basis of the triumphal Easter and is incapable of showing the intrinsic relation between the experience of Easter and the tragic reality of the "empty" time of Holy Saturday, the time in which death and silence reign.

60. This is what Metz calls the *Ichwerden an den Anderen* as expression of a solidarity, a Christian love of the neighbor as the stranger, the other, rather than the one at hand (see Johann Baptist Metz and Tiemo Reiner Peters, *Gottespassion: Zur Ordensexistenz heute* [Freiburg im Breisgau: Herder, 1991] 40, where Metz discusses his anthropology of the self as firmly anchored in the reality of the others).

61. Salvation therefore is both proleptic and "negative" in Adorno's sense. It is this innerly tensional aspect of negative dialectics that interests Metz most.

62. See *TL*, 281.

63. This is something that clearly separates Gutiérrez's theology from Metz's. Both seek to enhance the political implications and the transformative character of Christianity. However, whereas Metz adopts a "negative" perspective, Gutiérrez's approach is rather "positive." For Metz, the central category is the memory of suffering understood as a salvific category on the basis of God's eschatological salvation. This memory of suffering, best represented by the *memoria passionis, mortis et resurrectionis Jesu Christi*, interrupts history continually and changes it radically in view of the eschatological horizon of salvation. In other words, salvation acts in history as an ongoing "negative" to every historical achievement on the basis of the radically interruptive eschatological salvation. For Gutiérrez, the historical program is far less "negative," grounded as it is in the liberating salvation in history, to be sure within the dialectical paradigm already–not-yet, which occurred in Jesus Christ the liberator. In this respect, Gutiérrez's theology has a far more "identical" understanding of salvation than Metz's notion of salvation based on his radical experiences of "nonidentity."

64. Once again, the differences with Metz are striking. In Gutiérrez's section on *Cristo liberador* (see *TL*, 281–87), human sin plays the central role in understanding the presence of evil in history. Therefore, Christ's redemption, the liberation from sin, is interpreted as the foundation of integral, full liberation in all senses. Metz, however, thinks that the reduction of the *Theodizeefrage* to the question of sin and its soteriological solution through Christ's redemption are inadequate. For him, there remains always an *Unversöhnheit* in relation to God concerning the presence of evil and suffering in the world (see Metz, in Schuster and Boschert-Kimming, *Trotzdem Hoffen*, 52–55, where he asks "What is the status of the question of theodicy? Is it simply solved by the Christian doctrine of redemption? I have still questions to address to God, for which I have a language but no answer").

The differences with Tracy's Christology are also important. Tracy acknowledges the importance of soteriology for Christology, but soteriology is not the focal point of his Christology. Rather, within his understanding of Christian salvation on the basis of the whole system of symbols—creation, Messiah, Christology, ecclesiology, eschatology—he considers Christology necessary to understand soteriology correctly (see "The Christian Understanding of Salvation-Liberation," *Face to Face* 14 (spring 1988): 36). Jesus Christ is the decisive manifestation of the God who saves. Therefore, Christology becomes crucial to know who is this God who saves. Tracy, however, also acknowledges both the appropriateness and the necessity of using the Jesus Christ–Liberator model for contemporary theology (ibid., 40).

65. See, in this respect, *DV,* 170–83.

66. This latter view of Christ is predominant in Gustavo Gutiérrez, *En busca de los pobres de Jesucristo* (hereafter *BPJ*) (Lima: Instituto Bartolomé de Las Casas, Centro de Estudios y Publicaciones, 1992), English translation, *Las Casas: In Search of the Poor of Jesus Christ* (Maryknoll, N.Y.: Orbis Books, 1993), and is theologically worked out in *HD.*

67. It is important to insist on this point in order to avoid simplifications. The new approach is in no way a denial of the intrahistorical-ethical dimension of Christ's salvation. The point is rather that this transformative dimension must be understood within the bigger picture of a God who, although totally close to human beings in Jesus Christ, is always beyond the logic and the limits of human action and plans.

68. After discussing the existential meaningfulness of christological language, Tracy concludes that "The heart of Christian self-understanding, therefore, remains radically christocentric" (see *BRO,* 221).

69. *ONP,* 32–33.

70. On the question of orthodoxy and orthopraxis, see *GGG,* 122–28. The interesting point in this analysis is Metz's original understanding of orthodoxia and dogmatic tradition in relation not to the rational notion of truth but to their original content as remembrance of the historical ways in which God had acted and come to be known by creatures. This practical memory must be both recovered and acted out as the only way to make the dogma meaningful.

71. See, in this respect, Metz, *Jenseits bürgerlicher Religion,* 115–18.

72. Ibid., 118–25.

73. This is a constant in Gutiérrez from his *Líneas pastorales de la iglesia en América Latina* (Lima: Centro de Estudios y Publicaciones, 1970) to this day. In this respect, see Gustavo Gutiérrez, "Die Theologie: Eine kirchliche Aufgabe," *Münchener Theologische Zeitschrift* 2 (1996): 163, where he writes that "the theological work springs from the center of the church community and must be practiced in it" (my trans.). See also Gustavo Gutiérrez, "The Task of Theology and Ecclesial Experience," *Concilium* 176 (1984), an interesting article in which Gutiérrez analyzes his personal development and the irruption of the experience of the poor in his life and in his theology. Although Gutiérrez's theology stems from the Latin American church, its contribution is in many respects truly catholic in that it presents its claims to the entire church. At the same time, it would be a mistake to think, using Tracy's terms, that this theology is addressed only to the public of the church. On the basis of both its nature and intention, this theology is also addressed to the academy and to society at large.

74. Gutiérrez follows here not only Vatican II but also the universal character of

Christian salvation as understood in Rahner's theology of universal grace. In other words, Gutiérrez is fighting here the preconciliar principle *nulla salus extra ecclesiam* (see *TL,* 370–74).

75. This is to say, although the church is grounded in the Lord and always under the judgment of the word, Gutiérrez insists that its relation with the world must be so close that "the church must turn to the world, where Christ and the Spirit are present and active; it must allow itself to be inhabited and evangelized by the world" (*TL,* 378). This way of understanding the relation world-church is the expression of the correlational character of the theology of Vatican II and of Gutiérrez.

76. See, in this respect, *TL,* 379.

77. This is a crucial point in Gutiérrez. Two different dimensions of the church are intertwined here: the hierarchical and the spiritual. In principle the church is one and must be understood as "the people of God" guided and inhabited by the Spirit. This means that the people itself, the community of believers, must be the central element in any theoretical and practical understanding of the church. The way the hierarchy fulfills its task must be guided by this principle. This is the kind of church that is expressed by the grassroots communities in Latin America. Within this understanding of the church, the mission of the hierarchy is not to run the church as organization in a top-down way. Rather, this mission consists in accompanying the long journey of the people of God in history, favoring the inner life and dynamism of this community, and guiding it, in the light of the word and through the practice of discipleship, in its pursuit of liberation (see, in this respect, Gutiérrez's section on the bishops in *TL,* 192–94).

78. Ibid., 181.

79. See, in this respect, among other works, David Tracy and Stephen Happel, *A Catholic Vision* (Philadelphia: Fortress, 1984). Tracy explores the double dimension, the institutional and the communitarian, of the church as bearer of shared meanings within an ongoing tradition in *AI,* 21–22.

80. It must be noticed that Tracy himself, being of Irish descent, bears the marks of this unique American-Catholic experience.

81. See in this sense his works *A Catholic Vision* and the last part *AI.* This "Catholic" approach is an important particular trait of Tracy's enterprise vis-à-vis the more general "Christian" approach of both Gutiérrez and Metz in which the reflection upon the specific character and identity of the "Catholic" does not come to the fore.

82. It must be repeated once again that Tracy's theology can only be understood as an original result of a double, and apparently "counterintuitive," movement: an intensification of particularity (Catholic in his case) and a defense of the public character of this particularity.

83. *AI,* 244n.17, where Tracy explains how this ecumenical perspective is relevant for each of the particular traditions within Christianity.

84. See ibid., 23, 43n.90, 422, and, especially, 442n.29, where he writes that "The ecclesial mediation, in sum, is defined by the eschatological event it mediates and is thereby itself an always-already, not-yet sign of that reality as always-already, not-yet present *in the world.*"

85. Here there is a correspondence with Gutiérrez's notion of reading of the Bible

as an ongoing actualization of a dialogue between the experience, story, faith, and history of the apostolic community and the experience, story, faith, and history of the church community that reads the apostolic writings. The mediating character of the church must always be both under the judgment of the eschatological reality of the Kingdom of God and under the correcting power of the hermeneutics of suspicion in order to unmask and correct the systemic distortions embedded in any tradition. Moreover, each particular Christian tradition, whether Orthodox, Protestant, or Catholic, must open itself to the disclosive correcting power of the other traditions in order to remain faithful to the Christ event (see *AI*, 235–37, 251–53, 320–25, 328–29, 422–25, and David Tracy, *Plurality and Ambiguity: Hermeneutics, Religion, Hope* [hereafter *PA*] [San Francisco: Harper and Row, 1987], 66–81).

86. See *AI*, 390–98, 422–25; *PA*, 113–14.

87. *GGG*, 157 (my trans.). In interpreting Metz's apocalyptic theses, the corrective character of his theology must be taken into account. Metz's radical affirmations must be dialectically understood (see in this respect his introductory remarks to the theses in *GGG*, 149).

88. Johann Baptist Metz, "Im Eingedenken fremden Leids: Zu einer Basiskategorie christlicher Gottesrede," in Johann Baptist Metz, Johann Reitkerstorfer, and Jürgen Werbick, *Gottesrede* (Münster: LIT, 1996), where he writes: "The Christian time-message is based on the structuring of time through that memory and spiritual remembrance in which the name of God is narrated as eschatological name and as permanent end of time" (4 [my trans.]).

89. Schuster and Boschert-Kimming, *Trotzdem Hoffen*, 51, 53.

90. *GGG*, 71.

91. Ibid., 109–14.

92. For Gutiérrez's early assessment of political theology, see *TL*, 332–42. However, this assessment only takes into account Metz's early work on political theology. Since then, the positions of both Metz and Gutiérrez have evolved in important ways, and the former mutual criticism and distance have disappeared. This, of course, does not mean that there are no differences between the two theologies.

93. See in this respect Gustavo Gutiérrez, *Entre las calandrias: Un ensayo sobre José María Arguedas* (hereafter *EC*) (Lima: Instituto Bartolomé de Las Casas–Rimac, Centro de Estudios y Publicaciones, 1990), esp. 55–61.

94. At the beginning of the 1980s liberation theology changed toward a more positive approach to popular religiosity. However, Gutiérrez was already in 1971 hinting at a more positive assessment of the nature and values embedded in popular forms of religion (*TL*, 145–46, 146n.20).

95. See, in this respect, David Tracy, "A Response to Fr. Metz," in William J. Kelly, S.J., ed., *Theology and Discovery: Essays in Honor of Karl Rahner, S.J.* (Milwaukee: Marquette University Press, 1980), 184–87. In this work, Tracy insists on the necessity of taking into account the different, tensional aspects of the gospel narratives, both the aspects that underline the "already" and those that put the stress on the "not-yet." Tracy interprets Metz's and Rahner's positions as expressions of the "unity-in-difference" present in every analogy. This interpretation of the differences between the two in analogical terms has somehow been altered by Tracy's later insistence on interruption.

96. See Tracy, "Evil, Suffering, and Hope."

97. In the case of Gutiérrez, this criticism is also made from the Latin American point of view and refers mainly to the Eurocentric character of modernity that ignores other cultures, especially the colonized and dependent ones. One consequence of this Eurocentric and triumphalistic view of history is the failed theory of "development" concerning the future of the "underdeveloped" countries.

98. Metz, *Gottespassion*, 17.

99. In this sense, he also criticizes those theologies that, like Moltmann's, take into account the reality of suffering and develop a theology of the cross but try to find an intratrinitarian way of talking about God in relation to that experience of suffering.

100. Metz, *Gottespassion*, 31 (my trans.).

101. Metz, "Gotteskrise" (my trans.). Metz fully coincides with Derrida's opinion that theology must start with prayer, when he writes: " 'Begin with prayer,' requires Jacques Derrida in his investigation on negative theology. I concur" (ibid. [my trans.]). This is one of the instances where Metz's position concerning postmodern thought shows its tensional character. On the one hand, he opposes Derrida's insistence on dissemination, but, on the other hand, he fully coincides with Derrida's postmodern insistence on changing the center of theology, founding it not on argumentative reason but on prayer.

102. See, in this respect, Metz, *Landschaft aus Schreien: Zur Dramatik der Theodizeefrage* (Mainz: Matthias-Grünewald, 1995), where he writes, "Which kind of compassive love would be the one not threatened by the danger of radical futility?" (93 [my trans.]).

103. Metz, *Gottespassion*, 28–29 (my trans.). Vattimo's formulation of postmodernity as an age of *pensiero debole* resounds powerfully in Metz's "weak" categories to depict God, despite Metz's strong critique of postmodernity. However, the difference between the two lies in the fact that Metz's notion of weakness is strictly theological.

104. Metz is convinced that the God of postmodernity is a mere myth, a consoling, compensatory, psychological-aesthetic myth void of the eschatological, restless, uneasy dimension that characterizes the Christian God. Therefore, Metz thinks that postmodernity welcomes a mythological-compensatory religion but flatly opposes the God of Abraham, Isaac, Jacob, and Jesus (see *Gottespassion*, 24).

105. Ibid., 27 (my trans.).

106. *HD*, 18 (my trans.).

107. See in this respect Gutiérrez's own view concerning these differences between his approach and Metz's, in *HD*, 222–23. This is in no way a denial either of the importance of actual suffering in history in the case of Metz or of the relevance of the historical memory of suffering in Gutiérrez. Gutiérrez stresses through and through the importance of memory as a capacity for rebellion and liberating struggle (see, for instance, *EC*, 39, where he writes that "the memory of the poor is subversive because it is a factor of historical identity. That is why the powerful want to destroy it. A people without memory is a weak people" [my trans.]). Metz, in turn, seeks a universal and actual solidarity that expresses itself in concrete actions in favor of justice, recognition of the other, and peace. The question here highlighted is rather related to

the historical-theological approach of each author. For Metz, only an eschatological salvation that includes the dead and forgotten of history can be a foundation for hope. For Gutiérrez, only a radical discipleship in favor of the historical poor can do the truth of the Christian promise and message of salvation.

108. Actually, Gutiérrez goes beyond the realm of theology and claims that, also in the domain of human sciences, true knowledge is only possible when reason and understanding are based on practical and concrete experience (see, in this respect, Gutiérrez's comparative assessment of the way of reasoning of Vitoria, the brilliant and humanist but uncommitted and distant intellectual, and Las Casas, the intellectual whose reasoning is based on the knowledge of reality and the commitment to the poor, concerning the question of the nature and rights of the Indians, in *BPJ*, 459–96, and, esp. 490–91). In this respect, there are important similarities between Gutiérrez and Metz concerning their critique of autonomous reason and their epistemology. For both of them, reason must have a practical foundation. In the case of Metz, this practical foundation must be anamnestic. A reason without memory produces monsters, becoming frightening and destructive. For Gutiérrez, this practical foundation is experience, direct knowledge of reality, and, most important, commitment to the liberation of the oppressed.

109. This is Arguedas's way both to name the community of the poor in their search for justice and liberation and to insist that only on the basis of solidarity and fraternity, and not through individualism, can a just and human society be built (see *EC*, 12–21). The two *calandrias* (calandra larks) are symbols for alienating consolation and for liberation (see *EC*, 5–7, 58–61). Both Gutiérrez and Metz affirm that the Christian God does not console, does not put to rest the disturbing experience of the contradictions and suffering encountered in history. Quite the opposite, the Christian God is a source of resistance and liberation. Although Gutiérrez believes that there can be a liberation that brings consolation, the consoling God, understood as a symbol of resignation, is not the Christian God but an idol or a myth. Unlike Metz, who constantly uses the term "myth," Gutiérrez uses the term "idol" to differentiate the true God from the false one. In fact, Gutiérrez, very close to a culture and a religiosity in which myths play an important role, has a far more positive understanding of myths than Metz. Far from being an instrument of alienation, a myth can liberate powerful resources to oppose and resist the project of modernity imposed upon the dependent countries of Latin America (see in this sense Gutiérrez's quote of Pedro Trigo concerning the role of myth in Arguedas, in *EC*, 14n.6; also *EC*, 29).

110. Ibid., 67–68 (my trans.).

111. Ibid., 66–75; *BPJ*, 587–615.

112. This is Gutiérrez's way of expressing what Metz calls an *empathischer Gott* understood with "weak categories."

113. Washington Delgado, referring to the dialectical, tensive character of Vallejo's poems, observes that "Vallejo's poetry bears a high tension" and that it "is a mimesis of human life in its contradictory and unstoppable dynamism." He also notices the relationship between Vallejo's poetry and Gutiérrez's theology and, even more generally, among the works of Mariátegui, Arguedas, Vallejo, and Gutiérrez. In this respect, he writes: "There is a copious flow of sympathy between César Vallejo's

poetry and Gustavo Gutiérrez's intellectual work. There is a copious flow of sympathy among the most important Peruvian writers of this century: César Vallejo, José Carlos Mariátegui, José María Arguedas, and, now, Gustavo Gutiérrez" (see Washington Delgado, "Discurso de orden," *Páginas* 114–15 [1992]: 156–57 [my trans.]).

114. Gutiérrez gives several examples of this parallelism between Job and Vallejo. In this respect, see *HD*, 47, 50–51, 143, 147, 191.

115. Metz constantly insists that religion, biblically understood, does not provide answers to the ultimate questions of meaning. The questions remain open, as a source of irritation, of creative uneasiness. God does not console. Also God has "open flanks." This Metzian insight is masterfully expressed in Vallejo's poem "Las ventanas se han estremecido...," where he dismisses theodicy as a vain attempt to appease human restlessness (see César Vallejo, *Obra poética completa* [Madrid: Alianza Editorial, 1982], 184–87).

116. Personal suffering and human suffering in general are the raw material of Vallejo's work. Gutiérrez analyzes very perceptively the role of suffering in Vallejo and its relation to life and to hope, beyond sadness and despair (see the interview with Gustavo Gutiérrez, "Vamos a hablar de Vallejo," *Páginas* 114–15 [April-June 1992]: esp. 117–19). On the question of limit-hope, of hope in "negative," in the midst of intense suffering, see Vallejo's poem, "Voy a hablar de la esperanza," in *Obra poética completa*, 187–88.

117. See the poems "Los heraldos negros," "Dios," "Espergesia," "La de a mil," and "Los dados eternos" in *Obra poética completa*, 59, 108, 114–15, 96, and 105, respectively. The poem "Los dados eternos" is perhaps one of the poems in which the Metzian *leiden an Gott* is most powerfully expressed. On the contrast between hope and intense suffering in Vallejo, see Américo Ferrari, "César Vallejo entre la angustia y la esperanza," in *Obra poética completa*.

118. See *Páginas* 114–15 (April-June 1992): 123, where, referring to Vallejo, he writes that there are people who "refer so powerfully to the roots of every human being that are universal" (my trans.); *HD*, 33, concerning the universality of Job's experience.

119. *HD*, 21. Innocent persons can suffer because of the injustice and the moral evil of other people. In this sense, the oppressed, the dispossessed, and the marginalized are examples of this kind of suffering. They have done nothing wrong to deserve it, and, in this sense, they are innocent. However, Job's suffering is neither the consequence of his immoral behavior nor has it been caused by the moral evil of his fellow human beings. In this sense, it is an "innocent" suffering on the two accounts. Job accuses God of being directly responsible of his suffering. His situation is the clearest biblical example of *leiden an Gott*. On the question of how Gutiérrez interprets the sense of "innocent suffering," see *HD*, 20–21. On the one hand, Gutiérrez accepts the distinction between "guilty evil" and "innocent evil." On the other hand, he insists that the responsibility of those who cause evil cannot be overlooked. It is clear that, for Gutiérrez, the key question is related rather to the "suffering of the innocent" than to the "innocent suffering." See, in this respect, ibid., 28, where Gutiérrez points out that the suffering of the innocent in Latin America is "most of all, the result of unjust social structures that favor the few" (my trans.).

120. Again, Gutiérrez's way does not deny the validity of Rahner's discovery. The point is rather that when confronted with the existence of real suffering in history, the discovery of God's gratuitousness-mystery can only take place through this experience of suffering. The experience of suffering belongs to the discovery of God and cannot be avoided or bypassed through the transcendental route.

121. *HD*, 90–123.

122. Ibid., 125–31.

123. Ibid., 151–202.

124. Tracy insists that postmodernity has made it clear that modernity has become just another tradition, thus ceasing to be *the* emancipatory project vis-à-vis "tradition." By so doing, postmodernity has become a liberating force as regards modernity's absolute claim to be the only way to enlightenment and emancipation (see "Theology and the Many Faces of Post-Modernity," *Theology Today* 51, no. 1 [April 1994], where Tracy writes that "Many moderns, with a kind of vestigial Enlightenment prejudice against the very category 'tradition,' find it hard, perhaps impossible, to believe that modernity itself can now be viewed as one more tradition. But so it is. And like all traditions, modernity is deeply ambiguous").

125. This could be Tracy's final understanding of tradition: an ongoing and ever-renewed way of interpreting and imagining reality based on a founding, stable yet open, and lasting "constitutive experience," itself endlessly reinterpreted through its own classics.

126. He comes here very close to both Gutiérrez and Metz in their increasingly becoming negative theologians. In this respect, Tracy's central route to negative theology is neither gratuitousness nor interruption nor *Gottesbildersverbot* (God-representation ban) but radical "otherness." In this way must be interpreted his insistence on speaking of God's love as excess and, following Marion, of "God without being." These are ways of expressing the unfathomableness of God. Besides, with his insistence on "fragments" as opposed to grand narratives, he also comes very close to Metz's "weak" categories of speaking about God.

127. This is to say, the God of resistance and hope, the God who interrupts in order to open new possibilities.

Select Bibliography

Karl Rahner

"Warum uns das Beten nottut." *Leuchtturm* 18 (1924/1925).

Worte ins Schweigen. Innsbruck: Felician Rauch, 1938.

Geist in Welt. Munich: Kösel, 1957. English translation, *Spirit in the World* (New York: Herder and Herder, 1968).

Lexikon für Theologie und Kirche. Edited with J. Höfer. Freiburg im Breisgau: Herder, 1957.

Theological Investigations. Vol. 1, *God, Christ, Mary, and Grace.* Baltimore: Helicon, 1961.

"Einführender Essay." In *Christliche Anthropozentrik: Über die Denkform des Thomas von Aquin,* by Johannes Baptist Metz. Munich: Kösel, 1962.

The Christian Commitment. New York: Sheed and Ward, 1963.

Hörer des Wortes: Zur Grundlegung einer Religionsphilosophie. Revised by Johannes Baptist Metz. Munich: Kösel, 1963. English translation, *Hearers of the Word* (New York: Herder and Herder, 1969).

"Allgemeine Grundlegung der Protologie und theologischen Anthropologie." In *Mysterium Salutis: Grundriss heilsgeschichtlicher Dogmatik,* edited by Johannes Feiner and Magnus Löhrer, 2:406–20. Einsiedeln: Benziger, 1965.

"Der dreifaltige Gott als transzendenter Urgrund der Heilsgeschichte." In *Mysterium Salutis: Grundriss heilsgeschichtlicher Dogmatik,* edited by Johannes Feiner and Magnus Löhrer, 2:317–401. Einsiedeln: Benziger, 1965.

The Church after the Council. New York: Herder and Herder, 1966.

"Das Zweite Vatikanische Konzil: Allgemeine Einleitung." In *Kleines Konzilskompendium: Sämtliche Texte des Zweiten Vatikanums,* edited by Karl Rahner and Herbert Vorgrimler. Freiburg im Breisgau: Herder, 1966.

Theological Investigations. Vol. 4, *More Recent Writings.* Baltimore: Helicon, 1966.

"Grace." In *Sacramentum Mundi,* edited by Karl Rahner et al. New York: Herder and Herder, 1969.

"Modernism." In *Sacramentum Mundi,* edited by Karl Rahner et al. New York: Herder and Herder, 1969.

"La nouvelle théologie." In *Sacramentum Mundi,* edited by Karl Rahner et al. New York: Herder and Herder, 1969.

Theological Investigations. Vol. 6, *Concerning Vatican II.* Baltimore: Helicon, 1969.

"Some Critical Thoughts on 'Functional Specialties in Theology.'" In *Foundations of Theology: Papers from the International Lonergan Congress 1970,* edited by Philip McShane. Dublin: Gill and Macmillan, 1971.

Theological Investigations. Vol. 10/2, *Writings of 1965–1967.* New York: Herder and Herder, 1973.

Theological Investigations. Vol. 11/1, *Confrontations.* New York: Seabury, 1974.

The Trinity. New York: Seabury, 1974.

Theological Investigations. Vol. 13, *Theology, Anthropology, Christology.* New York: Seabury, 1975.

Theological Investigations. Vol. 14, *Ecclesiology, Questions of the Church, the Church in the World.* New York: Seabury, 1976.

Meditations on Freedom and the Spirit. New York: Seabury, 1978.

Theological Investigations. Vol. 16, *Experience of the Spirit: Source of Theology.* New York: Seabury, 1979.

Theological Investigations. Vol. 18, *God and Revelation.* New York: Crossroad, 1980.

Theological Investigations. Vol. 20, *Concern for the Church.* New York: Crossroad, 1981.

Im Gespräch. Edited by Paul Imhof and Hubert Biallowons. Vol. 1, 1964–1977. Munich: Kösel, 1982.

Im Gespräch. Edited by Paul Imhof and Hubert Biallowons. Vol. 2, 1978–1982. Munich: Kösel, 1983.

I Remember. New York: Crossroad, 1985.

Politische Dimensionen des Christentums: Ausgewählte Texte zu Fragen der Zeit. Edited by Herbert Vorgrimler. Munich: Kösel, 1986.

Foundations of Christian Faith: An Introduction to the Idea of Christianity. New York: Crossroad, 1987.

"Towards a Fundamental Theological Interpretation of Vatican II." In *Vatican II: The Unfinished Agenda: A Look to the Future,* edited by Lucien Richard, Daniel Harrington, and John W. O'Malley. Mahwah, N.J.: Paulist, 1987.

Strukturwandel der Kirche als Chance und Aufgabe. Freiburg im Breisgau: Herder, 1989.

Sehnsucht nach dem Geheimnisvollen Gott: Profil, Bilde, Texte. Edited by Herbert Vorgrimler. Freiburg im Breisgau: Herder, 1990.

Theological Investigations. Vol. 22, *Humane Society and the Church of Tomorrow.* New York: Crossroad, 1991.

Johann Baptist Metz

"Heidegger und das Problem der Metaphysik." *Scholastik* 28 (1953).

Advent Gottes. Munich: Ars Sacra, 1959.

"Theologische und metaphysische Ordnung." *Zeitschrift für katholische Theologie* 83 (1961). English version, "The Theological World and the Metaphysical World," *Philosophy Today* 10, no. 4/4 (1966).

Armut im Geiste. Munich: Ars Sacra, 1962.

Christliche Anthropozentrik: Über die Denkform des Thomas von Aquin. Munich: Kösel, 1962.

"Konkupiszenz." In *Handbuch theologischer Grundbegriffe,* vol. 1, edited by Heinrich Fries. Munich: Kösel, 1962.

Preface to *Hearers of the Word,* by Karl Rahner. New York: Herder and Herder, 1963.

"Freiheit als philosophisch-theologisches Grenzproblem." In *Gott in Welt: Festgabe für Karl Rahner,* vol. 1, edited by Johannes Baptist Metz et al. Freiburg im Breisgau: Herder, 1964.

"Widmung und Würdigung: Karl Rahner, dem Sechzigjährigen." In *Gott in Welt: Festgabe für Karl Rahner,* vol. 1, edited by Johannes Baptist Metz et al. Freiburg im Breisgau: Herder, 1964.

"Der Mensch als Einheit von Leib und Seele." With Francis Peter Fiorenza. In *Mysterium Salutis: Grundriss Heilsgeschichtlicher Dogmatik,* vol. 2, edited by Johannes Feiner and Magnus Löhrer. Einsiedeln: Benziger, 1965.

"Gott vor uns: Statt eines theologischen Arguments." In *Ernst Bloch zu ehren: Beiträge zu seinem Werk,* edited by Siegfried Unseld. Frankfurt: Suhrkamp, 1965.

"Preface." *Concilium* 6, no. 1 (June 1965).

"Unbelief as a Theological Problem." *Concilium* 6, no. 1 (June 1965).

"Preface." *Concilium* 16 (1966).

"Verantwortung der Hoffnung: Vier Diskussionsthesen." *Stimmen der Zeit* 177, no. 6 (1966).

"The Controversy about the Future of Man: An Answer to Roger Garaudy." *Journal of Ecumenical Studies* 4, no. 2 (1967).

"Die Verantwortung der christlichen Gemeinde für die Plannung der Zukunft." In *Die neue Gemeinde,* edited by Adolf Exeler, Johann Baptist Metz, and Walter Dirks. Mainz: Matthias-Grünewald, 1967.

"The Church's Social Function in the Light of 'Political Theology.' " *Concilium* 6, no. 4 (1968).

"Foreword: An Essay on Karl Rahner." In *Spirit in the World,* by Karl Rahner. New York: Herder and Herder, 1968.

"Religion and Society in the Light of a Political Theology." *Harvard Theological Review* 61, no. 4 (1968).

Zur Theologie der Welt. Mainz: Matthias-Grünewald, 1968. English translation, *Theology of the World* (New York: Herder and Herder, 1969).

"Apologetics." In *Sacramentum Mundi,* edited by Karl Rahner et al. New York: Herder and Herder, 1969.

Can a Christian Be a Marxist?: A Dialog among a Marxist Philosopher and Two Christian Theologians. With Milan Machoveč and Karl Rahner. Chicago: Argus, 1969.

" 'Politische Theologie' in der Diskussion." In *Diskussion zur "politischen Theologie,"* edited by Helmut Peukert. Mainz: Matthias-Grünewald, 1969.

Befreiendes Gedächtnis Jesu Christi. Mainz: Matthias-Grünewald, 1970.

"Does Our Church Need a New Reformation? A Catholic Replay." *Concilium* 4, no. 6 (1970).

Kirche in Prozess der Aufklärung. With Jürgen Moltmann and Willi Oelmüller. Munich: Kaiser, 1970.

"The Future in the Memory of Suffering." *Concilium* 76 (1972).

"Zu einer interdisziplinär orientierten Theologie: Skizze des Fragestandes." In *Begegnung: Beiträge zu einer Hermeneutik des theologischen Gesprächs,* edited by Max Seckler et al. Graz: Styria, 1972.

"Erlösung und Emanzipation." *Stimmen der Zeit* 3 (1973).

Meditations on the Passion: Two Meditations on Mark 8:31–38. With Jürgen Moltmann. New York: Paulist, 1974.

"Iglesia y pueblo o el precio de la ortodoxia." In *Dios y la ciudad: Nuevos planteamientos en teología política,* by Karl Rahner et al. Madrid: Ediciones Cristiandad, 1975.

"Ermutigung zum Gebet." In *Ermutigung zum Gebet.* With Karl Rahner. Freiburg: Herder, 1977.

Glaube in Geschichte und Gesellschaft: Studien zu einer praktischen Fundamentaltheologie. Mainz: Matthias-Grünewald, 1977. English translation, *Faith in History and Society: Toward a Practical Fundamental Theology* (New York: Seabury, 1980).

Zeit der Orden? Zur Mystik und Politik der Nachfolge. Freiburg im Breisgau: Herder, 1977. English translation, *Followers of Christ: The Religious Life and the Church.* New York: Paulist, 1978.

Toward Vatican III: The Work That Needs to Be Done. Edited with David Tracy and Hans Küng. New York: Seabury, 1978.

"Ökumene nach Auschwitz—Zum Verhältnis von Christen und Juden in Deutschland." In *Gott nach Auschwitz: Dimensionen des Massenmords am jüdischen Volk,* by Eugen Kogon et al. Freiburg: Herder, 1979.

"An Identity Crisis in Christianity? Transcendental and Political Responses." In *Theology and Discovery: Essays in Honour of Karl Rahner, S.J.,* edited by William J. Kelly, S.J. Milwaukee: Marquette University Press, 1980.

Jenseits bürgerlicher Religion: Reden über die Zukunft des Christentums. Munich: Kaiser, 1980. English translation, *The Emergent Church: The Future of Christianity in a Postbourgeois World.* New York: Crossroad, 1987.

Unterbrechungen: Theologisch-politische Perspektiven und Profile. Gütersloh: Gütersloher Verlagshaus Gerd Mohn, 1981.

Den Glauben lernen und lehren: Dank an Karl Rahner. Munich: Kösel, 1984.

"Facing the Jews: Christian Theology after Auschwitz." *Concilium* 175 (1984).

"Facing a Torn World." *Concilium* 190 (1983).

"Unterwegs zu einer nachidealistischen Theologie." In *Entwürfe der Theologie,* edited by Johannes B. Bauer. Graz: Styria, 1985.

"Thesen zum theologischen Ort der Befreiungstheologie." In *Die Theologie der Befreiung: Hoffnung oder Gefahr für die Kirche?* edited by Johann Baptist Metz. Düsseldorf: Patmos, 1986.

"Communicating a Dangerous Memory." In *Communicating a Dangerous Memory: Soundings in Political Theology,* edited by Fred Lawrence. Atlanta: Scholars Press, 1987.

Zukunftsfähigkeit: Suchbewegungen im Christentum. With Franz-Xaver Kaufmann. Freiburg im Breisgau: Herder, 1987.

"Ein Dialog der Theologen: Rückblick auf einen Kongreß." In *Lateinamerika und Europa: Dialog der Theologen,* edited by Johann Baptist Metz and Peter Rottländer. Munich: Kaiser, 1988.

"Theologie gegen Mythologie: Kleine Apologie des biblischen Monotheismus." *Herder Korrespondenz* (April 1988).

"Wider die zweite Unmündigkeit: Zum Verhältnis von Aufklärung und Christentum." In *Die Zukunft der Aufklärung,* edited by Jörn Rüsen, Eberhard Lämmert, and Peter Glotz. Frankfurt am Main: Suhrkamp, 1988.

"Anamnetische Vernunft: Anmerkungen eines Theologen zur Krise der Geisteswissenschaften." In *Zwischenbetrachtungen: Im Prozeß der Aufklärung,* edited by Axel Honneth, Thomas McCarthy, and Claus Offe. Munich: Suhrkamp, 1989.

"Fehlt uns Karl Rahner?." In *Freiburger Akademiearbeiten 1979–1989,* edited by Dietmar Bader. Munich: Schnell and Steiner, 1989.

"Lateinamerika mit den Augen eines Theologen." *GI Prisma* 2 (1989).

"Theology in the New Paradigm: Political Theology." In *Paradigm Change in Theology: A Symposium for the Future,* edited by Hans Küng and David Tracy. New York: Crossroad, 1989.

"Unity and Diversity: Problems and Prospects for Inculturation." *Concilium* 204 (1989).

"An der Schwelle zum dritten Jahrtausend oder Wohin ist Gott?." Contribution to the Concilium International Theological Congress, Louvain, September 9–13, 1990.

"Das Konzil—'der Anfang eines Anfangs'?" *Orientierung* 22 (1990).

"Geist Europas—Geist des Christentums." Unpublished manuscript, 1990.

"Gott und Aufklärung." Unpublished manuscript, 1990.

"Theologie als Theodizee?" In *Theodizee—Gott vor Gericht?* edited by Willi Oelmüller. Munich: Wilhelm Fink, 1990.

"Theologie versus Polymythie oder Kleine Apologie des biblischen Monotheismus." In *Einheit und Vielheit: XIV Deutscher Kongreß für Philosophie,* edited by Odo Marquard. Hamburg: Felix Meiner, 1990.

Welches Christentum hat Zukunft? With Dorothee Sölle and Karl-Josef Kuschel. Stuttgart: Kreuz, 1990.

"Zur Rettung der Vernunft: Der Geist Europas und der Geist des Christentums." *Süddeutsche Zeitung* 27/28 (October 1990).

"Die Verantwortung der Theologie in der gegenwärtigen Krise der Geisteswissenschaften." In *Wissen als Verantwortung: Etische Konsequenzen des Erkennens,* edited by Hans-Peter Müller. Stuttgart: W. Kohlhammer, 1991.

"Ende der Zeit?" *Frankfurter Allgemeine Zeitung,* July 13, 1991.

Gottespassion: Zur Ordensexistenz heute. With Tiemo Reiner Peters. Freiburg im Breisgau: Herder, 1991.

"Kirche nach Auschwitz." In *Israel und Kirche Heute: Beiträge zum christlich-jüdischen Dialog,* edited by Marcel Marcus, Ekkehard W. Stegemann, and Erich Zenger. Freiburg im Breisgau: Herder, 1991.

"Religion, ja—Gott, nein." In *Gottespassion: Zur Ordensexistenz heute.* With Tiemo Reiner Peters. Freiburg im Breisgau: Herder, 1991.

"So viele Anlitze, so viele Fragen: Lateinamerika mit den Augen eines europäischen Theologen." In *Augen für die Anderen: Lateinamerika—eine theologische Erfahrung.* With Hans-Eckehard Bahr. Munich: Kindler, 1991.

"Viele Kulturen—Eine Gesellschaft? Die Verantwortung der Christen." Unpublished manuscript, 1991.

"Was ist mit der Gottesrede geschehen? Überlegungen zur Kirche in der Welt der Massenmedien." *Herder Korrespondenz* 9 (1991).

"Das Christentum und der europäische Geist." In *Europa imaginieren: Der europäische Binnenmarkt als kulturelle und wirtschaftliche Aufgabe,* edited by Peter Koslowski. Berlin: Springer, 1992.

"Die Rede von Gott angesichts der Leidensgeschichte der Welt." *Stimmen der Zeit* 117 (1992).

"Ende der Zeit?" *Universitas* 6 (1992).

"Gotteszeugenschaft in einer Welt der religionsfreundlichen Gottlosigkeit." *Ordensnachrichten* 2 (1992).

"Plädoyer für mehr Theodizeempfindlichkeit in der Theologie." In *Vorüber man nicht schweigen kann,* edited by Willi Oelmüller. Munich: Fink, 1992.

Preface to *Theologie der Befreiung,* by Gustavo Gutiérrez. New edition. Mainz: Matthias-Grünewald, 1992.

"Solidarische Freiheit: Krise und Auftrag des europäischen Geistes." *Concilium* 2 (1992).

"Vorwort zur 5. Auflage." In *Glaube in Geschichte und Gesellschaft: Studien zu einer praktischen Fundamentaltheologie.* 5th ed. Mainz: Matthias-Grünewald, 1992.

"Das Christentum und die Fremden: Perspektiven einer multikulturellen Religion." In *Schwierige Fremdheit: Über Integration und Ausgrenzung in Einwanderungs-ländern,* edited by Friedrich Balke et al. Frankfurt: Fischer Taschenbuch, 1993.

"Die Dritte Welt und Europa: Theologisch-politische Dimensionen eines unerledigten Themas." *Stimmen der Zeit* 211 (1993).

"Die elektronische Falle: Theologische Bemerkungen zum religiösen Kult im Fernsehen." *Concilium* (1993).

"Gotteskrise: Ein Porträt des zeitgenössischen Christentums." *Süddeutsche Zeitung am Wochenende* 168 (1993).

"In der Spur des Lebens." In *Sie wandern von Kraft zu Kraft: Aufbrüche—Wege-Begegnungen.* Kevelaer: Butzon and Bercker, 1993.

"Gotteskrise: Versuch zur 'geistigen Situation der Zeit.' " In *Diagnosen zur Zeit,* by Johann Baptist Metz et al. Düsseldorf: Patmos, 1994.

Faith and the Future: Essays on Theology, Solidarity, and Modernity. With Jürgen Moltmann. Maryknoll, N.Y.: Orbis Books, 1995.

"Theodizee-empfindliche Gottesrede." In *Landschaft aus Schreien: Zur Dramatik der Theodizeefrage,* edited by Johann Baptist Metz. Mainz: Matthias-Grünewald, 1995.

Gottesrede. With Johann Reitkerstofer and Jürgen Werbick. Münster: LIT, 1996.

"Mit den Augen der Opfer." In *Mit dem Gesicht zur Welt,* edited by Peter Hertel. Würzburg: Echter, 1996.

"Monotheismus und Demokratie: Über Religion und Politik auf dem Boden der Moderne." In *Demokratiefähigkeit,* edited by Jürgen Manemann. Münster: LIT, 1996.

"Wie ich mich geändert habe." In *Wie ich mich geändert habe,* edited by Jürgen Moltmann. Gütersloh: Kaiser/Gütersloher Verlagshaus, 1997.

A Passion for God: The Mystical-Political Dimension of Christianity. Edited and translated by J. Matthew Ashley. New York: Paulist, 1998.

Poverty of Spirit. Edited and translated by John Drury. New York: Paulist, 1998.

Love's Strategy: The Political Theology of Johann Baptist Metz. Edited by John K. Downey. Harrisburg, Pa.: Trinity Press International, 1999.

Trotzdem Hoffen: Mit Johan Baptist Metz und Elie Wiesel im Gespräch. With Ekkehard Schuster and Reinhold Boschert-Kimming. Mainz: Matthias-Grünewald, 1993. English translation, *Hope against Hope: Johann Baptist Metz and Elie Wiesel Speak Out on the Holocaust* (New York: Paulist, 1999).

Gustavo Gutiérrez

"Tres comentarios a la declaración sobre la libertad religiosa." *IDOC* (Rome) 13 (1966).

Líneas pastorales de la iglesia en América Latina: Análisis teológico. Lima: Centro de Estudios y Publicaciones, 1970.

Teología de la liberación: Perspectivas. Lima: Centro de Estudios y Publicaciones, 1971. English translation, *A Theology of Liberation* (Maryknoll, N.Y.: Orbis Books, 1973).

"Marxismo y Cristianismo." In *CEDIAL, Cristianos latinoamericanos y socialismo.* Bogotá: Ediciones Paulinas, 1972.

"Liberation, Theology, and Proclamation." *Concilium* 96 (1974).

"Liberation Movements and Theology." *Concilium* 93 (1974).

"Statement by Gustavo Gutiérrez." In *Theology in the Americas,* edited by Sergio Torres and John Eagleson. Maryknoll, N.Y.: Orbis Books, 1976.

"Freedom and Salvation: A Political Problem." In *Liberation and Change,* edited by Gustavo Gutiérrez and Richard Shaull. Atlanta: John Knox, 1977.

"Two Theological Perspectives: Liberation Theology and Progressivist Theology." In *The Emergent Gospel: Theology from the Underside of History: Papers from the Ecumenical Dialogue of Third World Theologians, Dar es Salaam, August 5–12, 1976,* edited by Sergio Torres and Virginia Fabella. Maryknoll, N.Y.: Orbis Books, 1978.

Beber en su propio pozo: En el itinerario espiritual de un pueblo. Lima: Centro de Estudios y Publicaciones, 1983. English translation, *We Drink from Our Own Wells: The Spiritual Journey of a People* (Maryknoll, N.Y.: Orbis Books, 1984).

The Power of the Poor in History. Maryknoll, N.Y.: Orbis Books, 1983.

"The Task of Theology and Ecclesial Experience." *Concilium* 176 (1984).

Hablar de Dios desde el sufrimiento del inocente: Una reflexión sobre el libro de Job. Lima: Instituto Bartolomé de Las Casas, Centro de Estudios y Publicaciones, 1986. English translation, *On Job: God-Talk and the Suffering of the Innocent* (Maryknoll, N.Y.: Orbis Books, 1987).

La verdad los hará libres: Confrontaciones. Lima: Instituto Bartolomé de Las Casas–Rimac, Centro de Estudios y Publicaciones, 1986. English translation, *The Truth Shall Make You Free* (Maryknoll, N.Y.: Orbis Books, 1990).

"The Church and the Poor: A Latin American Perspective." In *The Reception of Vatican II,* edited by Giuseppe Alberigo, Jean-Pierre Jossua, and Joseph A. Komonchak. Washington, D.C.: Catholic University of America Press, 1987.

Evangelización y opción por los pobres. Buenos Aires: Ediciones Paulinas, 1987.

El Dios de la vida. Lima: Instituto Bartolomé de Las Casas, Centro de Estudios y Publicaciones, 1989. English translation, *The God of Life* (Maryknoll, N.Y.: Orbis Books, 1991).

Dios o el oro en las Indias: Siglo XVI. Lima: Instituto Bartolomé de Las Casas–Rimac, Centro de Estudios y Publicaciones, 1989.

Entre las calandrias: Un ensayo sobre José María Arguedas. Lima: Instituto Bartolomé de Las Casas–Rimac, Centro de Estudios y Publicaciones, 1990.

"Mirar lejos." In *Teología de la liberación: Perspectivas.* 7th ed. Lima: Centro de Estudios y Publicaciones, 1990.

Teología de la Liberación: Perspectivas. 7th ed. Lima: Centro de Estudios y Publicaciones, 1990.

En busca de los pobres de Jesucristo: El pensamiento de Bartolomé de Las Casas. Lima: Instituto Bartolomé de Las Casas, Centro de Estudios y Publicaciones, 1992. English translation, *Las Casas: In Search of the Poor of Jesus Christ* (Maryknoll, N.Y.: Orbis Books, 1993).

"Hacia el quinto centenario." In *Quinto centenario y nueva evangelización,* edited by Juan Ansión et al. Lima: Centro de Estudios y Publicaciones, 1992.

"Vamos a hablar de Vallejo." *Páginas* 114–15 (1992).

"Una agenda: La IV Conferencia de Santo Domingo." *Paginas* 119 (1993).
"Liberación y desarrollo: Un desafío a la teología." In *Liberación y desarrollo en América Latina: Perspectivas,* edited by Catalina Romero and Ismael Muñoz. Lima: Instituto Bartolomé de Las Casas, Centro de Estudios y Publicaciones, 1993.
Compartir la Palabra: A lo largo del Año Litúrgico. Lima: Instituto Bartolomé de Las Casas, Centro de Estudios y Publicaciones, 1995. English translation, *Sharing the Word through the Liturgical Year* (Maryknoll, N.Y.: Orbis Books, 1997).
"Die Theologie: Eine kirchliche Aufgabe." *Münchener Theologische Zeitschrift* 2 (1996).
Densidad del presente. Lima: Centro de Estudios y Publicaciones, Instituto Bartolomé de Las Casas, 1997. English translation, *The Density of the Present: Selected Writings* (Maryknoll, N.Y.: Orbis Books, 1999).

David Tracy

Lonergan's Interpretation of St. Thomas Aquinas: The Intellectualist Nature of Speculative Theology. Rome: Pontificia Universitas Gregoriana, Facultas Theologica, 1969.
The Achievement of Bernard Lonergan. New York: Herder and Herder, 1970.
"Method as Foundation for Theology." *Journal of Religion* 50 (July 1970).
"Lonergan's Foundational Theology: An Interpretation and a Critique." In *Foundations of Theology: Papers from the International Lonergan Congress 1970,* edited by Philip McShane. Dublin: Gill and Macmillan, 1971.
"The Task of Fundamental Theology." *Journal of Religion* 54 (1974).
Blessed Rage for Order: The New Pluralism in Theology. New York: Seabury, 1975.
"Modes of Theological Argument." *Theology Today* 33, no. 4 (1977).
"Theological Classics in Contemporary Theology." *Theology Digest* 25, no. 4 (winter 1977).
Celebrating the Medieval Heritage: A Colloquy on the Thought of Aquinas and Bonaventure. Edited by David Tracy. Special supplement of *Journal of Religion* 58 (1978).
"A Response to Fr. Metz." In *Theology and Discovery: Essays in Honor of Karl Rahner, S.J.,* edited by William J. Kelly, S.J. Milwaukee: Marquette University Press, 1980.
The Analogical Imagination: Christian Theology and the Culture of Pluralism. New York: Crossroad, 1981.
"Author's Response." *Journal of the College Theology Society* 8, no. 2 (fall 1981).
"Defending the Public Character of Theology." In *Theologians in Transition,* edited by James M. Wall. New York: Crossroad, 1981.
"Theologies of Praxis." In *Creativity and Method: Essays in Honor of Bernard Lonergan, S.J.,* edited by Matthew L. Lamb. Milwaukee: Marquette University Press, 1981.
"The Foundations of Practical Theology." In *Practical Theology,* edited by Don S. Browning. San Francisco: Harper and Row, 1983.
A Catholic Vision. With Stephen Happel. Philadelphia: Fortress, 1984.
"Tillich and Contemporary Theology." In *The Thought of Paul Tillich,* edited by James Luther Adams et al. San Francisco: Harper and Row, 1985.

"Particular Classics, Public Religion, and the American Tradition." In *Religion and American Public Life: Interpretations and Explorations,* edited by Robin W. Lovin. Mahwah, N.J.: Paulist, 1986.

"Christianity in the Wider Context: Demands and Transformations." In *Worldviews and Warrants: Plurality and Authority in Theology,* edited by William Schweiker and Per M. Anderson. Lanham, Md.: University Press of America, 1987.

Plurality and Ambiguity: Hermeneutics, Religion, Hope. San Francisco: Harper and Row, 1987.

"The Christian Understanding of Salvation-Liberation." *Face to Face* 14 (spring 1988).

"Argument, Dialogue, and the Soul in Plato." In *Witness and Existence: Essays in Honor of Schubert M. Ogden,* edited by Philip E. Devenish and George L. Goodwin. Chicago: University of Chicago Press, 1989.

"On Naming the Present." *Concilium* 1 (1990).

"On Reading the Scriptures Theologically." In *Theology and Dialogue: Essays in Conversation with George Lindbeck,* edited by Bruce D. Marshall. Notre Dame, Ind.: University of Notre Dame Press, 1990.

"Approaching the Christian Understanding of God." In *Systematic Theology: Roman Catholic Perspectives,* edited by Francis Schüssler Fiorenza and John Galvin. Minneapolis: Augsburg Fortress, 1991.

Dialogue with the Other: The Inter-religious Dialogue. Grand Rapids, Mich.: Eerdmans, 1991.

"God, Dialogue, and Solidarity: A Theologian's Refrain." In *How My Mind Has Changed,* edited by James M. Wall and David Heim. Grand Rapids, Mich.: Eerdmans, 1991.

"Literary Theory and Return of the Forms for Naming and Thinking God in Theology." *Journal of Religion* 74, no. 3 (July 1994).

On Naming the Present: God, Hermeneutics, and Church. Maryknoll, N.Y.: Orbis Books, 1994.

"The Return of God in Contemporary Theology." Unpublished manuscript, 1994.

"Theology and the Many Faces of Post-Modernity." *Theology Today* 51, no.1 (April 1994).

"Evil, Suffering, and Hope: The Search for New Forms of Contemporary Theodicy." Unpublished manuscript, 1995.

"Iris Murdoch and the Many Faces of Platonism." In *Iris Murdoch and the Search for Human Goodness,* edited by William Schweiker and Maria Antonacio. Chicago: University of Chicago Press, 1996.

"The Tenderness and Violence of God: The Return of the Hidden God in Contemporary Theology." *Lumière et Vie* (1996).

Index